The Minor Prophets

Robertson's Notes

Bible Books 28-39 of 66

A Bible Book Commentary

By

John C Robertson

Copyright © 2013 John C. Robertson
All rights reserved.
ISBN-13:978-1502829986
ISBN-10:1502829983

Max-

"It is all very well to be ambitious, but ambition should not kill the nice qualities in you."

Never change who you are no matter how far you go!

Jeremy + Grace

Abbreviations

AG Arndt and Gingrich, A Greek-English Lexicon of the NT

AHD American Heritage Dictionary

ASV 1901 American Standard Version Bible

ESV English Standard Version

ISBE International Standard Bible Encyclopedia

KJV King James Version Bible

LS Liddell and Scott, A Greek-English Lexicon of the NT

LXX The Septuagint with Apocrypha

Thayer Thayer's Greek-English Lexicon of the New Testament

Moulton The Analytical Greek Lexicon

NM Nestle and Marshall Interlinear Greek-English NT

Strong's Strong's Exhaustive Concordance of the Bible

Contents

Foreword	1
Introduction to Minor Prophets	3
Hosea	4
Joel	111
Amos	144
Obadiah	208
Jonah	223
Micah	254
Nahum	308
Habakkuk	331
Zephaniah	356
Haggai	381
Zechariah	404
Malachi	525
Bible Topic Index	567
Bibliography	588

FOREWORD

The objective of Robertson's notes is to explain Bible text in a precise and simple format. You will not read opinions, personal convictions, preconceived religious ideas, or a dogma of a particular denominational body. You will find a study that permits the word of God to explain itself. An expositor's best tools are context, cross references, terms of equivalences, and defining the original Greek meaning of words. Any study of God's word must take fearful consideration of the authoritative nature of divine revelation. God is the sovereign creator of earth and time. No man has the right to add or subtract from the mind of God.

Using Robertson's notes affectively means understanding the simple system of references and studies. The reader will encounter abbreviations for references used in parenthesis with their corresponding page number such as (Moulton 340). The reader will also encounter English words with the translated Greek word in parenthesis. Sometimes the author has written this out as follows, "deacon (Greek *diakon*)." Other times the Greek word stands alone as follows (*diakon*). Greek words will always be in italics and their respective definitions given. There are questions at the end of each chapter so that the reader may have a complete Bible study of the text.

There are also parenthetical studies that are referenced at the end of this book titled, "Bible Topics Index." The reader will encounter parenthetical numbers that corresponds to the appropriate Special Study as follows, (30p). When you come across these parenthesis with a number simply look to the back of this book for the study reference. A separate book examines these special studies in detailed fashion.

Lastly, the Bible text used in this study is the 1901 American Standard Version Bible (ASV) unless otherwise noted. The ASV is recognized as a "Formal Equivalence" text as opposed to a "Dynamic Equivalence." The Formal Equivalence method of translating Bible text into another language occurs by taking the original words and moving them over to the target language without too much concern over continuity and fluidity of reading. This is known as a "literal translation" or a "word for word translation" of God's word. The Dynamic Equivalence method of translating the Greek to English language occurs by translating the original language into the target language by means of paraphrasing the meaning. The value of a Formal Equivalence text is that human thought is removed from the meaning of the original words. The words say what they originally said rather than what someone paraphrases them to say. The author has taken the liberty to remove all archaic words such as "thee," "thou," "saith," and so forth seeing that the ASV is in the public domain.

The Minor Prophets

A study of the Minor Prophets will leave one with a greater reverence and respect for the authorized words of God. As we read these twelve books we are inserted into the lives of those who made the choice to live lives of righteousness and those who chose sin. Those who did not follow God's word were chastised by God as a father would an unruly child. The Lord punished his erring people by way of droughts, pestilence, sword, and famine. The object of the punishment was to cause the people to feel sorrow over their sins and return to the Lord. The Minor Prophets prove Solomon's words about the consequences of living a life of sin. Those who choose to sin have nothing but a thorny life of troubles (see Proverbs 22:5). Studying the Minor Prophets will bring wisdom to your life so that you will think twice before choosing sin. Christians are thankful to God that he will forgive the meek and lowly that repents when sin is permitted into one's life.

Hosea

Robertson's Notes

Bible Books 28 of 66

"For the spirit of whoredom has caused them to err"

Hosea 4:12

Introduction

During the days of Jehu God had pronounced the end of the Northern kingdom (see 2 Kings 9 and Hosea 1:3-5). Hosea comes on the scene just after the civil war between Israel and Judah (2 Kings 14:8ff). Israel, under the reign of Jehoash, attacked Judah (Amaziah) and defeated him taking much spoil. Jeroboam continued the wars against Judah that his father participated in and took Damascus and Hamath by force from Judah (2 Kings 14:28f). The next king of Israel, Zechariah, ruled only six months over Israel before being assassinated by Shallum. Shallum's reign lasts only one month before being killed by Menahem.

Israel first came in contact with Assyria during the reign of Menahem. Hosea had been prophesying in Israel for around fifteen years at this point. Tiglath-pileser (Pul), king of Assyria, had marched on Israel, and Menahem taxed his people to pay off the Assyrians (2 Kings 15:17-22). Pul accepted the money and left (750 BC). Five years later Tiglath-pileser marched again on Israel. The tribes of Naphtali, Gad, Reuben and Manasseh were carried away as captives during the days of Pekah, king of Israel (2 Kings 15:29). After this successful campaign against Israel, Assyria became weakened and preoccupied by the rising power of Babylon. Israel regained its strength. Pekah formed an alliance with Rezin, king of Syria, to attack its brother nation Judah (2 Kings 16:5-6). Ahaz foolishly offered Tiglath-pileser all the treasures of the temple of Jehovah for help (2 Kings 16:7-10). Tiglath-pileser agreed and defeated Israel and Syria at Damascus.

Hoshea conspired against Pekah, murdered him and took the throne of Israel in 725 BC (2 Kings 15:30). These were not only the final days of Israel as a nation but the final days of Hosea as a prophet. Eight years were spent in power struggles as Hoshea held office in Israel. During this time Shalmaneser V, the successor of Tiglath-pileser, came up against Israel and utterly defeated them, making them tributary. One last effort was made by Israel to maintain their independence through an alliance with Egypt; however, it failed (2 Kings 17:4). 722 BC effectively ended the kingdom of Israel for good. God's rod of correction had run its full course.

Judah alone was left as God's faithful people, yet they too were sinful and subject to God's wrath. Hezekiah replaced Ahaz as king of Judah around 725 BC. The author of 2 Kings said that Hezekiah "3 *did that which was right in the eyes of Jehovah, according to all that David his father had done*" (2 Kings 18:3). Sennacherib came up against Hezekiah as recorded at 2 Kings 19. Hezekiah prayed unto the Lord and Judah was delivered from the Assyrians. God killed 185,000 Assyrians and gave Judah peace from their enemy. It was during these days of war with Assyria and luxurious living that Isaiah came on the scene to warn God's people of their ungodly works and motivate them to repent. Israel had previously cried out for help from Syria (see 2 Kings 16:5-6) and Egypt (2 Kings 17:4ff) in the time of their calamity. Judah too called out to Assyria for help (2 Kings 17:7ff). The Lord's anger was kindled against Israel and Judah not only for not following his commandments and participating in idolatry (2 Kings 17:16) but also for their reliance on other nations for help when they should have prayed to God as did Hezekiah (2 Kings 16:5ff).

Author and Date

Hosea 1:1 gives us both the author and date. The book is clearly written by Hosea during the days Jeroboam II king of Israel. Jeroboam reigned forty-one years (2 Kings 14:23) (793 to 753 BC). Hosea's days were likely around 760 to 725 BC (the dates that the kings of Israel and Judah occupy as listed at Hosea 1:1).

The Message of Hosea

Hosea, by divine inspiration, depicted Israel as a wife that had "*departed*" from her husband (i.e., God) (Hosea 1:2 and 9:1). Israel's departure was a heart-wrenching experience for the Lord. She had committed adultery against her first love. Hosea wrote, "2 *Contend with your mother, contend; for she is not my wife, neither am I her husband; and let her put away her whoredoms from her face, and her adulteries from between her breasts;*" (Hosea 2:2). To effectively communicate God's feelings toward his departed wife, he requests Hosea to take a wife of whoredom (Hosea 1:2). Hosea faithfully obeyed the Lord and takes Gomer as his wife. Gomer committed adultery against Hosea and had three children (two sons and one daughter - Jezreel, Loruhamah, and Loammi). The meaning of Loammi's name (the last son) gives a summary of the book. Loammi's name means "9 *you are not my people, and I will not be your God*" (Hosea 1:9).

Israel's Sin

Hosea wrote that God had a *"controversy with the inhabitants of the land"* due to their sinfulness (Hosea 4:1). The people were *"defiled"* in their harlotry (Hosea 5:3 and 6:10). Their sins included sexual immorality (Hosea 4:14), ungratefulness (Hosea 2:8-9; 9:10, 13 and 11:3-4), idolatry (Hosea 4:17; 11:2 and 13:1), pride (Hosea 5:5 and 7:10), walking after *"man's commands"* (Hosea 5:10-11 and 11:6), drunkenness (Hosea 4:11 and 7:5), lying (Hosea 10:4), and cheating (Hosea 12:7). Furthermore, Israel had completely forgotten God (Hosea 4:6; 8:14 and 13:6). The deeper they went into sin the less they called upon the name of Jehovah for help in time of need (Hosea 7:7). Rather than looking to God for help and comfort they turned to idols (Hosea 4:12 and 11:2), their king (Hosea 10:3 and 13:10), Assyria and Egypt (Hosea 5:13 and 7:11), their mighty men of war (Hosea 10:13), and their wealth (Hosea 12:8). Every aspect of Israel's society was corrupt. Israel's prophets (Hosea 9:7-8), princes (Hosea 9:15), king (Hosea 10:3), judges (Hosea 7:7), and priest (Hosea 6:9 and 10:5) had perverted justice.

Consequences of Sin

God's wrath against the disobedient would be poured out upon Israel in the form of the Assyrian Empire (Isaiah 10:5 and Hosea 11:5). Israel was to be exiled to Assyria for her refusal to return to the Lord in repentance (Hosea 10:6). Samaria would bear her guilt and she was to die grievous deaths (Hosea 13:16). No king, judge, prophet, priest, idol, other nation, riches, or mighty men would be able to save them from God's wrath (Hosea 13:10). God had chastised Israel with a drought yet they continued in their sinful ways (Hosea 6:3). The time of their judgment had come.

Misdirected Thinking of Israel

Hosea used the contrast of the patriarchs Jacob and Israel to illustrate the people's misdirected and unspiritual thinking (Hosea 12:3ff). The more Israel sinned the deeper they sunk and the further from God they went (Hosea 7:13; 9:9 and 13:2). It was not long until Israel viewed God's laws as *"strange"* (Hosea 8:12). Israel was simply not thinking right. Hosea wrote, "4 *their doings will not suffer them to turn unto their God; for the spirit of whoredom is within them, and they know not Jehovah*" (Hosea 5:4). The **"spirit of whoredom"** is Israel's problem (Hosea 4:12). The idea of a *"spirit"* is the direction of one's thinking. Israel cheated, lied, committed sexual immorality, drank intoxicants, turned to everyone but God for help, and was filled with pride because she had a *"spirit of whoredom."* She was *"bent on backsliding"* (Hosea 11:7). God's people no longer cared about him. They looked to the surrounding nations and desired their ways and deities (Hosea 2:13). The grass appeared greener on the other side. When they walked in the counsel of the wicked; however, they produced trouble with God.

God's Desire for His People Then and Now

Though the book of Hosea brings out the truth that God will not allow sin to go unpunished it also tells of God's mercy (Hosea 1:10-11; 2:14-17, and 21-23). God's earnest desire was that his people would repent of their sins (Hosea 14:1). God wants us all to serve him because that is what our hearts truly desire to do. He wants our *"words"* to reveal a heart of humility and subjection to His will (see Hosea 14:2). God desires his people to *"acknowledge"* (Hosea 5:15) and confess (Hosea 14:2) their sins. The Lord wants to hear his people reject the help of other entities (such as idols and the Assyrians / see Hosea 14:3) in spiritual matters. To such people God will turn away his anger (Hosea 14:4). Hosea's final words define the *"wise"* and *"prudent"* of all history as those who will humble themselves to God and follow him with all their hearts (Hosea 14:9). Nothing has changed through the years. God still demands our interest, humility, subjection, and overall heart (Matthew 12:33). The Christian today must be careful not to allow an interest in this world to interfere with their eternal interest in God.

Hosea's References to the book of Revelation

Hosea 2:6 to Revelation 15:1-2 and 16:8-11, 21

Hosea 2:8-10 to Revelation 18:4-20

Hosea 2:19 to Revelation 19:7-9

HOSEA CHAPTER 1

Synopsis

Hosea's work involved many years of warning a rebellious people regarding the consequences of their sins. The beginning of his lengthy work was defined by the Lord. Hosea was to take a harlot for a wife that would commit adultery against him. The pain of having an unfaithful wife was to symbolize God's feeling toward his wife Israel. Though the Lord loved and cherished his wife Israel she left him for other lovers. Gomer has three children that would symbolize God's ultimate mercy on those who love him and his unyielding position toward those who reject his authority. Eventually, there would be a faithful wife that would serve God in faithfulness, fear, and reverence.

Application

The Apostle Paul's use of Hosea 1:10 at Romans 9:25 prove that Hosea's work was primarily in the area of encouraging the faithful to have hope. The Lord would fulfill his promise to Abraham, through Jesus, and his church would be established. People of all races and nations would have the opportunity to be forgiven of their sins. Meek people will comprise God's future kingdom and they will be saved from the day of wrath and condemnation. All who would answer the call of the gospel message (2 Thessalonians 2:13-14) to repent of sins (Acts 17:30), confess the name of Jesus (Romans 10:9), and be buried with him in baptism (Acts 2:38 and Romans 6:1-11) would enter into the eternal kingdom of God (Acts 2:38-

41). Baptized believers would comprise the Lord's church and stand as a faithful, fearful, and reverential wife to the Lord.

Hosea 1

Gomer has Three Children (1:1-9)

"**1** *The word of Jehovah that came unto Hosea the son of Beeri, in the days of Uzziah, Jotham, Ahaz, and Hezekiah, kings of Judah, and in the days of Jeroboam the son of Joash, king of Israel*" **(1:1).**

There is not much personal information about Hosea revealed other than that his father's name was Beeri. Hosea and Amos prophesied to the Northern tribe of Israel. The date of Hosea's work is given by the kings of Judah that are associated with his work. Jeroboam 2 began his reign as king over Israel (the northern kingdom) around the year 788 BC and he ruled until approximately 747 BC. The kings of Judah (i.e., Uzziah to Hezekiah) span a period of approximately 90 years (i.e., 785 to 695 BC). The dates given by Hosea (Hosea 1:1), Amos (Amos 1:1), Isaiah (Isaiah 1:1), and Micah (Micah 1:1) are all overlapping. These four prophets worked as God's mouth piece to warn both Israel and Judah of the consequence of their continued disobedience.

Hosea began his work during the days of Uzziah and Jeroboam 2. Uzziah's reign lasts for fifty two years and he began during the twenty seventh year of Jeroboam 2. Jeroboam 2's reign went on for another twelve years while Uzziah reigned in Judah for another thirty five years. Hosea began his work as prophet of God in Israel sometime within the twelve years that both Jeroboam 2 and Uzziah's reigns overlapped (i.e., 749 BC to 737 BC). Hosea continued his work in Israel through at least part of Hezekiah's reign as king of Judah. The scriptures tell us that Uzziah's reign lasts fifty two years (2 Chronicles 26:3), Jotham reigned sixteen years (2 Chronicles 27:1), Ahaz reigned sixteen years (2 Chronicles 28:1), and Hezekiah reigned 29 years (2 Chronicles 29:1). The most Hosea could have worked during the years of Uzziah would be thirty five years. If he worked as Israel's prophet through the reigns of

Jotham (16 years), Ahaz (16 years), and Hezekiah (29 years) that would entail, at the most, 96 years of service as a prophet to Israel. The least amount of years would involve Hosea coming on the scene in the last year of Jeroboam 2 (i.e., 737 BC) and the first year of Hezekiah which would be a total time of 56 years. Hosea's work in Israel goes from the reign of Jeroboam 2 of Israel to the reign of Hezekiah over Judah somewhere between 56 and 96 years.

The word of God reveals Israel's wickedness under Jeroboam 2 at 2 Kings 14:24. Speaking of the king the scriptures read, "*And he* (Jeroboam 2) *did that which was evil in the sight of Jehovah: he departed not from all the sins of Jeroboam* (1) *the son of Nebat, wherewith he made Israel to sin*." The Lord would bring down Israel due to her sin and rejection of God's pleas for their repentance through the prophets. Assyria would be the rod of God's correction for Israel (see Isaiah 10:5-6). Latter, the Lord would use the Babylonians as a battleaxe in his hand to punish sinful Judah (see Jeremiah 51:20). Hosea comes on the scene through Israel's greatest century of wickedness.

"**2** *When Jehovah spoke at the first by Hosea, Jehovah said unto Hosea, Go, take a wife of whoredom and children of whoredom; for the land commits great whoredom, departing from Jehovah*" **(1:2).**

The Lord's "*first*" words to Hosea must have been given to the prophet during the years of Jeroboam 2 (King of Israel) and Uzziah King of Judah. Hosea was a very young man at this point. The Lord's plan was to use Hosea as a living illustration so that Israel would see how offensive their conduct was. Israel had not followed God's commandments and went so far as to participate in idolatry (2 Kings 10). Later, the people would turn to other nations for help rather than putting their trust in God (see 2 Kings 16:5-6 and 17:4ff). Hosea would stand figuratively as the innocent mate of an adulterous marriage. God was the husband and Israel was the wife. Israel was an unfaithful wife who went to other gods and put her trust in others. A marriage covenant is based on trust and faithfulness yet Israel did not hold up her side of the oath.

It is fascinating to take note of God's use of signs or lively illustrations to get across his message. The Lord took the life of Ezekiel's wife to serve as sign to Judah that their wives and children would likewise die in the Babylonian siege for their disobedience (see Ezekiel 24:16, 24). The prophets and apostles of Jesus Christ also performed signs to produce faith in their audiences (see Hebrews 2:1-4). Jesus performed signs, wonders, and miracles too yet the world rejected and killed him (see Acts 2:22-24). Jesus said, "*An evil and adulterous generation seeks after a sign; and there shall no sign be given to it but the sign of Jonah the prophet:*" (Matthew 12:39). Jesus had one last sign to give to the unbelieving. As Jonah was in the depths of the ocean for three days even so Christ would die and three days latter be resurrected. The Lord was giving Israel signs to help them yet, as so often in their history, they turned a blind eye to his marvelous acts of love.

"**3** *So he went and took Gomer the daughter of Diblaim; and she conceived, and bare him a son.* **4** *And Jehovah said unto him, Call his name Jezreel; for yet a little while, and I will avenge the blood of Jezreel upon the house of Jehu, and* **will cause the kingdom of the house of Israel to cease.** **5** *And it shall come to pass at that day, that I will break the bow of Israel in the valley of Jezreel*" **(1:3-5).**

The prophet of God marries "*Gomer the daughter of Diblaim.*" Gomer is a prostitute that likely worked at some other deity's temple before Hosea is married to her. Though Gomer would not otherwise be a wise choice of a life long partner the prophet of God follows the Lord's instructions and takes the harlot as his wife. God knows that such a woman will not remain faithful to his prophet and so she would serve his divine purpose as a sign to Israel. Hosea must have been a well known prophet in Israel for the people to take note of his daily affairs and make this sign viable.

The scriptures tell us that Gomer bore Hosea a son that they named Jezreel by divine decree. The name "*Jezreel*" means "God saves" (ISBE volume 2 page 1059). The Greek Septuagint translates the word as

"*Hiezrael*" (LXX 1070) meaning "God sows" (ISBE volume 2 page 1059). The object of the Lord naming this child is to bring Israel to remember the sins of Jehu in relationship to Jezreel.

Jehu was the tenth king of Israel. God had anointed him king and commanded him to "7 *smite the house of Ahab your master, that I may avenge the blood of my servants the prophets, and the blood of all the servants of Jehovah, at the hand of Jezebel*" (see 2 Kings 9:6-8). Jehu did as God commanded (2 Kings 10:1ff) and the Lord commended him (2 Kings 10:30). Jehu had the opportunity to change the way the kings of Israel had sinfully operated; however, he chose to participate in the same sinful activity as did his forefathers (2 Kings 10:29-31). Though Jehu followed God's command regarding Jezreel he did not continue in those faithful steps as did Abraham his forefather. Due to Jehu's unwillingness to follow God's laws perfectly the Lord would "*cause the kingdom of the house of Israel to cease.*"

The son's name of Jezreel is a sign of God's **mercy**. Though Jehu, and many other Israelite kings and the people, rejected God's commands and served other deities the Lord would have mercy on them. God would save Israel to fulfill his promise that he had made to Abraham (see Hosea 1:11 and 2:22-23). Jezreel, the son of a harlot, would serve as a sign of God's mercy. Though he was born into a world of wickedness he would stand as a living symbol of mercy. This is the exact idea behind David's statement made a Psalms 51 when the king wrote, "*Behold, I was brought forth in iniquity; and in sin did my mother conceive me*" (Psalms 51:5). David was not responsible for the sins of the world that he was born into yet he stood as a living example of faithfulness and meekness.

"**6** *And she conceived again, and bare a daughter. And Jehovah said unto him, Call her name Loruhamah; for I will no more have mercy upon the* **house of Israel**, *that I should in any wise pardon them*" **(1:6).**

Gomer bore a second child and the Lord commanded Hosea to name the girl "*Loruhamah*" which means "not shown compassion or not pitied" (ISBE volume 3 page 170). While Jezreel's name stood for future hope and mercy through the Messiah and God's fulfilled promise to Abraham Loruhamah stood as a symbol of immediate punishment. The second child's name symbolized God's disposition toward Israel. Jezreel is said to be born of Gomer by Hosea yet this daughter appears to be someone else's child.

Israel, the Northern kingdom, had been destined by God to be destroyed because of her wickedness in the days of Jehu. Nothing would change the Lord's heart that he may "*pardon*" and save them as a nation. Two hundred years were spent in wickedness (the length of time that Israel remained as a nation separate from Judah).

"**7** *But I will have mercy upon the **house of Judah**, and will save them by Jehovah their God, and will not save them by bow, nor by sword, nor by battle, by horses, nor by horsemen*" **(1:7).**

No immediate mercy for Israel but mercy for Judah. Hosea will go on to expose the sins of Judah as well in this book; however, it was God's intention to save a remnant of people to bring forth his eternal promise of the forgiveness of sins.

The Lord saved Judah without sword when during the days of Hezekiah he struck 185,000 Assyrians dead (see Isaiah 37:36). The returning captives of Babylon, under Zerubbabel and Esther, rebuilt the city of Jerusalem and restored the people's faith without sword or battle (Ezra and Nehemiah). Lastly, Jehovah will save all of humanity from the consequences of their sins without sword. The Lord's people shall use his word as their sword (Ephesians 6:17) and the battlefield will be life itself as Satan attempts to destroy each person's soul (1 Peter 5:8).

"**8** *Now when she had weaned Loruhamah, she conceived, and bare a son.* **9** *And Jehovah said, Call his name Loammi; for you are not my people, and I will not be your God*" **(1:8-9).**

A third child is born to Gomer. Again, nothing is said of this child belonging to Hosea as was said about Jezreel. The child's name has to do with Israel not being the people of God. The International Standard Bible Encyclopedia defines the Hebrew word for "*Loammi*" as "not my people" (ISBE volume 3, page 149). The inference is that Gomer has had children in an adulterous affair (see Hosea 2:1-2). Hosea, as the prophet of God and standing sign, illustrated the pain that God experienced as he watched his people commit spiritual adultery against him. He was their God yet they rejected him for other deities and nations.

Hope for Both Israel and Judah (1:10-11)

"*10 Yet the number of the children of Israel shall be as the sand of the sea, which cannot be measured nor numbered; and it shall come to pass that, in the place where it was said unto them, You are not my people, it shall be said unto them, You are the sons of the living God*" **(1:10).**

Though Israel, the Northern kingdom, would be cast off by God it was not to be permanent. At the point of the gospel of Jesus Christ being preached to the world the Lord would take those who were "*not my people*" (*Loammi*) and recognize them as "*the sons of the living God.*"

The Apostle Paul quotes from this verse at Romans 9:25-26 and the Apostle Peter at 1 Peter 2:10. The indication is that both Jew and Gentile are on equal ground when it comes to salvation from past sins through the blood of Jesus Christ. Those whom the Lord rejected (i.e., the disobedient Jews and Gentiles) will now be accepted through their faith in Jesus Christ (Romans 9:30-33). There is always hope for any man or woman who seeks diligently after it. Those who by faith live obediently to the Lord shall be "*sons of the living God*" (see Galatians 3:26 and 1 John 3:9-10). Though we are all enemies of God before conversion he nonetheless is merciful to forgive any and all who would obey the gospel message.

"*11 And the children of Judah and the children of Israel shall be gathered together, and they shall appoint themselves one head, and shall go up from the land; for great shall be the day of Jezreel*" **(1:11).**

The "*day of Jezreel*" is a reference to Hosea 1:4 where God would put an end to the Northern kingdom of Israel because of her sins. All those of the spirit of Jehu (i.e., those who reject the commandments of Jehovah God) will have their end likened unto sinful Israel's kingdom.

The "*day of Jezreel*" looks to the future when Christ would bear the sins of the world on the cross and establish his eternal kingdom (see Isaiah 53 and Daniel 2:44-45). People of all races and nations shall be attracted to the kingdom of God because it offers forgiveness (see Zechariah 2:11; 3:10; 8:20-23 and Revelation 15:4 and 21:24). The Lord's people (Isaiah 50:1; 54:5; 57:3ff and Ezekiel 16:1ff) or the church of Jesus Christ (Romans 7:4; 2 Corinthians 11:2 and Ephesians 5:22ff) are often portrayed in scriptures as the Lord's wife. The Apostle Paul said, "*2 I espoused you to one husband, that I might present you as a pure virgin to Christ*" (2 Corinthians 11:2). The word "*espoused*" (Greek *hermosamen*) means "to fit, adapt, prepare, make ready...of marriage, to betroth one's daughter to any one; to betroth to oneself, or take to wife" (LS 118). The Lord looked to the future when he would have a faithful wife serve him spiritually.

Questions over Hosea Chapter 1

1. When did Hosea's prophecy take place?

2. Why did God tell Hosea to take a "*wife of whoredom*?"

3. What were the names of Gomer's three children and what did those names mean?

4. What two apostles quoted from Hosea 1:10?

5. When would God have a faithful wife that would serve him in fear and reverence?

6. Who will represent the faithful wife of God in New Testament times?

HOSEA CHAPTER 2

Synopsis

God has thoroughly exposed the adulterous sins of Israel and has figuratively divorced her. Israel has made her foolish choice and God is displeased. Israel's adulterous relationship soon takes a turn for the worse. She has run to her lovers for satisfaction, comfort, and sustenance yet they are no where to be found. Those she thought so highly of are now gone. The wicked have been sexually satisfied and now want nothing to do with her. Israel sought to attract the world with her wickedness and she succeeded. To Israel's dismay the world of wicked men were no where to be found when she was in need. Israel was left destitute and lonely.

Application

Hosea chapter two reminds us of the parable of the prodigal son found at Luke 15. The prodigal son desired the ways of the world and sowed his wild oats yet when the hardships of God's chastening hand hit him his worldly buddies were no where to be found. Many Christians walk through life as though it were the University of Hard Knocks. We often learn lessons the hard way. We find that though the world of wickedness appeared so alluring, fun, and exciting its end was truly disappointing. When Christians get decked out to attract the world rather than God they set themselves up for great disappointment and anguish. The world of sinners cannot save us and neither can we find true happiness and contentment in the things of this world (see 1 John 2:15-17).

Hosea 2

Israel tries to be Attractive to the World Rather than God (2:1-13)

"*1 Say unto your brethren, Ammi; and to your sisters, Ruhamah. 2 Contend with your mother, contend; for she is not my wife, neither am I her husband; and let her put away her whoredoms from her face, and her adulteries from between her breasts; 3 lest I strip her naked, and set her as in the day that she was born, and make her as a wilderness, and set her like a dry land, and slay her with thirst*" **(2:1-3).**

God instructs Hosea to speak to his brethren "*Ammi and Ruhamah*" (i.e., my people that have obtained mercy - 1901 American Standard Version footnotes). The Hebrew names given the brothers and sisters of Israel indicate their past relationship with God. The Lord had blessed them and granted great mercy toward them as he brought them out of Egypt and fed them in the wilderness yet they were ungrateful (see the prayer of Ezra at Nehemiah 9:6-38). God had found Israel as a new born baby that no one cared for. The Lord washed her and took care of her health and entered into a covenant agreement with her (see Ezekiel 16:1-9). Yet through time she forsook the Lord and committed adultery against him by going to other deities and nations for hope and help.

The Lord tells Hosea to speak to this unfaithful wife on his behalf. There will be grave consequences for her adulterous and sinful ways. If Israel will not repent of her wickedness God will strike her naked with great shame. Her sins are depicted in very graphic sexual language as she commits "*adulteries between her breasts.*"

"*4 Yea, upon her children will I have no mercy; for they are children of whoredom; 5 for their mother has played the harlot; she that conceived them has done shamefully; for she said, I will go after my lovers, that give me my bread and my water, my wool and my flax, mine oil and my drink*" **(2:4-5).**

It is apparent that the children born to Gomer were not Hosea's. The prophet's wife has committed adultery against him and bore "*children of whoredom.*" She has "*played the harlot.*" Gomer has turned to other men for her love, trust, help and hope in this life. She has broken not only the covenant she made in marriage but also her loving husband's heart.

Hosea, Gomer, and their children play only a small part in the big picture that God is relaying to Israel. If only they could see with their eyes the great sin that they're in. If only they would look to Hosea, Gomer, and their children of adultery and see the changes that must be made. Often times people have the ability to see the sin in other's lives yet fail to look with the same examining eyes to their own lives (see Romans 2:17-24). God has given his divine words to the people, sent the prophets Amos, Hosea, and Isaiah to help them see their error, and even used Hosea and Gomer's relationship to help them open their eyes to their sin. Far too often; however, the eyes of man are blinded by stubborn pride. Personal desire takes the place of God's commands. A willful man puts his own wishes above the laws of God (see Matthew 13:14-15) (14f).

"**6** *Therefore, behold, I will hedge up your way with thorns, and I will build a wall against her, that she shall not find her paths*" **(2:6).**

A universal lesson is displayed in both the Old and New Testaments regarding God's method of causing sinful men to repent. Israel had lost her way as God's wife and people. The Lord will "*hedge up your way with thorns*" and "*build a wall against her*" to chastise her for her wickedness. The way of the sinful Israelite will be made intensely hard. Israel's walk in life will be confronted with thorns and high walls of great difficulty. Solomon said, "5 *Thorns and snares are in the way of the perverse: He that keeps his soul shall be far from them*" (Proverbs 22:5).

God continues to chastise his people with hardships in New Testament days so that they may repent (see Hebrews 12:3-11; Revelation 15:1-2 and 16:8-11). The Lord knows that most people will be furthered hardened against him as they are chastised (Matthew 13:14-15) yet the faithful will feel the sting of shame and be moved to repentance (2 Corinthians 7:8-11). Those who do not truly love the truth are sent "*a working of error*" by God in the form of plagues that frustrate the wicked rather than cause them sorrows (see 2 Thessalonians 2:11 and Revelation 16:21). The Apostle Peter writes, "*The Lord knows how to deliver the godly out of temptation* (trials - Common English Bible) *and to keep the unrighteous under punishment unto the day of judgment*" (2 Peter 2:9) (17d). God knew before the foundation of the world that there would be people who were softened by the gospel message and those who would be further hardened against him (see Romans 8:29; 2 Corinthians 2:15-16; Ephesians 1:3-6 and 2 Thessalonians 2:13-14) (29j).

"**7** *And she shall follow after her lovers, but she shall not overtake them; and she shall seek them, but shall not find them: then shall she say, I will go and return to my first husband; for then was it better with me than now*" **(2:7).**

Gomer (the adulterous Israelites) follow after those they truly love rather than God yet she finds no real satisfaction and fulfillment of the soul. Pleasures of life and one's own pride can only take a man so far. When true want settles in there is no man of flesh and blood that can satisfied the soul's great need. The true Zion says, "2 *Behold, God is my salvation; I will trust, and will not be afraid: for Jehovah, even Jehovah, is my strength and song; and he is become my salvation*" (Isaiah 12:2). Some people trust in other people. The Apostle Paul commands "*Have no confidence in the flesh*" (Philippians 3:3). The Psalmist wrote, "*It is better to take refuge in Jehovah than to put confidence in man*" (Psalms 118:8). Some people put their confidence in government and politicians. David writes, "*It is better to take refuge in Jehovah than to put confidence in princes*" (Psalms 118:9). Still others look for trust and confidence in the riches of this world (see Job 31:24-25; Zephaniah 1:18; Luke 18:18-30).

Let us learn to put our trust and confidence in the one true living God. Solomon wrote, "*The fear of man brings a snare; But whoso puts his trust in Jehovah shall be safe*" (Proverbs 29:25) (11b).

Like the prodigal son of Luke 15 Gomer has had her fill of sin and now feels the sting of her filth. Her lovers have taken Gomer sexually and now want nothing more to do with her. Though she searches after them they want no more of her. The wicked are satisfied and want no more of what she has to offer. God chastens her with despair and loneliness and his hand is heavy upon her (see Psalms 32:4-5). She remembers how that Hosea loved and cared for her and now she desires to return to her first love. The sign of Hosea and Gomer ought to produce a remembrance in the hearts of the Israelites of God's tender love and affection for them. God had always cared for them and he alone was to be trusted and hoped in. Sometimes it takes people going through the University of Hard knocks to figure out how well they have it while with God and his saints.

"**8** *For she did not know that I gave her the grain, and the new wine, and the oil, and multiplied unto her silver and gold, which they used for Baal.* **9** *Therefore will I take back my grain in the time thereof, and my new wine in the season thereof, and will pluck away my wool and my flax which should have covered her nakedness.* **10** *And now will I uncover her lewdness in the sight of her lovers, and none shall deliver her out of my hand*" **(2:8-10).**

Israel's adultery is now clearly revealed as idolatry. Israel gave the blessings grain, new wine, and oil that they received from God to Baal. The people of God would not acknowledge or admit that it was God that had given them the great blessings of life. God will have no part of their adultery. The Lord takes back his blessings and leaves the people totally dependant upon those they thought would help them (i.e., Gomer's lovers - Baal and the world of sinful men). The Lord puts her away as an unfaithful wife (Hosea 2:1-2).

As the days go by and Baal and the sinful men of the world offer no blessings the eyes of Gomer (Israel) ought to be opened as to who she should truly love. After her lover received from her what they lustfully desired they wanted no more part of her. She is left alone and destitute. The Apostle John spoke of these very issues at Revelation 18:4-20. Babylon is depicted as the world of sinful men who suffer great plagues because of their wickedness. Often the saints of God think that the world of wickedness is the place they will attain happiness, contentment, and joy yet as time wears on they find no such things. The Baal's and Babylon's of the world suffer immensely and those found within her suffer too. Though the world may appear to have much to offer in relationship to happiness and contentment nothing can be further from the truth. The wicked of the world are only looking out for their personal interest. God cares for others well being now and forevermore. There is much to be said about receiving comfort, hope, and love in this life. God offers such things whereas the world of sinners does not (1 Peter 5:7).

God would take away his blessings for her unfaithfulness and she would be left in shame with her children of adultery. The Assyrians would eventually destroy Israel and take away all her treasures leaving her stripped.

"***11** I will also cause all her mirth to cease, her feasts, her new moons, and her Sabbaths, and all her solemn assemblies. **12** And I will lay waste her vines and her fig-trees, whereof she has said, These are my hire that my lovers have given me; and I will make them a forest, and the beasts of the field shall eat them. **13** And I will visit upon her the days of the Baalim, unto which she burned incense, when* **she decked herself with her earrings and her jewels, and went after her lovers, and forgot me, said Jehovah**" **(2:11-13)**.

God would visit Israel due to her sins. Israel has decked herself in beauty not for God but for her unlawful lovers. She has put on beautiful apparel and jewels to attract the eye of the world rather than God. She has sacrificed the blessings of God to Baal. Israel has burned the incense of devotedness and hope to Baal. Israel has put Jehovah God out of her mind in that she has run to the world for her pleasures and joy.

All married men can relate to the fury and hurt within the heart over such actions on the part of the one we love. Our expectation is that our wives would love us as we love them. A husband expects his wife to pretty herself up for him rather than for a secret lover. Christians are guilty of doing this very thing when we seek to attract the world for sinful reasons rather than considering God. When a Christian man or woman dresses immodestly they must asks themselves why they're doing this. When a Christian speaks like the sinners of the world they should asks why they are doing this. When the Christian laughs at filth in the world they must asks why they're doing this. When we seek to appease, attract, and fit in with the world of sinners we lose our sanctification (see Romans 6:19) (25s).

Gomer (Israel) has looked to others for her satisfaction and broke the heart of God. The Lord takes away his blessings from Israel and consequentially all happiness and joy comes to an end. The reality of having the blessings of God taken away is now realized. All that she was and has was because God cared for her. When she removed God out of her life happiness was removed. She should have been able to deduce that God was the source of her true happiness and blessings.

Future Restoration and Betrothal for Israel (2:14-23)

"*14 Therefore, behold, I will allure her, and bring her into the wilderness, and speak comfortably unto her. 15 And I will give her vineyards from thence, and the valley of Achor for a door of hope; and she shall make answer there, as in the days of her youth, and as in the day when she came up out of the land of Egypt. 16 And it shall be at that day, said Jehovah, that you shall call me Ishi, and shall call me no more Baali. 17 For I will take away the names of the Baalim out of her mouth, and they shall no more be mentioned by their name*" **(2:14-17).**

The alluring of God toward Israel would come by his unmerited love and mercy exercised upon her. She (Israel) would be brought to the valley of Achor (west of the North side of the Dead Sea). As the Lord brought Israel out of Egypt into the wilderness of Sinai to give her law and hope so now the Lord was to bring Israel out of her captivity of sin through doors of hope. Israel would have to spend years in Assyrian captivity and dominance yet there would be hope for her.

A day comes in which Israel would return to the Lord and call him "*Ishi*" (Hebrew for 'my husband') rather than "*Baali*" (Hebrew for 'my master' - a term that only equated God with other idols they worshipped). At this time the Lord would take the names of Baalim and other idols from Israel's mouth so that their names are not even mentioned in his presence for he is a jealous God. True repentance will move the harlot nation to abhor the name of Baal rather than speak about her past lover with words of fond remembrances. True Zion will want to put as much space between them and their past sins as possible. The penitent people of God will want no part of the worldly Babylon that John speaks of at Revelation 18:4.

"**18** *And in that day will I make a covenant for them with the beasts of the field, and with the birds of the heavens, and with the creeping things of the ground: and I will break the bow and the sword and the battle out of the land, and will make them to lie down safely.* **19** *And* **I will betroth you unto me for ever**; *yea, I will betroth you unto me* **in righteousness, and in justice, and in lovingkindness, and in mercies**. *I will even betroth you unto me in faithfulness; and you shall know Jehovah*" **(2:18-20).**

The day in which Israel had a change in heart would be the day that she calls upon Jehovah God as her Husband rather than simply master. God has persuaded her to do so with his divine mercy. This renewed heart is the time of her betrothal. Israel is depicted as an unfaithful wife who has gone through much agonizing emotional and physical duress to come to understand that her true love is God. At this state of mind Jehovah God would once again "*betroth*" her as a wife for ever. Vows or a "*covenant*" shall be made and the Lord shall promise, in faithfulness, that his righteousness, justice, loving-kindness, and mercies shall not depart from his faithful wife if she will remain faithful to him.

The Apostle John spoke of this day of marriage at Revelation 19:7-8 saying, "7 *Let us rejoice and be exceeding glad, and* **let us give the glory unto him**: *for the marriage of the Lamb is come, and his wife has made herself ready.* 8 *And it was given unto her that she should array herself in fine linen, bright and pure: for the fine linen is the righteous acts of the saints*." Hosea divinely looks to a day in the future when God's people will give him glory rather than the Baal's and Babylon's of this world (i.e., to have interest in worldliness). Israel would deck herself out in fine jewels and make herself pretty for God rather than for the world of wickedness.

How is it that Christ's wife, known as the saints of God, gets ready for the "*marriage of the Lamb*?" John sees that she is clothed in fine, bright, and pure linen. These clean and pure clothes are identified as "*the righteous acts of the saints*." Righteousness and justice are the standard requirements of God for his people (see Isaiah 28:17). Righteousness is the foundation of Jehovah's throne (Psalms 97:2). All who walk in the righteousness of God walk in his light and are in fellowship with him (1 John 1:1-7). Righteous "*acts*" infer a peculiar way of life.

The parable of the marriage feast at Matthew 22:1-14 tells the precise story of these verses. The "*works of righteousness*" (Revelation 19:9) are the required clothes to wear if one expects to be with the Lord (9e). Those not clothed in "*works of righteousness*" are cast out into utter darkness where there is the agony of weeping and gnashing of teeth (see Matthew 22:13). There are, as Jesus said, "*many called but few chosen*" (Matthew 22:14). A stark contrast is drawn between the seductive clothing of the harlot (Revelation 17:1-5) and the saints of God (obedient acts of righteousness) (20b). Gomer and Israel was the harlot yet some, through repentance, would cast off these garments and put on the works of righteousness.

"**21** *And it shall come to pass **in that day**, I will answer, said Jehovah, I will answer the heavens, and they shall answer the earth;* **22** *and the earth shall answer the grain, and the new wine, and the oil; and they shall answer Jezreel.* **23** *And I will sow her unto me in the earth; and **I will have mercy upon her that had not obtained mercy**; and I will say to them that were not my people, You are my people; and they shall say, You are my God*" **(2:21-23)**.

The "*day*" under consideration is the day of God's rich blessings through his beloved Son Jesus (see Ephesians 1:3-7). We know this conclusion is solid because Paul and Peter quote from these verses at Romans 9:25-26 and 1 Peter 2:10. The meek will attain the garments of righteousness through the forgiveness of sins and continued obedience to God's laws (see Romans 3:20-21, 27).

Questions over Hosea Chapter 2

1. What parable of Jesus is similar to the words of Hosea chapter 2?

2. What did God make the path of Israel like thorns and a high wall to climb?

3. Why were Israel's lovers no where to be found?

4. How are Christians today guilty of decking themselves in worldliness to attract sinners?

5. Who would be betrothed to God forever?

6. Why would God have mercy on those who had not obtained mercy?

HOSEA CHAPTER 3

Synopsis

Hosea is told to purchase back his wife. The prophet illustrates a heart of compassion and love by still loving one who had done such terrible things against their marriage. Hosea will once again receive and love his wife yet this will not happen without conditions that she must meet. If Gomer agrees to come back to him she must remain faithful.

Application

The Lord is filled with love and care for his beloved saints. The Apostle Peter tells us that he is not willing that any should perish but that all should come to repentance (2 Peter 3:9). Those who would come to themselves and seek out God's love and mercy must make a covenant with the Lord. When people are baptized into Christ they purpose never to return to a sinful style of life again (see Romans 6:1-11). God will receive all sinners who purpose to remain faithful to him. Our lives, as Christians, are often compared to Abraham. Abraham was a man who purposed to serve God in complete obedience. Abraham's works of obedience are praised by Jesus (John 8:39) as well as the New Testament writers (see James 2:20-24 and Hebrews 11:8-19). The Apostle Paul tells us that God will forgive and receive us if we will walk in the faithful and obedient steps of Abraham (Romans 4 all).

Hosea's relationship with Gomer serves as a very clear warning to the wicked. No one in their right mind would forgive and receive an adulterous wife back if she does not show remorse for her actions and prove to us that she will not do the same adulterous things again. Likewise, the Christian is one who was lost in sin yet now purposed to live in obedience to the Lord.

Hosea 3

God Would Receive Israel back as a Wife in the "*latter days*" (3 all)

"*1 And Jehovah said unto me, Go again, love a woman beloved of her friend, and an adulteress, even as Jehovah loves the children of Israel, though they turn unto other gods, and love cakes of raisins. 2 So I bought her to me for fifteen pieces of silver, and a homer of barley, and a half-homer of barley; 3 and I said unto her, You shall abide for me many days; you shall not play the harlot, and you shall not be any man's wife: so will I also be toward you*" **(3:1-3).**

The adulterous woman that Hosea is instructed to buy back is apparently Gomer. Hosea is the "*friend*" who loves her dearly. Though Gomer has committed adultery against her beloved husband he nonetheless continues to have feelings for her. The obvious conclusion is that though Israel has loved other deities and put her trust in them God continues to have loving feelings for them. We are reminded of the Apostle Peter's words at 2 Peter 3:9 when he said that God is not willing that any perish.

Gomer is purchased by Hosea yet not without conditions. She once again belongs to Hosea and she must remain faithful to him alone. If she is faithful to her husband he will be faithful to her. These words remind us of Paul's instructions to the Roman and Corinthian Christians. God bought them by the price of his own Son's blood (see 1 Corinthians 6:20 and 7:23). They were now servants of God rather than servants of another (Romans 6:6, 17-18). The Romans and Corinthians were not free to go back to their old sinful lives. Gomer (Israel) was bound by law to keep the covenant of marriage (see Romans 7:1-6). Gomer was bought and she was not free to return to her adulterous affairs. She was to honor the law of the marital relationship with Hosea. When Christians put away the old man of sin they are bound to the law of Christ (Romans 6:1-11).

"**4** *For the children of Israel shall abide many days without king, and without prince, and without sacrifice, and without pillar, and without ephod or teraphim:* **5** *afterward shall the children of Israel return, and seek Jehovah their God, and David their king, and shall come with fear unto Jehovah and to his goodness in the **latter days**"* **(3:4-5).**

Gomer's days of adultery and servitude to other lovers is likened unto Israel's days without king, prince, sacrifice, pillar, ephod, and teraphim. These are all parts of the kingdom of God and belong to the true worshippers of God. While serving other gods in sin they had no part in these divine and holy things. The people were separated from God in their iniquity (see Isaiah 59:1-2). God would not hear their prayers nor relieve them from his chastising plagues (Revelation 16:8-11, 21).

Hosea looks to "*latter days*" when Israel would "*return and seek Jehovah*." Israel decked their bodies out for other deities. She committed spiritual adultery and experienced the alienation of God (Hosea 2:13 and Revelation 17:4 and 18:16). They were chastised with thorns and high walls in life (Hosea 2:6 and Revelation 15:1-2). They had felt the full brunt of God's chastening hand and the alienation of the divine creator of heaven and earth. Chastisement and alienation moved them to repentance.

Hosea tells the story of not only his day but a day in the future when the church would be established and all nations shall flow to it for safety and eternal sustenance (see Isaiah 2:2-3; Daniel 2:28; Joel 2:28; Acts 2:17 and 3:24-26). This would be a time of merciful forgiveness on the part of God. The Lord never stopped loving his people.

Questions over Hosea Chapter 3

1. True or False: God continued to love his people even though they had sinned against him.

2. What conditions did Gomer (Israel) have to meet if they expected God to buy them back?

3. Do the conditions that Hosea placed on Israel apply to New Testament Christians today?

4. Why were the people of God separated from the divine things of God?

HOSEA CHAPTER 4

Synopsis

Hosea exposes Israel true sin. The people of God lacked knowledge of God's laws and a desire to keep them (Hosea 4:6). Due to their lack of knowledge they would be rejected of God and punished (Hosea 4:9). Those steeped deep in their wickedness would in no way repent of their sins but rather grow harder against the Lord (Hosea 4:16).

Application

Problems within the church of Christ today can always be traced back to a "*lack of knowledge*" on the part of someone (Hosea 4:6). Those who lack knowledge of the Word of God are easy prey for sin. The more they sin the more they experience the punishing hand of God (Hosea 4:9). Much of the world of wicked men are angered by God's punishment. The wicked will curse the name of God due to their hardships in this life rather than seeking out the reason for their suffering (see Revelation 16:21 and Haggai 1:6-11). The lesson of Chapter four is that we ought to take notice of the consequences of not having knowledge of God's words. People without knowledge are more likely to be misled by a false teacher, desire the riches of the world, or get caught up in vain glory. Acquaint yourself with the word of God now so that you may be strengthened in the day of trials. There is no excuse for not knowing God's laws. God has fully delivered his divine revelation to instruct man to receive eternal life. Those who will look into God's laws and obey them will be greatly rewarded.

Hosea 4

Hosea Exposes Israel's Sin (4 all)

"**1** *Hear the word of Jehovah, you children of Israel; for Jehovah has a controversy with the inhabitants of the land, because there is no truth, nor goodness, nor knowledge of God in the land.* **2** *There is not but swearing and breaking faith, and killing, and stealing, and committing adultery; they break out, and blood touches blood*" **(4:1-2).**

Jesus would often explain his parables to the disciples who desired to know the meaning (see Matthew 13:18ff). Likewise, the Lord now explains to the rebellious house of Israel, by way of Hosea, what the adulterous relationship between his prophet and Gomer means. Israel is Gomer in that they have walked away from the God that truly loved them. Israel was so far removed from God that he depicted them as having no truth, goodness, and or knowledge of him. They had decked themselves out in beauty for the wickedness of the world and put God far behind them. They swore, broke faith, murdered, were thieves, and committed sexual immorality. The prophet of God fearfully writes, "*For Jehovah has a controversy with the inhabitants of the land.*"

"**3** *Therefore shall the land mourn, and every one that dwells therein shall languish, with the beasts of the field and the birds of the heavens; yea, the fishes of the sea also shall be taken away.* **4** *Yet let no man strive, neither let any man reprove; for your people are as they that strive with the priest.* **5** *And you shall stumble in the day, and the prophet also shall stumble with you in the night; and I will destroy your mother*" **(4:3-5).**

Hosea appears to compare the people of Israel themselves to the adulterous children of Gomer and Israel as a whole to God's wife Gomer. God has put away Gomer (Israel) because of her adulteries listed. She shall be made to feel the chastising heavy hand of God as do all who walk contrary to his statutes and laws (see Psalms 32:4-5). The Lord will eventually bring the Assyrian Empire upon Israel for her wickedness yet there will be a remnant saved. Those who meekly acknowledge their error will turn to God in compliance to his divine laws and shall comprise the new bride of Christ. The faithful will come to be God's bride in the "*latter days*" (i.e., the days of the New Testament church) (see Hosea 2:21-23 and 3:5).

"***6** My people are destroyed for lack of knowledge: because you have rejected knowledge, I will also reject you, that you shall be no priest to me: seeing you have forgotten the law of your God, I also will forget your children*" **(4:6).**

Jeremiah would latter convict Judah of the same sin. The prophet writes, "*7 the stork in the heavens knows her appointed times; and the turtledove and the swallow and the crane observe the time of their coming; but my people know not the law of Jehovah*" (Jeremiah 8:7). Forgetting God's laws is equated to forgetting God himself. Those who do not stand by God's moral standard in any society will be given over to corruption and violence.

It was a lack of knowledge that caused Gomer to get decked out to attract the wicked of the world. It was a lack of knowledge that caused Gomer to commit adultery against her loving husband. It was a lack of knowledge that caused Gomer to turn to other deities for hope, sustenance, and protection. Likewise, in every generation of man it is a lack of knowledge that causes people to teach and practice unlawful things. Fear of God and knowledge are often found together in the scriptures. Solomon wrote, "*The fear of God is the beginning of knowledge but the foolish despise wisdom and instruction*" (Proverbs 1:7). People today often seek out their own ways in life rather than turning to the authorized words of God (Proverbs 14:12). Those willing to submit to God and be instructed will be wise and have true hope. Jesus said, "*45 It is written in the prophets, And they shall all be taught of*

God. Every one that has heard from the Father, and has learned, comes unto me" (John 6:45).

Having a "*lack of knowledge*" when we have the completed word of God is shameful (Jude 3). Those who don't know the scriptures and do things contrary to God's laws are without excuse (Romans 1:20). Whether the ignorant person is too lazy, is a lover of self acclaimed invented doctrines and opinions, or lacks respect for the almighty sovereign position of God matters not. Those who reject the knowledge of God will have God reject them.

"***7** As they were multiplied, so they sinned against me: I will change their glory into shame. **8** They feed on the sin of my people, and set their heart on their iniquity. **9** And it shall be, like people, like priest; and **I will punish them** for their ways, and will requite them their doings. **10** And they shall eat, and not have enough; they shall play the harlot, and shall not increase; because they have left off taking heed to Jehovah*" **(4:7-10).**

The people multiplied in number as they also multiplied their sins. The priests were actually encouraging the people's sins so that they may benefit from the burnt offerings. God determined to "*punish*" them for their "*ways.*" Punishment comes in the form of plagues throughout the word of God (see Deuteronomy 28:58-62 and 29:22-25 as well as Revelation 15:1-2). God would drive his people back to him in repentance by starving them and keeping the wombs of the women from producing children. As the days of hunger and no children pass the people ought to be moved to asks why these things were happening to them (Haggai 1:6-11). When they see that it is God's chastisement they should be moved, with godly sorrow, to repent of their sins.

Chastisement and or "punishment" have always been the way God moves the sinner to repentance. Those who choose a life of sin choose a thorny life of obstacles, hardships, and anguish (Proverbs 22:5).

"***11** Whoredom and wine and new wine take away the understanding*" **(4:11).**

Hosea list three things that "*take away the understanding*." First there is "*whoredom*" that takes away people's understanding. To be intoxicated with the sinful things of this world is spiritual whoredom. Israel decked herself out in beauty and sacrificed the very blessings of corn, oil, and wine to Baal and consequentially angered the Lord (see Hosea 2:8). When God's people take their bodies and minds and use it for unholy things they act as adulterous women.

Secondly, Hosea said that "*wine*" (Hebrew *yayin*) has taken away their understanding. *Yayin* is an intoxicating wine that has the power to seduce man's judgment and reason (see Proverbs 23:32-33 and 31:5). Those who sin against God's laws through temptations of lust and the vain glory of life are as the drunkard who loses sight of reality.

Lastly, Hosea said that "*new wine*" (Hebrew *tirosh*) has taken away the people's understanding. *Tirosh* is the freshly squeezed juice of the grape. *Tirosh* is not an intoxicating wine but rather grape juice. How could basic grape juice take away the people's understanding? *Tirosh* is associated with luxury at both Amos 6:1-6 and Micah 2:6-11. Wine of this sort was considered a blessing throughout the scriptures; however, the more Israel obtained the greater their wealth. Wealth has a way of deluding one's ability to reason in the areas of morality. The seducing qualities of money are well known by all. When people obtain wealth there is a sense of self sufficiency and contentment with the materials of this world. The rich are tempted to push God and his blessings of future salvation out of their hearts because they have so much now (see 1 Timothy 6:9).

The Apostle John, writing of the power of Babylon's worldliness, said "3 *For by the wine of the wrath of her fornication all the nations are fallen; and the kings of the earth committed fornication with her, and the merchants of the earth waxed rich by the* **power of her luxury**" (Revelation 18:3). The luxury of extravagant comfort is very powerful and alluring to all peoples of the world. Those who fall prey to such temporary glories of comfort will lose sight of God's eternal plan of man's salvation. Israel had grown to be very worldly minded and left off knowing and learning of God.

"**12** *My people ask counsel at their stock, and their staff declares unto them; for the spirit of whoredom has caused them to err, and they have played the harlot, departing from under their God*" **(4:12).**

Note that the "*spirit of whoredom has caused them to err.*" The word "*spirit*" is an interesting word study throughout the word of God. At times one's "*spirit*" indicates the spirit of man and at other times it is a disposition, character, or teaching of an individual (see Ephesians 2:2 and 1 John 4:1). Rather than having knowledge of God Israel exercised a knowledge and faith in idols (stock) and magic (staff). The "*spirit*" (teaching or character) of error has been around a long time. God's people did not learn to sacrifice and worship idols from the Lord but rather from their own fleshly reasoning that had been distorted by their dull and seduced minds (see Hosea 4:7-10 and Deuteronomy 4:9-16). This appears to be the **theme** of Hosea. Not that Israel practiced idolatry but that their minds were more bent toward worldliness than on God's ways (see Hosea 2:13). Israel was thinking in all the wrong directions.

"**13** *They sacrifice upon the tops of the mountains, and burn incense upon the hills, under oaks and poplars and terebinths, because the shadow thereof is good: therefore your daughters play the harlot, and your brides commit adultery.* **14** *I will not punish your daughters when they play the harlot, nor your brides when they commit adultery; for the men themselves go apart with harlots, and they sacrifice with the prostitutes; and the people that do not understand shall be overthrown*" **(4:13-14).**

Hosea had previously said that Gomer would "*follow after her lovers but she shall not overtake them*" (Hosea 2:7). Gomer's lovers were other men while Israel loved other deities. Idolatry often occurred under the green trees. Rather than worshipping Jehovah God under his guidance in his holy temple they worshipped by their own will under the trees. Their worship was perverted. Sexual acts often accompanied many idolatrous ways. The people justified their fornication and adultery (lustfulness for one another) by calling it worship to another deity. Note that the Lord would not hold the women accountable for this debauchery but rather the men who led them into these wicked practices.

"*15 Though you, Israel, play the harlot, yet let not Judah offend; and come not unto Gilgal, neither go up to Beth-aven, nor swear, As Jehovah lives. 16 For Israel has behaved himself stubbornly, like a stubborn heifer: now will Jehovah feed them as a lamb in a large place*" **(4:15-16)**.

A stern warning is delivered to Judah to not follow her sister Israel into the depths of spiritual whoredom that she has sunk. Israel, the wife of Jehovah, has conducted herself like a stubborn cow that will not be directed by the laws of its owner. Again, the focus is on the people's unwillingness to submit and obey the authorized words of God. God would punish them for their spiritual whoredoms by taking them to large open fields to be fed like lambs to the slaughter because there was not much protection. As they are being devoured by their adversaries maybe then they would open their eyes to the laws of God and fearfully obey him.

God has fully revealed his expectations to man. The Lord has always expected perfect obedience to his laws (Deuteronomy 27:26 and 1 Peter 1:15-16). The Lord is upset with his people because they are not meeting his expectations or even trying to.

"*17 Ephraim is joined to idols; let him alone. 18 Their drink is become sour; they play the harlot continually; her rulers dearly love shame. 19 The wind has wrapped her up in its wings; and they shall be put to shame because of their sacrifices*" **(4:17-19)**.

"*Ephraim*" is used as a term of endearment toward the people of God (see Isaiah 7:9; Jeremiah 31:9 and Hebrews 12:23). Other times the tribe of Ephraim is used as a term to identify the Northern Kingdom of Israel (see Hosea 5:1-3). Ephraim was one of the two sons of Joseph that were somewhat adopted by Jacob. Jacob loved Ephraim and his brother Manasseh so much that he gave both of them a portion of land in

Canaan with the patriarch's immediate sons. Though God's expectation of Ephraim was holiness they were, at this time, joined unfaithfully to idols. Ephraim, in fact, was so steeped in idolatry that the Lord considers it a waste of time to try to convince them to repent. Their minds are bent on serving their own ways. The Lord commands "*let them alone*."

Though their intoxicating drinks make them sick they continue in their wicked works like so many in our world today. The negative affects of smoking, doing drugs, and alcohol will not detour the one whose mind is dulled to God's ways. Such a one is deluded in the hardness of their hearts. The wicked will not hear nor will they repent of their evil deeds no matter what plague is upon them (Revelation 16:8-11, 21). Not only were the common people hardened in their shameful conduct but also Israel's rulers were involved in these things.

Questions over Hosea Chapter 4

1. What did Israel lack? (Hosea 4:1)

2. How does Hosea 4:2-3 compare to Hosea 2:11-13?

3. What was the cause of Israel's destruction at the hands of the Assyrians?

4. Why would the people be left feeling unsatisfied?

5. How does Hosea 4:11-13 compare to Hosea 2:7?

6. What was Israel's true love?

7. What would God do about Israel's adultery?

HOSEA CHAPTER 5

Synopsis

The Lord rebukes both Israel and Judah for their apostasy. Israel is defiled in her whoredoms of pride and walking after the commandments of men (Hosea 5:5, 11). Judah was guilty of removing God's ancient landmarks of truth (Hosea 5:10). The Lord has come to rebuke the wicked in judgment because he has seen it all. The wickedness of Judah and Israel has offered testimony or proof of their guilt. The Lord comes as a lion to pass fierce judgment and punishment upon all of his sinful people. The Lord will afflict his people so that they will be moved to acknowledge their trespasses against him (Hosea 5:14-15).

Application

There is nothing that escapes the all seeing eyes of God. The Lord knows of our pride and willful ways that seek to change or altar his holy commandments. Man's sins stand as testimony against him in God's spiritual courtroom. All who sin stand with not valid excuse. The verdict is pronounced against the wicked after all evidence has been assessed. The wicked shall be "*afflicted*" until they acknowledge their trespasses (Hosea 5:14-15). God moves man to earnestly seek him in truth and obedience by way of affliction and judgment. The lesson that we should all learn is that we will bring hardship and affliction to our lives and the lives of our loved ones as long as we persist in sin (see Proverbs 22:5). God's method of correcting us is affliction (Revelation 16:8-11). When the "*day of rebuke*" comes let us humble ourselves before the Almighty God and acknowledge our error.

Hosea 5

Israel's Spirit of whoredom Exposed (5:1-7)

"**1** *Hear this, O priests, and hearken, O house of Israel, and give ear, O house of the king; for unto you pertains the judgment; for you have been a snare at Mizpah, and a net spread upon Tabor.* **2** *And the revolters are gone deep in making slaughter; but I rebuke them all*" **(5:1-2).**

God has a "*controversy*" with Israel due to her sin and now calls upon her to listen carefully to his consequential judgment (Hosea 4:1). Israel had a "*spirit of whoredom*" that had caused her to "*err*" from God's will (Hosea 4:12). Hosea compares the people to "*a stubborn heifer*" that will not do what it is suppose to do (Hosea 4:16). Israel is exposed as a people of ill and misguided affections (Hosea 2:13). Judgment awaits the sinful people of Israel.

The nation's priests, king, and princes ought to have guided them in the paths of righteousness yet these leaders set a snare at Mizpah and Tabor for the entire nation to fall. Mizpah, in Hebrew, means "lookout or watch tower" (ISBE, volume 3, page 387). The location is somewhat obscure but appears to be in the region of Gilead north of the Jabbok River. Tabor is a limestone mountain that rises 1843 feet above sea level and located just south west of the Sea of Galilee. Were these two high elevated areas places of idolatrous worship? Were these two places representative of all Israel? It seems that the two sights must have been landmarks for unlawful acts of worship. The Day of Judgment was upon Israel.

"**3** *I know Ephraim, and Israel is not hid from me; for now, O Ephraim, you have played the harlot, Israel is defiled*" **(5:3).**

Notice the equivalences between Ephraim and Israel (see notes above at Hosea 4:17). Ephraim came to be "*defiled*" by her whoredoms (see

Hosea 4:1-2). To be defiled is to exist in a state of sin (see Leviticus 18:30 and Numbers 6:9-11). The word "*defile*" (Greek *koinoo*) means "to make common, to defile, profane... to deem or pronounce profane (irreverence toward God or things held sacred... disrespect of a sacred name by word or deed) (LS 440 and AHD 988). Another Greek word for "*defile*" is (*molusmos*) which means "to stain, sully; to defile and contaminate morally" (Moulton 272). The Hebrew word used here (i.e., *tame*) indicates a moral stain upon the soul of man. While Israel should have been a pure and faithful wife to God she was rather stained by the sin of spiritual adultery.

"**4** *Their doings will not suffer them to turn unto their God; for the spirit of whoredom is within them, and they know not Jehovah*" **(5:4).**

What causes a wife to be unfaithful to her husband? What causes a child or member of the church to be unfaithful? Hosea continues to enlighten us by answering these questions. If I am unfaithful to the Lord, my wife, or parents it is because "*the spirit of whoredom is within and I know not Jehovah*" (see also Hosea 4:12). The human mind has a choice in the direction it takes in this life. If I choose to serve God and keep his commandments I have chosen a life of the Spirit (Romans 8:1-9). If I choose to walk after the manner of the world seeking worldly gain and favor I have a spirit of error. We all have the choice as to which direction we will take. The Apostle Paul tells us that we either serve in obedience to unrighteousness or righteousness (Romans 6:16). As long as Israel put their personal pleasures and comfort above the laws of God they would not to turn to God.

The "*spirit of whoredom*" is defined as a "*defiled*" life. Hosea reveals to us that those who "*know not Jehovah*" are defiled with a spirit of whoredom. Though many claim to know God their ignorance of his truths and lack of faith and conviction reveal otherwise (see 1 John 2:4). If I am unfaithful to my Lord, wife, and or parents it is because I care more about the things of this world than God. I have erred in judgment and shall pay a high price as those of Israel did.

"**5** *And the pride of Israel testifies to his face: therefore Israel and Ephraim shall stumble in their iniquity; Judah also shall stumble with them*" **(5:5).**

Israel made manifest her "*pride*" by not giving effort to know and keep God's laws (see Hosea 4:1-6). A proud man is a self sufficient and arrogant man. Israel displayed a spirit of pride by not seeking out God's laws and turning to those things that they deemed good. Those with pride issues put their own agendas, opinions, and convictions above those of God. The proud believe they are so important in life that they can make new moral laws or change the ones that are in place. Solomon said that, "13 *the fear of Jehovah is to hate evil: Pride, and arrogance, and the evil way, and the perverse mouth, do I hate*" (Proverbs 8:13). If I have pride issues it is because I don't fear God and neither do I know my place before him.

"**6** *They shall go with their flocks and with their herds to seek Jehovah; but they shall not find him: he has withdrawn himself from them.* **7** *They have dealt treacherously against Jehovah; for they have borne strange children: now shall the new moon devour them with their fields*" **(5:6-7).**

Israel had committed adultery against the Lord and sought out different loves of life. After a while of sinful living they find no more fulfillment in their wickedness and decide to return to the Lord (see Hosea 2:7). Hosea now explains that though they come to see the great blessings of God and seek to return to him he will have no part of her. The Lord would only take back Israel as a wife if she decides to remain faithful to him (see Hosea 3:1-3).

Why was God no where to be found for these Israelites who were seeking him out? Like many in the denominational and so called Christian world today these Israelites went looking for God in all the wrong places. God is to be found in the saving knowledge of his truths (Romans 1:16). Those who seek to change God for their own personal preferences will never find him (see Isaiah 6:9-10 and Acts 28:23-28). A universal principle is established firmly in the minds of all those who study God's word. Sin separates one from God and without humble repentance there is no hope (see Isaiah 59:1-2 and 1 John 1:5ff) (14c).

As a loving husband departs from an unfaithful wife even so Jehovah departed from sinful and adulterous Israel. Their whoredoms of idolatry and the offspring produced thereof have manifested their true love.

Judgment pronounced upon Ephraim (5:8-15)

"**8** *Blow the cornet in Gibeah, and the trumpet in Ramah: sound an alarm at Bethaven; behind you, O Benjamin.* **9** *Ephraim shall become a desolation in the day of rebuke: among the tribes of Israel have I made known that which shall surely be*" **(5:8-9).**

The Lord establishes his deity by pronouncing the end of a matter before it begins (see Isaiah 46:9-10). The "*day of rebuke*" has come upon the house of Israel. Gibeah, Ramah, and Bethaven were to sound the alarm now for danger of the enemy was knocking at their doors because of Ephraim's sin. Assyria would come in the force of war overpowering a nation that ought to have been impervious to the threats of mere flesh.

"**10** *The princes of Judah are like them that remove the landmark: I will pour out my wrath upon them like water*" **(5:10).**

Judah was also in danger of judgment. The princes of Judah "*are like them that remove the landmark.*" Landmarks identify the corners and boundaries of property. To move a landmark was a despicable thing to do because it confused the true parameters of the property. People did this to gain more than what was actually theirs. Likewise, spiritually speaking, the princes of Judah had changed God's commands and confused the lines of right and wrong among the people. It is fascinating to find such an illustration as a landmark in comparison to God's commandments. God's commands are set like landmarks yet the ungodly move and pervert the lines. Isaiah, speaking for God, said "17 *I will make justice* **the line**, *and righteousness* **the plummet**; *and the hail shall sweep away the refuge of lies, and the waters shall overflow the* *hiding place*" (Isaiah 28:17). The ancient landmarks of God's word were justice and righteousness yet the people moved them to do their works of unrighteousness. If the property lines are moved one **trespasses** against God in that they do works that are contrary to God's laws (see Leviticus 26:40 and 1 Chronicles 10:13), they are rebellious (Joshua 22:16), sinful (2 Chronicles 28:13; Ezekiel 18:24 and Romans 5:18) and evil acts (Nehemiah 13:27).

Though man may pervert truth it nonetheless stands the test of time and ungodly men. Truth remains in its place as the world revolves on its axis and wicked men come and go. The word of God has been revealed and is set in the hearts of men. Though some may try to change truth it remains unaltered in the pages of God's word. The Apostle Paul wrote, "*19 Howbeit the firm foundation of God stands, having this seal, the Lord knows them that are his: and, let every one that names the name of the Lord depart from unrighteousness*" (2 Timothy 2:19 see also Zechariah 1:5-6).

"**11** *Ephraim is oppressed, he is crushed in judgment; because he was content to walk after man's command*" **(5:11).**

The Lord leaves nothing to our imagination. We see clearly the picture and justification of his wrath. Ephraim (Israel) will be "*oppressed*" and "*crushed*" by the enemy in judgment because "*he was content to walk after man's command.*" Previously the prophet of God referred to this oppression and crushing as "*punishment*" (Hosea 4:9) and later he will refer to it as "*chastisement*" (Hosea 7:12). Israel and Judah would be chastised "*because*" they had a closer relationship with the world of men than they did with God. Rather than gaining knowledge of God and his laws Israel sought out to know Baal and idolatry (see Hosea 2:8). The commandments and ways of the nations around them were more beloved than the commandments of God. Jesus said, "*7 you hypocrites, well did Isaiah prophesy of you saying, 8 This people honors me with their lips but their heart is far from me. 9 But in vain do they worship me teaching the doctrines and precepts of men*" (Matthew 15:7-9). When

God's people of any age replace his authorized words with their own doctrines they commit spiritual adultery (2 Peter 2:1-12). The Bible tells us that there is only one truth or gospel and we are all responsible for knowledge and practice of its teachings (Ephesians 4:1-4; Colossians 3:17 and 2 John 9-11) (9f).

"**12** *Therefore am I unto Ephraim as a moth, and to the house of Judah as rottenness*" **(5:12).**

Both Ephraim and Judah sought to change God's laws to fit their own personal conscience. Their attempts to look and speak like the world would result in their lives, cities, and ways of life being eaten away as a moth would do to one's clothing. Their existence would be as rottenness as God pours out his divine wrath upon a people of disobedience.

"**13** *When Ephraim saw his sickness, and Judah saw his wound, then went Ephraim to Assyria, and sent to king Jareb: but he is not able to heal you, neither will he cure you of your wound*" **(5:13).**

Another source of Ephraim and Judah's spiritual whoredoms was going to others in their time of need rather than turning to Jehovah God. Israel had before cried out for help from Syria (2 Kings 16:5-6) and Egypt (2 Kings 17:4ff) in the time of their calamity. Judah called out to Assyria for help (2 Kings 17:7ff, turned from the Lord and placed their confidence in other men (Isaiah 31:1-3), nations (Isaiah 30:1-5, 12), idols (Isaiah 42:17), and even money (see Isaiah 2:10-17). Israel and Judah sought for help in the wrong places. The physicians of Jareb king of Assyria, whom Israel and Judah contended with, would be unable to heal their spiritual wounds. The very act of reaching out for help from the enemies of Jehovah are once again indicators of a perverted and whoredom filled heart of error.

The Apostle Paul commands "*Have no confidence in the flesh*" (Philippians 3:3). The Psalmist wrote, "8 *It is better to take refuge in Jehovah than to put confidence in man. 9 It is better to take refuge in Jehovah than to put confidence in princes*" (Psalms 118:8-9). To put one's trust and confidence in self (2 Corinthians 1:9), the riches of this world (Job 31:24-25; Zephaniah 1:18), governments of men (Psalms 118:9), or a friend and neighbor (Micah 7:5) above God is the height of foolishness. God demands man's whole heart of trust, love, and confidence (see Deuteronomy 10:12-13 see also Matthew 22:37). Let us place our trust and confidence in the Lord whether we are living in times of plenty or desperation (see Job 4:6; Psalms 65:5; Proverbs 3:26 and 14:26). Solomon wrote, "25 *the fear of man brings a snare; But whoso puts his trust in Jehovah shall be safe*" (Proverbs 29:25). There is only one who is truly worthy of our trust and confidence and that is the Lord (see Jeremiah 17:5-8 and Acts 4:12). We must all walk by God's standard of righteousness (see Luke 1:74-75 and 2 Timothy 2:22).

"**14** *For I will be unto Ephraim as a lion, and as a young lion to the house of Judah: I, even I, will tear and go away; I will carry off, and there shall be none to deliver.* **15** *I will go and return to my place,* **till they acknowledge their offence, and seek my face**: *In their affliction they will seek me earnestly*" **(5:14-15).**

Like a powerful lion that thrashes and devours its prey the Lord would attack and consume Israel and Judah. No one can deliver them from the powerful might of the lion. Their only hope is to repent of the spirit of whoredoms and their pride. God knows this and so he will **punish** them severely (Hosea 4:9; 7:12; 10:2 and 12:2). Jeremiah wrote of Judah's punishment at the hands of the Babylonians saying, "*How can a living man complain about the punishment of his sins*" (Lamentations 3:39)? Assyria would be God's rod of anger against the wicked of Israel (Isaiah 10:5). Babylon would be God's battle-axe against the wicked of Judah (Jeremiah 51:20).

The Lord's desire is that his people would be faithful to him as a wife should be to her husband. God has blessed and given cause for rejoicing by promising man a Savior in Jesus the Christ. The Lord desires man's obedience in return for his blessings. When I sin, God wants me to "*acknowledge my offence*" and then "*seek my* (God's) *face*" (i.e., set the heart to follow his ways) (see also Jeremiah 3:13). Until that moment comes God continues to punish the wicked with affliction. When a man can take it no more he is driven to seek out God's mercy. Affliction continues in man's life until he acknowledges his error (see Romans 5:3; Hebrews 12 and Revelation 16:8-11) (17d).

God demands a spirit of humility within the hearts of those who would serve him. When we sin against God there ought to be a sense of shame within our hearts that compels us to seek out God's forgiveness. This principle is established in the book of Leviticus. God's people were to acknowledge their sin, confess it, and take the revealed steps to remedy the sin (Leviticus 5:5-6). Such an attitude on the part of the worshipper was recognized as one who, when he sins through error, does all within the instructions of God's word to make amends to the situation. The other side would be the man or woman who sins with a *"high hand."* This person has no intentions to follow God's laws of atonement and is to be cast out of the camp of Israel (Numbers 15:30). One represents the humble man of faith and the other the proud man of fleshly will. The humble are those God seeks to be his (Isaiah 57:15).

Questions over Hosea Chapter 5

1. How was Israel considered "*defiled*" (see Hosea 5:3)?

2. How did pride play into Israel's spirit of whoredom?

3. What sinful thing did Judah do (Hosea 5:10)?

4. Why would Ephraim be crushed in judgment?

5. What nation did Israel seek help from?

6. How long would God remain separated from Israel and Judah?

HOSEA CHAPTER 6

Synopsis

God is just in punishing the wicked of Judah and Israel with drought and war (see Hosea 5:11-12 and Romans 3:26). The people of God have dealt "*treacherously*" with the Lord as an unfaithful wife does against her husband (Hosea 6:7). The prophet of God describes Israel's treachery of spiritual adultery as something that is "*horrible*" (Hosea 6:10). The people's sins have been listed as seeking help from other nations rather than God (Hosea 5:13), sexual immorality (Hosea 4:14), ungratefulness (Hosea 2:8-9), and idolatry (Hosea 4:12, 17). God has a controversy with the people due to these adulterous acts (Hosea 4:1). The only way to get the people back into a loving and respectful relationship with God was a heavy dose of chastisement.

Application

Sacrifices of burnt offerings were commanded of sinners under the Mosaic Law (see Exodus 29; Leviticus 1:3-17 and 6:8-13). The one doing the sacrifice would place his hands upon the animal's head and symbolically transfer his sins to the animal and then kill it. Through time this ordinance obviously became ritualistic and people were killing animals without true remorse for their sins. Hoses explains to the people that God desires the people to be truly good and knowledgeable rather than simply going through the motions of killing animals as burnt offerings (Hosea 6:6). Living righteously is more than ritualistic service to

God. Living by God's commandments involves a heart that truly loves God and is broken hearted when failure comes. Those whose hearts are not broken because of their sins will have no problem returning to those same sins. Jesus and his apostles tell us that those who truly **love** the Lord will obey his commands (John 14:15). Those who claim to **know** God will keep his commandments (1 John 2:4). Those who claim to **believe** in Jesus will be obedient (John 3:36; Acts 14:1-2 and Hebrews 11:1ff). Keeping the commandments of God makes manifest a heart that loves, believes, and knows God.

Hosea 6

The Lord reveals His will for Israel and Judah (6 all)

"**1** *Come, and let us return unto Jehovah; for he has torn, and he will heal us; he has smitten, and he will bind us up.* **2** *After two days will he revive us: on the third day he will raise us up, and we shall live before him*" **(6:1-2).**

Hosea prophetically looks to a day when the affliction of Israel, at the hands of our punishing God, will move the people to "*return unto Jehovah*" (see also Hosea 5:14-15). God's disciplinary methods will work with those who truly love him (see 1 Corinthians 5:1ff) (12o). There is an obvious implication of Christ's death, burial and resurrection as a type of death that the Christian undergoes at baptism. Men will come to die to the ways of sin and be raised, through baptism, to walk in newness of life (see Romans 6:1-3). The spiritual "*balm of Gilead*" (forgiveness) will be effectively applied to the wounds produced by God's chastening hand against Israel and Judah when people acknowledging and repent of their sins (Jeremiah 8:22). God will "heal" the punished people whereas the king of Assyria can do nothing (Hosea 5:13).

"**3** *And let us know, let us follow on to know Jehovah: his going forth is sure as the morning; and he will come unto us as the rain, as the latter rain that waters the earth*" **(6:3).**

The inference is that God has withheld the rains and water from the earth because of the people's sins. Throughout the scriptures we see drought being a form of God's chastening hand against the wicked (see Psalms 65:9-13 and Haggai 1:6-11). The solution to the drought, and any other affliction that is due to man's sins, is for the people to come to knowledge of God and his laws. Those who seek out the knowledge of God and obey him will be blessed as the waters return to the earth.

"*4 O Ephraim, what shall I do unto you? O Judah, what shall I do unto you? For your goodness is as a morning cloud, and as the dew that goes early away*" **(6:4).**

The Lord reasons with his people as they're distressed. What else could they expect God to do to change their hearts other than drought and war with surrounding nations? God is just for punishing his people due to their repeated sins (see Hosea 5:11-12). Their moments of goodness (lawful living) are compared to the "*morning cloud and dew that goes early away.*" As soon as the sun beats upon the dew it disappears. Anything that caused Israel or Judah discomfort caused them to turn away from God rather than to him (see the parable of the sower at Matthew 13). God's people ought to be strengthened and caused to draw closer to God during days of affliction yet some are angered by their distress (see 1 Peter 1:5-7 and Revelation 16:8-11).

"*5 Therefore have I hewed them by the prophets; I have slain them by the words of my mouth: and your judgments are as the light that goes forth*" **(6:5).**

The Lord is just by punishing the wicked for their sins. There is little good within Judah and Israel. The Lord's objective with the affliction of his people is to cause them to see their error and repent. God is good and seeks the betterment and welfare of all men.

"*6 For I desire goodness, and not sacrifice; and the knowledge of God more than burnt offerings*" **(6:6).**

There is a connection between God desiring the people's "*goodness*" and having knowledge of his laws (Hosea 4:1, 6). Due to the people not conducting themselves in righteousness (goodness) and having knowledge of God they were led into sin. Their sin moved God to punish his people with grievous drought and war so that they may come to repentance. Apparently the people had been following the ordinances of the Mosaic Law, in that they were performing sacrifices, yet their hearts were far from God. The prophet Samuel once replied to a confused and rebellious King Saul saying, "*22 has Jehovah as great delight in burnt offerings and sacrifices as in obeying the voice of Jehovah? Behold, to obey is better than sacrifice, and to hearken than the fat of rams. 23 For rebellion is as the sin of witchcraft, and stubbornness is as idolatry and teraphim. Because you have rejected the word of Jehovah, he has also rejected you from being king*" (1 Samuel 15:22-23). The Israel and Judah of Hosea's day had manifest a heart displaced from God by following the commandments of men and turning to other nations and deities for help all while holding to a deluded relationship with God (see Hosea 5:10-13).

Jesus quotes from Hosea 6:6 when answering the self righteous Pharisees who condemned him for eating with sinners. The Lord said, "*13 Go and learn what this means, I desire mercy, and not sacrifice: for I came not to call the righteous but sinners*" (Matthew 9:13). The Pharisees of Jesus' day were guilty of performing their sacrifices and adhering to the Mosaic Law not because they had a genuine love for God but because they loved the ways of the world and wanted to hold on to a deluded relationship with God. If they truly loved God they would have seen Jesus for who he was and obeyed him (John 14:15). The Pharisees would have acknowledged their sins and sought after the glory of God rather than men. Likewise, those who truly love God today will not just go through the motions of religion but come to a knowledge of God and perform the works of Abraham in righteousness (see John 8:39). If we find ourselves in a state of conviction that denies God's mercy to others we are no better than the Pharisees of Jesus' day. Jesus desires to have mercy on sinners if they will repent (3n). The ways of the Pharisees were not the ways of Jesus.

When David's sin with Bathsheba was exposed by Samuel the king acknowledged and confessed his great error. David writes a beautiful prayer about this situation at Psalms 51. The king shamefully acknowledges his error and pours his heart out to God in prayer. David writes, "16 *for you will not delight in sacrifice, or I would give it; you will not be pleased with a burnt offering.* 17 *the sacrifices of God are a broken spirit; a broken and contrite heart, O God, you will not despise*" (Psalms 51:16-17). David knew exactly what God expected. There was no redo of the situation. There was no amount of animals to sacrifice upon the altar of burnt offering that would restore the life and family of Uriah and Bathsheba. God's request for all who violate his laws and ruin the lives of other people is to have a "*broken and contrite heart.*" "A contrite heart or spirit is one in which the natural pride and self-sufficiency have been completely humbled by the consciousness of guilt (see Isaiah 66:1-2 and Jeremiah 23:29)" (ISBE volume 1; page 767-768). The prophet Isaiah said, "15 *For thus said the high and lofty One that inhabits eternity, whose name is Holy: I dwell in the high and holy place, with him also that is of a contrite and humble spirit, to revive the spirit of the humble, and to revive the heart of the contrite*" (Isaiah 57:15). God's word has the power to humble the hardened hearts of sin (see Jeremiah 23:29 and 2 Corinthians 2:14-16). David's heart was truly broken over his sin. The Apostle Paul said, "10 *Godly sorrow works repentance unto a salvation that brings no regret*" (2 Corinthians 7:10) (19q).

"**7** *But they like Adam have transgressed the covenant: there have they dealt treacherously against me*" **(6:7).**

The LXX uses the term Greek term *anthropos* (man) rather than the name Adam. The translators of the 1901 American Standard Version Bible may have believed that Adam was inferred though the name is not italicized but rather footnoted. Though Adam's name is not in many original manuscripts one must admit that the sins of "*man*" (*anthropos*) are traced back to him (Romans 5). Adam would certainly be included in the *"they"* that have sinned.

Hosea's audience lived in the days of the Mosaic Law or covenant and they were guilty of violating its precepts (Hosea 8:1). Adam lived during days of law too (see Romans 5:13-14). The laws that both the people during the days of Adam and Moses were under are deemed *"covenants"* (see Psalms 78:10). The sins of Adam were the beginning point of the entire world's struggle against sin (see Romans 3:23 and 5:12). God, after Adam's failure, permitted Satan to cease upon the opportunity of his laws to tempt man to sin (see Revelation 13:5-7 as compared to Romans 7:5-9). Though all men would fall prey to Satan's devices not all would walk in unrighteousness (see Romans 3:23-27).

To sin against God, no matter the circumstance, is to deal *"treacherously"* (unfaithfully) against God. No man in his right mind would hold on to a wife who deals unfaithfully in the marital relationship. A man with an adulterous wife would demand that she stop her affair or leave the marriage. Likewise God commands man to either stop their sin or remain alienated from him and his promised blessings.

"**8** *Gilead is a city of them that work iniquity; it is stained with blood.* **9** *And as troops of robbers wait for a man, so the company of priests murder in the way toward Shechem; yes, they have committed lewdness*" **(6:8-9).**

As Adam transgressed God's laws even so does Ephraim. The people of God are depicted as a city, Gilead, that is filled with those who *"work iniquity"* (i.e., their works are against the authorized will and laws of God - see Matthew 7:21-23). Nothing escapes the omniscient all seeing eyes of God (Jeremiah 23:23-25).

Gilead had become a refuge for sinners and murderers. Priests acted in unity as a gang of thugs to spill innocent blood and practice lewdness (acts of indecency). Israel was filled to the brim with sin and a mind of error.

"**10** *In the house of Israel I have seen a horrible thing: there whoredom is found in Ephraim, Israel is defiled.* **11** *Also, O Judah, there is a harvest appointed for you, when I bring back the captivity of my people*" **(6:10-11).**

The prophet Jeremiah said a similar thing. Jeremiah writes, "*30 A wonderful and horrible thing is come to pass in the land:* **31** *the prophets prophesy falsely, and the priests bear rule by their means; and my people love to have it so: and what will you do in the end thereof*" (Jeremiah 5:30-31 see also Jeremiah 23:14). The "*horrible thing*" that Israel has done is to commit spiritual adultery against the Lord who loves them (14e). They have sought the ways of the world and put their trust in other deities, man, and nations. "*Israel is defiled.*"

Though Hosea's primary work is with Israel he nonetheless is given a vision of Judah's sin too. God would squeeze Judah in his great wrath and preserve a remnant from the "*captivity*" (see Revelation 14:14-19). Zerubbabel, Ezra, and Nehemiah would work among the returning captives of Babylon to restore the kingdom of God.

Questions over Hosea Chapter 6

1. Compare and contrast Hosea 6:1-3 and Romans 6:1-3.

2. True or False: God is being unfair to Israel and Judah by punishing them for their sins.

3. Why did Jesus quote from Hosea 6:6 at Matthew 9:13?

4. What did Adam have to do with the transgressions of Israel and Judah?

5. What "*horrible thing*" did God see in the house of Israel?

HOSEA CHAPTER 7

Synopsis

Hosea depicts the mercy of God in this chapter. The Lord desires to heal Ephraim of her wickedness yet she refuses to accept his help. Ephraim will not call out to God for help but rather goes to Egypt and Assyria looking for relief from the chastising drought of God. The Lord is depicted as a father to Israel in this chapter. The Lord chastises his erring children with the hope that they would see their wrong and turn away from it. Israel; however, is like a spoiled brat that refuses to turn from their bad behavior. The Lord does not give up on them but he rather continues to strike them with punishment until they open their eyes to their sin.

Application

Christians today ought to "*consider*" why they suffer (see Hosea 7:2 and Haggai 1:6-11). The wise saints of God will be aware of God's punishing and chastising ways so that they see the cause of their misery. The Lord continues to chasten and punish people today when they sin (see Hebrews 12:7-12). God forbid that we would turn our backs upon his chastening rod and harden our hearts against him (Revelation 16:8-11, 21).

Hosea 7

Israel did not Consider why they Suffered (7:1-7)

"**1** *When I would heal Israel, then is the iniquity of Ephraim uncovered, and the wickedness of Samaria; for they commit falsehood, and the thief enters in, and the troop of robbers ravages without*" **(7:1).**

The Bible in Basic English reads, "*When my desire was for the fate of my people to be changed and to make Israel well, then the sin of Ephraim was made clear, and the evil-doing of Samaria; for their ways are false, and the thief comes into the house, while the band of outlaws takes property by force in the streets.*" The Lord truly wanted to heal and relieve Israel of her affliction of drought; however, they continued to do wicked things such as lie and rob each other (see Hosea 6:1-2). The Lord had no choice but to keep afflicting his people so that they may open their eyes to their error.

"**2** *And they consider not in their hearts that I remember all their wickedness: now have their own doings beset them about; they are before my face*" **(7:2).**

Israel's lack of knowledge and faith in God was the reason they did so many wicked things. The Lord afflicted them with drought yet they did not "*consider*" the cause of their affliction. Hosea's prophetic duties mirror that of Haggai's. Haggai's duty was to cause the released Babylonian captives to remember their responsibility to rebuild the temple of God. When God's people failed to fulfill the command to build the temple God afflicted them with drought. Haggai tells the people to "*consider*" why they were going through the hardships of drought and lack of crops (see Haggai 1:6-11). The object of God's affliction is to cause the people to open their eyes to their sin. If people will not follow God's commands there are consequences now and forevermore. The Lord would rather see people suffer now for wrong doing rather than letting them go on in the comfort of their wickedness.

Israel would not; however, consider their ways of wickedness. God would continue to afflict them so long as they remained obstinately opposed to his divine will (see Hosea 5:15). God is willing to forgive and forget one's iniquities only if the sinner acknowledges and repents of the error. Jeremiah foretold of a day when God would remember the sins of man no more (Jeremiah 31:34). The fulfillment of this promise was realized under the law or covenant of Jesus Christ (Hebrews 8:12). The sins that God will remember no more are the sins that man repents of, in a spirit of humility, asking God to forgive them (see Acts 8:22 and 1 John 1:8-10).

"**3** *They make the king glad with their wickedness, and the princes with their lies.* **4** *They are all adulterers; they are as an oven heated by the baker; he ceases to stir the fire, from the kneading of the dough, until it be leavened*" **(7:3-4).**

The contagious leaven of sin has spread throughout Israel. The shepherds of Israel are all wicked. The king, princes, and even priests have proved to be opposed to the righteousness of God. God's rulers should have viewed the sins of the people as a horrible thing; however, they were actually glad (see Hosea 6:10).

Israel had come to be like an adulterous man or woman who burns in their lust for one that they have no right to. There is no turning them away from the heat of their passion. Israel is like an oven that is so hot that it needs no help throughout the bread making process.

"**5** *On the day of our king the princes made themselves sick with the heat of wine; he stretched out his hand with scoffers.* **6** *For they have made ready their heart like an oven, while they lie in wait: their baker sleeps all the night; in the morning it burns as a flaming fire.* **7** *They are all hot as an oven, and devour their judges; all their kings are fallen: there is none among them that calls unto me*" **(7:5-7).**

The "*day of our king*" may have been some sort of birthday or anniversary. The people took the opportunity to blast themselves with alcoholic wine to the point of being sick. The king commended and enjoyed the sinful actions of his subjects yet it all backfired on him. When the opportune time arises Israel murdered their kings and judges. The society was sin sick from the sole of the foot to the head. Sad words in the Bible are found when the Lord proclaims, "*There is none among them that calls unto me*." Who shall call upon the name of the Lord today (Acts 22:16)? Shall we allow our minds to enter into a stupor of delusion having never prayed unto the Lord or call upon him in times of joy and pain and somehow expect that I will receive his grand award of heaven? (15h)

Israel's Deceptive Ways (7:8-16)

"**8** *Ephraim, he mixes himself among the peoples; Ephraim is a cake not turned.* **9** *Strangers have devoured his strength, and he knows it not: yea, gray hairs are here and there upon him, and he knows it not*" **(7:8-9).**

God's people were called upon to be separate; i.e., sanctified from the surrounding nation's error (see Leviticus 20:7, 23). When God's people "*mixed*" with those erring nations round about them they learned their ways of idolatry and whoredoms (see Psalms 106:35ff). God sees his bride Israel as a "*cake not turned*" i.e., burned on one side and good for nothing and raw on the other. Ephraim was so steeped in their mixing with the sinful nations around them that they had forgot God and did not even know the horrid state of their souls. The shame of their circumstances is exposed in that even the gray haired men had little to no knowledge of God and their sins. Grayed haired men, by reason years upon the earth, are expected to have greater wisdom and knowledge. Solomon writes, "*The hoary head* (gray hair) *is a crown of glory; It shall be found in the way of righteousness*" (Proverbs 16:31).

Though Ephraim lacked knowledge of God's laws they were nonetheless held responsible for their actions. Many today live by the principle "ignorance is bliss" yet we find throughout the word of God that ignorance is no excuse for violating law (14j).

"**10** *And the pride of Israel testifies to his face: yet they have not returned unto Jehovah their God, nor sought him, for all this*" **(7:10).**

Once again we find pride at the source of Israel's troubles with God (see Hosea 5:5). Israel's pride "*testifies*" to God that the people are defiled. Pride is the proof of their wickedness and God's just punishment against them. They have been given the evidence by the prophets yet they ignore their words and refuse to return to God. The drought has been dreadful yet they do not "*consider*" why they are suffering through it (see Hosea 7:2). "*All this*" (warnings and drought) have come upon them yet they are ignorant of their sinful ways.

"**11** *And Ephraim is like a silly dove, without understanding: they call unto Egypt, they go to Assyria.* **12** *When they shall go, I will spread my net upon them; I will bring them down as the birds of the heavens;* **I will chastise** *them, as their congregation has heard*" **(7:11-12)**.

God has sent his prophets and he has struck them like a lion with drought yet the people remain "*like a silly dove*" that has no "*understanding*." As an animal that flies through the air with no care but to seek immediate relief from the elements and sustenance so is Israel. God had blessed them with human minds of intelligence yet they rejected God's natural order of the human mind and ignored his divine efforts to restore them to spirituality. The people were like animals that lack respect for authority (2 Peter 2:12). The proof of their complete ignorance is that when they suffered by drought they turned to the Egyptians and Assyrians for help.

The Lord would not give up on his people. He would spread a net over them as one to capture birds of the heavens. The Lord would bring these silly and ignorant birds down to the ground and "*chastise them*" (17d). Notice that the people's ignorance of God was not a just cause for their sins and neither was it reason for God not to punish them. Though Israel was ignorant God would continue to strike them with a heavy hand of chastisement until they either fell in death or repented. Solomon said, "*Withhold not correction from the child; for if you beat him with the rod he will not die.* **14** *You shall beat him with the rod, and shall deliver his soul from Sheol*" (Proverbs 23:13-14) (33d). The Lord knows that it would be better for him to continue to strike the erring and disobedient than to let them perish in their sins. Man must come to see that there is nothing worth loosing out on heaven. Similarly, Jesus said, "*8 And if your hand or your foot causes you to stumble cut it off and cast it away: it is better for you to enter into life maimed or halt, rather than having two hands or two feet to be cast into the eternal fire. 9 And if your eye causes you to stumble, pluck it out, and cast it from you: it is good for you to enter into life with one eye, rather than having two eyes to be cast into the hell of fire*" (Matthew 18:8-9).

"**13** *Woe unto them! For they have wandered from me; destruction unto them! For they have trespassed against me: though I would redeem them, yet they have spoken lies against me*" **(7:13).**

The Lord has ever stood ready to "*redeem*" Israel; however, their lies have sealed their fate of punishment. God's true desire was to have mercy on the people if only they would acknowledge their wickedness and repent (see Hosea 6:6). Jesus once said, "*37 O Jerusalem, Jerusalem, that kills the prophets, and stones them that are sent unto her! How often would I have gathered your children together, even as a hen gathers her chickens under her wings, and you would not*" (Matthew 23:37).

They have denied the one true God and have gone after other deities and nations in their whoredoms. Nothing but a woeful punishment awaits them at the chastising hands of the Almighty God.

"**14** *And they have not cried unto me with their heart, but they howl upon their beds: they assemble themselves for grain and new wine; they rebel against me.* **15** *Though I have taught and strengthened their arms, yet do they device mischief against me.* **16** *They return, but not to him that is on high; they are like a deceitful bow; their princes shall fall by the sword for the rage of their tongue: this shall be their derision in the land of Egypt*" **(7:14-16).**

Israel cries out in anguish not because they're sorry about their sins but because they have lost their material wealth and freedom to Assyria. Their hearts were not with God though they said it was. They deceitfully promise to return to the Lord; however, the moment the opportunity of sin is there they seize it without thinking twice about the eternal consequences thereof (Hosea 6:4, 7) (14d). God, as a father figure to Israel, had taught them and strengthened them yet they rebelled against him.

Israel is likened unto a bow that is designed to thrust an arrow at the bull's eye. Israel has missed the mark, however, and deceitfully at that. They made empty and deceitful promises to God that they would walk in his statutes yet they lied and fulfilled the lust of their flesh. Egypt will be far from a safe haven for Israel. Assyria would soon destroy them.

Far too many times sinful man does the same things today. When God's heavy hand of chastisement is upon the sinner they make vows to never sin again. As soon as the tribulation of God's punishment is lifted the sinner is right back to his old ways. When an opportunity to sin arises the sinner jumps on it without considering the ordeal that was just suffered at the hands of our angry God.

Questions over Hosea Chapter 7

1. What happened when God attempted to heal Israel of her affliction?

2. How many people called out to God for help during the days of their affliction?

3. What relationship is there between Ephraim having gray hair and no understanding?

4. Who did Israel call out to for help during the time of their affliction?

5. **True or False:** Though Israel was chastised by God they continued to do sinful things.

HOSEA CHAPTER 8

Synopsis

Hosea is given a vision of the coming fierce armies of Assyria descending upon Israel like an Eagle after prey. While Israel worships their calves God prepares for war. God had sent his prophets to warn Israel. The Lord cursed the land with a dreaded drought. Furthermore God gave his people ten thousand things of his law to instruct the people yet they refused it all (Hosea 8:12). The time of God's just punishment has come upon a rebellious people and he would "*remember their iniquity*" (Hosea 8:13).

Application

When a people walk in continuous sin they may expect nothing less that God's divine wrath. One may claim that they love, know, and believe in God all they want but the Lord looks to man's actions. Those who truly love, know, and believe in God are those who hear his words and obey them. When a man or woman does not spend time studying God's actual words they depend upon their own preconceived ideas of religion for understanding. The longer such a foolish approach to one's eternal soul goes on the more foreign God's word actually is. When the real laws of God are examined they sound strange (Hosea 8:12). The rebellious often choose their own ways over the ways of God because they forget their true Maker (Hosea 8:14). The best remedy for any man or woman who truly wants to make it to heaven is to look into the laws of God and learn now before its everlasting too late.

Hosea 8

Israel has Sown the Wind and shall now reap the Whirlwind (8:1-7)

"*1 Set the trumpet to your mouth. As an eagle he comes against the house of Jehovah, because they have transgressed my covenant, and trespassed against my law*" **(8:1).**

The watchmen of Israel are instructed to blow the trumpet as an alarm because the "*eagle comes against the house of Jehovah.*" The eagle is apparently the Assyrian Empire. Assyria would swoop down upon Israel and destroy her. Once again Hosea is careful to list the cause of Israel's destruction; i.e., "**because** *they have transgressed my covenant and trespassed against my law.*" Keeping God's laws have always been important with the Lord from the days of Adam to Moses to Christ and beyond to our days (see Deuteronomy 27:26; Galatians 3:10 and Romans 6:16-17). When Israel rebelled against God he sent drought and his prophets to turn the people back in repentance. Seeing that there is no response to the Lord's efforts to turn the people he ratchets up the degree of punishment.

Israel's casual approach to the laws of God and sin are the cause of all her troubles. Secondly, the prophet of God is careful to let every man and woman know that they are getting their just reward. God will punish them and they have no cause for complaint.

"*2 They shall cry unto me, My God, we Israel know you. 3 Israel has cast off that which is good: the enemy shall pursue him. 4 They have set up kings, but not by me; they have made princes, and I knew it not: of their silver and their gold have they made them idols, that they may be cut off*" **(8:2-4).**

Hosea continues to add to the sins of whoredom that Israel has been involved in. The prophet of God exposes Israel's evil character in that they cast off what is good rather than receiving it. They set up kings and princes over Israel without even praying to God about it. God was not a part of their lives. Instead of consulting with God they took their blessings of silver and gold and constructed idols of heathen deities and called them their gods.

As a last resort; i.e., when all else has failed, Israel now cries unto God claiming "*we know you*." God will not hear their cries of distress because they had cast off all that was good and right. Jesus said that many will say the same thing on the final Day of Judgment (Matthew 7:21-23). Let us learn the lesson today. The Apostle John tells us that those who truly know God are those who obey his commandments (see 1 John 2:4). Let us truly love (John 14:15), believe (John 3:36 and Acts 14:1-2), and know (1 John 2:4) God now by our acts of obedience before it's everlastingly too late.

"**5** *He has cast off your calf, O Samaria; mine anger is kindled against them: how long will it be ere they attain to innocence?* **6** *For from Israel is even this; the workman made it, and it is no god; yea, the calf of Samaria shall be broken in pieces.* **7** *For they sow the wind, and they shall reap the whirlwind: he has no standing grain; the blade shall yield no meal; if so be it yield, strangers shall swallow it up*" **(8:5-7).**

Hosea is so confident in his words that God has given him to speak that he said the "*calf of Samaria*" is already cast off. The day of God's vengeance and punishment has come. Israel's idolatry kindled God's anger like hay to a fire. Israel's continued ignorance and misunderstanding of spiritual matters is a sub theme of Hosea. Israel was so deluded in ignorance toward God that they fabricated an idol out of silver, gold, or wood and actually called it a god. Hosea questions Israel's folly by asking if the work of man's hands had the power or ability to help them in the day of their calamity. Would the idol actually help, aid, or deliver the people from the Almighty God's wrath? The answer is obvious. An idol made with man's hands is absolutely nothing. The idol cannot speak much less help someone.

Israel has sown to the wind in foolishness by putting their hope in other nations and pagan deities. The harvest of their wickedness will be the whirlwind of God's wrath in the form of Assyria. Solomon said, "*8 He that sows iniquity shall reap calamity; and the rod of his wrath shall fail*" (Proverbs 22:8 see also Galatians 6:7-8). The calamity of Israel would be God's chastening hand against them in the form of the Assyrian army.

Israel has totally Forgotten God (8:8-14)

"*8 Israel is swallowed up: now are they among the nations as a vessel wherein none delights. 9 For they are gone up to Assyria, like a wild ass alone by himself: Ephraim has hired lovers. 10 Yea, though they hire among the nations, now will I gather them; and they begin to be diminished by reason of the burden of the king of princes*" **(8:8-10).**

Earlier Hosea had wrote of Gomer saying, "*7 And she shall follow after her lovers, but she shall not overtake them; and she shall seek them, but shall not find them: then shall she say, I will go and return to my first husband; for then was it better with me than now*" (Hosea 2:7). At a time of Gomer's greatest need her lovers (the idols she constructed with her own hands, the Assyrians, and the Egyptians) are no where to be found. They had received their full of sexual immorality with the harlot and have no more need for her.

Hosea now depicts Israel as a woman at the end of her rope. Israel, in a state of desperation, sends ambassadors to Assyria seeking peace yet they do not receive her. Israel is like a wild ass that stands alone before the nations. No one will help her. Israel is depicted as a foolish whore that has given herself out for pay and expects people to respect her. She is a piece of trash in their sight and they want nothing to do with her. The nations cast Israel away after they have received what they desired of her.

"*11 Because Ephraim has multiplied altars for sinning. 12 I wrote for him the ten thousand things of my law; but they are counted as a strange thing*" **(8:11-12).**

Israel did not have the calf alone at Samaria but other deities were multiplied throughout the land. Their allegiance was to the multitude of idols rather than God. God had delivered to them "*the ten thousand things of my law*." These laws were designed to instruct, sanctify, protect and defend the people yet they not only were ignorant of these laws but rejected them. The numerous laws were designed to direct each step of Israel yet she wanted nothing of subjection and obedience (see Jeremiah 10:23).

When God's commands or laws come to be "*strange*" to those who would claim to be his disciples then there is a serious problem between that person and the law giver. Some today believe that it is a "*strange*" thing to name false teachers by name, to withdraw from unruly and unfaithful brethren, to suffer calamity for sin, and to live faithfully to God's commands. Some Christians think it's a strange thing to actually find men who meet the qualifications of a Bishop or elder listed at 1 Timothy 3. Some also believe that it is strange for a church not to support the needy of the world, to exclude musical instruments in worship, and to not use the building for social events. The idea of seeing God's commands as strange is that they do not meet the people's preconceived ideas of what religion should be. When man is ignorant of God's actual laws they become strange when heard (11h).

"**13** *As for the sacrifices of mine offerings, they sacrifice flesh and eat it; but Jehovah accepts them not: now will he **remember their iniquity**, and visit their sins; they shall return to Egypt*" **(8:13).**

The sacrifices Israel makes to God are nothing more than eating a common meal for them. God does not recognize nor accept their worship because their hearts are far from him. Israel needed to repent and make their lives right with God. They needed to illustrate to God that they were serious about serving him before he would accept their worship (see Isaiah 1:11ff and Hebrews 11:1ff). Now is the time of Israel's punishment for the sins she has committed. She shall go into captivity to Assyria as she once was in Egypt. Again, we see the just cause of God's wrath and chastisement against Israel. They were sinners who did not acknowledge their wrong.

"**14** *For Israel has forgotten his Maker, and built palaces; and Judah has multiplied fortified cities: but I will send a fire upon his cities, and it shall devour the castles thereof*" **(8:14).**

Earlier God revealed through his prophet that he was responsible for the drought they experienced (see Hosea 6:3). The drought did not curve the people's sinful passions. The Lord now prepares the people for warfare. The Assyrians would conquer Israel by burning their cities and castles down to the ground.

Israel's "*Maker*" is God yet they neither acknowledged him nor knew him. They walked rebelliously making idols in their cities and worshipping them. When man becomes so secure in his riches and fortifications the time of worrying ought to begin. The Lord would devour all that Israel and Judah put their trust in.

Questions over Hosea Chapter 8

1. Did Israel really "*know*" God?

2. Compare and contrast Hosea 8:7 and Galatians 6:7-8.

3. What did God give Ephraim that was considered so strange by the wicked?

4. Why didn't God accept the sacrifices of Ephraim?

5. What was so wrong about Israel and Judah building palaces and fortified cities?

HOSEA CHAPTER 9

Synopsis

Hosea exposes Israel's "*deep corruption*" (Hosea 9:9). Israel's harlotry would bring them to such a terrible relationship with God that he is depicted as departing from them (see Hosea 9:12) and casting them (Hosea 9:17). Though God had blessed his people they were not grateful to him but rather went to other deities and nations for their joy. The time had come for God to visit Israel with "*days of recompense*" for their evil deeds (Hosea 9:7).

Application

There is only so much bad behavior a parent or God can stand before a time of reckoning judgment is passed down to the rebellious. God will chasten Israel with death, exile, and starvation (see Hosea 4:9; 7:12; 10:2 and 12:2). No man or woman alive today will be overlooked when it comes to their moral decisions in this life. People that live their lives good and right will be rewarded now and forevermore with joy and peace. Those who do evil will experience pain now and forevermore. Jesus said, "28 *Marvel not at this: for the hour cometh, in which all that are in the tombs shall hear his voice,* 29 *and shall come forth; they that have done good, unto the resurrection of life; and they that have done evil, unto the resurrection of judgment*" (John 5:28-29).

Hosea 9

Israel is "deeply corrupted" (9:1-9)

"**1** *Rejoice not, O Israel, for joy, like the peoples; for you have played the harlot, departing from your God; you have loved hire upon every grain-floor*" **(9:1).**

Israel, under the lengthy reign of Jeroboam II, had experienced wealth and prosperity. Their "*joy*" was not over their spiritual relationship with God but with their prosperity. They had built palaces and fortresses with their excess and put their trust in many things other than God (see Hosea 8:14). Now; however, was not the time for rejoicing but for mourning over their sins.

Hosea helps the ignorant and hard hearted people draw the connection between what he experienced with Gomer and what God is now experiencing with Israel. Israel had been unfaithful to their God just as Gomer was unfaithful to her husband Hosea. Israel's spiritual idolatry is summed up as a "*departure from God*" (see also Hosea 1:2). Israel had participated in idolatry (2 Kings 17:16ff and Hosea 8:11) and rejected knowledge of God and his commands (Hosea 4:1). God's commands had become "*strange*" to Israel (Hosea 8:12) and they cared more for the ways of the world than God (Hosea 2:13). Israel only compounded their problems with God by seeking help from other nations like Egypt and Assyria (2 Kings 16:5-6; 17:4ff and Hosea 7:11-12).

"**2** *The threshing-floor and the winepress shall not feed them, and the new wine shall fail her.* **3** *They shall not dwell in Jehovah's land; but Ephraim shall return to Egypt, and they shall eat unclean food in Assyria*" **(9:2-3).**

The blessings of grain and new wine will not always be there for Israel. Israel was about to face difficult days of bondage as in the days of Egypt. Eventually, Israel would find herself exiled to Assyria where they would eat "*unclean bread*" (i.e., bread sacrificed to the idols of Assyria). God would punish and chastise his people for their gross error (see Hosea 4:9; 5:14-15; 7:12; 10:2 and 12:2) (17d). God would not merely act out in anger but the Lord would correct his people so that they may repent.

"**4** *They shall not pour out wine-offerings to Jehovah, neither shall they be pleasing unto him: their sacrifices shall be unto them as the bread of mourners; all that eat thereof shall be polluted; for their bread shall be for their appetite; it shall not come unto the house of Jehovah.* **5** *What will you do in the day of solemn assembly, and in the day of the feast of Jehovah?*" **(9:4-5)**

As a captive in Assyria the people would have no access to the temple in Jerusalem to make their solemn sacrifices of praise, thanksgiving, and oblations for their sin. There would be no way to celebrate and worship God on the set feasts days. The people will be captives and their eating would be to satisfy their starvation rather than being a joyous moment of blessings from God. The Lord asks the people "*What will you do in the day of solemn assembly and in the day of the feasts of Jehovah?*" The people ought to be concerned now. There comes a day when they will be taken captive into Assyria and there will be no observance of the Sabbath or set feasts.

"**6** *For, lo, they are gone away from destruction; yet Egypt shall gather them up, Memphis shall bury them; their pleasant things of silver, nettles shall possess them; thorns shall be in their in their tents.* **7** *The days of visitation are come, the days of recompense are come; Israel shall know it: the prophet is a fool, the man that has the spirit is mad, for the abundance of your iniquity, and* **because** *the enmity is great*" **(9:6-7).**

Memphis was a great city in Egypt and would be the burial place for the treasures of Israel. The comforts of ease will now leave them and in the place of comfort will be thorns and nettles. The day of Jehovah's visitation or recompense had come to Israel for her iniquities. There was a great gulf of enmity between God and Israel due to their sins. The prophet was a fool and the one who claimed to have the spirit of God was actually a mad man. False prophets were proclaiming days of comfort whereas the true prophets; i.e., Hosea, were proclaiming doom and gloom for the people's iniquity.

Hosea is careful to let the people know why they are being taken captive by Assyria. God has warned them through the prophets and drought yet they would give no heed to his divine words. Israel's day of great punishment has come "*because*" they refused to obey their heavenly father's commands. The word "*because*" is very significant to our study. God's punishment or chastisement of Israel is "*because*" of her sins. God does not act out in anger for no reason. The Lord's anger is because of Israel's sins. The only way to get Israel back to obedience and love of God is to chastise them as a parent would do to an unruly child.

"**8** *Ephraim was a watchman with my God: as for the prophet, a fowler's snare is in all his ways, and enmity in the house of his God.* **9** *They have deeply corrupted themselves, as in the days of Gibeah: he will remember their iniquity, he will visit their sins*" **(9:8-9).**

God had set prophets up as watchmen to watch and warn the people against the onslaught of error yet Ephraim actually watched "*against*" God (see footnote at bottom of ASV). God's ways, laws, and commands were "*strange*" to the people (see Hosea 8:12). Israel was consequentially carefully, watchfully, and purposefully alienated from God. Such a state of mind is considered a "*deep corruption*" (14e). When people reject the words of God there is no hope. Jesus said that those who blaspheme the Holy Spirit will receive no forgiveness (see Mark 3:29 and 1 John 5:16).

Hosea compares present Israel with God's people during the days of "*Gibeah*" (see Judges Chapters 19-20). At that time the Benjaminites of Gibeah raped and abused a man's concubine all night and she died. The owner cut the woman into twelve parts and delivered them to the twelve tribes of Israel. Israel rallied and nearly exterminated the Benjaminites for their wickedness. Israel now is no different than the base Benjaminites of the days of Gibeah.

A Lack of Interest is the cause of Israel's Destruction (9:10-17)

"**10** *I found Israel like grapes in the wilderness; I saw your fathers as the first-ripe in the fig-tree at its first season: but they came to Baalpeor, and consecrated themselves unto the shameful thing, and became abominable like that which they loved*" **(9:10).**

God compared Israel to fresh grapes in the wilderness and the first ripe figs upon the tree. The Lord was excited about Israel; however, it was not long that their fruit proved to be rotten. That "*shameful*" deed done at Baalpeor (the Baal of Peor) is recorded at Numbers 25:1ff (14e). Israel played the harlot with the daughters of Moab by sexual immorality and by making sacrifices to the gods of Moab.

Israel's desire was to be like the surrounding nations. They wanted their freedoms from God and the ability to worship and play with those who rejected Jehovah's creation. Many Christian's are likewise casting off their first love of God for the "fun" and "freedoms" that are offered by the world around us.

"**11** *As for Ephraim, their glory shall fly away like a bird: there shall be no birth, and none with child, and no conception.* **12** *Though they bring up their children, yet will I bereave them, so that not a man shall be left: yea, woe also to them when I depart from them!*" **(9:11-12)**

All those worldly interest that Israel had put her trust in shall fly away like a bird. She decked herself out in beauty to attract the world yet she was treated shamefully (see Hosea 2:13). Children will be scarce due to miscarriages and those who do make it will be bereaved by Jehovah so that eventually no one is left. Israel's alienation has been caused with by their sin. God will "*depart*" from Israel because they chose to depart from him (see Hosea 9:1).

"**13** *Ephraim, like as I have seen Tyre, is planted in a pleasant place: but Ephraim shall bring out his children to the slayer.* **14** *Give them, O Jehovah – what will you give? Give them a miscarrying womb and dry* *breasts.* **15** *All their wickedness of their doings I will drive them out of my house; I will love them no more; all their princes are revolters"* **(9:13-15).**

Jehovah planted his people in a land that was likened unto Tyre (i.e., secure from the west by the Mediterranean Sea and to the East by the mountains). Though Israel had the same security they would bring out their children to the slayer for their sin. Jehovah would drive them out of the land so that the slayer would destroy them. Hosea's prayer for Israel is not that they would seek security but rather that God's full wrath would be completed in the unfruitful wombs of women. King David is often found praying these same types of prayers against the enemies of God (see Psalms 69:24 and Matthew 5:43-45).

"**16** *Ephraim is smitten, their root is dried up, they shall bear no fruit: yea, though they bring forth, yet will I slay the beloved fruit of their womb.* **17** *My God will cast them away,* **because** *they did not hearken unto him; and they shall be wanderers among the nations"* **(9:16-17).**

Israel is like a tree that dies due to lingering drought conditions. The Lord is very careful to let Ephraim know why they are withering away. Hosea writes, "*Because they did not hearken unto him*." The idea of "*hearkening*" is to not only listen but to obey (to listen attentively or give heed [AHD 600]). One who listens is one who has interest in the topic at hand. To obey is to believe in a cause. Israel neither had interest in God nor believed in his ways. Israel was so wrapped up in desiring to be like the world that they completely forgot about the Lord and his prescribed ways.

Questions over Hosea Chapter 9

1. Why would Ephraim eat unclean food in Assyria?

2. What are the "*days of recompense*" that are upon Israel (see Hosea 9:7)?

3. Who did Israel erroneously consecrate or separate to?

4. Why would God drive Ephraim out of his house?

HOSEA CHAPTER 10

Synopsis

Israel had come to a cross road in their faith. They understood what God expected of them; however, their personal desires were in another direction. Hosea tells us that their "heart is divided" between God and worldliness (Hosea 10:2). The people's language and actions displayed a heart that was more interested in serving the idols of the pagan nations around them than God. Israel was so deeply steeped in their love of worldliness that when God chastised them for their wickedness they choose death over repentance (Hosea 10:8). The prophet depicts Ephraim as a stubborn heifer that refuses to consider wisdom and righteousness. Rather than trusting God the stubborn people put their trust in their fortresses, mighty men of valor, idols and other nations of men.

Application

Jesus and the Apostle John quote from Hosea 10:8 to illustrate just how wicked men have always been and will continue to be. Rather than letting the gospel of Jesus Christ soften their hearts the wicked choose to continue in their sins (see 2 Corinthians 2:16). Rather than choosing repentance the people choose the chastening hand of God even if it means death (see Luke 23:28-31 and Revelation 6:16). When men choose death and the things of this world what more can God do for them?

Hosea 10

Internal Corruption shall cause Assyria to march on Israel plundering and Exiling God's People (10:1-8)

"**1** *Israel is a luxuriant vine, that puts forth his fruit: according to the abundance of his fruit he has multiplied his altars; according to the goodness of their land they have made goodly pillars*" **(10:1)**.

Israel stood out among the nations like a fruitful and healthy grapevine. Rather than attributing their abundance and wealth to God they built "*pillars*" (obelisks) to make their sacrifices and thanksgivings to other deities.

"**2** *Their heart is divided; now shall they be found guilty: he will smite their altars, he will destroy their pillars.* **3** *Surely now shall they say, we have no king; for we fear not Jehovah; and the king, what can he do for us*?" **(10:2-3)**.

The hearts of the people were divided. They knew of their history with Jehovah God yet their hearts longed for the deities of other nations. A part of them wanted to serve God yet another part desired to be like the surrounding nations. Jesus said, "13 *No servant can serve two masters: for either he will hate the one, and love the other; or else he will hold to one, and despise the other. You cannot serve God and mammon*" (Luke 16:13).

The Bible in Basic English reads as follows for Hosea 10:3 - "Now, truly, they will say, We have no king, we have no fear of the Lord; and the king, what is he able to do for us?" When God smites the people's altars and destroys the pillars (obelisks) they will open their eyes and "*surely*" see their great folly.

"**4** *They speak vain words, swearing falsely in making covenants: therefore judgment springs up as hemlock in the furrows of the field.* **5** *The inhabitants of Samaria shall be in terror for the calves of Bethaven; for the people thereof shall mourn over it, and the priests thereof that* *rejoiced over it, for the glory thereof, because it is departed from it.* **6** *It also shall be* **carried unto Assyria** *for a present to king Jareb: Ephraim shall receive shame, and Israel shall be ashamed of his own counsel"* **(10:4-6).**

The kings of the land of Israel have spoken "*vain words, swearing falsely in making covenants.*" The kings of Israel had the integrity of a mad fool among the nations and so they were despoiled. Israel's prophets were also seen as "*fools*" (Hosea 9:7). The princes of Israel were "*revolters*" (rebellious) (Hosea 9:15) and now we see that the priests were just as lost as the other shepherds of Israel. The priests are seen rejoicing over the idolatrous calves of Samaria and Dan. All positions of authority were lost to ignorance and irreverence toward God.

The "*calves of Bethaven*" shall be shamefully carried away in defeat to Assyria and presented as a present to the king of Assyria. God's people will be utterly shamed for their wickedness and hardness of heart.

"**7** *As for Samaria, her king is cut off, as foam upon the water.* **8** *The high places also of Aven, the sin of Israel, shall be destroyed: the thorn and the thistle shall come up on their altars; and they shall say to the mountains, Cover us; and to the hills, Fall on us*" **(10:7-8).**

The omniscient eyes of God are upon his nation and he sees wickedness. The Lord will cut off the king of Israel and all the nobles and the nation will fall. The Lord will also destroy all the places of idolatry among the people of Israel. The places of idolatry at "*Aven*" will be so thoroughly destroyed that there will be nothing but thorns and thistles growing in their place. Aven is the Beth-aven of the scriptures. "Hosea (4:15 and 10:5) uses the term Beth-aven as a symbol of reproach for Bethel and Amos 5:5 makes a pun on the name, 'Bethel shall come to nought' from the Hebrew word *awen*... A prophetic guild appears to have existed in Bethel and had some contact with Eisha (2 Kings 2:3); but according to Amos and Hosea, Canaanite religion with its terrible moral, social, and religious degradations was dominate at Bethel. Because it was synonymous with the very worst elements of paganism and idolatry, these two prophets launched the most scathing denunciations against it" (ISBE volume 1, page 464-466).

When the people see the high places and pillars destroyed by the hand of Jehovah God they will cry out in their shame to the mountains saying, "*Cover us; and to the hills, Fall on us*." Jesus made this same statement to the weeping women who cried and bewailed as he carried his cross to be crucified. Jesus turns to the women and said that people would soon say, "*cover us and to the hills, Fall on us*" and then he explains the words saying, "*For if they do these things in the green tree, what shall be done in the dry*?" (Luke 23:31). The Lord's point was that the people were wicked and without shame. While the object of punishment and chastisement is repentance many would rather die in the hardness of their hearts than repent (see Revelation 16:9). Furthermore we find the Apostle John making this statement at Revelation 6:16 in relationship to people choosing death rather than repenting at the behest of their wrathful and punishing God. Hosea, Jesus, and John's point is that many will choose death in this life rather than softening their hearts and acknowledging the error of their ways (17d).

Israel's Bleak Future (10:9-11)

"**9** *O Israel, you have sinned from the days of Gibeah: there they stood; the battle against the children of iniquity does not overtake them in Gibeah.* **10** *When it is my desire,* **I will chastise them**; *and the peoples shall be gathered against them, when they are bound to their two transgressions*" **(10:9-10).**

The ASV foot note states that the sin of Israel was "more than in the days" of Gibeah rather than sinning "*from the days of Gibeah*." We know that Israel had sinned previous to the days of Gibeah so that it is more likely that the thought is "more than in the days of Gibeah." The sin that occurred in Gibeah of Benjamin was discussed at Hosea 9:9 (see notes).

At a time that Jehovah determines he shall punish Israel for two transgressions. The two transgressions are likely two sins that sum up their "*spirit of whoredom*" (Hosea 4:12). Israel turned to other gods (Hosea 4:12) and other nations (Hosea 7:11) for comfort, hope, and identity.

"**11** *And Ephraim is a heifer that is taught, that loves to tread out the grain; but I have passed over upon her fair neck: I will set a rider on Ephraim; Judah shall plow, Jacob shall break his clods*" **(10:11).**

Ephraim has already been compared to a "*stubborn heifer*" in behavior at Hosea 4:16. The stubborn heifer shall no longer find the pleasantries of grain in Palestine but rather be forced into hard labor in the fields of foreigners for her food.

True hope rest in Jehovah God (10:12-15)

"**12** *Sow to yourselves in righteousness, reap according to kindness; break up your fallow ground; for it is time to seek Jehovah, till he come and rain righteousness upon you.* **13** *You have plowed wickedness, you have reaped iniquity; you have eaten the fruit of lies; for you trust in your own way, in the multitude of your mighty men*" **(10:12-13).**

Rather than sowing seeds of wickedness and reaping a whirlwind of God's wrath the people ought to sow seeds of righteousness and reap peace (see Hosea 8:7). The only way such a spiritual harvest will happen is if the wicked of Israel "*break up your fallow ground*." Uncultivated ground is hard and needs tilling to get it in shape to plant seeds. Likewise, the people's hearts were hardened in sin and needed to be softened by the gospel of Jesus Christ so that they may bear fruits of righteousness (see 2 Corinthians 2:16 and Galatians 5:22-24). The gospel of Jesus Christ has the power to save anyone who is willing to hear, learn, and obey (Romans 1:16).

Rather than repenting and sowing seeds of righteousness in their minds they had plowed and sowed wicked seeds in the wicked fields of their minds. The harvest is nothing but sin, lies, and consequential punishment. Rather than trusting in God they put their trust in "*their mighty men*." We find a fourth part of the equation to the spirit of whoredom. Not only did Israel trust in other deities, nations, and their fortifications (Hosea 8:14) but they also put their trust in the mighty men of Israel (i.e., men of war). No comfort; however, would ever be found in any source other than Jehovah.

"**14** *Therefore shall a tumult arise among your people, and all your fortresses shall be destroyed, as Shalman destroyed Betharbel in the day of battle: the mother was dashed in pieces with her children.* **15** *So shall Bethel do unto you because of your great wickedness: at daybreak shall the king of Israel be utterly cut off*" **(10:14-15).**

Jehovah has pronounced sure doom for their wicked acts. All that they trusted in would be destroyed (i.e., their fortresses, mighty men of valor, idols, and nations of men).

Hosea gives the example of "*Shalman*" destroying Betharbel. Though nothing is known about this person or place it is apparent that Israel was fearfully knowledgeable of the incident, as they were the events of Gibeah, else the illustration would have no meaning. Some believe "*Shalman*" to be the Shalmanezer of Assyria. The Assyrians' method of war was terrifying. Israel is told that they will experience the full force of this callous and cold blooded army of killers.

Questions over Hosea Chapter 10

1. What shameful thing does Hosea reveal about Israel at chapter 10:1-3?

2. What type of words did Israel speak?

3. What shall be carried to Assyria?

4. Why would the people call upon the mountains and hills to fall upon them?

5. Why did Jesus and John quote from Hosea 10:8?

6. Hosea has mentioned Gibeah several times in this study. What significance is there to Gibeah in relationship to Ephraim (Israel)?

7. What did Israel put her trust in?

HOSEA CHAPTER 11

Synopsis

God cared for Israel as though he were his own son. Israel; however, rebelled against God. The people put their trust in their mighty men, fortified cities, other nations, and other gods. The Lord sent his prophets to admonish them yet they rejected their divine instructions. The people were bent on destruction. There was nothing the Lord could do more for them except send the sword of war (Hosea 11:6). Out of the dust cloud of sword and war a remnant would arise trembling toward God and acknowledging their error.

Application

People prove themselves to be the sons of God today when living by faith and faithfully enduring the various suffering that come with this life (Romans 8:14-17). The true sons of God will be moved to repentance after being chastised for sins. God's true sons will be heart broken over their error and they will fearfully seek out God's forgiveness (see 2 Corinthians 7:10). Hosea reveals God's great love for his people in this chapter. God chastens his sons because he loves them and wants to see them following his divine instructions. The author of Hebrews writes, "*7 it is for chastening that you endure; God deals with you as with sons; for what son is there whom his father chastens not?*" (See Hebrews 12:7). Hosea chapter 11 explains to us that God will always have a class of men and women who will respond favorably to his chastening punishment.

The favorable reaction to chastisement is to acknowledge one's wrong doing and repent of those things (see Hosea 11:10-11). There will also be a class of people bent on their own destruction as they live by their own standards and enjoy sin on this earth.

Hosea 11

Israel's Doom is due to their spirit of Rebellion (11:1-7)

"*1 When Israel was a child, then I loved him, and called my son out of Egypt*" **(11:1).**

The Lord appears to be pondering the more pleasant days of Israel's youth as he did at Hosea 9:10 and 10:9. During the infant years of the nation of Israel God blessed them and brought them out of Egypt. God "*loved him*" as a son and cared for them as a mother (see Exodus 19:4).

Fascinatingly, we find Matthew quoting from Hosea 11:1 at Matthew 2:15. Matthew tells us that Joseph and Mary were commanded to take their baby Jesus to Egypt because Herod sought to kill the child. Joseph, Mary, and Jesus remained in Egypt until Herod died. Matthew writes, "*15 and they were there* (in Egypt) *until the death of Herod: that it might be fulfilled which was spoken by the Lord through the prophet, saying, Out of Egypt did I call my son*" (Matthew 2:15). Hosea identifies God's people as his beloved sons that he delivered from Egyptian bondage here. Matthew speaks of God's beloved son Jesus that was delivered out of the hands of Herod. God truly cares for his people and for his Son Jesus. Egypt was a place of protection for Jesus and a place of spiritual development for Israel. Israel was delivered out of Egypt by the mighty hand of God just as God has the mighty power to deliver man from the servitude of sin (see John 8:31-36 and Romans 6:15ff). God truly loves his sons and wants the very best for them.

Matthew's use of Hosea 11:1 in relationship to Jesus helps us understand how prophecy is used in the New Testament. Old Testament quotes found in the New Testament often have duel meanings. The point is often made in relationship to the types of Christ that are found in the Old Testament (Abraham and David etc.). Men displayed the mind of the future Christ when they said things that Jesus would later say. David literally said, "*My God, my God, why have you forsaken me*" at Psalms 22:1 just as Jesus did while on the cross (see Matthew 27:46). The Old Testament was revealing the mind and character of Christ far before the Lord would come into the world. Men should have known how to be conformed to the image of Christ before Jesus lived (see Romans 8:29).

While it is true that Matthew reveals the ultimate unfolding of Hosea's prophecy regarding Jesus it is equally true that God viewed the Israelites that came out of Egypt as his own sons. Israel then stood as a type of the Christ as God's sons (see Exodus 4:22 and Romans 8:14) (see also Jesus' temptation in the wilderness for forty days as compared to Israel's forty years in wilderness wandering) (10q).

"**2** *The more the prophets called them, the more they went from them: they sacrificed unto the Baalim, and burned incense to graven images*" **(11:2).**

Through time, Israel sinned and the Lord chastened them by the mouth of prophets. Israel rejected the admonition of the prophets and left Jehovah in the lurch by sacrificing to the Balaam and burning incense to other graven images. It is here that we begin to see the object of Hosea and Matthew speaking of God's sons coming out of Egypt. The Lord would always have a remnant of faithful people who would in no way bow down to Baal or any other graven image (see Romans 11:1-5). This remnant would be the true Christ like people that God had foreknowledge of (Romans 8:29 and Ephesians 1:3-7). The true sons of God would be led by the Spirit rather than the flesh (Romans 8:14).

David helps us understand God's ordinance of predestination as it relates to Paul's teaching at Ephesians 1:3-7 and Romans 8:29. David writes, "*For God is with the generation of the righteous*" at Psalms 14:5. The word "*generation*" in Hebrew is *dowr* and translated by the Greek Septuagint as *genea* (LXX 705). The Greek *genea* is defined as,

"Characterized by quality, condition, or class of men" (Strong's 1755). Liddell and Scott define the word as "of the persons in a family, race, stock or family. Of horses, a breed or kind, a race or generation" (LS 161). "*Righteous*" people are a class or breed of men in the same family. God has always been with and blessed the class or breed of people known as "*righteous*" (see Isaiah 28:17). The righteous are a class or breed of people who are "*conformed to the image of his Son*" (Romans 8:29). Generations upon generations of people pass with time yet there is one thing that unites God's sons and daughters together for all time and that is righteousness (a Christ like life). God has always known that his special family would exist. There will always, in every generation, be a class or breed of people who love truth and obey God's laws to attain righteousness (see Romans 11:2-5) (29j).

"**3** *Yet I taught Ephraim to walk; I took them on my arms; but they knew not that I healed them.* **4** *I drew them with cords of a man, with bands of love; and I was to them as they that lift up the yoke on their jaws; and I laid food before them*" **(11:3-4).**

God, as a loving Father to Israel, took them to his own and taught them the ways of law. The Lord healed their wounds, loved them, and provided food for them. God's tenderness, love, and care for Israel is depicted at Exodus 19:4 when Moses records that He "*bare you on eagles' wings, and brought you unto myself.*" Though Israel faced hardships God was always there for them setting food before them that they perish not. Yet for all this care Israel cast God away and went to serve the deities of the Canaanites. Why did Ephraim depart from the loving care of God and worship idols? The Apostle John answers our question by saying, "19 *and this is the condemnation, that light is come into the world, and men loved darkness rather than light, because their deeds were evil*" (John 3:19).

The point is obvious. God gave man a choice to follow him in faithfulness or follow the ways of man. The Lord's true sons that he brought out of Egypt would always choose him in service and obedience.

The events that transpire throughout Israel's lives, as well as our own, separates the good from the evil as the chaff is blown by the wind. There will always be people who God does much for yet they could care less about him. There will also always be those who see God's blessings and love and serve him in obedience.

"**5** *They shall not return into the land of Egypt; but the Assyrian shall be their king, because they refused to return to me.* **6** *And the sword shall fall upon their cities, and shall consume their bars, and devour them, because of their own counsels*" **(11:5-6)**.

Due to Israel's refusal to return from their wicked ways and their ingratitude toward Jehovah God they will be given over to another king; i.e., Assyria. With clear language the prophet now reveals their fate. They had been brought into Egypt to learn lessons of trust and faith. The time of such basic lessons have past. God's mercy in Egypt is gone. The only place for the hardened wicked is Assyria. Israel foolishly trusted in their mighty men, fortified cities, other nations, and pagan gods and now they would be punished (see Hosea 10:13).

Notice again that we see the word "*because*." God is just in punishing Ephraim because they refused to repent of their sins but rather turned to their own council. God's laws were rejected for their own ways. Israel had proved herself not to be a son of God. The Lord now rejects the wicked.

"**7** *And my people are bent on backsliding from me: though they call them to him that is on high, none at all will exalt him*" **(11:7)**.

One's "*bent*" is equated to one's purpose, objective, interest, and or one's ways. God's people were "*bent*" on "*backsliding*." We now have a further definition of the "*spirit of whoredom*" mentioned at Hosea 4:12. Israel's "*bent*" or "*spirit of whoredom*" is characterized by their "*backsliding*" ways. To backslide is to "revert to sin or wrongdoing, esp. in religious practice" (AHD 150). Israel had reverted back to ways of a lack of faith and trust in God. Their minds were bent away from God and they would in no way exalt the mighty name of Jehovah God. God's mercy would only be established in the hearts of those who followed his commandments rather than their own will (see Romans 9:16 in its context).

Jehovah's Compassion to be fully revealed in the Gospel Age (11:8-12)

"*8 How shall I give you up, Ephraim? How shall I cast you off, Israel? How shall I make you as Admah? How shall I set you as Zeboiim? My heart is turned within me, my compassions are kindled together*" **(11:8).**

Admah and Zeboiim were the two other wicked cities that were destroyed along with Sodom and Gomorrah. The heart of the Lord is turned within due to his anguish and sorrow over his people's departure. It is not God's will that his people be destroyed as in the days of Sodom and Gomorrah. The tender mercy and kindness is stirred within the heart of God and he does not want to crush his people by the Assyrians but they leave him no choice (2 Peter 3:9). God is just and will punish the wicked of every generation (see Jeremiah 9:23).

"*9 I will not execute the fierceness of mine anger, I will not return to destroy Ephraim: for I am God, and not man; the Holy One in the midst of you; and I will not come in wrath. 10 They shall walk after Jehovah, who will roar like a lion; for he will roar, and the children shall come trembling from the west. 11 They shall come trembling as a bird out of Egypt, and as a dove out of the land of Assyria; and I will make them to dwell in their houses, said Jehovah*" **(11:9-11).**

Through God's compassion he will not utterly destroy Israel even though they deserve it. Man may exercise such extreme destruction yet not so with the merciful God. There will be those in the future who shall walk after God's laws (a far cry from those who "*refused to return*" unto the Lord at Hosea 11:5). These people that shall "*walk after Jehovah*" are those who hear the roaring of the Jehovah lion and heed to his ways in fear. Earlier the prophet of God had said, "*14 For I will be unto Ephraim as a lion, and as a young **lion** to the house of Judah: I, even I, will tear* and go away; I will carry off, and there shall be none to deliver. 15 I will go and return to my place, **till they acknowledge their offence, and seek my face**: In their affliction they will seek me earnestly" (Hosea 5:14-15). The Lord is obviously addressing those who "*acknowledge their offence and seek my face*" at Hosea 11:10. These men and women come to God "*trembling*" out of Egypt and Assyria and God will have mercy on them.

Consider the words of the prophet Isaiah. Isaiah writes, "1 *thus said Jehovah, Heaven is my throne, and the earth is my footstool: what manner of house will you build unto me? And what place shall be my rest? 2 For all these things has my hand made, and so all these things came to be, said Jehovah: but to this man will I look, even to him that is poor and of a contrite spirit, that that* **trembles** *at my word*" (Isaiah 66:1-2). The remnant of God's people, his sons out of Egypt, will be those who tremble at his words (i.e., fearfully respect and reverence the laws of God). Today all who will call upon the name of God with fear and trembling shall be saved (Acts 22:16 and Romans 10:9-10). The gospel message would reveal the mind and will of God to men and those who humbly receive and obey those words would be saved (Romans 1:16).

"**12** *Ephraim compasses me about with falsehood, and the house of Israel with deceit; but Judah yet rules with God, and is faithful with the Holy One*" **(11:12).**

Falsehood of error is another indicator of Israel's whoredom. God would have no choice but to punish them. A remnant would rise to the top in fear and trembling toward God as they acknowledge their error in the face of his ferocious tearing and punishing them as a roaring lion.

The footnote in the American Standard Version reads, "*And Judah is yet unstedfast with God and with the Holy One who is faithful*." Due to the comments made at chapter 12 it is more probable that the footnote version is more correct. Judah was just as much a disappointment to the Lord as was her northern sister Israel.

Questions over Hosea Chapter 11

1. Why did Matthew quote from Hosea 11:1?

2. Why would the Assyrian be Ephraim's king?

3. What were God's people "*bent*" on doing?

4. What difficult position did Ephraim put God in (Hosea 11:8)?

5. Why would some of Israel come trembling before God?

HOSEA CHAPTER 12

Synopsis

Chapter 12 reads as a father who is disappointed in his son. An assessment is made of Ephraim's life and it is wretched. God's own children were not faithful and obedient to him. The problem of disinterest is exposed. If only God's people would return to the spirit of Jacob who would do anything to attain God's favor and blessings.

Application

A great spiritual problem in every generation is spiritual interest. If I am not interested in the things of righteousness and justice I am most likely not to study my Bible, attend worship service faithfully, and or pray to God often. Hosea calls upon Israel to look to their brother Jacob for guidance. Jacob was so absorbed in attaining God's blessings that he went through many sorrows and hard service to attain it. If only God's people today would value truth the way Jacob did we may find ourselves doing all things possible to attain it.

Hosea 12

A Contrast between the faithful character of Jacob and the wicked people of God during Hosea's Day (12:1-6)

"**1** *Ephraim feeds on wind, and follows after the east wind: he continually multiplies lies and desolation; and they make a covenant with Assyria, and oil is carried into Egypt*" **(12:1).**

The erring councils of the priests, princes, and rulers were taken hook, line and sinker by Israel's people. They "*feed*" on these falsehoods (see Ephesians 4:14). The "*lies*" of Ephraim appear to be their words of change yet no change comes (Hosea 6:7 and 10:4). Ephraim speaks words of faith yet their actions are far from obedience (Hosea 4:2). Ephraim's prophets have lied saying that God has spoken when the Lord said no such things (see Hosea 7:13 and 9:7).

Lip service was the order of worship. Ephraim was saying the right things but doing all the wrong things. Jesus similarly said, "**18** *this people honors me with their lips; But their heart is far from me*" (Matthew 15:18). One example of their wrong doings is found in the covenants they made with Assyria and Egypt rather than turning to God for help (see also Hosea 7:11 and 8:9).

"**2** *Jehovah has also a controversy with Judah, and will **punish** Jacob according to his ways; according to his doings will he recompense him*" **(12:2).**

The footnote examined at Hosea 11:12 now gains greater acceptance. Judah and Israel (i.e., Jacob) will be punished for their wrong doings. Punishment is due to those who reject the ways of God for their own ways. God's punishment is intended to cause sinners to acknowledge their error and repent (see notes above at Hosea 11:9-11).

"**3** *In the womb he took his brother by the heel; and in his manhood he had power with God:* **4** *yea, he had power over the angel, and prevailed; he wept, and made supplication unto him: he found him at Bethel, and there he spoke with us,* **5** *even Jehovah, the God of hosts; Jehovah is his memorial name.* **6** *Therefore turn to your God: keep kindness and justice, and wait for your God continually*" **(12:3-6).**

Hosea reminds Israel and Judah of the faith of Jacob. The events brought up in these few verses indicate Jacob's resolve and intense interest in God's blessings as opposed to Esau who despised his birthright. Let the people of God have such an intense interest in the blessings of the Lord; i.e., the forgiveness of sins through the blood of Jesus Christ. Jacob illustrated this intense interest for the blessings of God even in the womb by grasping hold of Esau's heel. It is as though Jacob held on to Esau because he was the first born and due the birthright. The birthright of blessings was important to Jacob from his earliest days. Jacob was so fascinated with the birthright of blessings that he tried to physically take it from Esau (Genesis 25:23ff).

Latter we find Jacob wrestling with the angel of Jehovah God (see Genesis 32:24ff). Jacob was to learn, during his wrestling match, that God's blessings cannot be wrestled away from him by physical strength, craft, or deceit but by faithfulness, humility of life, and prayer. The angel assures Jacob of Jehovah's great power by touching his thigh and moving it out of socket. Jacob now had no doubts regarding God's favor, power, and protection and neither did he doubt God's promises.

Jacob was a man of prayer. There is a marked change in Jacob's character after serving Laban twenty years for the hand of Rachel and Leah. When Jacob was distressed and filled with fear over the coming of Esau with 400 men he prayed to God and revealed his new spirit of humility. Jacob prays saying, "*I am not worthy of the least of all the lovingkindnesses, and of all the truth, which you have showed unto your servant...*" (Genesis 32:7, 10). Conviction of the reality of God's promises, a determination to obtain these promises, and prayerful humility were traits exercised by Jacob. A far contrast between this patriarch of faith and the people of God during Hosea's day (30d). The wicked people of Hosea's day were governed by pride, ignorance, and a spirit of whoredom (Hosea 4:12). The call to Ephraim is to "*turn to God*" and seek "*kindness and justice*" and "*wait*" upon the Lord's coming promises in faithfulness and meekness. There must be a transformation take place in wicked people's hearts (see Colossians 1:13 and Romans

12:1-2). This change will only occur as one takes on a genuine spiritual interest as did Jacob. We must all learn the value of truth and the longevity of eternity to come to love truth. Solomon said, "*Buy the truth and sell it not*" (Proverbs 23:23).

The book of Hosea continues to mirror Paul's discussion of predestination at Romans chapters 8 and 9. Paul explains to his Jewish kinsmen that it is not one's heritage, skin color, or race that determines their standing with God but rather their direction of life. God has always known that there would be a class or type of people that would receive his chastisement and love him. He also knew that there would be a class of people who did not see the value of truth and they would reject righteousness and justice. Paul also uses the illustration of Jacob and Esau to prove this point of a predestined righteous class of people at Romans 9:10-13.

Self Delusion and Ingratitude Lead to God's Wrath (12:7-14)

"**7** *He is a trafficker, the balances of deceit are in his hand: he loves to oppress.* **8** *And Ephraim said, Surely I am become rich, I have found me wealth: in all my labors they shall find in me no iniquity that were sin*" **(12:7-8).**

Israel had a reputation of being cheaters. Rather than following the godly ways of Jacob and seeking justice Ephraim had become a "*trafficker*" (one who participates in trade) using balances of deceit. Produce and grain was sold by weight. Ephraim had perverted scales so that it favored them. When weighing produce the scales were calibrated to read less than what was actually being weighed. Such a deceitful balance would bring the buyer more money for less fruit and grain.

Trafficking became so much a part of their ways that they did not see any wrong in their actions (see Jeremiah 2:35) (38). Ephraim reasoned that since they had become rich using the faulty scales then "*they shall find in me no iniquity that were sin.*" Ephraim was guilty of the greatest deception of all; i.e., self delusion. There is a danger today that our sin may produce a seemingly good outcome yet let us not consider it a blessing from God or a sign of no wrong committed. God's laws determine right from wrong.

"**9** *But I am Jehovah your God from the land of Egypt; I will yet again make you to dwell in tents, as in the days of the solemn feast.* **10** *I have also spoken unto the prophets, and I have multiplied visions; and by the ministry of the prophets have I used similitudes*" **(12:9-10).**

The Lord reminds Israel that he alone is "*Jehovah your God*." God had brought them out of Egypt with a mighty arm and caused them to dwell in tents in the wilderness and so they would return. The days of tent dwelling were days Israel was learning to be dependant upon Jehovah God for all their protection and sustenance.

The Lord had not only trained them through the University of Hard Knocks but he also had revealed his will to them through the prophets in "*visions*" and "*similitudes*" (see also Hosea 11:12 notes). The prophet Zechariah is best known for delivering eight visions to the people of God. The Lord had revealed visions to his prophet and he in turn revealed these things to the people. Furthermore God gave his people the prophet's ministry of "*similitudes.*" A "*similitude*" (Greek LXX *homoiothen*) means "to make like, cause to be like or resemble, assimilate; to be made like, become like, resemble, or to liken or compare" (Moulton 288). God used Gomer to affectively teach Israel by way of "*similitude.*" Her adulteries were 'compared' to Israel's whoredoms of disobedience. The current mind set of Israel was inexcusable in relation to where God had brought them and where they should have been at this point in history. God used Ezekiel and his wife as a similitude as well as David and his sufferings (see Ezekiel 24:24 and Psalms 71:7). Again, we are seeing that God is doing all things possible to save his beloved people.

"**11** *Is Gilead iniquity? They are altogether false; in Gilgal they sacrifice bullocks; yea, their altars are as heaps in the furrows of the field*" **(12:11).**

Gilead was the sin city of their day (see Hosea 6:8). Gilgal was located about 15 miles due north of Jerusalem. The temple of Jehovah was located in the city of David (i.e., Jerusalem). Sacrifices were to be made there alone rather than in other parts of the country. Israel had their worship and intentions all whacked.

"**12** *And Jacob fled into the field of Aram, and Israel served for a wife, and for a wife he kept sheep.* **13** *And by a prophet Jehovah brought Israel up out of Egypt, and by a prophet was he preserved.* **14** *Ephraim has provoked to anger most bitterly: therefore shall his blood be left upon him, and his reproach shall his Lord return unto him*" **(12:12-14).**

Once again Hosea goes back to the comparison with Jacob. Jacob had left his home in Canaan traveling to Haran to find a wife of his kindred. Fourteen years would pass as he served Laban by keeping sheep for two wives (7 additional years for Rachel due to Laban's deception). Why do this Jacob? Because his grandfather Abraham (Genesis 24:1-3) and father Isaac (Genesis 28:1) had spoke by divine revelation commanding not to take a wife from among the Canaanites.

Jacob was obedient even though it caused him much grief and time of life. Ephraim; however, will not obey the voice of God. Ephraim illustrates a spirit of ungratefulness for all that God has done by removing them from Egypt and making them into a mighty nation. They shall pay the price of God's wrath for their ingratitude, self deception, and false ways.

Questions over Hosea Chapter 12

1. Why does Hosea mention the Old Testament character of Jacob?

2. Why did Ephraim conclude that they were not guilty of sin?

3. **True or False:** Ephraim was guilty of cheating people in their business affairs.

4. What methods of teaching did God offer to Israel by way of the prophets?

5. How did the obedience of Jacob put Ephraim to shame?

HOSEA CHAPTER 13

Synopsis

The day of God's punishing judgment against Israel was very near. God would roar as a lion and tear the wicked to shreds. There would be no king of another land or great wealth to save them from the wrath of God.

Application

There will, as in every generation, be a remnant that will rise above the punishing blows of God and in repentance return to his gracious favor. Death will not be able to hold the redeemed (Hosea 13:14). God will raise the righteous from the dead to die no more in paradise (1 Corinthians 15:54-55). Now is the time to gain favor and interest in the things of God.

Hosea 13

Israel's Progression of Sin has lead them to be winnowed by the wind of God's Wrath (13:1-3)

"**1** *When Ephraim spoke, there was trembling; he exalted himself in Israel; but when he offended in Baal, he died*" **(13:1).**

There was a time when Ephraim (Israel) spoke that they were feared as a nation due to God's favor. Israel was exalted high. The nations "*trembled*" when they heard of Israel's might. Israel; however, fell from the lofty heights of God's favor to the depths of sin as they worshipped "*Baal.*" When Israel committed spiritual adultery against God they died spiritually and lost favor with the Lord.

"*2 And now they sin more and more, and have made them molten images of their silver, even idols according to their own understanding, all of them the work of the craftsmen: they say of them, Let the men that sacrifice kiss the calves*" **(13:2).**

Israel's sin grew deeper and deeper. To begin with, Israel worshipped God through the calf. Jeroboam I had convinced Israel to worship at Samaria and Dan rather than going all the way to Jerusalem. The calf stood as a symbol of God yet was indeed a perversion of God's will (see Deuteronomy 4:9ff). Israel eventually left off God in the calf worship and moved toward serving Baal. Those who sacrificed to the idols "*kiss the calves*" in that they showed forth their faith, love, and devotion to the idol. Such a sight moved Jehovah to great jealousy and anger as a woman that cheated on her husband would do (i.e., the story of Hosea and Gomer). The Lord wants to know where the spirit of Jacob is at (see Hosea chapter 12). Where is the faith, love, devotion, and spiritual interest in the things of God?

"*3 Therefore they shall be as the morning cloud, and as the dew that passes early away, as the chaff that is driven with the whirlwind out of the threshing-floor, and as the smoke out of the chimney*" **(13:3).**

Hosea gives four illustrations to indicate the futility and short lived pleasure of idolatry among the Israelites. Israel will fade away as the morning fog, as the dew that dissipates with the midmorning heat, as the chaff that is thrown into the air to be separated from the good grain, and as smoke that comes from the chimney that is carried away by the wind. The passing pleasures of sin are short lived (see Hebrews 11:25). When a sinner's life ends so does the pleasure he earnestly sought after in this life.

God will devour the ungrateful, disobedient, and self deluded people of contentment of all Ages (13:4-8)

"**4** *Yet I am Jehovah your God from the land of Egypt; and you shall know no god but me, and besides me there is no savior*" **(13:4).**

Who should Israel look for in this prophetic time of calamity? Shall the Baal and or any other idol saved them? God will bring Assyria upon his wicked people to punish them and Baal will be no where to be found. Isaiah quoted from God saying, "9 *Remember the former things of old: for I am God, and there is none else: I am God, and there is none like me*" (Isaiah 46:9). This same principle is established at Acts 4:12 when Peter had addressed the Sanhedrin council saying, "12 *and in none other is there salvation: for neither is there any other name under heaven, that is given among men wherein we must be saved*." Though the people of Hosea's day looked to Balaam, their fortified cities, their mighty men, and other nations for help and comfort there would be nothing of the sort found. God was the only source of true help out of their dire situation.

"**5** *I did know you in the wilderness, in the land of* **great drought**. **6** *According to their pasture, so were they filled; they were filled, and their heart was exalted: therefore have they forgotten me*" **(13:5-6).**

God had used a drought to chastise his people as mentioned as Hosea 6:3. The "*drought*" of this verse is speaking of a different day. The "*land of great drought*" was obviously the wilderness of Sinai. God fed them manna and quail in a place where no food could be found. When they were thirsty in the dry land God gave them water from the rocks. Truly God had born Israel "*on eagle's wings*" as he divinely cared for them (Exodus 19:4). Israel was filled with the blessings and care of God yet they quickly forgot the Lord in their comfort.

A similar danger exists today. When all is well in our lives we tend to take the credit rather than giving God the glory and thanksgiving he deserves. When all is well in man's life they have tendency to forget all about God and his great eternal blessings. Throughout the history of God's people they are found forgetting God when things went well (see Isaiah 17:10; Jeremiah 3:21; Ezekiel 22:12; Hosea 4:6; 8:14 and here at 13:6).

"**7** *Therefore am I unto them as a lion; as a leopard will I watch by the way; I will meet them as a bear that is bereaved of her whelps, and will rend the caul of their heart; and there will I devour them like a lioness; the wild beast shall tear them*" **(13:7-8).**

The greatest folly of all is to lose conscience of one's sin and standing with Jehovah God. When we think all is well, while living in sin, let us beware of the all powerful God. Like a lion, leopard, and bereaved bear that has lost her cubs will the Lord tear to shreds the disobedient, unthankful, and deluded content peoples of all ages. Hosea has used the "*lion*" illustration a few times previously in this study (see Hosea 5:14-15). The prophet said that as God tore the wicked to pieces as a ferocious lion there would be a remnant who would consider their wickedness and return to the Lord in repentance (see Hosea 11:9-11).

Destruction for the Foolish and hope for the Wise (13:9-14)

"**9** *It is your destruction, O Israel, that you are against me, against your help.* **10** *Where now is your king, that he may save you in all your cities? And your judges, of whom you said, Give me a king and princes?* **11** *I have given you a king in mine anger, and have taken him away in my wrath*" **(13:9-11).**

Israel was so deluded that they did not see that they had set themselves against the one who was truly there to help. Nothing but a lion tearing and destroying them stood in their way because of their rebellion. The very lion that sought their destruction had the power and will to help them yet they rejected him. Israel put their trust in everything but God. The people of God turned to their riches (Hosea 12:8), mighty men (Hosea 10:13), king (Hosea 10:3 and 13:10), judges (Hosea 13:10), princes (Hosea 9:15 and 13:10), priests (Hosea 10:5), idols (Hosea 8:6;

11:2 and 13:2), and the kings of Assyria and Egypt (Hosea 7:11; 8:9 and 12:1). The very things Israel thought would help them only turned out to be their destruction. The ways of God were not interesting to them or pleasurable. They turned their backs on God to be like the nations around them. They wanted lives of sin rather than lives of righteousness.

"**12** *The iniquity of Ephraim is bound up; his sin is laid up in store.* **13** *The sorrows of a travailing woman shall come upon him: he is an unwise son; for it is time he should not tarry in the place of the breaking forth of children*" **(13:12-13).**

God has taken a reckoning of the sins of Ephraim and has remembered them in their folly. There are grave consequences for the sinful people to meet out due to their iniquity. The English Standard Version Bible reads as follows for verse 13 - "*The pangs of childbirth come for him, but he is an unwise son, for at the right time he does not present himself at the opening of the womb.*" If Israel was a wise son he would find his way to the opening of the womb to be delivered yet they are foolish and remain in the womb. The point is that Israel does foolish things rather than being wise. Their minds are bent on their own destruction in that they loved the ways of sin above the laws of God (see Hosea 11:7).

"**14** *I will ransom them from the power of Sheol; I will redeem them from death: O death, where are your plagues? O Sheol, where is your destruction? Repentance shall be hid from mine eyes*" **(13:14).**

The Bible in Basic English reads for this verse as follows - "*I will give the price to make them free from the power of the underworld, I will be their savior from death: O death! Where are your pains? O underworld! Where is your destruction? My eyes will have no pity.*" The "*ransom*" or price to free them from spiritual death would be the blood of Jesus Christ (see Acts 20:28 and Ephesians 1:7). Those chastised and who come trembling before God as they acknowledge their trespasses will be saved from the consequences of spiritual death (see notes at Hosea 11:9-11). Though these blood bought people die they will not be held in the grave of Sheol forever. God will raise them from the dead to ascend in glory into the heavens forevermore (see Romans 8:22-25).

The Apostle Paul quotes from Hosea 13:14 verse at 1 Corinthians 15:54-55 to indicate the Christian's victory over sin and death through the blood of Jesus Christ. The Christian can be forgiven of sins and be raised from the dead to die no more. The prophet Hosea foretold of the resurrection far before it would actually occur. Even to this day the resurrection has not yet occurred yet for the faithful they have this hope. Hosea is looking to a day when the true Israel would awaken from their folly, acknowledge, and confess their sins to God. The power of Sheol (realm of the dead) shall not hold such a one. God will not "*repent*" from giving men this opportunity. It is his promise to mankind and sealed by the blood of his dear Son Jesus.

Ephraim shall bear her guilt for Rebellion (13:15-16)

"**15** *Though he be fruitful among his brethren, an east wind shall come, the breath of Jehovah coming up from the wilderness; and his spring shall become dry, and his fountain shall be dried up: he shall make spoil of the treasure of all goodly vessels*" **(13:15).**

At one time Ephraim was fruitful yet now the harvest of grain, wine, and oil are scorched by an east wind because of their refusal to repent of their sin. Assyria will make spoil of their possessions and carry them off as captives to a foreign land.

"**16** *Samaria shall bear her guilt; for she has rebelled against her God: they shall fall by the sword; their infants shall be dashed in pieces, and their women with child shall be ripped up*" **(13:16).**

Samaria, the capital city of Israel, would bear the consequences of her rebellion against the Lord. Gruesome deaths await man, woman, child, and even the pregnant women. One can visualize a lion ripping people to shreds (see Hosea 5:14-15 and 11:9-11) or a sword ripping through the flesh of men (see Hosea 7:16 and 11:6). God will chastise and punish his people as a lion and sword against a defenseless people.

Questions over Hosea Chapter 13

1. Why did the people of Ephraim say, "*Let the men that sacrifice kiss the calves?*"

2. Why would God tear the people to shreds like a lion or wild beast?

3. **True or False:** Ephraim is compared to an unwise son.

4. Why did the Apostle Paul quote from Hosea 13:14 at 1 Corinthians 15:54-55?

HOSEA CHAPTER 14

Synopsis

The prophet of God finishes his work with a final plea for Israel to see the chastening hand of God in their lives. Not all Israel would fall to the sword, pestilence, and famine. Not all Israel would be torn to shreds in their sin. Some will come to see God's great love and with broken hearts they shall come back to him in repentance.

Application

People of all ages must come to recognize the chastening hand of God in their lives. Those who acknowledge their sins and say words that illustrate a broken heart over their sins will be saved. It is very difficult for some to say "*words*" that admit self error (Hosea 14:2). Those who swallow their pride and repent with a broken heart will be received by God (see 2 Corinthians 7:10). Wisdom and foolishness is exposed in the reactions of one to the chastening hand of God during sinful days. The wise will see with spiritual vision the love of God and turn from their wickedness whereas the sinful will be hardened in their sins. The prophet's final call to Israel is to be wise and repent.

Hosea 14

What God wants to hear Ephraim Say (14 all)

"**1** *O Israel, return unto Jehovah your God; for you have fallen by your iniquity.* **2 Take with you words**, *and return unto Jehovah:* **say unto him**, *Take away all iniquity, and accept that which is good: so will we render as bullocks the offering of our lips*" **(14:1-2)**

The "*words*" that the Lord desires to hear from his people are words of repentance. The Lord desires that his people would "*acknowledge*" their sin with a spirit of humility (Hosea 5:15 and 11:9-11). Furthermore the Lord desires to hear the "*offering of our lips.*" **Words** that not only acknowledge sin but words that indicate the worshippers' desire to have his or her iniquity taken away. One may offer animals upon the altar of burnt offering yet do it out of mechanical motions of habit. God wants much more from his people (Hosea 6:6). God's people must come to have rivers of tears flow down their cheeks as they acknowledge the sin in their lives with a heart that is broken over their actions (see Psalms 51:17).

The Lord desires to hear the people say, from the honesty of their heart, that they have made a mistake and desire God to forgive them. Such words would indicate a desire toward spiritual matters as Jacob illustrated in his life. Words are not all the Lord wants. God wants to see our actions improve; i.e., "*accept that which is good.*" A complete change of heart was called for. Ephraim needed to move from a heart that had misplaced trust to a heart that loved, trusted, and believed in God and his laws (10y).

"**3** *Assyria shall not save us; we will not ride upon horses; neither will we say any more to the work of our hands, You are our gods; for in you the fatherless finds mercy*" **(14:3).**

The "*words*" God wants to hear are as stated here at Hosea 14:3. God wanted to hear the people say that Assyria, horses of might, and the gods of the nations have no power to save us. All those things that Israel found comfort in are to be cast away (i.e., Assyria, Egypt, idols, mighty men, fortified cities and riches). Those moved to tremble at the word of God and say these things will find mercy.

"**4** *I will heal their backsliding, I will love them freely; for mine anger is turned away from him.* **5** *I will be as the dew unto Israel; he shall blossom as the lily, and cast forth his roots as Lebanon*" **(14:4-5).**

The "*backsliding*" of Israel was discussed at Hosea 11:7. Though the people had performed acts of wickedness God would freely love them and turn away his anger from them if only they would acknowledge their guilt and the true power of God (see Hosea 14:3 above). If only they would say the "*words*" above from an honest and genuine broken heart.

These verses spell out submission and obedience. To admit that you are wrong about a direction you took and to ask for forgiveness and then turn to that course you spurned is the definition of submission. God's desire is that people would turn themselves over to him in obedience (see Colossians 1:22-23). If their hearts would be changed from enmity to friendship and fellowship with God he would heal them. Jehovah God is creator and sovereign ruler of the world and man must come to believe, trust, and obey him. Throughout the Old and New Testaments we see God's demand for absolute lawful perfection (see Leviticus 11:44 and 1 Peter 1:16-17; Deuteronomy 27:26; Matthew 5:48; Romans 8:4; Galatians 3:10; 2 Peter 1:4 and 1 John 4:17). Those who conform their lives to the sinless Christ shall be as beautiful and aromatic as the lily and strong as the cedars whose roots grow deep within the earth.

"**6** *His branches shall spread, and his beauty shall be as the olive-tree, and his smell as Lebanon.* **7** *They that dwell under his shadow shall return; they shall revive as the grain, and blossom as the vine: the scent thereof shall be as the wine of Lebanon*" **(14:6-7).**

The world shall feel the influence of the humble and penitent. They shall be beautiful as the olive tree and fragrant as Lebanon. Many others shall benefit from their beauty and fragrance. Forgiven sinners live with a spirit of love and mercy toward others. Those who are restored to the Lord are likened unto beautiful things.

"**8** *Ephraim shall say, What have I to do any more with idols? I have answered, and will regard him: I am like a green fir-tree; from me is your fruit found*" **(14:8).**

The success of God's chastisement and or punishment is depicted in these final verses. God has chastened his people with drought (Hosea 6:3) and war with Assyria (Hosea 5:8-9). A remnant will rise above the pain and come trembling back to God in repentance (Hosea 1:7; 6:11 and 11:10-11). The true Israel of God will come up out of Egypt like the Son of God and they shall be faithful to the Lord till their dying day. God will once again have "*regard*" for Ephraim.

"**9** *Who is wise, that he may understand these things? Prudent, that he may know them? For the ways of Jehovah are right, and the just shall walk in them; but transgressors shall fall therein*" **(14:9).**

The people of Israel have been compared to an unwise son who did not do those things that were beneficial for life (see Hosea 13:13). There will; however, be a remnant that comes trembling before the Lord as they acknowledge their sin and put their trust, faith, and hope in God. These are the true Israel that Hosea identifies as the "*wise and prudent*."

Solomon spends a considerable amount of time defining wisdom in the book of Proverbs. Solomon writes, "*I wisdom have made prudence my dwelling, and find out knowledge and discretion*" (Proverbs 8:12). Wisdom is identified as prudence, knowledge, and discretion. The word "*prudence*" "expresses caution and wisdom in the conduct of affairs. Prudence implies not only caution but the capacity for judging in advance the probable results of one's actions" (AHD 998). "*Discretion*" is "to be discreet, having or showing a judicious reserve in one's speech or behavior; prudent, lacking ostentation or pretension or modest" (AHD 403). "*Knowledge*" is "familiarity, awareness, or understanding gained through experience or study. Knowledge is the sum or range of what has been perceived, discovered, or learned" (AHD 705). Wisdom is defined having all three of these attributes. "*Wisdom*" may be defined then as the ability to gain understanding of life issues and to exercise reserve due to a perception of probable outcomes. Knowledge, prudence, and discretion will keep man out of much trouble in life and bring a great deal of happiness now and forevermore.

The wise man or woman will hear and give heed to God's laws. The wise will have spiritual vision that sees the outcome of sinful living and decisions. The wise will be voluntarily subject to God's laws. When the wise violates God's laws they tremble and acknowledge their wrong doing and the Lord forgives them. The call for an adulterous people who had caused God much grief and pains was that they love, trust, and put their faith in God rather than anything else. To get the people to this frame of mind God would chasten and punish the people. The remnant would rise above the ashes of war and sword and with a penitent heart be restored to the Lord. The redeemed will come trembling in repentance with a changed heart after God has chastened them by way of Assyria (see Hosea 11:9-10).

Questions over Hosea Chapter 14

1. What "*words*" did God want to hear from Ephraim and all sinners today?

2. Would God heal his backsliding people?

3. **True or False:** Only the wise will give heed to God's instructions.

Joel

Robertson's Notes

Bible Books 29 of 66

"*26 And you shall eat in plenty and be satisfied, and shall praise the name of Jehovah your God, that has **dealt wondrously with you**; and my people shall never be put to shame.*"

Joel 2:26

Introduction

Not much is known about Joel other than he is the son of Pethuel. Dating the book of Joel depends upon one's interpretation of God's "*great army*" of locust, canker-worms, caterpillars, and the palmer-worm (Joel 2:25). If this "*great army*" is the Babylonians, then the date would likely be during a similar time of Jeremiah (i.e., 605 to 586 BC). There are strong hints that the Babylonians are under consideration in the book itself. Joel refers to God's "*great army*" as a "*nation*" (Joel 1:6) and then again as the "*northern army*" (Joel 2:20). We know that the Babylonian nation is often referred to as the army from the "*north*" in the writings of the Major Prophets (Jeremiah 10:22). If Joel is speaking about a literal insect attack there is virtually no telling when the book was written (Joel 1:7). Many have concluded, with little evidence, that the book was written as early as 830 BC. We do know that Joel belongs among the books of the Bible. The Apostle Peter quotes from Joel 2:28-32 at Acts 2:17ff. The apostle Paul quotes from Joel 2:32 at Romans 10:13.

Gloomy Days for God's People

Joel chapters 1:1 through 2:11 paint a vivid picture of **doom and gloom** upon the land and inhabitants of Palestine (more evidence that this is Babylon - compare with the doom and gloom of Lamentations). God's *"great army"* of locust, canker-worm, caterpillar, and the palmer-worm cause widespread desolation upon the land. This *"great army"* is well organized and determined to achieve its purpose of desolating the land (Joel 2:4-11). The destruction caused by this army affects the grazing fields, grain, new wine, oil, fig, pomegranate, palm, apple, *"and even all the trees of the field are withered"* (Joel 1:8-12). The land is also plagued with drought (Joel 2:23) and fire (Joel 1:19). Joel depicts these days as *"darkness and gloominess, a day of clouds and thick darkness..."* (Joel 2:2). A land that has been desolated of all vegetation will surely cause famine and pestilence to settle in among the inhabitants (Joel 1:15). Joy and laughter is no where to be found (Joel 1:15). Israel faces dark, gloomy, and depressing days. Joel writes, *"For joy is withered away from the sons of men"* (Joel 1:12b).

The Day of Jehovah

One may confidently argue that the theme of the book of Joel is *"the day of Jehovah"* (see Joel 1:15; 2:1, 11, 31 and 3:14). The day of Jehovah is depicted as a dark and gloomy day of judgment upon the disobedient in the form of plagues. As we travel through the book of Joel it becomes evident that the prophet of God is revealing the universal dealing of God with sinful man. The wicked of every generation have no joy, laughter, or blessings of this life to enjoy due to their sin and dire condition of the soul. Judah was plagued by drought, fire, famine, pestilence, and sword because of their sins (see Jeremiah 25:8-9 and 51:35). God moves the wicked to repentance in every generation by way of plagues (see Revelation 15-16). Joel is a study that exposes the loving yet chastening hand of God against sinners.

Joel's time of work was obviously similar to that of Jeremiah. It was during these days that the good king Josiah made many valiant attempts to reform the people of God. The more Josiah tried; however, the deeper Judah slipped into sin. The hearts of men would only return to the Lord by the intense fires of plagues at the hand of God. The Lord brought upon Israel the "*rod of mine anger*" (Assyria) (Isaiah 10:5-6) and now he would bring the Babylonians upon Judah (Jeremiah 25:9ff; Habakkuk 1:5-11 and Zephaniah 1:12-18). God referred to Babylon as the "*wilderness of the sea*" and the "*destroyer*" (Isaiah 21:1-2). As molten gold is purified by the fiery furnace so the Babylonians would unmercifully decimate the land of Judah for a future cleansing.

The Blessings and Future Joy for those who Humble themselves to God

Joel writes, "12 *turn unto me with all your heart, and with fasting, and with weeping, and with mourning: and rend your heart, and not your garments, and turn unto Jehovah your God*;" (Joel 2:12). The prophet's request, by inspiration, for God's people to repent infers that the cause of all this doom and gloom is their sin. The lesson we learn is no different that that which we learn when studying virtually every book in God's word. God wants man to serve him not because it is what he has to do, or because it is always what we have done, or to get gain. Neither does the Lord desire men to serve him by way of mechanical worship where one goes through the motions of service with no emotional involvement. The Lord wants his people to serve him because they love him and desire to know more about him. When people have a true and loving relationship with God their sin will break their hearts. God wants to see rivers of water rolling down the cheeks of sinners as they repent (see Psalms 51:16-17). Samuel had instructed Saul to have such a heart at I Samuel 15:22-23. The prophet Isaiah prescribed such a heart at

Isaiah 57:15 and 66:1-2. The apostle Paul spoke of such a humble hearted disposition at 2 Corinthians 7:10.

Joel foretells of God's saving work in the New Testament church age. God will save men in the future church the same way he saved people by way of plagues during the days of Babylon's siege of Jerusalem. The Lord plagues the wicked with his strong chastening hand and those who humble themselves in sorrow and meekness will call out to him for help. Joel explains this method of God by revealing the future work of the Holy Spirit and church. God will pour out his Holy Spirit upon men and women, young and old, slave and free (Joel 2:28-29). Those immersed in the Holy Spirit will deliver a soul-saving message through prophesy, dreams, and visions. The Apostle Peter quotes from these verses of Joel at Acts 2:17-21. Those who recognize the words of revelation as divine help shall "*call*" upon the name of Jehovah God (Joel 2:32). Those who so call upon the name of the Lord shall be saved (Acts 2:21). Today, if sin governs my life and I experience the heavy hand of God's chastisement I too can call out to God in sorrow and expect to receive his divine help in the form of forgiveness and blessings (see Psalms 32:4-5 and 1 Corinthians 1:1-2).

There will be, throughout the ages, men and women who are hardened in their sins. God will tread the wicked under his feet in the great wine press of anger (see Joel 3:12-13). The more the Lord shall chastise and punish the hard hearted wicked the more these people will gnash their teeth in anguish and blaspheme the name of God for their suffering (see Revelation 16:9). There will also be, in every generation of men, those who will receive God's chastisement and with broken hearts repent of their sins. Joel refers to these people as the "*remnant*" (Joel 2:32). The Apostle Paul spoke of these predetermined remnant people at Romans 8:29-30; 9:6-11, 23-24 and 11:1-5). The New Testament apostles were simply reaffirming what the prophets of old had already revealed.

Important Revelation References found in the book of Joel

Joel 1:15; 2:1-2, 4, 5, 11 and 3:4 compared to Revelation 9:7-9, 16-21; 16:8-11 and 18:8

Joel 3:9-13 compared to Revelation 14:19-20 and 19:15

Joel 3:14-17 compared to Revelation 16:13-16, 21 and 20:10-15

JOEL CHAPTER 1

Synopsis

Joel, like Jeremiah, is prophetically looking into the city of Jerusalem at the time of the Babylonian siege. The chapter reads as a diary of one who is cataloguing all the devastation that is going on around them during a time of war. The picture is terrifying and leaves one trembling at the thought of what God's wrath is capable of. The Lord brings war, drought, fire, and pestilence to his sinful people to move them to repentance. It is better that they suffer now then for all eternity in hell.

Application

The saints of God in every generation must be reminded of the Lord's divine hatred for sin. There will always be great consequences to sinful living. Solomon writes, "15 *Good understanding gives favor; But the way of the transgressor is hard*" (Proverbs 13:15). The life of the fool is likened making your way through a "*hedge of thorns*" (Proverbs 15:19). As we face the heavy hand of God for our sins we would be wise to open our eyes to our faults before we are utterly expired in this life (see Psalms 32:4-5). All of God's actions are for our betterment, strength, and eternal well being. Let us all open our eyes to the sin in our lives and repent before its everlasting too late. If you are suffering in this life you should "*consider*" the reason (see Haggai 1:5). If you are suffering due to your sins, by way of God's chastening hand, then acknowledge the error and be relieved now and forevermore. It may be that you are being put to the test by God (1 Peter 1:6-7). During days of God testing the saints we should learn from the experience and give God thanks (Job 23:10 and James 1:1-4). Judah was suffering because of her sins and needed to repent.

Joel 1

Joel paints a Picture of Devastation, Desolation, and Depression among the remaining Inhabitants of the Land (1 all)

"*1 The word of Jehovah that came to Joel the son of Pethuel. 2 Hear this, you old men, and give ear, all you inhabitants of the land. Has this been in your days, or in the days of your fathers? 3 Tell your children of it, and let your children tell their children, and their children another generation. 4 That which the palmer-worm has left the locust has eaten; and that which the locust has left the canker-worm has eaten; and that which the canker-worm has left has the caterpillar has eaten*" **(1:1-4).**

Joel sets the tone for his prophetic words by describing the current state of the people of God's land. A great plague of worm, locust, canker-worm, and caterpillar has laid waste the land and the people's moral. Wave after wave of devastation has struck the land till there is not much left. The affects of the attack is demoralizing. Generation after generation is to be told of these days so that they may learn the valuable lessons. The consequence of sin in men's lives is devastation now and forevermore.

There are two possible interpretations of the source of destruction. First, the insects could very well be literal (see Ezekiel 31:14). Secondly, the insects could be figurative; i.e., the Babylonians (see Jeremiah 5:14-18). Jeremiah had spoke of such devastation in the days of Babylonian conquest in the form of sword, famine, and pestilence (Jeremiah 14:12) (see discussion in the introduction). Furthermore, Joel refers to these insects and worms as a "*nation*" (Joel 1:6), "*the northern army*" (Joel 2:20), and the "*great army*" (Joel 2:25). This study will bear out the fact that the devastation under consideration has been brought on by God through the Babylonian Empire due to the sins of Judah. God's heavy hand of punishment was upon his own people because of their gross immorality.

"**5** *Awake, you drunkards, and weep; and wail, all you drinkers of wine, because of the sweet wine; for it is cut off from your mouth.* **6** *For a* **nation** *is come up upon my land, strong, and without number; his teeth are the teeth of a lion, and he has the jaw teeth of a lioness.* **7** *He has laid my vine waste, and barked my fig-tree: he has made it clean bare, and cast it away; the branches thereof are made white*" **(1:5-7).**

The wicked people of Judah are depicted as "*drunkards*" that are clueless to the coming devastation for their sins. Jeremiah has a similar assessment of Judah during the impending days of Babylonian siege and conquest. The prophet of God describes Judah as a, "**22** *people that are foolish, they know me not; they are* **sottish** *children, and they have no understanding; they are wise to do evil, but to do good they have no knowledge*" (Jeremiah 4:22). The word "*sottish*" means to be deluded as one that is intoxicated. The Lord looked down from heaven and saw the true state of Judah (Jeremiah 7:11). The people had **no fear of God** (Jeremiah 5:22-24), **no shame for their sin** (Jeremiah 6:15), and **no knowledge of God** (Jeremiah 8:7). Judah was **rebellious** (Jeremiah 6:16) and given to **covetousness and falsehood** (Jeremiah 8:10). They practiced **idolatry** and even sacrificed their sons to Baal (Jeremiah 16:10-11 and 19:5). The people of Judah were **liars** (Jeremiah 9:1ff), **Sabbath breakers** (Jeremiah 17:19ff), **covenant breakers** (Jeremiah 34:18ff), and they had completely **put God out of their lives** (Jeremiah 18:15). Judah's **rulers led many astray** with their lies (Jeremiah 2:33). These rulers did what they considered to be right rather than following the laws of God (Jeremiah 7:24; 8:6). Judah's **prophets and priests were wicked** as well (see Jeremiah 5:30-31). Judah was ripe for a thrashing at the hands of God.

Jeremiah also speaks of the Babylonian Empire as a devouring lion saying, "**7** *The lion is come up from his thicket, and the destroyer of the*

Gentiles is on his way; he is gone forth from his place to make your land desolate; and your cities shall be laid waste, without an inhabitant" (Jeremiah 4:7). This same "*nation*" that has teeth as a lion is obviously likened unto a devastating swarm of insects as well. The prophet's design for the insects is figurative not literal. Babylon would be like a devouring lion and insects upon the land of a deluded sinful people. It would take acts of great **violence** to open the sinful people's eyes to their error (see Lamentations 2:6).

The joy of fresh squeezed grape juice (sweet wine) and the more intoxicating wines are gone from the people. Let those addicted to intoxicants weep and wail because it is all gone. With such calamity before them it would seem as though they would "*awake*" out of their drunken stupor and recognize that God was punishing them for their rebellious spirit.

"**8** *Lament like a virgin girded with sackcloth for the husband of her youth.* **9** *The meal-offering and the drink-offering are cut off from the house of Jehovah; the priests, Jehovah's ministers, mourn.* **10** *The field is laid waste, and the land mourns; for the grain is destroyed, the new wine is dried up, the oil languishes.* **11** *Be confounded, O husbandmen, wail, O vinedressers, for the wheat and for the barley; for the harvest of the field is perished.* **12** *The vine is withered, and the fig-tree languishes; the pomegranate-tree, the palm-tree also, and the apple-tree, even all the trees of the field are withered: for joy is withered away from the sons of men*" **(1:8-12).**

The joy that wine brought to Judah is now turned into deep sorrows and weeping. The blessing of oil is gone. The crops of wheat and barley have perished. The fruit trees have been stripped and uprooted. Even the basic trees of the land are destroyed by the chastening hand of God. The people are called upon to mourn as a virgin who was betrothed to a man from her youth only to have him die before they are able to be married. Deep dark sorrows await the people who are deluded in great sin.

Jeremiah similarly wrote a lamentation about the loss of Judah's joy. The prophet of God said, "15 *the joy of our heart is ceased; our dance is turned into mourning*" (Lamentations 5:15 see also Isaiah 16:10; 24:8 and Jeremiah 48:33). When Babylon crushed Judah by siege, burning down their temple, and destroying the walls of the city the people were left demoralized. The siege of Jerusalem left people in desperation of starvation. Some even resorted to eating their own children to stay alive (see Lamentations 4:10).

"**13** *Gird yourselves with sackcloth, and lament, you priests; wail, you ministers of the altar; come, lie all night in sackcloth, you ministers of my God: for the meal-offering and the drink-offering are withheld from the house of your God.* **14** *Sanctify a fast, call a solemn assembly, gather the old men and all the inhabitants of the land unto the house of Jehovah your God, and cry unto Jehovah*" **(1:13-14).**

There was no place for laughter as the full force of Babylon was bearing down on Judah. The land has been desolated and the crops are gone. God had also stricken the land with a terrible drought (see Joel 2:23). Starvation settles in and with this comes pestilence and death. Deep dark days of sorrow as each watches their family members and friends die. There is nothing to sacrifice to God. The priests were left mourning in sackcloth because they had nothing wherewith to do their work at the altar. Joel suggests that the priests call an assembly of the survivors that they may gather at the Lord's temple fasting and praying. Joel speaks as though the siege has already occurred; however, the next verse as well as chapter 2:1 reveals that this day of God's judgment against the wicked of Judah is yet in the future.

"**15** *Alas for the day! For the day of Jehovah is at hand, and as destruction from the Almighty shall it come.* **16** *Is not the food cut off* **before our eyes***, yea, joy and gladness from the house of our God?* **17** *The seeds rot under their clods; the garners are laid desolate, the barns are broken down; for the grain is withered.* **18** *How do the beasts groan!*

The herds of cattle are perplexed, because they have no pasture; yea, the flocks of sheep are made desolate" **(1:15-18).**

The prophet of God takes an assessment of the current plight of people being invaded by Babylon. Joel catalogues the events as they take place. The prophet looks out upon the land and sees the devastation that happens "*before our eyes*." Joel prophetically looks upon the animals as they suffer for a lack of food. Things are slowly dying and there is carnage of suffering that is unbearable. The "*day of Jehovah*" has arrived! This is a day that God judges the wicked and chastises them so that they may be moved to acknowledge their sins and repent (see more on this topic at chapter 3).

The prophet of God acknowledges that it is the "*Almighty*" God that is the source of all this devastation to the land. The cattle and sheep have no land to graze. Fire has devoured the fields, insects have denuded all living vegetation, and the Babylonians have devoured many with sword. God has stricken the land with a crippling drought (Joel 2:23). Starvation and disease settle in and the remaining peoples and beasts cry aloud in misery. The prophet Jeremiah is also very careful and deliberate to reveal God as the source of all devastation to Judah because of her sins. Let no man say that Babylon conquered Judah by her own power (see Jeremiah 25:8-9; 27:5-6; 30:15; 31:10-11; 33:2 and 44:15-23). The Lord said, "**5** *I have made the earth, the men and the beasts that are upon the face of the earth, by **my** great power and by **my** outstretched arm; and I give it unto whom it seems right unto **me**.* **6** *And **now I have given** all these lands into the hand of Nebuchadnezzar the king of Babylon, my servant; and the beasts of the field also have I given him to serve him*" (Jeremiah 27:5-6 see also Daniel 2:20-22).

"**19** *O Jehovah, to you do I cry; for the fire has devoured the pastures of the wilderness, and the flame has burned all the trees of the field.* **20** *Yea, the beasts of the field pant unto you; for the water brooks are dried up, and the fire has devoured the pastures of the wilderness*" **(1:19-20).**

Under the strain of war, drought, wildfires, hunger and disease Joel cries out unto Jehovah God for relief. There is; however, no where to run to get respite. There is no water and neither is their grazing grass for the animals. All living things have died or are in the process of dying. The blackness of death is about the land and leaves its inhabitants, along with all those who pass by, in a state of shock (see Jeremiah 18:16 and 19:8). Surely the world will see the hand of God in these things and come to fear his awesome name.

Questions over Joel Chapter 1

1. Why would it be so important for the current generation to tell their children and their children's children about these events?

2. Who is the lion that comes upon the land of Judah to devour her?

3. What affects does Babylon have on the land of Judah?

4. Why are the people called upon to lament and mourn?

JOEL CHAPTER 2

Synopsis

Judah would face the fierce wrath of God in the form of the Babylonian Empire. The Babylonians would strip all joy and sustenance from the land. Additionally, God brought a terrible drought (Joel 2:23), and fire (Joel 1:19) upon the land to chastise the wicked people of Judah. The prophet of God pleads with the people to acknowledge their error with a broken heart so that God would return his blessings upon them. If repentance occurs, due to God's plagues, they would be richly blessed now and forevermore. Not only would the rains return and the land be restored to its former Garden of Eden appearance but they would also find eternal salvation. Joel looks to a day in the future when the church would be established and man would have the opportunity of having their sins removed by the blood of Christ. If only the sinners of Judah would call out to God for help they would have all these blessings.

Application

Joel, like all of the prophets, speaks a common language with the New Testament writers. The prophet of God helps us understand that there is nothing but the fierce wrath of God's chastening hand that sinful man can expect to experience. God uses his plagues of horsemen in every generation to bring sinners to repentance (see Joel 2:4-5 and Revelation 9:7-9, 16-21 and 16:8-11). God will bring the true meek of Zion to be broken hearted over their sins by way of chastisement (Joel 2:12-14).

God's blessings will return when we acknowledge our error and turn to him in repentance.

Joel 2

A Description of Jehovah's Destructive Army (2:1-11)

"**1** *Blow the trumpet in Zion, and sound an alarm in my holy mountain; let all the inhabitants of the land tremble: for* **the day of Jehovah** *comes, for it is nigh at hand;* **2** *a day of darkness and gloominess, a day of clouds and thick darkness, as the dawn spread upon the mountains; a great people and a strong; there has not been ever the like, neither shall be any more after them, even to the years of many generations*" **(2:1-2)**.

Joel calls upon the inhabitants of Jerusalem to sound the alarm in Jerusalem. The "*day of Jehovah comes*" (see also Joel 1:15). The nearness of the event is depicted in the prophet's instructions to sound the alarm now. The watchers (God's prophets) upon the wall see the devastation coming and are called upon to warn the inhabitants of the city. Joel tells us that there has never been nor will there be for many generations to come such an awful experience. When we consider the brutality of the Assyrians as they raided lands, impaled their conquered victims upon poles throughout the cities, and covered walls with the skins of human flesh we tremble to think of what comes.

Joel uses dramatic language that illustrates to the inhabitants of the land what they're about to experience. Their pain and anguish for the sins they committed would be the greatest darkness and gloomy state that has ever been experienced by man. Such a state of doom will cause the joyous city to wail in pain and agony. Fascinatingly, the entire event reminds us of the crucifixion of Jesus Christ. The Lord's trial of beating (Matthew 26:62-68), being mocked (Luke 23:11), scourged by the Roman soldiers (John 19:1-6), and ultimately killed in a most brutal way by crucifixion (John 19:17-22) happened on a world stage so that the would may see God's view of sin and his love for all humanity so that they may be saved (see Isaiah 53 all). There is nothing but dark, gloomy, and or cloudy days that await the wicked in every generation. God's chastening hand will bring such doom and gloom to a man's life so that they may repent and be saved.

"**3** *A fire devours before them; and behind them a flame burns: the land is as the Garden of Eden before them, and behind them a desolate wilderness; yea, and none has escaped them*" **(2:3).**

The great Babylonian army, as a host of devouring insects, destroys all that is in their path. Land resembling the Garden of Eden for beauty and greenery turns black as it is scorched by the fire of their fury. Jeremiah writes the words of God saying, "10 *for I have set my face upon this city for evil, and not for good, said Jehovah: it shall be given into the hand of the king of Babylon, and he shall burn it with fire*" (Jeremiah 21:10 see also Joel 1:19-20).

"**4** *The appearance of them is as the appearance of horses; and as horsemen, so do they run.* **5** *Like the noise of chariots on the tops of the mountains do they leap, like the noise of a flame of fire that devours the stubble, as a strong people set in battle array.* **6** *At their presence the peoples are in anguish; all faces are waxed pale.* **7** *They run like mighty men; they climb the wall like men of war; and they march every one on his ways, and they break not their ranks.* **8** *Neither does one thrust another; they march every one in his path; and they burst through the weapons, and break not off their course*" **(2:4-8).**

The alarm has been sounded. The watchmen have seen with their eyes the power and might of this foe. An army of horsemen is their appearance and their goings has the sound of many chariots and a devouring fire. When the people under attack see the army their hearts are melted and filled with anguish. The people's faces are "*pale*" for they're sickened at the thought of what they are about to experience. The devouring army is driven by a purpose of destruction and they do not break their ranks but rather march in astonishing order that they may achieve their goal.

These horsemen are doing the bidding of God due to Judah's great sin. The terrifying horsemen are the chastening hand of God against a greatly disobedient and rebellious people. These comments mirror the events of the book of Revelation. God sends his horsemen of great plagues to devastate the land and inhabitants yet many harden their hearts and refuse to repent (see Revelation 9:7-9, 16-21) (17d). God's objective with the armies of Babylon was man's repentance (Jeremiah 18:8, 11) and likewise his objective with the devastating armies of plagues today is man's repentance (see Hebrews 12:5-13 and Revelation 16:8-11). Judah was in sin and God would move them to repentance by violent plagues (Jeremiah 51:35).

"*9 They leap upon the city; they run upon the wall; they climb up into the houses; they enter in at the windows like a thief. 10 The earth quakes before them; the heavens tremble; the sun and the moon are darkened, and the stars withdraw their shining. 11 And Jehovah utters his voice before his army; for his camp is very great; for he is strong that executes his word; for **the day of Jehovah is great and very terrible**; and who can abide it?*" **(2:9-11).**

This destructive army that leaves the land and people desolated is now revealed to belong to Jehovah God. Jeremiah had warned Israel that God would fight against them due to their hardened hearts (Jeremiah 21:5). The Babylonians were to be God's battle axe in his hand to destroy his rebellious people (Jeremiah 51:20). The Lord's destructive forces have arrived for judgment against the ungodly inhabitants of the land. The destroying army comes upon the city covering and invading it like water that invades a dry sponge by saturation. Joel writes, "*The day of Jehovah is great and very terrible*" (see also Joel 1:15 and 2:1). The day of God is not a final day of judgment but rather a day when God chastens the wicked to move them to repentance. When man sins he can expect nothing but doom and gloom in his life.

There is a reference to Revelation 18:8 regarding the strength of God in performing these acts against the ungodly at Joel 2:11. The Apostle John depicts Babylon as the great harlot of worldliness in every generation of mankind. God brings swift and violent destruction to her in the forms of great plagues and judgment. The admonition to the saints is that they would come up out of her and have no part in her wickedness (Revelation 18:4). Worldliness shall in no way prevail over God. All those who partake in the pleasures of sins will face a dark and gloomy day of judgment now and forevermore!

Joel Suggests that the People turn their hearts to God before its Everlasting too Late (2:12-17)

"*12 Yet even now, said Jehovah, turn unto me with all your heart, and with fasting, and with weeping, and with mourning: 13 and rend your heart, and not your garments, and turn unto Jehovah your God; for he is gracious and merciful, slow to anger, and abundant in lovingkindness, and repent him of the evil. 14 Who knows whether he will not turn and repent, and leave a blessing behind him, even a meal-offering and a drink-offering unto Jehovah your God?*" **(2:12-14).**

Yet even in this time of immediate danger there is hope. The people can avert the calamity of utter destruction if only they would turn back unto God "*with all your heart*." God's desire for his people is that they would serve him because that's what is in their heart to do rather than simply going through the mechanical motions of service. The "*day of Jehovah*" comes as God's heavy hand of chastisement will be upon a disobedient people for their own good. Sinful people of all ages are to look at the doom and gloom in their lives and conclude that their own iniquities have brought their current situation of hardships. The remedy now and forevermore is repentance. Once we have experienced the chastening hand of God we should never want to return to such dark and gloomy days. It is the days of God's chastening hand that produces fear in our hearts and a driving purpose to not return to sin.

Rending the garments would be a typical reaction to one who was in sorrows; however, such activity did not necessarily mean that there was true sorrow in the heart. The Lord desires Israel to "*rend your heart*" in turning back to Jehovah in repentance. The worshipper of God must truly have a broken or torn heart due to their knowledge of violating the Lord's commands. We must all be bothered by our sin to do something about it (14e). Though David had committed a terrible sin against God by destroying the family of Uriah he nonetheless found forgiveness through a broken heart and confession. David writes, "*For you delight not in sacrifice; else would I give it: you have no pleasure in burnt offerings. 17 The sacrifices of God are a broken spirit: a broken and a contrite heart, O God, you will not despise*" (Psalms 51:16-17). It is not until we see our great guilt and pour rivers of water from our eyes in tears that we may be moved to acceptable repentance and restoration.

The Lord's request is that his people would earnestly turn to him in repentance and purpose within their heart to follow his laws to the best of their abilities. When one is broken hearted over their sins and moved to repentance they illustrate the spirit of one who believes in the reality of God, heaven, and hell. Such an individual voluntarily places self under the authoritative commandments of God out of a sense of reverence, fear, and respect for the Almighty. People who earnestly give effort to follow God's precepts and ways are the people that God desires to serve him (Philippians 3:13-15).

Note the fact that God is depicted not only as a destroying force (Joel 2:11) but also a "*gracious and merciful*" God that is "*slow to anger, and abundant in lovingkindness.*" Judah had tried God's patience, grace, and mercy for years. Though the strong arm of God was about to be unleashed upon them it was still not too late for them to repent. God gives man a chance to turn to him till their dying day.

"*15 Blow the trumpet in Zion, sanctify a fast, call a solemn assembly; 16 gather the people, sanctify the assembly, assemble the old men, gather the children, and those that suck the breasts; let the bridegroom go forth from his chamber, and the bride out of her closet. 17 Let the priests, the ministers of Jehovah, weep between the porch and the altar, and let them say, Spare your people, O Jehovah, and give not your heritage to reproach, that the nations should rule over them: wherefore should they say among the peoples, Where is their God?"* **(2:15-17).**

Joel gives the people within the walls of Jerusalem quick instructions to avert the disaster that is about to take place. The admonition is to call for a national fast and assembly of young, old, male, and female. The assembly should be one of great mourning. All should come to see their great sin and call out to God in sorrows as they acknowledge their error. The prophet of God speaks about the urgency of the matter. Babylon is marching toward Zion with sword and devastation. Now is the time to awake in repentance!

Joel gives the exact words that God desires to hear from his people. The prophet Hosea did a very similar thing at Hosea 14:1-3 in relation to the words God wanted to hear from Israel. When a man makes statements of confession his words illustrate a heart that is compliant (meek) to God's divine revelation. Such words illustrate a man's acknowledgement of God's divine being. Such words illustrate a man's fear and reverence toward the holy name of the Almighty God. These are the words that God wants to hear. These words will reveal to him the man's heart of love and devotion.

Such a state of mind will move Israel to understand that by their actions they have caused the surrounding nations to not believe that God is. How could a God of any people, so they would say, let all these horrific events occur? Neither the people of God nor the surrounding nations understood that it was the Almighty God who actually brought these calamities upon his own people. Israel had a rebellious spirit that needed correction. The rebellious attitude and consequential punishment has caused the world to say, "*Where is their God*." Joel prays that it would not come to this.

The Blessings that await the repentant Sinner (2:18-27)

"**18** *Then was Jehovah jealous for his land, and had pity on his people.* **19** *And Jehovah answered and said unto his people, Behold, I will send you* *grain, and new wine, and oil, and you shall be satisfied therewith; and I will no more make you a reproach among the nations;* **20** *but I will remove far off from you the northern army, and will drive it into a land barren and desolate, its forepart into the eastern sea; and its stench shall come up, and its ill savor shall come up, and because it has done great things"* **(2:18-20).**

Joel prophetically looks to a future day when Judah would be saved as a result of their understanding and repentance. The saved will be those who said the words God wanted to hear (see Joel 2:17 above). The humble people would once again be blessed with grain, new wine, and oil. Their stomachs would be full and their hearts made glad by the new wine and oil.

The swarming *"northern army"* would be removed by the might of God. This verse proves that a literal locust invasion was not the meaning of Joel's prophecy at Joel 1:2-4. Some believe that the locusts are still under consideration due to the winds driving them into the various seas. One must also consider the fact that the Babylonians were often referred to as those of the *"north"* by the prophets (see Jeremiah 1:13-15; 4:6; 6:1; etc.). Jeremiah writes, "**22** *the voice of tidings, behold, it comes, and a great commotion out of the* **north country**, *to make the cities of Judah a desolation, and dwelling-place of jackals*" (Jeremiah 10:22).

God would certainly judge the pride stricken Babylonians of the north (see Jeremiah 25:12). Their sin is revealed as pride (Jeremiah 50:29), covetous (Jeremiah 51:13), and they were filled with idolatry (Jeremiah 50:2 and 51:40, 52). Though the Lord would use Babylon to punish his people they would not escape judgment due to their own wickedness. Babylon had striven against the Lord (Jeremiah 50:24). Babylon would be punished for her evil deeds (Jeremiah 25:12; 50:14 and 50-51). God purposed to bring the Medes and Persians against Babylon and they would be conquered (Jeremiah 51:11).

"**21** *Fear not, O land, be glad and rejoice; for Jehovah has done great things.* **22** *Be not afraid, you beasts of the field; for the pastures of the* *wilderness do spring, for the tree bears its fruit, the fig-tree and the vine do yield their strength.* **23** *Be glad then, you children of Zion, and rejoice in Jehovah your God; for he gives you the former rain in just measure, and he causes to come down for you the rain, the former rain and the latter rain, in the first month"* **(2:21-23).**

God's true Zion would acknowledge their sins and repent. The righteous and meek of the earth would have nothing to fear. There would come a day when the fruit trees, pastures, and rains would be restored. God had divinely called for a drought upon the land in addition to the plague of fire, sword, famine and pestilence. Droughts are found throughout the Bible as a tool that God uses to chastise people to repentance (see Psalms 65:9-13; Hosea 5:11-12; 6:3-4 and Haggai 1:6-11). Man ought to "*consider*" why they are experiencing droughts, war, and plagues so that they may find relief (see Hosea 7:2 and Haggai 1:6). When man considers the why of their plagues and repents of sins God's blessings return. The inference is that God chastens man for sin by removing his blessings from them (17d).

"**24** *And the floors shall be full of wheat, and vats shall overflow with new wine and oil.* **25** *And I will restore to you the years that the locust has eaten, the canker-worm, and the caterpillar, and the palmer-worm, my great army which I sent among you.* **26** *And you shall eat in plenty and be satisfied, and shall praise the name of Jehovah your God, that has* **dealt wondrously with you***; and my people shall never be put to shame.* **27** *And you shall know that I am in the midst of Israel, and that I am Jehovah your God, and there is none else; and my people shall never be put to shame"* **(2:24-27).**

Joel's fear was that the nations of men would think that God was too weak to save his people from Babylon (see Joel 2:17). The Lord assures his prophet and people that when they repent there will be obvious blessings restored and the world would know of God's might. All that the army of locust, worms, and caterpillars took would be divinely restored. The land would once again look like the Garden of Eden (see

Joel 2:3). When all these things are restored the people would come to see the manner that God has "*dealt wondrously with you.*"

How does God "*deal wondrously*" with his people? Joel has told us that God is "*gracious, merciful, slow to anger, and abundant in lovingkindness*" (Joel 2:13). The Lord loves his created people and desires all of us to be saved (2 Peter 3:9). He "*deals wondrously*" with us by chastising, punishing, or plaguing us so that we may be moved to repentance. God's heavy hand of chastisement was upon the people in the form of the Babylonian Empire. To think that God had the power to move a mighty nation like Babylon to accomplish his will and then destroy them for their own wickedness is very wondrous (see Daniel 2:20-22). When all the atrocities of Babylon through drought, fire, sword, famine, and pestilence are miraculously displaced by Jehovah God then all would know that, "*I am Jehovah your God, and there is none else*" (see also Isaiah 46:9-10). God uses all creation to move man in the direction that he desires so that they may have eternal life. God wondrously brings a condemned sinner to repentance by way of chastisement (17d).

Future blessings through Christ (2:28-32)

"**28** *And it shall come to pass afterward, that I will pour out my Spirit upon all flesh; and your sons and your daughters shall prophesy, your old men shall dream dreams, your young men shall see visions:* **29** *and also upon the servants and upon the handmaids in those days will I pour out my Spirit*" **(2:28-29).**

After the days of Babylonian chastisement and a restoration of Zion there shall come even greater blessings at the hands of the Lord. God "*dealt wondrously*" with people in the days of Jeremiah and Joel so that they may have hope of eternal salvation. The Apostle Peter quotes from Joel 2:28-32 about six hundred years later at Acts 2:17-21 because the Lord continues to deal "*wondrously*" with his people. Joel foretells of what will take place in the "*last days*" (Acts 2:17 and see also Isaiah 2:2-3 and Daniel 2:28). God was to pour out his Holy Spirit upon the Apostles and "*upon all flesh*" in the form of divine revelation that would be confirmed as truth through the miracles that followed them (see Mark 16:20). Without partiality God would use male, female, young, old, slave, and free to distribute his message. Those immersed in the Holy Spirit would have the power to speak divinely inspired words of truth. God's truth or law would wondrously instruct people in the paths of righteousness.

The author of Hebrews tells us that God communicated his message to man in "***divers manners***" (Hebrews 1:1). God **spoke directly** to some prophets (Genesis 12:1ff; Exodus 12:1ff. etc.). God "*moved*" some men to speak divine truths by the **Holy Spirit** (2 Peter 1:21). The Holy Spirit "*entered into*" (Ezekiel 2:1-2) and "*fell upon*" (Ezekiel 11:5) the apostles and prophets in times past. Jesus said to his apostles, "*8 When the Spirit of truth is come, he shall **guide** you into all the truth: for he shall not speak from himself; but what things soever he shall hear, these shall he speak: and he shall declare unto you the things that are to come*" (John 16:8ff). Nehemiah records, "*Yet many years did you bear with them, and testified against them **by your Spirit** through your prophets*" (Nehemiah 9:30 and also see Ezekiel 1:3; 11:4-7). Others received "**visions**" and "**dreams**" from God to speak a divine message to the people (Daniel 7:1; Obadiah 1:1 and Joel 2:28ff). These men, that were moved by God to speak, **confirmed** their words as being of divine origin by the signs and wonders they performed (see Mark 16:20; John 20:30-31; Acts 2:22; Hebrews 2:2-4) (10d).

Take note of the association between "*pouring forth my Spirit*" and "*prophecy, wonders, and signs*." This would be the "*like gift*" of Acts 11:17. While it was only the apostles who received Holy Spirit baptism at Acts chapter two we know that the Holy Spirit was poured out upon many others as time went on. God would "*pour forth of my Spirit*" by means of the apostles laying their hands upon others (see Acts 8:14-17). Baptism of the Holy Spirit did not; therefore, occur simply because one was baptized into Christ. To have the ability to perform the power of God, through miracles, would only occur through the apostles' laying on of hands (see also Acts 19:1-7). The great miracles that the prophets and other inspired people did produce wonder (awe) within the minds of the witnesses (6d).

"**30** *And I will show wonders in the heavens and in the earth: blood, and fire, and pillars of smoke.* **31** *The sun shall be turned into darkness, and the moon into blood, before the great and terrible day of Jehovah comes*" **(2:30-31).**

The days of Acts chapter 2 would see unrepentant sinners just as there were during the days of Joel. Due to their hardened hearts God would bring doom, gloom, and blood upon them in judgment against their wicked deeds. Such men "*mock*" at the words of divine revelation rather than being humbled (see Acts 2:13). The "*day of the Lord*" awaits those who sin. The "*day of the Lord*" is used throughout the scriptures to illustrate a day of calamity and judgment (see Isaiah 13:9-11; Ezekiel 30:3; 2 Corinthians 1:14 and 1 Thessalonians 5:2). Judgment of doom awaits the un-repenting sinner. God plagues the sinner to cause him to repent (Revelation 16:8-11) and those who refuse God's chastisement will die in their sins (see John 8:24).

The dark gloomy days that Judah would experience at the hands of the Babylonians would also be experienced in subsequent generations of wicked men. Nothing would change, in relationship to God's chastening hand, from testament to testament. The "*day of the Lord*" would be the day that wicked men are divinely chastised for their sinful deeds. God will plague the wicked with his horsemen in every generation (see Joel 1:15; 2:1-2, 4, 11 and Revelation 9:7-9, 16-21).

"**32** *And it shall come to pass, that whosoever shall call on the name of Jehovah shall be delivered; for in mount Zion and in Jerusalem there shall be those that escape, as Jehovah has said, and among the remnant those whom Jehovah does call*" **(2:32).**

The Apostle Paul was told by Ananias to be baptized so that his sins might be washed away. Then he was instructed to "*call upon the name*" of Jesus (see Acts 22:16). The idea of *"calling upon the name of God"* is to "invoke" or "appeal" to the name of God for help (LS 292) (15h). This *"calling"* and being *"saved"* are inseparably connected. Those who suffer at the chastising hand of God are moved to call out to God in repentance and help. *"Deliverance"* from the dark, doom, and gloomy days of God's chastening hand is dependant upon one's reaction to the punishment.

The following verses are examples of men calling upon the name of Jehovah (see Psalms 3:1ff; Acts 2:21; 9:14, 21; 22:16; Romans 10:12-13; 1 Corinthians 1:2 and 2 Timothy 2:22). God calls upon men and women to be saved through the gospel message (2 Thessalonians 2:13-14). Man calls upon God by **appealing to him for help** in his time of needing forgiveness for sins. The meek and lowly will not only acknowledge their error but they will call out to God for mercy and forgiveness.

Joel continues saying, *"for in mount Zion and in Jerusalem there shall be those that escape, as Jehovah has said, and among the remnant those whom Jehovah does call."* Salvation is found at *"mount Zion and in Jerusalem."* Mount Zion is where the law of forgiveness would go forth (Isaiah 2:3). Those who come to Mount Zion through hearing and responding to the call of the gospel message have entered into the church of Jesus Christ and forgiven of sins (Hebrews 12:21ff). The forgiveness of sins is what brings *"escape"* of eternal condemnation and *"salvation"* (15e). All who conform their lives to the image of Jesus Christ will be identified as the *"remnant"* (see Romans 8:29 and 11:1-5). Those who call out to God for help in all generation are the elect and foreordained of God (Romans 9:11-13 and Ephesians 1:3-7). There will always be those who are willing to fearfully and meekly follow the Lord's authoritative words.

Questions over Joel Chapter 2

1. What is the "*day of Jehovah*" that is sure to come?

2. Compare and contrast the appearance of God's chastening hands at work here at Joel 2:4-5 and Revelation 9:7-9, 16-21).

3. What does God expect his people to do as they face this terrible destroying army?

4. What does Joel pray to God that the people of Judah would "*say*?"

5. True or False: If the sinful people of Judah would repent God would return the blessings to their land.

6. True or False: God had additionally plagued Judah with a drought.

7. Why did the Apostle Peter quote from Joel 2:28-32 at Acts 2:17-21?

JOEL CHAPTER 3

Synopsis

Joel sees a panoramic spiritual picture of the generations of men to come upon the earth. The wicked are called to the valley of Jehoshaphat to receive their judgment by God. The Lord will chastise them with heavy punishment so that they may repent. Most; however, blame God for their torment and develop hatred rather than softness of heart. Though the wicked persecute the righteous there is even hope that they too can be forgiven.

Application

The saints of God can gain great comfort from reading Joel chapter 3. God is in control of all things in this life. God sees all that the saints go through. Though the wicked persecute the saints they're comforted with the words of God's divine revelation. Though the wicked come up against the saints as the sand of the sea shore for number they will not prevail. Jesus said, "28 *and be not afraid of them that kill the body, but are not able to kill the soul: but rather fear him who is able to destroy both soul and body in hell*" (Matthew 10:28).

Joel 3

Judgment pronounced against all nations with emphasis on Tyre, Sidon, and Philistia (3:1-8)

*"**1** For, behold, in those days, and in that time, when I shall bring back the captivity of Judah and Jerusalem, **2** I will gather all nations, and will bring them down into the valley of Jehoshaphat; and I will execute judgment upon them there for my people and for my heritage Israel, whom they have scattered among the nations: and they have parted my land, **3** and have cast lots for my people, and have given a boy for a harlot, and sold a girl for wine, that they may drink"* **(3:1-3).**

The prophet of God continues to proclaim words that have to do with "*those days, and in that time*." The days under consideration, contextually, can be none other than the days of the kingdom of God being established on the day of Pentecost (Acts 2) (see previous chapter notes). Secondly, this would be a time of God's judgments being unleashed upon the wicked. Joel has repeatedly spoke of the "*day of Jehovah*" (see Joel 1:15; 2:1, 11 and 31). The day of Jehovah would be the day that God brings doom and gloom upon the wicked so that they may acknowledge their sins and repent. Some of the sinners due God's wrath would be those who persecute the saints for their stand in truth. The wicked of every variety will be called to the "*valley of Jehoshaphat*" (Literally, Valley of the Lord's Judgment) and God would execute his judgments against them in the form of plagues.

The prophet Amos also said that God would "*bring back the captivity of my people Israel*" at Amos 9:14. James quotes from the context of Joel and Amos at Acts 15:14-18. Contextually James speaks of God's eternal plan to include the Gentiles in his plan of salvation. Joel looks to a day when the gospel message will be preached in the entire world and anyone who obeys the word of God will be saved (Jew or Gentile). Those who rebel against the outpouring of the Holy Spirit will be chastised. Joel sees future judgments against those of the world that mirror what Judah went through at the hands of Babylon. The Holy Spirit would be poured out upon men and women during the days of the apostles and they would reveal divine revelation to the world. Many would persecute the saints of God for their stand in truth. Joel sees a day when God would judge the wicked of the world that have treated his saints with a sense of shame.

"**4** *Yea, and what are you to me, O Tyre, and Sidon, and all the regions of Philistia? Will you render me a recompense? And if you recompense me, swiftly and speedily will I return your recompense upon your own head*" **(3:4).**

The English Standard Version Bible reads for Joel 3:4 as follows: "*What are you to me, O Tyre and Sidon, and all the regions of Philistia? Are you paying me back for something? If you are paying me back, I will return your payment on your own head swiftly and speedily.*" Do the nations of wicked men believe that they're getting God back for being plagued when they persecute his beloved saints? There will be many who are judged in the valley of Jehoshaphat that are irritated with God when he plagues them for their wickedness. Though God is trying to help the wicked to acknowledge their error and repent the sinners are hardened and angry. The Apostle John said that this is exactly what the wicked of every generation would do rather than repent (see Revelation 16:21). Some are softened by God's divine revelation that is poured out upon man by the Holy Spirit and some are hardened in their sins (2 Corinthians 2:14-16). Again, some are angered by God's chastisement and a few are moved to repent in shame (see Revelation 16:8-9).

"**5** *Forasmuch as you have taken my silver and my gold, and have carried into your temples my goodly precious things,* **6** *and have sold the children of Judah and the children of Jerusalem unto the sons of the Grecians, that you may remove them far from their border;* **7** *behold, I will stir them up out of the place whither you have sold them, and will return your recompense upon your own head;* **8** *and I will sell your sons and your daughters into the hand of the children of Judah, and they shall sell them to men of Sheba, to a nation far off: for Jehovah has spoken it*" **(3:5-8).**

Though God used the wicked nations of Assyria and Babylon to chastise his people these ungodly nations were also subject to God's laws. As God chastised even the Gentile nations they lashed out at God in anger rather than to soften their hearts and acknowledge his divine and sovereign being. To get even with God the wicked stole treasures from his holy temple and sold his holy people as slaves. The wicked have no conscience when performing their dark deeds against the people of God (see John 16:1-2).

The Lord; however, will protect and guard his beloved children in every generation (see Zechariah 9:8, 15 and 1 Peter 1:5). The saints of God are the apple of his divine eyes (Deuteronomy 32:10; Psalms 17:8 and Zechariah 2:8). Isaiah said that the saints are a "*royal diadem in the hand of God*" (Isaiah 62:3). Those who treat the people of God with disdain will pay a high price. Jesus said, "6 *Whosoever shall cause one of these little ones that believe on me to stumble, it is profitable for him that a great millstone should be hanged about his neck, and that he should be sunk in the depth of the sea*" (Matthew 18:6).

A call to War and Identity of God's People (3:9-21)

"**9** *Proclaim this among the nations; prepare war; stir up the mighty men; let all the men of war draw near, let them come up.* **10** *Beat your plowshares into swords, and your pruning hooks into spears: let the weak say, I am strong.* **11** *Haste, and come, all nations round about, and gather yourselves together: cause your mighty ones to come down, O Jehovah.* **12** *Let the nations bestir themselves, and come up to the valley of Jehoshaphat; for there will I sit to judge all the nations round about.* **13** *Put in the sickle; for the harvest is ripe: come, tread you; for the winepress is full, the vats overflow; for their wickedness is great*" **(3:9-13).**

Joel sees future battles between the wicked and good. God is depicted as protecting and defending his true saints. As God crushed the wicked in the wine press of his divine wrath in Judah, by way of the Babylonian Empire, even so he will do in all generations to come (see Revelation 14:19-20 and 19:15). The Lord will plague the wicked in judgment at the valley of Jehoshaphat.

The wicked, which are hardened by truth and chastisement, resort to persecuting the saints of God. To turn one's wrath to God's saints is to fight against God. The wicked are called upon to make their farming tools into weapons and come to the valley of Jehoshaphat to meet God in battle. The idea is that if one fights against the saints of God they're actually fighting against God. The wicked of every generation will do this and they will always be defeated (Revelation 18:1-4 and 20:7-9).

"**14** *Multitudes, multitudes in the valley of decision! For the day of Jehovah is near in the valley of decision.* **15** *The sun and the moon are darkened, and the stars withdraw their shining.* **16** *And Jehovah will roar from Zion, and utter his voice from Jerusalem; and the heavens and the earth shall shake: but Jehovah will be a refuge unto his people, and a stronghold to the children of Israel.* **17** *So shall you know that I am Jehovah your God, dwelling in Zion my holy mountain: then shall Jerusalem be holy, and there shall no strangers pass through her any more*" **(3:14-17).**

The "*valley of decision*" is the "*valley of Jehoshaphat*" (Joel 3:12). Joel sees "*multitudes*" upon multitudes gathering together at this valley with their weapons of war. The Apostle John spoke of this gathering for war against the saints and Jehovah God at Revelation 16:13-14. John writes, "*And they gathered them together into the place which is called in Hebrew Harmagedon* (**Armageddon**)" (Revelation 16:16). Contextually, John sees God pouring out his bowls of wrath that are designed to get the wicked to repent yet they blaspheme the name of God for his punishments (see Revelation 16:21). Joel too is prophetically seeing the system of God at work in every generation of mankind. God will do all things within his power to save the most wicked of men yet those who refuse to change will be eternally judged and condemned. The Apostle John sees the wicked coming up against the saints of God numbering as the sand of the seashore for multitude (Revelation 20:10-15). Though the saints of God seem outnumbered by the world as they live a life of sanctification and holiness they have the greatest of all on their side (see Romans 8:31).

"**18** *And it shall come to pass in that day, that the mountains shall drop down sweet wine, and the hills shall flow with milk, and all the brooks of Judah shall flow with waters; and a fountain shall come forth from the house of Jehovah, and shall water the valley of Shittim.* **19** *Egypt shall be a desolation, and Edom shall be a desolate wilderness, for the violence done to the children of Judah, because they have shed innocent blood in their land.* **20** *But Judah shall abide for ever, and Jerusalem from generation to generation.* **21** *And I will cleanse their blood, that I have not cleansed: for Jehovah dwells in Zion*" **(3:18-21)**.

Joel writes, "*In that day*" which connects these thoughts to the thoughts and time table above. The time is during the revelation of Jesus Christ being poured out upon sons, daughters, old and young men, slave and free. The days are times when the saints that receive the gospel message in obedience shall be persecuted for their faith. The days are times when God would chastise wicked men, as he has in every generation, to cause them to repent. The days are times when the wicked will meet God in the valley of Jehoshaphat for battle.

The abundance of blessings listed must have to do with the satisfying word of God that is revealed by revelation through the prophets, apostles, and inspired people of the New Testament age. God's word would sustain, protect, guard, and guide the saints of God. Egypt and Edom stand in metonymy (see Obadiah study) for all the ungodly that reject the gospel message of salvation. The wicked will always dwell in a desolate place of hardships and divine chastisement.

The Common English Bible reads, "*I will forgive their bloodguilt, which I had not forgiven*." The word "*bloodguilt*" (Hebrew *dam*) "Ezekiel 18:13 seems to indicate that these terms do not necessarily signify bloodshed, but any grievous sin which, if it remains, will block God's favor to his land and people (see Deuteronomy 21:8 and Isaiah 1:15)" (ISBE volume 1, page 527). The body of man is depicted as having physical blood and spiritual blood. Those who wreck the spiritual condition of another is deemed guilty of that man's blood in that they cause their soul to be lost (see Acts 20:26). Though the wicked cause others to lose their soul there is hope even for those who do the persecuting. Zion will be comprised of some of the worst of sinners who have had a change of heart and newly directed in life (see 1 Corinthians 6:8-11).

Questions over Joel Chapter 3

1. What will happen in the valley of Jehoshaphat?

2. Why was the winepress full?

3. Why would God "*roar from Zion*" as a lion?

Amos

Robertson's Notes

Bible Books 30 of 66

"You only have I known of all the families of the earth: therefore I will visit upon you all your iniquities"

Amos 3:2

Introduction

Due to Israel's wickedness Amos proclaimed, "*Prepare to meet your God*" (Amos 4:12). God fearfully said, "*The end is come upon my people Israel*" (Amos 8:2). God would send the Assyrian army to accomplish his judgment upon Israel (see Isaiah 10:5; Hosea 11:5 and Amos 3:11; 5:27). Israel had only captivity (Amos 6:7, 14 and 7:9) and violent judgment (Amos 8:3 and 9:1-2, 10) to look forward to. The days of judgment would be times of great sorrow and darkness for the wicked (Amos 5:16-20 and 8:9-10). Not one single wicked man or woman would survive this day (Amos 9:1, 10).

Date

The days of Amos were "*evil times*" (Amos 5:13). Uzziah was king of Judah and Jeroboam II was king of Israel. Uzziah reigned 52 years in Judah (790 to 738 BC - 2 Chronicles 26:3). Jeroboam II reigned forty-one years in Israel (791 to 750 BC - 2 Kings 14:23). Amos' prophecy had to fall some time between 791 and 750 BC (the time that encompasses both reigns of Uzziah and Jeroboam II). The only other indicator of time is that this prophecy falls two years before the "*earthquake*" (Amos 1:1; see also Zechariah 14:5). During these days the Assyrian Empire was on the verge of world dominance. Assyria, under the reign of Tiglath-Pileser (five years after the days of Amos), began their westward trek of war and terror (around 745 BC).

God in Amos

Amos was careful to identify Jehovah as the "*God of hosts*" on eight occasions in this prophecy. The sovereignty of God over man, nations, nature, and animals is precisely identified by God's prophet (Amos 4:13; 5:8-9 etc.). Amos leaves no doubts in the minds of the wicked in Israel as to their lawless deeds and just judgment that they faced. No sin committed by Israel had escaped the all-seeing and all-knowing God (Amos 4:13). During these evil days the prophet proclaimed, "*Prepare to meet your God, O Israel*" (Amos 4:12).

Amos

The name "Amos" means "burden-bearer" (ISBE volume 1, page 114). God divinely appointed the burden of exposing the sins and doom of the northern kingdom of Israel (Amos 1:1 and 7:15). Amos' home town was Tekoa (six miles south of Bethlehem). Tekoa was high in elevation and overlooked the wilderness areas of Judah and Palestine. Amos lived here as a "*herdsman*" (Amos 1:1) and "*dresser of sycamore trees*" (Amos 7:14). Most of Amos' work was conducted at Bethel (Amos 7:13). Amos was a man of prayer (cf. Amos 7:2, 5) and deep conviction (Amos 7:14ff). Amaziah once demanded that Amos take his message of doom and gloom to the south yet the prophet continued with a "*thus said Jehovah*" (Amos 7:15). Amos was careful to always elevate God's commands above man's fleshly will (Acts 5:29).

Israel

Israel had come to be no different than the heathen Gentiles in the eyes of the Lord (Amos 9:7). God said of Israel, "*I know how manifold are your transgressions, and how mighty are your sins*" (Amos 5:12). Rather than viewing Israel as the kingdom of God they are referred to as "*the sinful kingdom*" (Amos 9:8). Israel had far removed itself from the plumb-line of truth and justice (Amos 7:7-8). Amos revealed Israel's lack of regard for the poor (Amos 2:6-7; 4:1; 5:11-12 and 8:4) and insatiable appetite for riches (Amos 3:12, 15; 5:11 and 6:1-3). Israel was ungrateful (Amos 2:9) and disrespectful toward God (Amos 2:11-12). God had given her his divine revelation yet she turned to her own ways (Amos 3:1-2, 10). The people were guilty of idolatry (Amos 3:14) and disingenuous worship (Amos 4:4-5; 5:21ff and 8:4-6). Israel was also spiritually deluded. She sincerely thought that God was with her while she conducted herself in unlawful ways (see Amos 5:14, 18; i.e. "*as you say*" compared to Jeremiah 2:35; 8:8; 13:22 and 16:10). She actually looked forward to the day of God's judgment (Amos 5:18) because she thought, "*The evil shall not overtake nor meet us*" (Amos 9:10). Israel was also filled with pride (Amos 6:8), self sufficient (Amos 6:13), and they cheated the poor (Amos 8:5-6).

Lessons learned from Amos

We, too, live in an "*evil time*" (Amos 5:13). A day of judgment is coming and shall fall upon the misguided masses that have put God out of their lives (Romans 2:3-8). God has sent his prophets and evangelist to save the sinners yet many reject their words. Furthermore God chastens sinners to move them to repentance yet many turn their backs in anger (Amos 4:6-11 and Revelation 16:8-11). Amos reveals a day when God's mercy and love runs out and the sinner meets his eternal doom.

Though there are thousands upon thousands of people who call themselves Christians it is the elected remnant that are the true people of God (see Amos 3:12; 5:14-15; 9:8; Romans 9:27 and 11:1-5). Many today are religiously deluded. Religious people in our society long for the day when Christ shall come again yet fail to realize that his coming will be a day of terror for all who did not subject themselves to his authority (Amos 5:18 and Matthew 7:21-23). Denominational bodies are worshipping the Lord and doing many things in his name yet we hear the words of Amos loud and clear as he says that the Lord *"hates, despises, and takes no delight in your solemn assemblies"* (Amos 5:21). Amos helps us to understand that God has a standard, his law, that man is measured by (Amos 7:7-8 and Galatians 6:2). If any man or woman does not meet that standard then violent judgment awaits. God's day of terror will not be a time that the wicked should look forward to. The wicked will not be able to hide on the mountain tops, clouds of the heavens, and depths of the earth or sea without being found (Amos 9:1-4). Now is the time to let God's word fashion my life rather than man's will (Amos 7:14ff and Romans 8:29).

AMOS CHAPTER 1

Synopsis

The roaring voice of Jehovah will be heard over many nations of men and women due to their wickedness. Each of the nations mentioned in this chapter had a common error. There was a lack of value for human life. Every wicked nation would face the *"fire"* of God's wrath (see seven references beginning at Amos 1:4). Joel compared Babylon to a fire that God would use to chastise the wicked of Judah (see Joel 2:3-5). The prophet Joel said that God would chastise the wicked with fire and drought (see Joel 1:19-20). Amos too reveals God's wrath upon the wicked nations to be in the form of fire.

Application

Amos reveals the universal sovereignty of God over the nations of men. There is not one nation of people in any given time period that is not subject to the authorized words of God (see Jeremiah 32:27 and Ezekiel 18:4). Each nation would be chastised or punished by the hand of God for their wickedness. Today, nations the world over continue to be chastened or punished by God for their wickedness because he alone is Lord. It is God's desire that people would come to repentance through their suffering (see Revelation 16:8-11).

Amos 1

Amos announces his prophetic work and the doom of the Ungodly (1:1-2)

"**1** *The words of Amos, who was among the herdsmen of Tekoa, which he saw concerning Israel in the days of Uzziah king of Judah, and in the days of Jeroboam the son of Joash king of Israel, two years before the earthquake*" **(1:1)**.

The dates of this book, as well as Amos of Tekoa, have been discussed in the introduction. Amos' words are things that he "*saw concerning Israel.*" God often communicated his message to the prophets by means of dreams and visions (see Daniel 7:1; Obadiah 1:1 and Joel 2:28ff). The Lord gave Amos a vision of what was to come of "*Israel*" (i.e., the northern nation). Amos sees three visions at chapter 7 and two more at chapters 8 and 9.

Amos speaks of an "*earthquake*" occurring two years before he began to reveal his divine visions and words. Zechariah also mentions the earthquake that occurred during the days of Uzziah the king of Judah (see Zechariah 14:5). Nothing more is known about this quake. The fact that both Amos and Zechariah mention the quake indicates that it must have been a historical event of significance and one the people were well aware of.

"**2** *And he said, Jehovah will roar from Zion, and utter his voice from Jerusalem; and the pastures of the shepherds shall mourn, and the top of Carmel shall wither*" **(1:2)**.

Zion was the mountain in Jerusalem where David had constructed the temple of Jehovah. Inspired Bible prophets often used this term to signify not only God's immediate kingdom but the future spiritual kingdom, the church, and those who would eventually dwell in heaven (see Hebrews 12:22-23).

Amos sees the Lord roaring as a fierce lion from this mountain and terror filling the hearts of the inhabitants of the land. The prophet Hosea also saw God roaring as a lion. Hosea writes, "14 *For I will be unto Ephraim as a lion, and as a young **lion** to the house of Judah: I, even I, will tear and go away; I will carry off, and there shall be none to deliver.* 15 *I will go and return to my place,* **till they acknowledge their offence, and seek my face**: *In their affliction they will seek me earnestly*" (Hosea 5:14-15). Many of Israel would come to fear and reverence the name of God as they "*acknowledge their offence and seek my* (God's) *face.*" Again, Hosea writes, "10 *they shall walk after Jehovah, who will roar like a lion; for he will roar, and the children shall come trembling from the west*" (Hosea 11:10). The roaring of God as a lion was the chastising punishment he sent upon Israel in the form of Assyria and Judah in the form of Babylon. Joel writes, "16 *Jehovah will roar from Zion, and utter his voice from Jerusalem; and the heavens and the earth shall shake: but Jehovah will be a refuge unto his people, and a stronghold to the children of Israel*" (Joel 3:16).

Judgments pronounced against 7 nations (including Judah and Israel) (1:3-2 all)

"**3** *Thus said Jehovah: For three transgressions of* **Damascus***, yea, for four, I will not turn away the* **punishment** *thereof; because they have threshed Gilead with threshing instruments of iron*" **(1:3).**

It is apparent that the number "*three yea four*" is not to be taken literal. The Lord states that for these three yea four sins the nations were to be punished yet gives only one example. The thought is that their sins are due God's punishment. Note that God's punishment is directly associated with the nation's transgression.

Damascus was the capital city of Syria located about 55 miles northeast of the Sea of Galilee. It was known as the "pearl of the east." The city was famous for its grapes, melons, and apricots (ISBE volume 1, page 852). Gilead was the region of land due east of the Jordan River (between the Dead Sea and Sea of Galilee). Gilead was occupied by the tribes of Manasseh and half the tribe of Gad. The error of Damascus is summed up in their threshing of Gilead with instruments of iron. Acts of cruelty are no doubt under consideration here. Damascus murdered the inhabitants of Gilead with crude instruments that indicated brutality.

*"4 But **I will send a fire** into the house of Hazael, and it shall devour the palaces of Benhadad. 5 And I will break the bar of Damascus, and cut off the inhabitant from the valley of Aven, and him that holds the scepter from the house of Eden; and the people of Syria shall go into captivity unto Kir, said Jehovah"* **(1:4-5).**

Hazael is known to have murdered king Benhadad so that he may take the throne of Syria by violence (see 2 Kings 8:7ff). God would punish Hazael and his house for his wickedness. Kir was "a country in Mesopotamia (Isaiah 22:6), from which Syrians came (Amos 9:7) and to which they were later exiled (2 Kings 16:9)" (Oxford Bible Atlas, page 133). Amos sees that God will send the advancing people of Syria back to their home lands defeated. Each of the following oracles or judgments against the nations includes *"fire"* being used by God to punish the wicked (see synopsis of chapter 1).

*"6 Thus said Jehovah: For three transgressions of **Gaza**, yea, for four, I will not turn away the punishment thereof; because they carried away captive the whole people, to deliver them up to Edom"* **(1:6).**

Gaza was one of the chief cities of Philistia (home of the Philistines). Gaza likely stands as a representative of the whole of Philistia. Gaza's punishment is due to their capturing innocent people (likely their neighboring Israelites) and selling them as slaves to Edom. When human beings are treated as treasures to be discovered and sold there is a problem with one's estimation of human life. God would *"punish"* the wicked of Philistia.

*"7 But **I will send a fire** on the wall of Gaza, and it shall devour the palaces thereof. 8 And I will cut off the inhabitant from Ashdod, and him that holds the scepter from Ashkelon; and I will turn my hand against*

Ekron; and the remnant of the Philistines shall perish, said the Lord Jehovah" **(1:7-8)**.

Jehovah's fiery judgments would come upon Gaza for her human trafficking and shall devour her palaces. The association of Gaza with all of Philistia is now made more probable as the prophet pronounces woes upon all the chief cities of Philistia (i.e., Gaza, Ashdod, Ashkelon, and Ekron). The Philistines were devoted to extinction for their part in human trade for money.

"**9** Thus said Jehovah: for three transgressions of **Tyre**, yea, for four, I will not turn away the punishment thereof; because they delivered up the whole people to Edom, and remembered not the brotherly covenant. **10** But **I will send a fire** on the wall of Tyre, and it shall devour the palaces thereof" **(1:9-10)**.

Tyre was a chief city in the region of Phoenicia. Tyre was known for their sea trade due to their location upon the Mediterranean Sea. Ezekiel had pronounced judgment upon Tyre due to her disposition toward Judah as God's nation fell to the Babylonians. Tyre thought that Judah got her just reward and scoffed at Judah (see Ezekiel 26 all). Amos reveals Tyre's chief sin to be slave trafficking (like as the Philistines) against a people that they had made covenant agreements with. Tyre was dishonest and treacherous for the sake of monetary gain (see Joel 3:4-6). God determined to punish Tyre with fire.

"**11** Thus said Jehovah: For three transgressions of **Edom**, yea, for four, I will not turn away the **punishment** thereof; because he did pursue his brother with the sword, and did cast off all pity, and his anger did tear perpetually, and he kept his wrath forever. **12** But **I will send a fire** upon Teman, and it shall devour the palaces of Bozrah" **(1:11-12)**.

Edom was located south of the Dead Sea (due south of Moab). Teman and Bozrah were chief and capital cities of Edom. The Edomites were descendants of Esau (twin brother of Jacob) (see Genesis 25:19-24, 30 and 36:8-9). The sins of Edom, throughout history, are summed up in the words pride and arrogance (Jeremiah 49:16). Edom had no real concern for the lives of their kinsmen of Israel and Judah (Ezekiel 35:6). Edom's corruption is depicted in their rejoicing over the fall of Israel and Judah (see Psalms 137:7 and Ezekiel 35:13-15). When the Lord brought upon Israel and Judah calamity from the Assyrians and Babylonians, the Edomites reasoned that they would now possess the land of these two nations (Ezekiel 35:10). There could be nothing further from the truth. Edom had even gone as far as attacking God's people in their weakened state after doing battle with the Babylonians (Ezekiel 25:12 and 35:4-6).

Ezekiel reveals the perpetual anger and envy against their brethren in Canaan (Ezekiel 35:10-12). This perpetual anger is now reiterated by Amos and is a symptom of their erroneous disease. Edom would be "*punished*" by God's judgment of fire for their unrepentant state of mind and acts of cruelty toward their brethren (see also Joel 3:19).

"*13 Thus said Jehovah: For three transgressions of the children of **Ammon**, yea, for four, I will not turn away the **punishment** thereof; because they have ripped up the women with child of Gilead, that they may enlarge their border. 14 But **I will kindle a fire** in the wall of Rabbah, and it shall devour the palaces thereof, with shouting in the day of battle, with a tempest in the day of the whirlwind; 15 and their king shall go into captivity, he and his princes together, said Jehovah*" **(1:13-15).**

The Ammonites (and Moabites) were the descendants of Lot (Genesis 19:30ff). Ammon was located due east of Gilead in the desert. Ammon's sins are like the nations listed above in that they treated human life with the basest of ways. God reveals that Ammon killed women and children (women who were pregnant with children) for the sole sake of gaining more territory. Once again, the value of human life was not important to this nation. God's fiery judgment would come against Rabbah, the capital city of Ammon, for her transgressions.

Ammon had long been an enemy of God's people. We find Jotham, King of Judah and son of Uzziah fighting against them at 2 Chronicles 27:5.

Jeremiah records that Baalis, King of the children of Ammon, decided to pay to have Gedaliah (appointed governor of Judah) assassinated probably to further disrupt Judah (Jeremiah 40:13-14).

Jeremiah pronounces an oracle against Ammon at Jeremiah 49:1-6 because they had taken possession of Gad (one of the territories east of the Jordan) at a point in time when Israel was weak. Ammon (along with Moab) had fallen into gross idolatry worshipping the god "*Malcom*" (Jeremiah 49:1-6). The long history of conflict and strained relations between Israel and Ammon is culminated in the statement by Ammon toward Judah saying, "3 *Aha, against my sanctuary, when it was profaned and against Israel, when it was made desolate; and against the house of Judah, when they went into captivity*" (Ezekiel 25:3). To say "*Aha*" is to exercise contempt and malicious joy. The Lord's main complaint against Ammon is that they exercised malicious joy over the fact that Judah had profaned the Lord's sanctuary with their idolatry (Ezekiel 5:11 and 23:38-39).

Questions over Amos Chapter 1

1. When did Amos do his work?

2. Where else have you read of God roaring like a lion?

3. Why would God punish Damascus?

4. Why would God punish Gaza?

5. Why would God punish Tyre?

6. Why would God punish Edom?

7. Why would God punish Ammon?

AMOS CHAPTER 2

Synopsis

Amos continues his vision of God's judgments against the ungodly nations of men. Judah and Israel are both mentioned among the nations that were due God's chastening hand of punishment.

Application

God shows no partiality when it comes to his divine expectations of men. Both Israel and Judah were chastised because of their sins. God cared not if the nation was Israel, Babylon, Assyria, or Moab. The Lord's universal and timeless expectations of all men is moral righteousness or perfection (see Deuteronomy 27:26; Matthew 5:48; 1 Peter 1:16-17; 2 Peter 1:4; 1 John 4:17 etc.).

Amos 2

A continuation of God's judgments against seven nations including Israel and Judah (2:1-8)

"**1** *Thus said Jehovah: For three transgressions of Moab, yea, for four, I will not turn away the **punishment** thereof; because he burned the bones of the king of Edom into lime.* **2** *But **I will send a fire** upon Moab, and it shall devour the palaces of Kerioth; and Moab shall die with tumult, with shouting, and with the sound of the trumpet;* **3** *and I will cut off the judge from the midst thereof with him, said Jehovah*" **(2:1-3).**

The land of Moab is due east of the Dead Sea. Moab, like Ammon, was a son of Lot by an incestuous act with his two daughters (Genesis 19:30ff). At some unrevealed time the Moabites had taken the dead body of the king of Edom and ground the bones into lime. Again, a sense of inhumane acts was done on the part of Moab as the previous mentioned nations. Ezekiel would later write an oracle against Moab saying, "*11 and I will execute judgments upon Moab; and they shall know that I am Jehovah*" (Ezekiel 25:11). Jeremiah would also write an oracle against the Moabites (Jeremiah chapter 48). Jeremiah tells us that Moab rejected God and worshipped "*Chemosh*" (Jeremiah 48:7-8). Moab had rejoiced over the fall of Judah as did Ammon (see Jeremiah 40:14). Jeremiah records the sin of **pride** being a primary issue with the profligate nation (Jeremiah 48:26-30). Isaiah said that Moab would not go unpunished (Isaiah 15-16). Amos reveals the uniform punishment by the fiery anger of God as is the case with all who sin.

"**4** *Thus said Jehovah: for three transgressions of **Judah**, yea, for four, I will not turn away the **punishment** thereof: because they have rejected the law of Jehovah, and have not kept his statutes, and their lies have caused them to err, after which their fathers did walk.* **5** *But **I will send a fire** upon Judah, and it shall devour the palaces of Jerusalem*" **(2:4-5).**

Judah will not escape the judgment of God for their iniquities. Judah, the southern nation, had participated in idolatry and irreverent acts of disobedience toward God. Amos exposes their error referring to them as "*liars*" and those who have "*rejected God's laws and not kept his statutes.*" Jeremiah would latter reveal many more sins. The prophet of God said that the Lord looked down from heaven and saw the true state of Judah (Jeremiah 7:11). The people had no fear of God (Jeremiah 5:22-24), no shame for their sin (Jeremiah 6:15), and no knowledge of God (Jeremiah 8:7). Judah was rebellious (Jeremiah 6:16) and given to covetousness and falsehood (Jeremiah 8:10). They practiced idolatry and even sacrificed their sons to Baal (Jeremiah 16:10-11; 19:5). The people of Judah were liars (Jeremiah 9:1ff), Sabbath breakers (Jeremiah 17:19ff), covenant breakers (Jeremiah 34:18ff), and they had completely put God out of their lives (Jeremiah 18:15). Judah's rulers led many astray with their lies (Jeremiah 2:33). These rulers did what they considered to be right rather than following the laws of God (Jeremiah 7:24; 8:6). Judah's prophets and priests were wicked as well (see Jeremiah 5:30-31). The reforms of Josiah had only affected Judah on the surface. Their hearts remained hardened against God.

"**6** *Thus said Jehovah: For three transgressions of* **Israel***, yea, for four, I will not turn away the* **punishment** *thereof; because they have sold the righteous for silver, and the needy for a pair of shoes –* **7** *they that pant after the dust of the earth on the head of the poor, and turn aside the way of the meek: and a man and his father go unto the same maiden, to profane my holy name:* **8** *and they lay themselves down beside every altar upon clothes taken in pledge; and in the house of their God they drink the wine of such as have been fined*" **(2:6-8).**

Israel, the northern kingdom, was likewise due God's punishing judgments for her sin. The punishment of fire is not mentioned against Israel until chapter 7:4. Israel was guilty of selling their poor brethren as slaves for silver and a pair of shoes to wear. They had little regard for the needy. The needy could sell themselves to others for services yet the rich of Amos' day was taking these needy people and selling them to others as slaves. Here again is an illustration of no regard for human life or God's laws. Israel lacked compassion and love for their fellow brothers.

Amos emphasizes Israel's wretched treatment of the poor among them by revealing their cruel behavior. The people of Israel took the poor among them and crushed them into the dust of the earth as though they were nothing of importance. Amos said that Israel took the coat of the poor and would not return it to them though the law commanded such to be done (Deuteronomy 24:12ff). Furthermore, the "*meek*" (truly compliant with God's laws) were mistreated as well.

Israel was sexually corrupt. Amos exposes the shameful act of sensuality by a father and son taking the same woman in a sexual intercourse

(Leviticus 20:10ff). The Israelites further profaned their self by bowing down and worshiping idols.

Lastly, Israel was guilty of drinking wine gained from fines against others within the temple of Jehovah God. The words of Amos signify that the Almighty and omniscient God saw all their wicked deeds done behind closed doors.

The burden that Amos would bear (prophecy against Israel) begins here. God had done much for his beloved Israel; however, they were Ungrateful and Disrespectful to his Laws (2:9-15)

"**9** *Yet destroyed I the Amorite before them, whose height was like the height of the cedars, and he was strong as the oaks; yet I destroyed his fruit from above, and his roots from beneath*" **(2:9).**

The term "*Amorite*" was sometimes used in place of Canaanite. The Bible often uses the name Amorites in the place of Canaanites that the people of God were commanded to exterminate (see Deuteronomy 20:17; Judges 6:10; 1 Samuel 7:14 etc.) (See ISBE volume 1, page 113). Israel and Judah seems to have forgotten that the very land they currently dwell in was given them by Jehovah God. No foe was too large or strong for God to defeat. Israel should have taken note of God's providential care yet they did not consider his love and protection.

"**10** *Also I brought you up out of the land of Egypt, and led you forty years in the wilderness, to possess the land of the Amorite*" **(2:10).**

Not only did God give giants into the hands of his people but he removed them safely from the world power of Egypt. He was with Israel for forty years while they wandered through the wilderness to be proved and strengthened. God fed them with manna and quail. God miraculously provided water to drink. The Lord providentially gave longevity to their clothes and shoes. The Lord cared for his people every step of their way (see Exodus 19:3-6).

"**11** *And I raised up of your sons for prophets, and of your young men for Nazirites. Is it not even thus, O you children of Israel? Said Jehovah.* **12** *But you gave the Nazirites wine to drink, and commanded the prophets, saying, Prophesy not*" **(2:11-12)**.

The Lord cared much for Israel. He revealed his mind to Israel through various prophets. There were some who heard the message of God by the prophets and earnestly desired to serve him with all their hearts. They took "*Nazirite vows*" that they may be separate from all that God revealed as unclean (see Numbers 6:1ff).

Yet there were those of Israel who displayed great disrespect for the revealed word of God and gave the Nazirites wine to drink and consequentially disqualifying the vow (Numbers 6:1ff). Those prophets who revealed law and sin were commanded not to prophesy such words of discomfort. Much of Israel illustrated a mind that was not dedicated to following God's laws (see also Isaiah 30:10).

"**13** *Behold, I will press you in your place, as a cart presses that is full of sheaves.* **14** *And flight shall perish from the swift; and the strong shall not strengthen his force; neither shall the mighty deliver himself;* **15** *neither shall he stand that handles the bow; and he that is swift of foot shall not deliver himself; neither shall he that rides the horse deliver himself;* **16** *and he that is courageous among the mighty shall flee away naked in that day, said Jehovah*" **(2:13-16)**.

The English standard Version Bible reads for Amos 2:13 as follows: "*Behold, I will press you down in your place, as a cart full of sheaves presses down.*" Amos has already spoken of God roaring like a lion at Amos 1:2 in relationship to his chastening hand being against the wicked. Now, Amos speaks of God "*pressing*" Israel due to her sins. Fascinatingly, when one examines the meaning of the word "tribulation" in the New Testament you find a similar meaning. The word "*tribulation*" (Greek *thlipsin*) means "to squeeze, press, encumber, distress, afflict, pressure, compress, distress of mind or circumstance, or a trial" (Moulton 195). The Apostle Paul uses this Greek word when speaking of God's judgments against the wicked at Romans 2:4-9. Paul writes, "**4** *or do you despise the riches of his goodness and forbearance and longsuffering, not knowing that the goodness of God leads you to repentance?* **5** *but after your hard and impenitent heart you treasure up wrath in the day of wrath and revelation of the righteous judgment of God;* **6** *who will render to every man according to his works:* **7** *to them that by patience in well-doing seek for glory and honor and incorruption, eternal life:* **8** *but unto them that are factious, and obey not the truth, but obey unrighteousness, shall be wrath and indignation,* **9 tribulation** *and anguish, upon every soul of man that works evil, of the Jew first, and also of the Greek.*"

Joel spoke of the "*day of Jehovah*" throughout his writings (see Joel 1:15; 2:1, 11, 31 and 3:14). This was a day when God would judge the deeds of man and bring plagues upon the wicked by way of punishment for their deeds. The object of this event was the sinner's repentance (see Joel 2:12-14). Likewise, Amos is telling his Israel audience that God's Day of Judgment comes when he will chastise them for their wickedness. There will be no man or nation that will have the power to deliver them from their distress. They will be called upon to repent or suffer the consequences of sin.

Questions over Amos Chapter 2

1. Why would God punish Moab?

2. Why would God punish Judah?

3. Why would God punish Israel?

4. Who had the height of cedars and the strength of oaks?

5. Why would courageous men be seen running naked and afraid?

AMOS CHAPTER 3

Synopsis

There is a high degree of responsibility placed upon the shoulders of God's people because he had chosen them, out of all the families of the earth, to fulfill his seed promise. Israel went against God original design and consequentially their actions are the cause of a great adversary coming against them. God had roared in the form of prophets warning Israel of their sins yet they turned a deaf ear to their words. Israel was so bent on attaining wealth and practicing idolatry that the fear of God, which should have existed in their minds, was not there.

Application

Amos chapter 3 teaches us the cause for man's sins. You, and everyone else, sin today when lured away from truth by the tempting vices of this world (see Amos 3:8; Romans 3:23 and James 1:12-15). When our sinful passions overwhelm our conviction of righteousness we fall to sin. The powerful pull of lust and worldliness overcomes our senses of righteousness and the fear of God is no where to be found in our mind. We often do not come to our original sense of conviction and love for God until our lust has been fulfilled. It is then that our hearts are broken and we regain conscience of our duty toward righteousness and fall to our knees in despair. We cry out to God for mercy and he forgives (1 John 1:8-10). Far too many; however, never turn back to God in repentance (see Matthew 7:13) (14d).

Amos 3

Egypt and Philistia are Summoned upon the Mountain tops to Witness the Judgment against the Sinful, Chaotic, Ruthless, and Wealth driven Nation of Israel (3 all)

"**1** *Hear this word that Jehovah has spoken against you, O children of Israel, against the whole family which I brought up out of the land of Egypt, saying,* **2** *You only have I know of all the families of the earth: therefore I will visit upon you all your iniquities*" **(3:1-2)**.

God had chosen Abraham to bring forth his seed promise by which all nations would be blessed with the opportunity of having their sins forgiven (Genesis 12:3). Abraham's descendants became the great nation of Israel because he obeyed the commandments of God (Genesis 22:18). Righteousness was reckoned unto Abraham due to his heart of faith and obedience (Genesis 15:6 and Romans 4:3). This original disposition of faith and obedience was not always carried over from generation to generation. Egypt subdued all of Jacob's family and made slaves of them for generations. God delivered the people from Egyptian bondage though the world would have seen this as an impossible task. God gave Israel the land of Canaan, fought their battles for them, and gave them farms and wells that they did not plant and dig. There was a relationship that existed between God and Israel that the rest of the world did not experience. The Apostle Paul said that the Jews had great advantage over all other nations due to their history with God (see Romans 3:1-2 and 9:4-5). God communicated his divine expectations of Israel yet they failed miserably. Due to Israel's lack of effort to obey God he said "*therefore I will visit you all your iniquities.*" Nothing but punishment awaited the rebellious nation.

"**3** *Shall two walk together, except they have agreed? Will a lion roar in the forest, when he has no prey?* **4** *Will a young lion cry out of his den, if he have taken nothing?* **5** *Can a bird fall in a snare upon the earth, where no gin is set for him? Shall a snare spring up from the ground, and have taken nothing at all?* **6** *Shall the trumpet be blown in a city, and the* *people not be afraid? Shall evil befall a city, and Jehovah has not done it?* **(3:3-6)**

Amos reasons with the people. Some may, like the days of the Apostle Paul, argue that they cannot possibly be due God's fiery wrath due to their Jewish heritage (see Romans 9:6). Amos reminds the people of God that those who do not follow God's commandments are due his divine wrath. Moses wrote, "23 *If you walk contrary to me* 24 *then will I also walk contrary unto you; and I will smite you, even I, seven times for your sins*" (Leviticus 26:23-24). One's "walk" is that governing factor in their life. The direction one walks is determined by the law they follow. God demands that man walk after his divine standard of righteousness and justice (see Isaiah 28:17 and Colossians 3:17). Israel's problem was that they went against God's expectations and design for them (see Romans 10:3).

To illustrate just how far apart God and Israel are the prophet uses seven illustrations. Israel went against God's design for them just as it would be unnatural for two to walk together without an agreement. Israel went against God's objective for them just as it would be odd for a lion to roar without having prey. As it is impossible for a bird to be caught in a trap where there is no trap or a snare even so it is impossible to give such great blessings to a nation and they do not follow your will. Furthermore, if a trumpet sounds upon the wall by a watchman people are naturally afraid and if evil comes upon a city it is because God is chastising them. Israel; however, had no fear when they should have been terrified. Israel, in every way, disappointed and frustrated God's divine objective for them.

7 *Surely the Lord Jehovah will do nothing, except he reveal his secret unto his servants the prophets.* **8** *The lion has roared; who will not fear? The Lord Jehovah has spoken; who can but prophesy?*" **(3:7-8)**.

The facts of the Lord's expectations for man's lawful lives, unwillingness to fellowship the wicked, and sure punishment are known to all through the law. God's chastening hand would not come upon a sinful people without a warning from his prophets. When one hears a lion roaring in the forest there is great fear for life. The roar is a warning that the lion has spotted his prey and prepares to tear it to shreds. The prophets are likened unto the lion roaring. God roars through his prophets warning the wicked before he tears them to shreds.

Amos asks, "*Who will not fear?*" How can someone not fear as they hear and see the ferocious lion that desires to thrash and eat them? The foolish one that has no fear is Israel. Israel, like Judah, refused repentance because of a lack of fear (Jeremiah 2:19 and 5:24). They were more concerned with experiencing pleasure than they were the fiery judgments of God. As a foolish insect is lured by the light of electricity only to be zapped so Israel was driven by their lust and lured to the ways of worldliness and their minds were dull to the consequences of their actions (14d).

"**9** *Publish in the palaces at Ashdod, and in the palaces in the land of Egypt, and say, Assemble yourselves upon the mountains of Samaria, and behold what great tumults are therein, and what oppressions in the midst thereof.* **10** *For they know not to do right, said Jehovah, who store up violence and robbery in their palaces*" **(3:9-10).**

The lion roars and the prophets warn! The prophets' warning words are to be published in the palaces of Ashdod and Egypt. All who have a mind of any reason are to assemble upon the mountains of Samaria and fearfully look at the carnage of chaos that occurs in the wicked nation of Israel. It is ironic that the Gentile sinners of heathen nations are called upon to look at the nation of Israel so that they may see the consequence of wickedness. Ashdod and Egypt are called upon to look at a nation chosen of God yet forsaken because they do not know him nor obey him.

"**11** *Therefore thus said the Lord Jehovah: an adversary there shall be, even round about the land; and he shall bring down your strength, and your palaces shall be plundered*" **(3:11).**

Due to Israel's irreverence, ungratefulness, and ignorance of the laws of God they shall be destroyed. The princes, kings, priests and all those of authority who have contributed to such a despotic state of mind shall be brought down and the city plundered by an enemy. The "*adversary*" would be the Assyrians (i.e., the "*rod of mine anger*" - Isaiah 10:5).

"**12** *Thus said Jehovah: as the shepherd rescues out of the mouth of the lion two legs, or a piece of an ear, so shall the children of Israel be rescued that sit in Samaria in the corner of a couch, and on the silken cushions of a bed*" **(3:12).**

The entire body of Israel will be devoured by the Assyrian lion save a few legs and an ear. The idea is that a small remnant will be spared from the mouth of the lion. The reason for a small number being saved is that the majority have approached life having considered that their luxuries and wealth should save them. Their minds were intoxicated with the things of this world and they did not consider God's will for them. "During the reign of Jeroboam II the northern kingdom reached its zenith of wealth and power with the attendant results of luxury and excess, a situation reflected constantly in the prophetic visions of Amos" (ISBE volume 1, page 115). A small remnant of people will always be saved because they will follow God's laws come what may in this life (see Matthew 7:13 and Romans 11:2-5) (15a).

"**13** *Hear, and testify against the house of Jacob, said the Lord Jehovah, the God of hosts.* **14** *For in the day that I shall visit the transgressions of Israel upon him, I will also visit the altars of Bethel; and the horns of the altar shall be cut off, and fall to the ground.* **15** *And I will smite the winter-house with the summer-house; and the houses of ivory shall perish, and the great houses shall have an end, said Jehovah*" **(3:13-15).**

Amos gives us a greater understanding of the mind dulling lure of temptation that caused the people of God to ignore the lion roaring in the field (see Amos 3:8). The people had little to no fear of God as the prophets roared against them because they had set their heart on riches and attained them (see 1 Timothy 6:9) (25h) (14d). Israel had attained riches at the expense of the poor and needy (see Amos 2:6). Their thirst for wealth led to attaining winter and summer homes laced with ivory at the expense of their souls (see Hosea 4:6).

The lion prophets roared of a "*day that God would visit the transgressions of Israel*" (i.e., punish them with fire - see Amos 7:4). God has watched a people driven by luxury and idolatry and will remain silent no longer. Bethel was the place Jeroboam I had set up a calf to worship God (see 1 Kings 12:25ff). God would smite the idolaters and their images to the ground.

Questions over Amos Chapter 3

1. Why would God no longer "*walk*" with Israel (see Amos 3:3)?

2. Why would the lion roar over Israel?

3. What does Amos 3:8 teach us about the workings of sin in our lives?

4. What two great sins of Israel does Amos expose in this chapter?

5. How would God "*visit the transgressions of Israel upon him?*" (see Amos 3:14)

AMOS CHAPTER 4

Synopsis

Israel had a delusional passion for riches and they would stop of at nothing to attain it. Though their actions were sinful they nonetheless zealously worshipped God as though nothing were wrong. God attempts to bring them to repentance with famine, drought, fungus and insects on their farms, pestilence, the sword of war, and fire. Though these seven plagues touched Israel they nonetheless refused to open their eyes and see their folly.

Application

God's people of every generation must be aware that unlawful desires have the power to cause us to forget our spiritual responsibilities. When we allow deep passions for sinful things to control our daily lives we come to be deluded to God's expectations. Though God punishes and the church exercises discipline on the erring they will remain in this stupor of sin until the end unless they soften their heart (2 Corinthians 2:15-16). The gospel has the power to break up the stony heart; however, it is up to the individual to respond in obedience.

Amos 4

Unauthorized Acts of Worship (4:1-5)

"**1** *Hear this word, you kine of Bashan, that are in the mountain of Samaria, that oppress the poor, that crush the needy, that say unto their lords, Bring, and let us drink*" **(4:1)**

The word "*kine*" is "an archaic plural of 'cow'" (ISBE volume 3 page 20). Bashan was a "fertile plateau east of the Sea of Galilee and North of Gilead... the region provided good pasture land" (ISBE volume 1, page 436). David spoke of the grand mountain range of Bashan as compared to the lowly Zion of Jerusalem at Psalms 68:16. The cows were fat on rich grazing in a land of plenty. Israel was like a cow of Bashan in that they were full yet did not give thought to those they crushed to get so much.

Amos is the lion prophet that roars out words of fierce warning to Israel. The people of God have repressed and afflicted the poor and needy while they sit around drinking like kings. Their delusional problem of sin continues to be revealed as a desire for the things of this world over a desire to perform acts of righteousness and justice (see notes at Amos 3:12, 15).

"**2** *The Lord Jehovah has sworn by his holiness, that, lo, the days shall come upon you, that they shall take you away with hooks, and your residue with fish-hooks.* **3** *And you shall go out at the breaches, every one straight before her; and you shall cast yourselves into Harmon, said Jehovah*" **(4:2-3).**

The Almighty God has watched the cruel manner Israel has dealt with the poor and needy and he is angry. God has watched Israel's sexual immorality (Amos 2:7), their idolatry (Amos 3:14), and their appetite for wealth and luxury (Amos 3:12) and determines to have his people pulled from their fat land with hooks. The Assyrians would conquer Israel, put hooks into their flesh, and exile them to "*Harmon*" (possibly Mount Hermon North of Bashan).

"**4** *Come to Bethel, and transgress; to Gilgal, and multiply transgression; and bring your sacrifices every morning, and your tithes every three days;*

5 *and offer a sacrifice of thanksgiving of that which is leavened, and proclaim freewill-offerings and publish them: **for this pleases you**, O you children of Israel, said the Lord Jehovah"* **(4:4-5).**

Amos, with a sense of sarcasm, calls upon the wicked of Israel to continue their unauthorized acts of worship. A people who have no respect, gratitude, or regard for God's laws could care less about worship the way God prescribed. Amos roars out God's warnings that two cannot walk together unless they have agreed (see Amos 3:3). Israel does not walk with God but rather their objective is self pleasure.

The self centered Israelites are called to the centers of idolatrous worship; i.e., Bethel and Gilgal, to continue their illegal and self prescribed worship. They brought sacrifices every morning, tithes three times twice a week, leavened offerings of thanksgiving, and proclaimed free-will offerings. The object of Amos is to illustrate not only a lack of respect, on the people's part, for worshipping God according to his authorized ways but also to show the zeal of their worship. To offer a sacrifice with leaven was a blatant violation of the Mosaic Law (see Leviticus 2:11 and 7:11). God did not command a three times a week tithing yet they did this zealously. Furthermore, they proclaimed to the world how that they offered, of their own free will, other sacrifices to show their supposed religious and loving ways toward God.

The Lord saw right through the wicked people's motives. The purpose of their worship was not to please God but their own selves. Jesus quoted from Isaiah 29:13 at Matthew 15:8-9 saying, "8 *this people honors me with their lips; but their heart is far from me. 9 But in vain do they worship me, teaching as their doctrines the precepts of men*." Unauthorized acts of worship never please God and are always designed to meet man's expectations (Colossians 2:23) (12e).

No man or woman would have a right to complain to God when the Assyrians come and take them away with hooks. Israel walked in sin rather than with God.

God calls to their Remembrance his Blessings and Curses in times of Obedience and Disobedience "*yet have you not returned unto me, said Jehovah*" **(4:6-11)**

"**6** *And I also have given you cleanness of teeth in all your cities, and want of bread in all your places; yet have you not returned unto me, said Jehovah*" **(4:6).**

Clean teeth and want of bread indicates times of famine. God providentially caused a famine to come to the land to chastise the people so that they may repent. Amos writes; however, "*you have not returned unto me*." God uses droughts, fire, famine, sword, and pestilence to chastise his people so that they may turn from their wickedness. Unfortunately the wicked are often found complaining and grumbling against God rather than acknowledging their sins and turning back to him (see Haggai 1:6-11 and Revelation 16:8-11).

"**7** *And I also have withheld the rain from you, when there were yet three months to the harvest; and I caused it to rain upon one city, and caused it not to rain upon another city: one piece was rained upon, and the piece whereupon it rained not withered.* **8** *So two or three cities wandered unto one city to drink water, and were not satisfied: yet have you not returned unto me, said Jehovah*" **(4:7-8).**

Drought is a mainstay of God's chastisement throughout history (see Psalms 65:9-13; Hosea 5:11-12; 6:3-4; Joel 2:23; Amos 4:7-8 and Haggai 1:6-11). The omnipotent God caused it to rain in designated areas at times for the designated purpose of the people's repentance. The dry areas and cities went to the watered cities for drink yet their thirst was not satisfied. The drought diminished and destroyed much of the crops yet the people rejected God's pleas of their repentance.

"**9** *I have smitten you with blasting and mildew: the multitude of your gardens and your vineyards and your fig-trees and your olive-trees has the palmer-worm devoured: yet have you not returned unto me, said Jehovah*" **(4:9).**

God chastened his people with a blasting wind and mildew fungus that destroyed the people's gardens, vineyards, and fruit trees. Again, God was chastening his people due to their transgressions. Though the Lord sent these irritants among the fields of the people they continued to reject God's request for their repentance. The texts in each of these instances indicate that the people were told, likely by a prophet, that God had caused the event due to their sinful lives.

"**10** *I have sent among you the pestilence after the manner of Egypt: your young men have I slain with the sword, and have carried away your horses; and I have made the stench of your camp to come up even into your nostrils: yet have you not returned unto me, said Jehovah*" **(4:10)**.

God plagued Israel with pestilence that was compared to the days of Egypt. The Lord chastised and punished Israel with the sword. Though God's people had been chastised with famine, drought, fungus, pestilence, and sword they would not return to God's laws and ways. Even though the people walked through the city streets smelling death and rotted flesh they refused repentance.

"**11** *I have overthrown cities among you, as when God overthrew Sodom and Gomorrah, and you were as a brand plucked out of the burning: yet have you not returned unto me, said Jehovah*" **(4:11)**.

Lastly, Amos reveals that God had sent fires to chastise his people. While the fires burned and cities were destroyed the people refused repentance. The Apostle John writes, "9 *And men were scorched with great heat: and they blasphemed the name of God who has the power over these plagues; and they repented not to give him glory*" (Revelation 16:9). Though the acts of drought, famine, pestilence, sword, and fire may sound cruel they were nonetheless necessary for the correction of the people. God was doing all things possible to save his people (17d).

"**12** *Therefore thus will I do unto you, O Israel; and because I will do this unto you,* **prepare to meet your God***, O Israel. **13** For, lo, he that forms the mountains, and creates the wind, and declares unto man what is his* *thought; that makes the morning darkness, and treads upon the high places of the earth – Jehovah, the God of hosts, is his name"* **(4:12-13).**

The above seven mentioned chastisements for Israel's sin did nothing to move them to repent. The Lord proclaims that there will be an unnamed judgment that comes upon them that will be worse that the above mentioned ones. Israel is to prepare to meet the God of war in judgment.

Israel should be horrified to hear that the "*God of hosts*" is preparing to do battle against them. The sins and hard hearted dispositions of the people have brought God against them. God is not one that lacks power or knowledge. God is omniscient ("*declares unto man what is his thought*"). God is omnipotent (he "*treads upon the high places of the earth*"). God is creator (he "*forms the mountains and creates the wind*"). The prophet Isaiah tells us that there is no comparison to the Almighty Jehovah God (see Isaiah 40:12-25). God would instill a fear into the people that they lacked in days gone by (see Amos 3:7-8).

Questions over Amos Chapter 4

1. Who is guilty of oppressing the poor and crushing the needy?

2. Why did God call Israel to Bethel and Gilgal?

3. What "*pleased*" the children of Israel?

4. List five things that God did for Israel that ought to have caused them to repent of their wickedness yet they refused to do so.

5. How does Amos 4:6-11 relate to Revelation 15 and 16?

6. Why is Israel called upon to be prepared to meet their God?

AMOS CHAPTER 5

Synopsis

Amos prophetically foretells of Israel's demise at the hands of the Assyrians. God had sent his prophets to roar out the message of warning, he brought plagues upon the land, and revealed his omnipotent power through creation yet Israel ignored these obvious things. Israel cheated the poor and needy and turned around the next hour to worship God in sacrifice and song. God commanded the wicked people of Israel to take their worship elsewhere because he wanted no part of it. God, with strong language, tells Israel he hates and despises their efforts to serve him. God's true desire was for the people to embrace justice and righteousness; however, most of them wanted no part of this. The Lord has no recourse but to act out in violence toward his own people. A stringent punishment by the hands of the violent and ruthless Assyrian army would cause some to contemplate their situation and repent.

Application

God has done much today for man's repentance. The Lord has given us his completed revelation to read and make application in our lives (2 Timothy 3:16-17). The Lord chastises the wicked for wrong doing (see Hebrews 12:7-13 and Revelation 16:8-11). Furthermore we have creation to examine and conclude that God is (Romans 1:20). There is absolutely no excuse for any man or woman of our day to reject God's instructions that identify righteousness (Amos 5:7, 24). Those who remain deluded in their personal opinions, convictions, or preconceived religious ideas have no part with God.

Amos 5

Amos calls upon Israel to "*seek*" the Lord (5:1-9)

"**1** *Hear this word which I take up for a lamentation over you, O house of Israel.* **2** *The virgin of Israel is fallen; she shall no more rise: she is cast down upon her land; there is none to raise her up.* **3** *For thus said the Lord Jehovah: The city that went forth a thousand shall have a hundred left, and that which went forth a hundred shall have ten left, to the house of Israel*" **(5:1-3).**

God has revealed his divine secrets to Amos regarding the end of Israel (see Amos 3:7). The Northern nation has been likened unto a virgin who has been defiled by sexual immorality. She has committed spiritual adultery in that she has turned to idolatry and wealth and consequentially forgotten God's commandments and expectations (see Hosea 11:2 and Amos 2:6-8; 5:26).

The Lord pronounces the fall of Israel as a nation. Though Israel may call upon other nations to help none will avail (see also Hosea 7:11). The Lord will cut down each city of Israel by 90 percent.

"**4** *For thus said Jehovah unto the house of Israel,* **Seek me, and you shall live**; *but seek not Bethel, nor enter into Gilgal, and pass not to Beersheba: for Gilgal shall surely go into captivity, and Bethel shall come to nothing. Seek Jehovah, and you shall live; lest he break out like fire in the house of Joseph, and it devour, and there be none to quench it in Bethel*" **(5:4-6).**

Amos, the prophet of God, is roaring out God's warnings like a lion (see Amos 3:7-8). The admonition is that Israel would "*seek God and live.*" To not seek the Lord is to die in your sins. The Assyrians will come with hooks to take away a deluded and sinful people. The word "*seek*" (Greek *ekzetesate* - LXX 1088) means to "seek out, investigate diligently, scrutinize, or seek diligently or earnestly" (Moulton 124). Liddell and Scott define the word as to "seek out, enquire, or to demand an account of a thing" (LS 238). The prophetic instruction is for God's people to seek or request God's ways rather than the ways of man at Bethel and Gilgal (the places of idolatrous worship). Israel is called upon to demand authoritative ways of living rather than doing things that please them. Jeremiah had similarly wrote, "*O Lord, I know that the way of man is not in himself; it is not in man that walks to direct his steps*" (Jeremiah 10:23). Joel said that that those who call out to God will be saved (see Joel 2:28-32 and Acts 2:21).

Amos pleads with the wicked of Israel to open their eyes to what is coming for their wickedness. Those who refuse to earnestly demand God's authoritative lawful ways in their lives will face the fiery wrath of God in the form of the Assyrian Empire.

"**7** *You who turn justice to wormwood, and cast down righteousness to the earth*" **(5:7)**

Justice and Righteousness is the standard that God expects man to measure up to (Isaiah 28:17). The word "*justice*" (Greek *krima* - LXX 1088) means a "judgment, a sentence, award, a judicial sentence, administration of justice, execution of justice, a lawsuit, judicial visitation, or an administrative decree" (Moulton 241). "*Righteousness*" (Greek *dikaiosune* - LXX 1088) means "fair and equitable dealing, justice, rectitude, virtue, investiture with the attribute of righteousness, acceptance as righteous or justification" (Moulton 102). These two words are very similar in meaning. **The Greek word *dikaiosune* has to do with one's right and just conduct while the Greek word *krima* indicates the actual instructions to be right and just.** Israel had taken God's commands to be righteous (i.e., live according to his divine laws) and turned it into "*wormwood*." Wormwood is "used figuratively of bitter things, the term denotes the result of illicit sexual relations (Proverbs 5:4), God's punishment due to sin (Jeremiah 9:15; 23:15; Lamentations 3:15, 19), and perverted justice (Amos 5:7; 6:12). In

Deuteronomy 29:18 (MT 17) the AV translates Hebrew *lana* as 'wormwood' (RSV 'bitter') in a description of the bitter results of practicing idolatry" (ISBE volume 4, page 1117). **God's instructions to Israel to be right and just was a bitter pill for them to swallow.** Israel cast down God's instructions as though they were worthless. The gospel of Jesus Christ does the same thing to the wicked today (see 2 Corinthians 2:14-16). Throughout man's history God has hardened the wicked with his commandments (see Romans 9:18) (14f).

"**8** *seek him that makes the Pleiades and Orion, and turns the shadow of death into the morning, and makes the day dark with night; that calls for the waters of the sea, and pours them out upon the face of the earth (Jehovah is his name);* **9** *that brings sudden destruction upon the strong, so that destruction comes upon the fortress*" **(5:8-9).**

Though Israel had acted out so disrespectfully toward God he nonetheless offered them hope. The God of mercy and love continues to call out to his people that they may put their trust in him and turn from their wicked ways. Amos reminds the people of God's omnipotence in that he has made the "*Pleiades and Orion.*" The **Pleiades** is "an open star cluster in the constellation Taurus, consisting of several hundred stars, of which six are visible to the naked eye" (AHD 952). **Orion** is "a constellation in the celestial equator near Gemini and Taurus containing the stars Betelgeuse and Rigel" (AHD 877). The Israelites, and the world, were in the habit of looking up into the heavens at the constellations. The clusters of stars were an incredible sight and the prophet of God reminds Israel that is God that had made these natural phenomena. The visage of these phenomena ought to have awakened a sense of faith within the minds of all men.

God's omnipotence is seen in that he "*turns the shadow of death into the morning.*" The dark shadows of judgment may be turned into rays of hope if men would turn and seek him. Furthermore God pulls water from the seas and cast them upon the dry earth in the form of rain. The Lord also has displayed his great power by bringing sudden destruction upon the strong (see the plagues of Egypt). Seeing that God is so Great Isaiah challenged his audience to find anyone anywhere close to the incomparable great God that created heaven and earth (see Isaiah 40:18-31). These facts of God's omnipotence ought to cause the mind to turn to him in great sorrow of heart as man repents (see Romans 1:20) (19q).

Amos' days were "*evil times***" (5:10-13)**

"*10 They hate him that reproves in the gate, and they abhor him that speaks uprightly. 11 Forasmuch therefore as you trample upon the poor, and take exactions from him of wheat: you have built houses of hewn stone, but you shall not dwell in them; you have planted pleasant vineyards, but you shall not drink the wine thereof* **(5:10-11).**

Israel had just judges that reproved sinful activity and spoke uprightly; however, they were passionately hated by the people. The swindlers that sought to get gain from the poor and needy "*abhorred*" the man who tried to make things right and just. When their cheating was exposed they in turn hated the one who exposed them because their great profits came to a halt. The wicked people of Israel robbed the poor and built beautiful houses for themselves. The Lord said that those who do such things will have no time in those luxurious homes to enjoy them because he will remove them.

A significant point to notice is that there were good, just, and righteous people in the days of Amos. These good and just people; however, had to suffer with the unjust. The punishment of plagues listed at Amos 4:6-11 landed upon both the just and the unjust as they together shared the land. What was punishment for the wicked became a test of faith for the righteous.

"*12 For I know how manifold are your transgressions, and how mighty are your sins – you that afflict the just, that take a bribe, and that turn aside the needy in the gate from their right*" **(5:12).**

The swindlers and cheaters of Israel ought to have been horrified as they heard Amos say, "*I know how manifold are your transgressions*." The omniscient God of heaven and earth saw all that the wicked were doing (see also Jeremiah 23:23) (3h). God named their sins as that of injustices enacted upon the poor and needy so that they may prosper in their beautiful homes in security. God exposes the supposed success of Israel's unjust entrepreneurs for what it truly was. The people's actions were identified by God as "*mighty sins*." They were crooks rather than successful business men.

"**13** *Therefore he that is prudent shall keep silence in such a time; for it is an evil time*" **(5:13).**

The just and the right are hated at the gates where buying and selling took place. Amos tells us that the righteous "*kept silent*" because the days were an "*evil time*." The wise and righteous men acted in "*prudence*" to preserve their life. Solomon said that "*21 the wise in heart shall be called prudent; And the sweetness of the lips increases learning*" (Proverbs 16:21). The word "*Prudence*" (Greek *phronesis*) means "a minding to do so and so, purpose, intention... thoughtfulness or prudence" (LS 872). The American Heritage Dictionary defines the word as, "careful management... the capacity for judging in advance the probable results of one's actions" (AHD 998). The prudent is cautious and careful in all his dealings. It is a sad day when God's people must remain silent or else face the wrath of the unrighteous who call themselves righteous.

The Day of Jehovah (5:14-20)

"**14** *Seek good, and not evil, that you may live; and so Jehovah, the God of hosts, will be with you, as you say.* **15** *Hate the evil, and love the good, and establish justice in the gate: it may be that Jehovah, the God of hosts, will be gracious unto the remnant of Joseph*" **(5:14-15).**

Amos gives Israel words of hope. They may live if only they would seek after "*the God of hosts*." Israel must come to pursue, desire, long for, be interested, participate, stretch after, work for, and or have justice and righteousness as the object of their desire. The people are instructed to listen to the prophets, learn from God's chastening hand, and look to creation to motivate them to attain conviction (16c).

God comes with his host against Israel for their wickedness. God would not be with them; however, "*as you say*." Israel was saying that God was with them even though they had cast off justice and righteousness. Mental delusion, through ignorance of God's will, governed their hearts. This type of delusion is described by Jeremiah regarding the Southern kingdom of Judah. They considered themselves to be without sin (Jeremiah 2:35 and 16:10) and believed that their worship was acceptable to God (Jeremiah 6:20; 11:15; 14:11-12 and 26:2). Judah had considered themselves wise (Jeremiah 8:8). When captivity came upon them they said, "Why are all these things happening to us?" (See Jeremiah 13:22 and 16:10)

A disposition and or character of "*hate*" toward "*evil*" deeds and "*love*" toward justice and righteousness would certainly reveal a heart that had turned to God (see Romans 12:9) (14e).

"**16** *Therefore thus said Jehovah, the God of hosts, the Lord: Wailing shall be in all the broad ways; and they shall say in all the streets, Alas! Alas! And they shall call the husbandman to mourning, and such as are skilful in lamentation to wailing.* **17** *And in all vineyards shall be wailing; for I will pass through the midst of you, said Jehovah*" **(5:16-17).**

God's judgment against Israel's wicked behavior will be a day of great mourning and wailing. Sad hearts will prevail as the people look out over a desolated land and dead loved ones. The joy of idolatry, wine, luxury and plenty will be taken away.

"**18** *Woe unto you that desire the day of Jehovah! Wherefore would you have the day of Jehovah? It is darkness, and not light*" **(5:18).**

Those who truly believe that God is with them, even though they do deeds of wickedness, are actually those who "*desire the day of Jehovah.*" The prophet Joel gives a precise definition of the "*day of Jehovah*" in his book. The "*day of Jehovah*" is not a final judgment against all mankind but rather a day of judgment against wicked men in the form of punishing plagues (such as drought, fire, pestilence, and or warfare) (Amos 4:6-11) (see notes at the introduction to Joel on "*the day of Jehovah*").

God asks the wicked why they would desire to see this dark and gloomy day of punishment? The obvious answer is that the wicked did not fear God's judgments because they do not think they are doing anything wrong. Israel is so far removed from God's word that they actually believed that all was well. Many live in the same manner today. As long as one believes his acts are right he has no fear of God. Unfortunately for the deluded, one's personal conscience, opinions, convictions, and ideas or beliefs of right and wrong will not be the standard they are judged by (see John 12:44). Israel's arrogance is depicted in that they measured their standing with God not by his word but by their own ideas of what was right for the times they lived in.

"**19** *As if a man did flee from a lion, and a bear met him; or went into the house and leaned his hand on the wall, and a serpent bit him.* **20** *Shall not the day of Jehovah be darkness, and not light? Even very dark, and no brightness in it*?" **(5:19-20).**

The deluded of Israel must open their eyes to the reality of God's dark and gloomy day of judgment that is coming against them. Amos tells the people that God's day of judgment will be a time of no escape from harm. People will run from a lion only to be met by a bear. The wicked will lean his hand upon a post in the house to rest only to be bitten by a serpent. The day of God's judgments will not be a pleasant time. Amos' point is that Israel needed to open their eyes now before it was everlasting too late.

God has rejected Israel's Worship (5:21-27)

"**21** *I hate, I despise your feasts, and I will take no delight in your solemn assemblies.* **22** *Yea, though you offer me your burnt-offerings and meal offerings, I will not accept them; neither will I regard the peace-offerings of your fat beasts.* **23** *Take away from me the noise of your songs; for I will not hear the melody of your viols.* **24** *But let justice roll down as waters, and righteousness as a mighty stream*" **(5:21-24).**

Israel had robbed the poor and needy to purchase luxurious things. Furthermore they had practiced idolatry and turned a blind eye to God's laws. Meanwhile, the deluded people worshipped the Lord with great conviction (see Amos 5:14). Israel assembled on the days of holy convocation, they made their sacrifices, and they sang songs from the heart about how they loved God. God responds to their delusional worship by telling them that he "*hates and despises*" it all. Imagine the shock upon the faces and minds of the wicked as they hear Amos say these words. The people honestly believe that their worship to God is awesome and accepted by him. The prophet of God; however, rains on their parade telling them what a sinful mess they are in.

God does not desire the people's worship through sacrifice and song. God demands the people's hearts be changed to "*justice and righteousness*" (see Amos 5:7 and Isaiah 28:17). To change their hardened hearts God sends plagues of punishment and ultimately the Assyrian army (see Amos 3:11 and 4:6-11). Repentance will also come to man today by way of God's plagues and punishment (see Revelation 16:8-11).

"**25** *Did you bring unto me sacrifices and offerings in the wilderness forty years, O house of Israel?* **26** *Yea, you have borne the tabernacle of your king and the shrine of your images, the star of your god, which you made to yourselves.* **27** *Therefore will I cause you to go into captivity beyond Damascus, said Jehovah, whose name is the God of hosts*" **(5:25-27).**

Apparently during the forty years that Israel wandered in the wilderness, for an evil report of the land of Canaan, they worshipped God by mingling idolatry with his prescribed worship. Amos refers to the idol that was introduced into Jehovah worship as "*the star of your god.*" Israel had made a shrine and worshipped the idol as though it were God. Israel had continued this melting pot religion even until this later date. Due to such depraved and self delusional worship the Lord would send them into captivity to the land of the Assyrians.

As Israel languished in captivity they would come to their senses. Days and months would pass as they contemplated their current plight of defeat and captivity. The design of God's day of judgment is to cause the remaining people to consider why this has all happened (see also Haggai 1:6-11). When they found the answer to their question they are instructed to lament with great tears so that God would restore a remnant to Israel.

Questions over Amos Chapter 5

1. What lamentation did Amos cry over Israel?

2. What did Amos instruct the house of Israel to do?

3. Who made the Pleiades and Orion?

4. What did Amos say about the number and strength of Israel's sins?

5. What did God think about Israel's feasts and assemblies?

6. Why would God cause Israel to go into Damascus as captives?

AMOS CHAPTER 6

Synopsis

Israel lived like kings and participated in revelry while God was preparing a mighty nation to conquer them. The foolish Israelites had no clue that their laughter and wealth was about to be lost forever. God would strike them because he abhorred and hated their haughty mind and luxuriant palaces. There was little to no love for God and his truths so the people would get their just reward.

Application

People seem to easily lose sight of God's judgments and eternity when there is so much wealth and health in their lives. All of us would do well to remember the brevity of this short life we live. If we set aside God for our personal earthly desires we risk losing our eternal well being with him. There is no amount of riches or glory in this world that is worth our eternal soul. The lesson for us all is that God's words should be sweet rather than bitter. If I am angered at his commands or find myself trying to justify my sinful actions it is time to open my eyes and consider what I am doing. The day of God's judgments come in every man and woman's life. God will chastise and punish the wicked with the desire to save us all. Let us not be foolish as the Israelites but rather see their demise and save ourselves before its everlasting too late.

Amos 6

Israel's False Sense of Security (6 all)

"**1** *Woe to them that are at ease in Zion, and to them that are secure in the mountain of Samaria, the notable men of the chief of the nations, to whom the house of Israel come!*" **(6:1).**

Amos had pronounced a "*woe*" upon Israel at 5:18 because the deluded sinful people actually "*desired the day of Jehovah.*" Jesus pronounced seven "*woes*" against the scribes and Pharisees at Matthew 23:13-36. There the Greek word for "*woe*" (*ouai*) means "calamity" (Moulton 294). The Greek *ouai* is used at Revelation 9:12 and 11:14 to signify judgment for misdeeds. The un-repenting and deluded sinners of Israel have nothing but a calamity of judgment to look forward to as long as their state of mind remains contrary to the way of God. The men of Israel have cheated the poor and needy and sit at ease while the same needy come to them for judgments. How can the poor and needy get justice from such crooked men? God chastises and plagues the wicked throughout history to move them to repentance.

Not only was Israel guilty of idolatry, injustice, erroneous worship, and unrighteousness but their root problem, according to Amos, is their quest for financial security. The problem was not in gaining financial security but rather their attitudes and methods of such gain. The wording of this verse indicates their trust in wealth and fortified city of Samaria rather than God (see 1 Timothy 6:9-10).

"**2** *Pass unto Calneh, and see; and from there go to Hamath the great; then go down to Gath of the Philistines: are they better than these kingdoms? Or is their border greater than your border?* **3** *You that put far away the evil day, and cause the seat of violence to come near;* **4** *that lie upon beds of ivory, and stretch themselves upon their couches, and eat the lambs out of the flock, and the calves out of the midst of the stall;* **5** *that sing idle songs to the sound of the viol; that invent for themselves instruments of music, like David;* **6** *that drink wine in bowls, and anoint* *themselves with the chief oils; but they are not grieved for the affliction of Joseph"* **(6:2-6).**

The text infers that these cities (i.e., Calneh, Hamath, and Gath) were considered great yet Judah and Israel far surpassed them in land mass and greatness of strength. God had truly blessed his people with land and power. Israel had not; however, considered God's blessings and by their wicked ways they were bringing the day of calamity and violence closer and closer.

Israel was currently living off of the past blessings of God. They were wealthy; i.e., lying on beds of ivory, content as they lounged without fear upon their couches, sang songs with instruments and invented new ways of playing to enrich their contentment and joy of life. They had all that a man could ever want in this day. They drank plenty of wine from bowls, ate the best of steak from lambs, and anointed themselves with the chief oils. Israel had come to be lost in a world of plenty. They were blind to the dangers of ease and to the need of the poor of their brethren. While they lived it up in the lap of luxury many of their own brethren were starving and being taken advantage of.

*"***7** *Therefore shall they now go captive with the first that go captive; and the revelry of them that stretched themselves shall pass away.* **8** *The Lord Jehovah has sworn by himself, said Jehovah, the God of hosts: I abhor the excellency of Jacob, and hate his palaces; therefore will I deliver up the city with all that is therein"* **(6:7-8).**

Due to Israel's sin of ease and unwillingness to help the needy among their brethren God will bring them into captivity at the hands of the Assyrians first and foremost (see Amos 3:11; 5:27 and Hosea 11:5). Amos identifies the activities of singing with instruments and the inventions of new music as "*revelry*" (i.e., "boisterous merrymaking... to engage in uproarious festivities... a noisy festivity" [AHD 1057]). While Israel was living it up in luxury and riotous living God's anger was smoking.

The Lord said that he hates their worship of sacrifice and singing (Amos 5:21-23). The Lord reveals his passionate hatred for Israel's "*excellencies*" (pride and arrogance regarding their riches at the expense of the poor and needy). God also hated Israel's palaces of ivory because they put their hope and trust in these things of the world rather than the laws of God and hope of heaven. Israel was focusing on their life in this world rather than in the world to come.

"*9 And it shall come to pass, if there remain ten men in one house, that they shall die. 10 And when a man's uncle shall take him up, even he that burns him, to bring out the bones out of the house, and shall say unto him that is in the innermost parts of the house, Is there yet any with you? And he shall say, No; then shall he say, Hold your peace; for we may not make mention of the name of Jehovah. 11 For, behold, Jehovah commands, and the great house shall be smitten with breaches, and the little house with clefts*" **(6:9-11).**

So complete will God's calamity fall upon the wicked of Israel that none will be left in a house to bury their dead. The nearest of kin, such as an uncle, will come to not bury but burn the bodies of the dead (possibly due to the fact that the dead are so numerous that there is no grave spaces to bury them). The name of Jehovah will carry much greater fear in the day of Israel's judgment. To mention the name of the great judge was to bring further destruction upon the house of the wicked.

"*12 Shall horses run upon the rock? Will one plow there with oxen? That you have turned justice into gall, and the fruit of righteousness into wormwood; 13 you that rejoice in a thing of nothing, that say, Have we not taken to us horns by our own strength? 14 For, behold, I will raise up against you a nation, O house of Israel, said Jehovah, the God of hosts; and they shall afflict you from the entrance of Hamath unto the brook of the Arabah*" **(6:12-14).**

Amos calls upon Israel to reason with him. The prophet poses two questions of which the answer was obvious. Horses have more sense than to run on rocks. Men do not plow in rocky areas. The point is that the matter of justice and righteous behavior is just as easily determined; however, Israel has muddied the waters of their responsibilities toward the Lord (i.e., they turned both justice and righteousness into such a mess that they were like people who foolishly plowed and ran horses on rocks).

Yet even more foolish was their conclusion that that they could obtain all blessings of life by "*our own strength*." Israel looked to idols (Hosea 11:2), other nations (Hosea 7:11), and now their own strength (Amos 6:13 and Hosea 10:13) for comfort in time of need. The Lord will judge the nation of Israel with Assyria from the northern most border to the southern most line (see Amos 3:11 and 5:27).

Questions over Amos Chapter 6

1. Who slept on beds of ivory?

2. **True or False:** God abhorred Jacob and his palaces.

3. What did Israel do to justice and righteousness (see Amos 6:12)?

4. **True or False:** God would rise up a nation against Israel.

AMOS CHAPTER 7

Synopsis

Amos sees three divine visions at chapter 7. God plans plagues of locusts, fire, and sword upon Israel for her wickedness. The prophet of God pleads with his Lord two times on behalf of "*Jacob*" (the elect remnant of God). God complies with the prophet's request to save Jacob; however, God will not repent of his objective to send the sword upon Israel for her sins.

There is a distinct difference between "*Jacob*" and "*Israel*." Jacob is depicted as the small in number elect where as the name Israel is used to describe the masses of wicked Jews. The determining factor that identifies one as Jacob or Israel is the plumb-line that establishes the true vertical of a wall. The inference clearly points to the standard of righteousness and justice being a standard that all Israel was measured by. Those found not measuring up to this plumb-line of righteousness and justice were to be devoted to destruction.

Application

There remains an elect remnant to this day (see Romans 11:5). The truth continues to divide the righteous from the unrighteous (see John 12:48-50). God's church will always have men and women who uphold the absolute truths of God's words. If it is not me or you that holds and demands truth from all it will be someone else (see Esther 4:14). Amos was God's man of this particular hour. You and I must be God's men and women of our hour. Let us demand book, chapter, and verse Bible authority from not only ourselves but everyone else.

Amos 7

Amos is showed Three Visions of God's Judgment against Israel (7:1-9)

"**1** *Thus the Lord Jehovah showed me: and, behold, he formed locusts in the beginning of the shooting up of the latter growth; and, lo, it was the latter growth after the king's mowings.* **2** *And it came to pass that, when they made an end of eating the grass of the land, then I said, O Lord Jehovah, forgive, I beseech you: how shall Jacob stand? For he is small.* **3** *Jehovah repented concerning this: it shall not be, said Jehovah*" **(7:1-3).**

The judgments, punishment, or chastisement for Israel's wickedness is under consideration in the three visions of verses one through nine. Amos has already revealed the plagues of famine, drought, fungus, and insects on crops, pestilence, sword, and war at chapter 4:6-11. Seven manners of plagues may be sufficient with one last; i.e., the nation of Assyria delivering a final blow to the wicked of Israel. Amos appears to have thwarted additional plagues of chastisement by communicating with God in prayer.

To take away all the grass by insects would be too much for Israel to bear. Amos petitions the Lord that this would not be done to Israel based upon their littleness. The name "*Jacob*" is a term indicating the elect remnant that belong to God (see Isaiah 59:20-22 and Romans 11:26). The number of God's true elect people is small in comparison to the masses of people who reject God and his laws (see Matthew 7:12-14 and Romans 11:1-5). God's prophet is concerned that the destruction of grass would be too much for the remnant to survive. Amos said, "*O Lord Jehovah, forgive, I beseech you:*" God heard the prayer of Amos and it repented him to perform such actions (i.e., he changed his mind).

"**4** *Thus the Lord Jehovah showed me: and, behold, the Lord Jehovah called to contend by fire; and it devoured the great deep, and would have* *eaten up the land.* **5** *Then said I, O Lord Jehovah, cease, I beseech you: how shall Jacob stand? For he is small.* **6** *Jehovah repented concerning this: This also shall not be, said the Lord Jehovah"* **(7:4-6).**

Again, the Lord "*showed*" Amos a divine vision of Israel being destroyed by fire. The destruction of the fire would run "*deep*" within Israel. Amos, once again, petitions the Lord in prayer that this disaster upon the land and people of Israel would not take place. Amos explains that Jacob is small in number and will not survive. The Lord hears Amos' prayer and it repents him that he would do such a thing.

"**7** *Thus he showed me: and, behold, the Lord stood beside a wall made by a plumb-line, with a plumb-line in his hand.* **8** *And Jehovah said unto me. Amos, what do you see? And I said, A plumb-line. Then said the Lord, Behold, I will set a plumb-line in the midst of my people Israel; I will not again pass by them any more;* **9** *and the high places of Isaac shall be desolate, and the sanctuaries of Israel shall be laid waste; and I will rise against the house of Jeroboam with the sword"* **(7:7-9).**

This is now the **third vision** that Amos sees. Amos beheld the Lord standing beside a wall that had been made perfectly vertical by use of a plumb-line. A plumb-line is a string with a weight attached at the end. The weight hangs suspended from a measuring device (such as a tripod) and is used to determine the absolute vertical over any given point. Such a device may be used to calculate elevations in surveying land. Amos sees the Lord standing next to a wall with a plumb-line in his hand to distinguish the true Jacob from all Israel. Fascinatingly, the prophet Isaiah said, "23 *if the number of the children of Israel be as the sand of the sea, it is the remnant that shall be saved*" (Isaiah 10:22-23 see also Romans 9:27).

God had spared the remnant of Jacob because of his promise that he made through Abraham to bless all nations by his seed (Genesis 12:1ff). The Lord; however, would not spare all Israel.

The Lord asks Amos what it is that he sees. Amos replies to the Lord by saying that he sees a plumb-line. God answers Amos saying that he will place a plumb-line in the midst of the people as if to check or measure the verticality of each person. The determining factor as to whether one was spared or destroyed was the plumb-line of righteousness and justice (see Isaiah 28:17).

God had made Israel upright (i.e., vertical) by use of the law yet many had transgressed it. Israel is measured by the vertical wall and what the Lord determines is that they are far off from the true standard that has been set in his laws. Like Daniel, who interpreted the hand writing on the wall to mean that God's people had been weighed in the balance and found wanting, even so Amos has seen God's measuring of his people (see Daniel 5:27) (10b).

Note that Amos does not pray to God on this occasion so that his judgments would not pass against Israel. What can one say when the standard of truth has exposed a people's error? Amos knew that the standard never lies and many of the people stand condemned. The Lord pronounced the punishing sword upon the wicked house of Jeroboam (king of Israel).

Amaziah's conversation with Jeroboam and Amos (7:10-17)

"*10 Then Amaziah the priest of Bethel sent to Jeroboam king of Israel, saying, Amos has conspired against you in the midst of the house of Israel: the land is not able to bear all his words*" **(7:10).**

Amaziah, the priest of Bethel, had gained intelligence of Amos' words of prophecy against Jeroboam, i.e., Jeroboam's house would die by the sword. The priest seems to urgently make his way to the king and reveal Amos' "*conspiracy.*" Though Amos was doing the work of God he was nonetheless despised and hated. Amos had revealed at chapter 5:10 that those who spoke of justice and righteousness were hated. Here is an example of that prophecy. The words of righteousness and justice condemned and stung the priest of Bethel and the king of Israel

(Jeroboam). Likewise, preachers of the gospel of Jesus Christ today will be viewed as the mean guy and the object of many people's hatred. Let the gospel preacher remember that duties belong to the man of God. The preacher must press forward no matter the wicked looks and actions of men (see Ezekiel 2:1-7) (18c).

"**11** *Amos has said that Jeroboam shall die by the sword, and Israel shall surely be led away captive out of his land.* **12** *Amaziah also said unto Amos, O you seer, go, flee away into the land of Judah, and there eat bread, and prophesy there:* **13** *but prophesy not again any more at Bethel; for it is the king's sanctuary, and it is a royal house*" **(7:11-13)**.

Amaziah tells Jeroboam all that Amos has said against the king and his house. Amos had prophesied that the king and his house would die by the sword and that the nation would be led captive by foreigners. These words of doom were more than the king or Amaziah the priest could bear. Rather than changing their unlawful works they request that Amos change his location of doomsday prophecy. Amos had been prophesying in the city of Bethel (a center for idolatrous worship - Amos 3:14). The prophet's words not only affronted the king and priest but the entire nation. Amos' words were contrary to the lifestyle of all. Such a state indicates how far from the plumb-line of God's law they had erred (both in mind and actions).

Israel was hardened by God's laws rather than softened. Rather than considering the plagues that God had sent and giving heed to the warning of Assyria conquering them they choose more rebellion. Israel, her king, and priests considered their way of life to have greater weight than the laws of God. Amaziah tells Amos to leave for Judah because his words were annoying. Many good and faithful preachers throughout the years have been asked to move on when they preach sermons on Bible authority, subjection, the absolute nature of truth, unity of the saints, and fellowship to name a few. Too many members of the body of Christ just do not know their Bible and the truth on many given subjects. The church today, and in every generation, needs seasoned preachers to stand firm, kind, and gentle in the pulpits handling the issues that come their way with wisdom and truth. Many churches could be held together with solid elders and preachers who know the scriptures and give Bible answers for the factions that arise.

"**14** *Then answered Amos, and said to Amaziah, I was no prophet, neither was I a prophet's son; but I was a herdsman, and a dresser of sycamore-trees: and Jehovah took me from following the flock, and Jehovah said unto me, Go, prophesy unto my people Israel*" **(7:14-15).**

Amaziah has displayed a spirit opposed to the words of God. Amos responds to the priest in a pointed way. Amos tells Amaziah that he has no history that would cause men to take notice of his words. Amos was a simple herdsman and a dresser of sycamore trees. Amos was divinely moved by God to speak the words he has to say. Amos would otherwise be tending to the flocks and trees yet God commanded him to speak. While king Jeroboam and Amaziah take out their frustration on Amos they must know that his words are divinely inspired. Jeroboam and Amaziah have a problem with God and his laws rather than the prophet Amos. Amos is simply doing what God commanded him to do.

"**16** *Now therefore hear the word of Jehovah: You say, Prophesy not against Israel, and drop not your word against the house of Isaac;* **17** *therefore thus said Jehovah: Your wife shall be a harlot in the city, and your sons and your daughters shall fall by the sword, and your land shall be divided by line; and you shall die in a land that is unclean, and Israel shall surely be led away captive out of his land*" **(7:16-17).**

Amos, with a spirit of boldness, openly declares Amaziah's folly. To tell one not to do something that God commands is the height of error. God's fury will be poured out not only upon the land and people of Israel but specifically upon Amaziah. Due to the wicked advice Amaziah gave to Amos he would die in an unclean land. Amaziah's sons and daughters would fall by sword. Lastly, Amos tells the erring priest that God would make his wife a harlot in the city. When these things happened people would know that a prophet of God had spoken.

Note the bold spirit of Amos the man of God. We would do well to take such a firm stand against the wicked today that condemn us for following God's laws. Let us rise up and address the wicked to their face rather than fearing them. If the wicked tell me that I do not have to be baptized to be saved let me pronounce woe unto their soul for so long as they hold such an erring view (Acts 2:38). If the wicked tell me that I do not have to call one a false teacher who teaches false doctrines then let me pronounce woe upon their soul as they hold to such erring views (1 Timothy 1:19-20). If the wicked tell me that I will not be condemned, even though I am disobedient, then let me pronounce woe upon their soul as they hold to such erring views (Romans 6:1). If the wicked tell me to do anything contrary to God's laws let me boldly proclaim that it is better to obey God than men (Acts 5:29).

Questions over Amos Chapter 7

1. What did God show Amos in the three visions of judgment against Israel at Amos 7:1-9?

      a.   First Vision:

      b.   Second Vision:

      c.   Third Vision:

2. What did Amaziah accuse Amos of doing?

3. How did Amos respond to Amaziah's accusations?

AMOS CHAPTER 8

Synopsis

Amos sees a fourth vision of ripe fruit in a basket. God explains to his prophet that Israel is ripe for punishment. God will decimate Israel so badly by the Assyrian empire that there will be dead bodies lying in the open streets. Assyria will flood the land of Israel as the Nile River was known to do during the flood season. The sounds of joy and happiness will no where be heard. Truth will be nowhere found and God will not hear the people's cries. Israel will fall and never rise again.

Application

When man's heart comes to be so hardened against God that truth is like a unknown foreign language he is lost and due God's wrath. Amos chapter 8 gives us insight into how a man's heart is hardened. God's laws demanded periods of holy convocations for the spiritual betterment of the people; however, they despised the days of worship. Many of the people of Israel could not wait for the holy days to be finished so that they could get back to the business of cheating the poor and building their wealth. Though God's truth was before their eyes they could not see it. A man's true interest and self view are often so skewed from spirituality that truth is unconsciously ignored. Truth is not received and accepted because it does not fit the wicked man's expectations of religion. Truth is different than the wicked man's opinions and personal conscience. The end of the wicked is the decision to reject truth and hold to personal conscience, opinion, and preconceived religious expectation. The meek of this world have the uncanny ability to set aside their own opinions and permit truth to form their conscience. The meek are lowly and subject to God whereas the wicked think very highly of their self (20b).

Amos 8

Israel is ripe for Judgment (Amos' fourth vision) (8 all)

"**1** *Thus the Lord Jehovah showed me: and, behold, a basket of summer fruit.* **2** *And he said, Amos, what do you see? And I said, A basket of summer fruit. Then said Jehovah unto me, The end is come upon my people Israel; I will not again pass by them any more.* **3** *And the songs of the temple shall be wailings in that day, said the Lord Jehovah: the dead bodies shall be many; in every place shall they cast them forth with silence*" **(8:1-3).**

Amos is showed a fourth vision. The prophet communicates with God as the Lord shows him a summer fruit basket. Summer fruit is ripe fruit. The inference is that the nation of Israel is ripe for the outpouring of God's wrath. The time of the people's joyful singing in the temple has come to an end. These were "*evil times*" (Amos 5:13) and a time when "*dead bodies*" shall fill the cities of Israel. Assyria would violently march upon Israel and crush them by the guidance and power of God (See Isaiah 10:5 and Hosea 10:6).

"**4** *Hear this, O you that would swallow up the needy, and cause the poor of the land to fail,* **5** *saying, When will the new moon be gone, that we may sell grain? And the Sabbath, that we may set forth wheat, making the ephah small, and the shekel great, and dealing falsely with balances of deceit;* **6** *that we may buy the poor for silver, and the needy for a pair of shoes, and sell the refuse of the wheat?*" **(8:4-6).**

Israel's ill treatment of the poor and needy of the land was one of three reasons God would punish Israel (see Amos 2:6). Israel's unjust handling of the poor, their unsatisfied hunger and thirst for wealth, and their disrespect for the laws of God came to be their demise.

Israel's state of mind is revealed in these verses. They understood the necessity of worship; however, their convictions lay only upon the surface. Like the future Pharisees they practiced their religion in hypocrisy. The wickedness of their minds is revealed in that they could not wait for the religious days of a new moon and Sabbath to be over so that they could get back to their fraudulent practices. Buying and selling was their true love whereas they ought to have looked forward to these holy days. David once said, "*I was glad when they said unto me, Let us go unto the house of God*" (Psalms 122:1). Israel's heart is fearfully viewed by God and he sees their disinterest in spiritual matters. Jesus would later quote from Isaiah 29:13 saying, "8 *this people honors me with their lips; but their heart is far from me. 9 But in vain do they worship me, teaching as their doctrines the precepts of men*" (Matthew 15:8-9). God's people today ought to delight in our times of worship. Many; however, seem to catch sicknesses on worship days and miraculously recover the next day for work or play (12e).

Israel shortchanged and overcharged the poor in that their balances were corrupt. Hosea said that Israel's scales were "*balances of deceit*" (Hosea 12:7). Produce and grain was sold by weight. Israel had perverted scales so that it favored them when selling and buying. When weighing produce the scales were calibrated to read more than what was actually being weighed if they were selling to the poor. If they were buying, their scales would read less than the actual weight. Such a deceitful balance would bring the merchants more money for less fruit and grain. Though they thought they were being clever God saw all their unjust ways.

"**7** *Jehovah has sworn by the excellency of Jacob, Surely I will never forget any of their works. 8 Shall not the land tremble for this, and every one mourn that dwells therein? Yea, it shall rise up wholly like the river; and it shall be troubled and sink again, like the River of Egypt*" **(8:7-8).**

Jehovah God should have been "*excellent*" in the eyes of Jacob; however, they were blinded by their quest for riches and glory. Their wickedness had brought upon them God's judgments and the Lord proclaims, "*I will never forget any of their works.*"

When the Assyrians flood Israel with violence then there shall be mourning and trembling. Isaiah had spoken of such a flood of destruction (see Isaiah 8:7ff). The Assyrian flood would be likened unto the Nile River that had a reputation and history of severe flooding and drought. The Assyrians would overflow Israel and the people would be violently conquered.

"**9** *And it shall come to pas in that day, said the Lord Jehovah, that I will cause the sun to go down at noon, and I will darken the earth in the clear day.* **10** *And I will turn your feasts into mourning, and all your songs into lamentation; and I will bring sackcloth upon all loins, and baldness upon every head; and I will make it as the mourning for an only son, and the end thereof as a bitter day*" **(8:9-10).**

Dark days of God's judgment was soon to come upon Israel (see Joel 2:31). These gloomy days of judgment would severely dampen any mood to sing songs of joy. The people will lament as they look out upon the dead bodies of brethren, loved ones, and family. They would lament as they're shackled in chains and exiled to Assyria. This was no day to look forward to without fear (Amos 5:18). Israel's heart would be broke as though they had lost their only son to death.

"**11** *Behold, the days come, said the Lord Jehovah, that I will send a famine in the land, not a famine of bread, nor a thirst for water, but of hearing the words of Jehovah.* **12** *And they shall wander from sea to sea, and from the north even to the east; they shall run to and fro to seek the word of Jehovah, and shall not find it*" **(8:11-12).**

Not only would Jehovah destroy Israel with the sword and captivity but he would cause a famine of divine revelation to his people. Though they seek council from God in the extreme corners of the world they will not find it. The wicked king Saul sought the help of God when the Philistines attacked yet the Lord would not answer him (1 Samuel 28:6). God's people will turn to him after all that they have heard comes to pass and there is no other to turn to yet he will not help (see Ezekiel 7:26 and Micah 3:6). God had already given his plagues for their eye opening repentance yet they rejected him (Amos 4:6-11). The final crushing judgment blow of Assyria was on its way.

Many today pray to God yet the Lord does not hear due to their sin (see Psalms 66:18; 109:7; Proverbs 28:9; Isaiah 1:11-15; Matthew 6:5-8; 7:7-11 and John 9:31).). Many today seek out God's truths yet they never find them because their preconceived ideas of religion do not meet expectation when they read the Bible (Matthew 13:10-14). The Apostle Paul said that these conscientious opinionated brethren are, "*7 ever learning, and never able to come to the knowledge of the truth*" (2 Timothy 3:7).

"**13** *In that day shall the fair virgins and the young men faint for thirst.* **14** *They that swear by the sin of Samaria, and say, As your god, O Dan, lives; and, As the way of Beersheba lives; they shall fall, and never rise up again*" **(8:13-14).**

"*That day*" is the day when God has hardened the hearts of men so that truth is repelled and lost. Jesus said that his words were the waters of life and all those who drink from it shall be saved (see John 4:10-11 and 7:38). The life sustaining waters of truth; however, would be withheld from Israel because they had put their trust in the idols of Samaria, Dan, and Beersheba. Though they search for truth they will not find it. Though the truth is right before their eyes they do not see it because it does not meet their preconceived ideas and opinions. Fascinatingly, we see with clear vision the process of a hardened heart against truth. Those who cannot see the truth before their eyes are blind because they value their own conscience, opinions, and preconceived ideas of religion above the words of God. The wicked put such great value and honor upon their opinions that it supersedes God's instructions. This is the day that God divinely moves Assyria against his own people for their error. God will watch in silence as his people are destroyed. God watches the blind wicked fall into the pit of destruction in every generation. Jesus said, "*14 Let them alone: they are blind guides. And if the blind guide the blind both shall fall into a pit*" (Matthew 15:14).

Questions over Amos Chapter 8

1. What did God show Amos in the forth vision?

2. **True or False:** God would forget some of the wicked works of Israel.

3. At what day would God turn the people's songs into lamentations?

4. What type of famine would God send upon the land?

5. Who will fall and never rise up again?

6. Describe the process of a hardened heart against truth.

AMOS CHAPTER 9

Synopsis

Amos chapter nine reveals the sure judgments of God against the wicked. Just as sure as the elements and animals of the earth obey God's sovereign will even so Israel shall fall in destruction. Assyria will obey the voice of God and they will march violently upon the ungodly nation of Israel. There will be no wicked man or woman that will survive the brutal attack. There will; however, be a remnant of righteous people that the Lord would preserve.

Application

The final chapter of Amos reveals the fearful consequences of living without the authority of God's will. Those who seek their own ways in this life will fail miserably. Those who lean upon their own understanding, personal judgments, conscience, or opinions shall forever fall. The meek; however, shall stand forever as God's elect remnant. The lesson of Amos is timeless. Let us all meekly subject ourselves to God's laws and live in eternal peace or forever suffer the consequences of a hardened heart.

Amos 9

Jehovah's Judgments are Unavoidable (Amos' fifth vision) (9:1-10)

"**1** *I saw the Lord standing beside the altar: and he said, Smite the capitals, that the thresholds may shake; and break them in pieces on the head of all of them; and I will slay the last of them with the sword: there shall not one of them flee away, and there shall not one of them escape*" **(9:1).**

Amos sees his fifth and final vision from the Lord. The Common English Bible reads, "*I saw the Lord standing beside the altar and the Lord said: Strike the pillars until the foundations shake, shatter them on the heads of all the people.*" God commands his angel to strike the pillars and thresholds of the idolatrous altars so that they would shake and be broke in pieces. Those that are not killed in the destruction of the buildings will be killed by the sword. No one shall be able to flee or escape. All the wicked shall perish; however, the piece of ear and two legs out of the lions mouth would escape (i.e., the elect remnant or few righteous of the day) (Amos 3:12).

"**2** *Though they dig into Sheol, thence shall my hand take them; and though they climb up to heaven, thence will I bring them down.* **3** *And though they hide themselves in the top of Carmel, I will search and take them out thence; and though they be hid from my sight in the bottom of the sea, thence will I command the serpent, and it shall bite them.* **4** *And though they go into captivity before their enemies, thence will I command the sword, and it shall slay them: and I will set mine eyes upon them for evil, and not for good*" **(9:2-4).**

A picture of utter destruction without hope is given. The saying, "You can run but you cannot hide" applies here. The wicked of Israel would not be able to hide in the depths of Sheol (probably a reference to the depths of the earth i.e., caves and so forth), the heavens, mountaintops, nor the bottom of the sea. Those who are captured by the enemy will not escape. The sword will devour them in captivity. The wickedness of God's people had reached its maximum status and the time of their judgment had come.

Note the authority of God. He commands the animals and they obey (i.e., serpents). Jehovah commands the nations and they bring their swords. All things and all peoples are subject to God (see Matthew 8:27).

Some may read these words and declare God everything but loving. Such a conclusion would prove one's ignorance of context. The word of God reveals the Lord's divine patience and longsuffering with the wicked as he sent prophet after prophet to turn them from their sins yet they would not. The Lord sent chastising plagues of drought, famine, fire, and pestilence yet many would not repent (see Amos 4:6-11). God gives a man chance after chance because he is not willing that any should perish (2 Peter 3:9). There comes a time; however, when God's patience and longsuffering run out (see Amos 4:12). The hearts of the wicked will continue to be wicked though truth is presented to them. When truth is right before their eyes they reject it because it does not meet their judgments, opinions, conscience, and conviction. Those who place their personal opinions and judgments above God's laws are forever doomed. The time of a hard hearted Israel's demise had come.

"**5** *For the Lord, Jehovah of hosts, is he that touches the land and it melts, and all that dwell therein shall mourn; and it shall rise up wholly like the River, and shall sink again, like the River of Egypt;* **6** *it is he that builds his chambers in the heavens, and has founded his vault upon the earth; he that calls for the waters of the sea, and pours them out upon the face of the earth; Jehovah is his name*" **(9:5-6).**

Amos describes the omnipotence of God as he simply touches the earth and all melts with destruction. God's destructive touch is likened to the Nile River that swells and dries and the land is washed away in its vigor (3j). God commands the elements of the world and they obey. Rain comes to the land as God takes hold of the waters of the sea and throws it on the dry land. Just as sure as God commands the elements and they obey so shall Israel we destroyed.

The prophet of God gives a fearful depiction of the Lord; however, Israel had no fear (see Amos 5:7). The wicked of every generation share this one trait. The Apostle Peter refers to the fearless wicked as daring (see 2 Peter 2:10). God's truths are like bitter pills to the wicked (see Amos 4:4-5). When one sets his own judgments, opinions, conscience, and or convictions on par or above the laws of God they prove themselves arrogant. The Apostle Paul commanded that no man think too highly of self (Romans 12:3). The meek and elect of God; however, think only as God directs them (Jeremiah 10:23).

"**7** *Are you not as the children of the Ethiopians unto me, O children of Israel? Said Jehovah. Have not I brought up Israel out of the land of Egypt, and the Philistines from Caphtor, and the Syrians from Kir?*" **(9:7)**.

Israel had become "*as the children of the Ethiopians*" to God. They were like the heathen in that they were far removed from the mercy of God. They had placed their personal judgments and opinions above the laws of God and were ripe for great punishment. The wicked of Israel could not fall back to their previous relationship with God saying, "But Lord, you brought us up out of Egypt." God, through Amos, tells the people that the Philistines could say the same thing about being brought out of Caphtor and the Syrians from Kir. God was responsible for it all yet man chose to stand above God and his laws. Remember the words of Daniel. The prophet of God writes, "21 *God changes the times and the seasons; he removes kings, and sets up kings; he gives wisdom unto the wise, and knowledge to them that have understanding*" (Daniel 2:21).

"**8** *Behold, the eyes of the Lord Jehovah are upon the sinful kingdom, and I will destroy it from off the face of the earth; save that I will not utterly destroy the house of Jacob, said Jehovah*" **(9:8)**.

Israel is not depicted as the kingdom of God but rather the "*sinful kingdom*." The all seeing omniscient eyes of God have seen the cheating of the people against the poor, their idolatry, their lack of interest in holy convocations, and their hardened hearts against his laws. The Lord loved Israel and attempted to discipline her with punishment to return to him yet they would not. The time of their final judgment has come. God would "*destroy the wicked from off the face of the earth.*"

There would; however, be a class of people saved. "*Jacob's house*" would not be destroyed as the rest of the wicked. Again, the name **Jacob** is used to indicate the elect remnant that does love God's laws and his days of holy convocation (see Amos 3:13-15 and Romans 11:26-27 as Paul quotes from Isaiah 59:20). The elect remnant could not possibly cheat their poor brethren. The elect remnant could not possibly conceive the thought of worshipping another deity. The elect remnant of God are small yet they love the Lord with all their heart, mind, and soul (see Matthew 7:12-14; Romans 9:27 and 11:1-5). God will not destroy these meek and gentle people (see Amos 7:2-6). Joel said, "*32 And whosoever shall call on the name of Jehovah shall be delivered; for in mount Zion and in Jerusalem there shall be those that escape, as Jehovah has said, and among the **remnant** those whom Jehovah does call*" (Joel 2:32). The plumb-line of righteousness and justice will distinguish between the wicked and meek of this earth for all times (see Amos 7:7-9) (15a).

"**9** *For, lo, I will command, and I will sift the house of Israel among all the nations, like as grain is sifted in a sieve, yet shall not the least kernel fall upon the earth.* **10** *All the sinners of my people shall die by the sword, who say, The evil shall not overtake nor meet us*" **(9:9-10).**

The wicked Jews of Israel will be no different than any other nation when it comes to God's judgment. Israel will be likened unto grain that is sifted to separate the chaff from the good grain. The chaff people will blow away and be consumed by the fires of God's judgment along with all other wicked Gentile nations that reject God.

The word "*sinner*" infers law. God's anger and destructive judgment against Israel is due to her unwillingness to follow his laws. God is no respecter of persons. The Jew is no different than the Gentile when walking in sin. The Apostle Paul taught this to a disobedient group of Jews in the book of Romans. Salvation belongs to the meek and lowly person who is willing to subject themselves to the righteousness of God. Paul writes, "3 *for being ignorant of God's righteousness, and seeking to establish their own, they did not subject themselves to the righteousness of God*" (Romans 10:3). The meek, on the other hand, will hear and obey all God's laws (see Matthew 26:39 and Luke 9:23).

A Final Message of Hope for those who wait patiently upon the Lord (9:11-14)

"**11** *In that day will I raise up the tabernacle of David that is fallen, and close up the breaches thereof; and I will raise up its ruins, and I will build it as in the days of old;* **12** *that they may possess the remnant of Edom, and all the nations that are called by my name, said Jehovah that does this*" **(9:11-12).**

Amos has clearly identified the elect remnant of God by referring to them as "*Jacob*" (see Amos 7:2-6 and 9:8). Jacob will be meek and lowly as they comply not with their personal opinions and judgments but rather with the laws of God. Amos and Paul reveal that not all of Israel; however, is of Israel (see Romans 9:6). The wicked will always lean upon their own understanding, judgments, and greatly value their opinions and personal convictions even over the Lord's laws.

Amos sees a future day when "*the tabernacle of David*" will be raised in glory. Isaiah used similar language with reference to the future church with Christ sitting upon the throne of David (see Isaiah 16:5). James quotes from Amos 9:11-12 at Acts 15:16-18 in reference to false teachers telling Christians that they must be circumcised and keep the Law of Moses to be saved (see Acts 15:5). The Jew's prejudice toward Gentiles was a major obstacle that was not easily overcome. Many of the New Testament preachers, prophets, and apostles taught the Jews from the Old Testament scriptures proving that God's kingdom, church, would be comprised of saved sinners from both Jew and Gentile races. Amos is telling the people that God will save the meek and lowly of all nations (i.e., the remnant). Though the Lord roars over the wicked like a lion devouring prey he will save a remnant of all nations.

"**13** *Behold, the days come, said Jehovah, that the plowman shall overtake the reaper, and the treader of grapes him that sows seed; and the mountains shall drop sweet wine, and all the hills shall melt.* **14** *And I will bring back the captivity of my people Israel, and they shall build the waste cities, and inhabit them; and they shall plant vineyards, and drink the wine thereof; they shall also make gardens, and eat the fruit of them.* **15** *And I will plant them upon their land, and they shall no more be plucked up out of their land which I have given them, said Jehovah your God*" **(9:13-15).**

When Amos said that the wicked would be destroyed and never rise again he spoke of those who die in their sins (see Amos 8:13-14). Though God's judgments would be fierce against Israel there would be a remnant of elect people that survive. The elect of God would meekly serve and receive an abundance of blessings. The remnant's blessings will be so abundant and rich that there is no end in sight.

Amos prophetically looks to the day when the tabernacle of David shall be raised. Zion, God's church, would be eternally established and indestructible. The rich blessings of forgiveness will be provided to the remnant (Ephesians 1:7).

Questions over Amos Chapter 9

1. What did Amos hear God say?

2. Who would God find though they hid in Sheol, in the heavens, at the top of Carmel, bottom of the sea, or even taken captive?

3. What happens to the land when God touches it?

4. Who did God have his eyes on?

5. Who would God not utterly destroy?

6. What will God raise up "*in that day?*"

Obadiah

Robertson's Notes

Bible Book 31 of 66

"The pride of your heart has deceived you O you that dwell in the clefts of the rock whose habitation is high; that says in his heart, Who shall bring me down to the ground?"

Obadiah 3

Introduction

The book of Obadiah gives the historical record of Edom's wickedness and consequential fall to the all-seeing eyes of Jehovah God (Ezekiel 35:13). Pride took hold of Edom and moved like a contagious disease throughout the nation (Jeremiah 49:16). The source of Edom's *"pride of heart"* (Obadiah 1:3) was to be found in the fortitude of their mountainous geographic location (Obadiah 1:3), allies (Obadiah 1:7), riches (Obadiah 1:6), wise men (Obadiah 1:8), and mighty men of war (Obadiah 1:9). Edom's longstanding feelings of animosity toward Israel caused them to be *"angry, hateful, and envious"* toward God's people (Ezekiel 35:11). A case point is delivered by Obadiah. Edom had rejoiced at the sight of Judah's calamity (Obadiah 1:12). Furthermore, Edom exercised "*violence*" toward Judah in that they stood by idly and even rejoiced while enemies killed and plundered them. Edom, with a callous eye of hatred and envy, plundered, captured, sold as slaves, and even killed many of the remaining Jews in Judah (Obadiah 1:10-14).

Obadiah reveals a true picture of every society and every generation. Esau and Edom represent a worldly approach to life whereas Jacob and Zion represent those who are godly and spiritual. The spirit of Esau and Edom is exhibited by men and women when their pride moves them to trust in self and other things rather than God. These wicked men shall fall to the eternal kingdom of God in burning flames (Obadiah 1:18ff). Obadiah does not leave the wicked nations without hope. "*Saviors*" shall come from the kingdom of God and teach the saving grace of God to the nations (Obadiah 1:21). Those who obey the gospel message of the apostles, preachers, and teachers shall be saved from the great Day of Judgment. At the conclusion of a study of Obadiah, one is left with a sense of the great and everlasting nature of the kingdom of God. Those who enter into it, through obedience, shall be victors with God throughout eternity. Those who reject the kingdom shall fall among the masses of humanity into the depths of despair and defeat in a place called hell (Revelation 20:10ff). God's kingdom is everlasting, all powerful, and shall never be defeated.

Edom

The Edomites were descendants of Esau (twin brother of Jacob) (Genesis 25:19-24, 30 and 36:8-9). The conflict between Jacob (Israel) and Esau (Edom) began in their early days. Esau was the first born son of Isaac and Rebekah and due the birthright of the family. God had made grand and eternal promises to Abraham regarding the future blessings of all men through his Christ (Genesis 12:1-3 and Galatians 3:16). The firstborn had the upper hand in being in the line that would eventually produce the Messiah. Esau had the opportunity of being in the lineage of Jesus Christ by way of his father Isaac; however, he did not value his first born birthright of the family as did Jacob. Esau eventually sells his birthright to his brother Jacob for bread, pottage, and lentils. The book of Genesis tells us that Esau "*despised*" the grand blessings of God through Abraham (see Genesis 25:33-34). The author of the book of Hebrews refers to Esau as "*profane*" or impure due to his lack of spiritual interest (see Hebrews 12:16). The Apostle Paul quotes the prophet Malachi, in the context of God's eternal knowledge of his elect and remnant people, saying "*Jacob I loved but Esau I hated*" (Malachi 1:2-3 and Romans 9:13).

God hated Esau because his life was a living contradiction to the will of God. Esau married a Canaanite women even though his grandfather Abraham had commanded not to do so (see Genesis 24:1ff and 26:34-35). Esau's descendants eventually form the nation of Edom. The Edomites were as their founding father Esau when it came to spiritual interest and the people of God. There was a perpetual animosity that Edom harbored for his brother nation Israel. While Edom despised spirituality and was a profane people Israel sought to live by the laws of God. Edom had no real concern for the lives of their kinsmen of Israel and Judah (Ezekiel 35:6). Edom, from the days of Esau, was both angry and envious of Israel (Ezekiel 35:10-12).

The animosity of Edom toward Israel is seen when Israel desired to pass through their land on the way to Canaan. The king of Edom refused Israel's request making them travel far out of their way to reach their destination (see Numbers 20:14-21). Furthermore Edom is found rejoicing in happiness when they saw and heard of Israel's hardships and defeats at the hands of enemies (see Psalms 137:7 and Ezekiel 35:13-15). The Edomites erroneously reasoned that they would possess the land of Israel and Judah when the Assyrians and Babylonians conquered them (Ezekiel 35:10). Edom had even gone as far as attacking and plundering God's people in their weakened state after doing battle with the Babylonians (Ezekiel 25:12 and 35:4-6).

Throughout the scriptures, the name of Edom is used as a representation of all Jehovah's enemies that love wickedness rather than righteousness (Isaiah 34:1-17; Jeremiah 49:7 and Obadiah 1:21). Jeremiah summed up the sin of Edom as being that of pride and arrogance (cf. Jeremiah 49:16). Jeremiah said that Edom, and all those who set their face against Jehovah God, would be brought down off their high horse of pride (Jeremiah 49:7-22). Isaiah depicts Edom as a sick man that continues to check the clock throughout the night anxiously awaiting the end of his illness that is brought on by God due to their disobedience (Isaiah 21:11-12). There would be, however, no relief for the pride-stricken people of Edom. World empire after empire would continue to press them (i.e., Assyria, Babylon, Medes and Persians, Grecians and then the Romans), and eventually they were non-existent (Malachi 1:2-4). "The archeological evidence also indicates the downfall of Edom by the end of the sixth century. Nomadic tribes infiltrated Edom, and it lost the power to control and profit from the trade between Arabia and the Mediterranean coast and Egypt. In the fifth century, an Arabian tribe, the Nabateans, forced their way into Edom and replaced the Edomites, many of whom went westward to southern Judea (later to become Idumea; cf. I Macc. 5:3, 65), while others were absorbed into the newcomers. By 312 B. C. the area around Petra also was inhabited by the Nabateans" (ISBE, Volume 2, page 20). The Edoms of all times are defeated by good (see Revelation 18:2).

Isaiah sees Edom as a place of judgment. The Lord is depicted as trampling to death the wicked of all nations in Edom (Isaiah 63:1-6). Similarly we read of Christ doing the same thing at Revelation 14:19-20. The Apostle Paul's depiction of Esau at Romans 9:13 and the clear denouncing of Edom in the Old Testament prove the figurative use of Esau and Edom to stand for the wicked now and forevermore. The wicked will always hate the righteous and persecute them (see John 15:18-16:3). Nothing but the wrath of God awaits all those who fall into the class of people ruled by the mind of Esau (see Romans 2:5ff). The same prophets and apostles use the name of Jacob to depict the elect remnant of God that will enjoy the peace and serenity of heaven forevermore (see Amos 3:13-15; Obadiah 1:10, 17-18 and Romans 11:26-27 as Paul quotes from Isaiah 59:20).

OBADIAH CHAPTER 1

Synopsis

Obadiah exposes Edom's sin of pride and misguided trust in their fortifications, allies, wealth, wise men, and mighty men. Furthermore, Edom acted out in malicious hatred toward his brother nation of Jacob when he joyously plundered and murdered those who sought refuge from their attackers. God will judge Edom in wrath and there will be no escape for the wicked. God's judgment, in fact, comes to all nations. Jacob, all those who dwell in mount Zion, shall be the only ones to escape the wrath of God. Though the nations of men appear to be mighty and powerful it is God's kingdom that occupies the true state of indestructible power now and forevermore.

Application

Edom and Esau stand for the wicked of all time whereas Jacob and Zion stand for the righteous and meek. Those who represent Edom in this life are hopeless whereas the meek of Jacob are God's remnant forevermore.

Obadiah 1

Edom to suffer destruction due to her Pride (1:1-9)

"**1** *The vision of Obadiah. Thus said the Lord Jehovah concerning Edom: We have heard tidings from Jehovah, and an ambassador is sent among* *the nations, saying, Arise, and let us rise up against her in battle.* **2** *Behold, I have made you small among the nations: you are greatly despised"* **(1:1-2).**

The name "*Obadiah*" means "servant (or worshipper) of Jehovah" (ISBE, volume 3, page 574). The name Obadiah was a very common name among the Jews in the Old Testament time. Consider all the different Obadiah's mentioned where it is difficult to determine who is who (see 1 Kings 18:3ff; 1 Chronicles 3:31; 7:3; 8:38; 9:44; 12:9; 27:19; 2 Chronicles 17:7-9; etc.). The first two verses read as an oracle or judgment against Edom. Isaiah, Jeremiah, and Ezekiel all delivered oracles against Edom; however, Obadiah's prophecy deals exclusively with Edom.

The Obadiah of this book has experienced a "*vision*" from God. Throughout the Old Testament we find other men who were inspired to write God's word by way of visions (see Daniel 1:1). Some prophets were moved to speak by the Holy Spirit (2 Peter 1:21) and others were spoken to directly by God (see Genesis 12:1 and Exodus 12:1). Interestingly, Obadiah said that not only has he received a word from God but that the people of Israel had as well (i.e., "*we have heard tidings from Jehovah*").

An "*ambassador*" has been sent to many nations to muster them up against Edom. The Lord identifies Edom as having their origins from God and that they are very small and despised. Edom is "*despised*" because of their wickedness and the time of their judgment comes quickly.

"**3** *The pride of your heart has deceived you, O you that dwell in the clefts of the rock, whose habitation is high; that says in his heart, Who shall bring me down to the ground?* **4** *Though you mount on high as the eagle, and though your nest be set among the stars, I will bring you down from thence, said Jehovah*" **(1:3-4).**

Jeremiah 49:16 records a very similar reading. Some believe that Jeremiah must have quoted from Obadiah, however, this is an uncertainty. Edom was a land engulfed by the Seir mountain range.

"Mount Seir is generally identified with modern Jebel esh-Shera', a range of mountains east of the Arabah, stretching from Wadi el-Hesa in the north to Wadi el-Hismah in the south, with peaks rising above 5000 ft.... Seir is generally used as a synonym of Edom (see Genesis 32:3; Numbers 24:18; Judges 5:4; 2 Chronicles 25:11, 14 and Ezekiel 35:15)" (ISBE; volume 4, page 383). The Edomites regarded their rocky dwellings as sure safety against any foes. Their place of dwelling; however, would not protect them from the all powerful Jehovah God. Though the Edomites *"should make their nest as high as the eagle, I will bring you down from thence."* Sometimes we similarly hear one say today, "He needs to be brought down off his high horse" or "you can run but you can't hide" (see Amos 9:1-5). God was going to bring the Edomites down in humiliation and shame and there would be nowhere for them to hide.

"**5** *If thieves came to you, if robbers by night (how are you cut off!), would they not steal only till they had enough? If grape-gatherers came to you, would they not leave some gleaning grapes?*" **(1:5)**

The wrath of Jehovah God against Edom will not stop as a thief or grape-gatherers. Such people take until they have had their fill, however, Jehovah will not stop till every leaf has been turned over and Edom completely devastated and destroyed. Both Malachi and Ezekiel prophesied of the extent of Edom's destruction (see Malachi 1:1-5 and Ezekiel 25:13-14).

"**6** *How are the things of Esau searched! How are his hidden treasures sought out!*" **(1:6).**

Obadiah uses Esau's name as the founder of Edom. The use of Esau's name connects his wickedness to the nation's wickedness. Though Edom had the protection of the Mount Seir range and plenty of wealth they would be cast down from their high eagle's nest. The nations know of Edom's treasure in the capital city of Petra. God will send treasure hungry nations to destroy and plunder the proud nation of Edom.

"**7** *All the men of your confederacy have brought you on your way, even to the border: the men that were at peace with you have deceived you, and prevailed against you; they that eat your bread lay a snare under you: there is no understanding in him*" **(1:7)**.

Those nations such as Ammon, Moab, Tyre and others, who at one time traded and gained wealth through Edom, would now turn against them and plunder them. Edom is depicted as a foolish nation because they did not see their downfall coming. Like foolish children they continued to play with those who were truly their enemies. Edom's pride and overconfidence blinded them to the deception that was taking place around them.

"**8** *Shall I not in that day, said Jehovah, destroy the* **wise men** *out of Edom, and understanding out of the mount of Esau?* **9** *And your* **mighty men***, O Teman, shall be dismayed, to the end that every one may be cut off from the mount of Esau by slaughter*" **(1:8-9)**.

Obadiah has exposed pride as being the cause of God's wrath being unleashed against Edom (Obadiah 1:3). Edom was proud of her geographic location because she considered herself untouchable (see Obadiah 1:3-4). Edom found comfort and peace in their riches and allies. A fourth area of Edom's erroneous thinking was that they put trust and confidence in both their wise and mighty men. These men were not wiser or mightier than God.

No wise or mighty man would stop the Lord from thrashing Edom to the point of utter destruction. Ezekiel spoke of the extent of Edom's destruction by mentioning the names of the two cities that lay to the extreme South (Teman) and North (Dedan) (see Ezekiel 25:13-14). The Lord will certainly and thoroughly wipe out Edom for her sin.

Why is Edom being Destroyed (1:10-16)

"**10** *For the violence done to your brother Jacob, shame shall cover you, and you shall be cut off for ever*" **(1:10)**.

Edom's pride is conjoined with their sins against their brother nation Israel. Pride (Proverbs 16:18 and 29:23) and a lack of concern over others well being (James 2:14-16 and 1 John 3:15ff) have never been admirable traits in the eyes of God. Esau is depicted as a representation of worldly minded men just as Jacob's name is used to signify God's elect remnant that follow God's laws (see Amos 3:13-15 and Romans 11:26-27 as Paul quotes from Isaiah 59:20).

Edom is charged by God with acting out in "*violence*" toward their brother nation Jacob. Edom had no care or concern about the lives of the people of Israel. Those who died at the hands of enemies were actually rejoiced over by Edom (see Ezekiel 35:4-6). Furthermore, Edom attacked with sword and plundered the people of God as they were in a weakened state (Ezekiel 35:4-6). The extent of the Lord's fierce wrath and judgment against Edom is now clearly stated. Edom would be "*cut off for ever.*"

"**11** *In the day that you stood on the other side, in the day that strangers carried away his substance, and foreigners entered into his gates, and cast lots upon Jerusalem, even you was as one of them*" **(1:11)**.

Obadiah divinely and fearfully exposes Esau's dark history. Edom stood by idly while the enemies of God attacked and plundered the city of Jerusalem. The Edomites were so calloused to the event that they not only watched but participated in the killing, capturing, and plundering of Judah (see introduction).

"**12** *But look not on the day of your brother in the day of his disaster, and rejoice not over the children of Judah in the day of their destruction; neither speak proudly in the day of distress*" **(1:12)**.

Obadiah helps us hear the unrecorded words of the Edomites that the omniscient eyes and ears of God knows. God heard all the words and thoughts of the Edomites as Babylon crushed the wicked nation of Judah. Rather than seeing the devastation and violence done to Judah and having fear of God and pity for the lost souls they "*rejoiced.*" Many in

Edom likely said bitter things with joy like, "Judah has received what she deserves." Though Judah suffered violence for her sins it was not the place of Edom to rejoice and partake of their spoils. One man's sins do not justify another man's error.

"**13** *Enter not into the gate of my people in the day of their calamity; yea, look not on their affliction in the day of their calamity, neither lay hands on their substance in the day of their calamity.* **14** *And stand not in the crossway, to cut off those of his that escape; and deliver not up those of his that remain in the day of distress*" **(1:13-14).**

Edom entered into the gates of the city of Jerusalem when the people were in a very week state, saw their vulnerability, and laid hands upon their substance rather than trying to help them. Not only did Edom plunder the left over people that were physically and emotionally wounded but they murdered those who tried to escape from the war zone. The remaining peoples of the city were handed over to the enemies as captives. Edom came in and cleaned up the residue of God's people to the point of near extinction.

"**15** *For the day of Jehovah is near upon all the nations: as you have done, it shall be done unto you; your dealing shall return upon your own head.* **16** *For as you have drunk upon my holy mountain, so shall all the nations drink continually; yea, they shall drink, and swallow down, and shall be as though they had not been*" **(1:15-16).**

The "*day of Jehovah*" is a day of judgment against the enemies of God. God's judgment day fell on several Old Testament peoples on several occasions due to their sins (see during the days of Noah, the Assyrians, Babylonians, Medes, etc.).

A timeless principle is delivered by Obadiah when he wrote, "*As you have done, it shall be done unto you*..." The Apostle Paul said that the wages of sin is death (Romans 6:23). God has not changed in his judgments. Those who live right and those who live condemned will all be judged by the word of God (John 12:44ff and Revelation 20:12). The Apostle John writes, "*12 And I saw the dead, the great and the small, standing before the throne; and books were opened: and another book was opened, which is the book of life: and the dead were judged out of the things which were written in the books, **according to their works**"* (Revelation 20:12). Those who have lived a godless life will drink the wine of God's wrath to the full (Jeremiah 25:15). Edom will have their fill of this wine. The point is that there are always consequences to one's sinful actions (see Proverbs 22:5).

The Final Judgment upon Edom (1:17-21)

"**17** *But in **mount Zion** there shall be those that escape, and it shall be holy;* **18** *and the house of **Jacob** shall be a fire, and the house of Joseph a flame, and the **house of Esau for stubble**, and they shall burn among them, and devour them; and there shall not be any remaining to the house of Esau; for Jehovah has spoken it*" **(1:17-18).**

Obadiah said that the "*day of Jehovah*" has come to all nations. God's judgment of wrath is due the wicked of Edom the world over. There is one class of people; however, that will escape the wrathful judgment of God. That class of people is "*Jacob*." Jacob is not a specific individual but rather a class of people who are meek and or compliant with God's will rather than their own. Perhaps no Old Testament scripture defines Obadiah's prophecy better than the words of David at Psalms 14:5 as he contrast the wicked with the righteous. David writes, "*5 There they* (the wicked) *are in great terror, for God is with the generation of the righteous*" (Psalms 14:5).

The deluded and short sighted unrighteous of the world are in "*great terror*" and don't even know it. David writes, "*For God is with the generation of the righteous*." While the wicked may appear to be confident in their disbelief they are actually in a terrifying state of being. David turns to God's care for his "*generation of the righteous*." The word "*generation*" in Hebrew is *dowr* and translated by the Greek Septuagint by the Greek word *genea* (LXX 705). The Greek *genea* is defined as, "Characterized by quality, condition, or **class of men**" (Strong's 1755).

Liddell and Scott define the word as "of the persons in a family, race, stock or family. Of horses, a breed or kind, a race or generation" (LS 161). The "*righteous*" of any age are a class or breed of men in the same family. God has always been with and blessed the class or breed of people known as "*righteous*" (see Isaiah 28:17). These words seal our understanding of God's predetermined or predestined people identified at Romans 8:29-30 and Ephesians 1:3-7. The righteous are a class or breed of people who understand and seek after God's divine will. Generations upon generations of people pass with time yet there is one thing that unites God's sons and daughters together for all time and that is righteousness. Those who choose to be directed by the Spirit of God through truth in obedience are the "foreordained" of God. God has always known that his special family would exist. There will always, in ever generation, be a breed of people who love truth and obey God's laws to attain righteousness. These people are referred to as "Jacob," "Zion," the "church," "elect of God," and or the "remnant" (see notes at Obadiah 1:10 - see Amos 3:13-15 and Romans 9:6-13 and 11:26-27 as Paul quotes from Isaiah 59:20... see also Romans 11:1-5).

Obadiah specifically mentions mount Zion in this text as it is related to Jacob. The prophet Zechariah reveals to us what "*mount Zion*" represents when he states, "3 *Thus said Jehovah: I am returned unto Zion, and will dwell in the midst of Jerusalem: and Jerusalem shall be called the city of truth; and the mountain of Jehovah of hosts, the holy mountain*" (Zechariah 8:3). When we compare Zechariah's words with those of Isaiah 2:1-4 and Hebrews 12:22-28 we find that the Lord's church is identified. The true church of Christ, Zion, is the elect remnant of Jacob and will stand by the authority of God's laws come what may in this life. The true Zion will be saved whereas the wicked of Edom shall be consumed in fiery judgment. Not one wicked man or woman shall escape!

"**19** *And they of the South shall possess the mount of Esau, and they of the lowland the Philistines; and they shall possess the field of Ephraim, and the field of Samaria; and Benjamin shall possess Gilead.* **20** *And the* *captives of this host of the children of Israel, that are among the Canaanites, shall possess even unto Zarephath; and the captives of Jerusalem, that are in Sepharad, shall possess the cities of the South.* **21** *And saviors shall come up on mount Zion to judge the mount of Esau; and the kingdom shall be Jehovah's"* **(1:19-21).**

Those of the "*South*" and the "*lowland*" represent Judah and Benjamin (the two remaining faithful tribes unto God at the time of Obadiah's writing). The enemies of God shall be possessed by God's people. The captives of God's people that had been taken as prisoners of war by their enemies (see Obadiah 1:11, 14) are now victors as members of God's eternal kingdom. These captives now rule in every direction (i.e., the whole world). God's kingdom has no geographical bounds and shall certainly never be defeated. To be in God's kingdom is to be a part of the greatest and most powerful kingdom ever known and ever will be known to mankind. It is indestructible! The saints of God reign in righteousness with Christ over the wicked of Edom (see 1 Corinthians 4:8 and Revelation 5:10).

Obadiah reveals that "*Saviors*" in the kingdom or church days shall "*judge the mount of Esau*." Saviors in New Testament church days would be the apostles, preachers, elders, and teachers that teach and represent truth as revealed by the mind of God. The words of God shall judge the ungodly world (i.e., the mount of Edom) (John 7:24 and 12:48). Those of ungodly Edom who reject their inspired truths shall be forever consumed. Those sinners who repent and obey the gospel message are added to the kingdom of God (Acts 2:38ff).

Obadiah delivers a picture of hopelessness for the wicked that opt out of obeying God's rule and desiring a place in the kingdom of God. The NT Christian is a part of a powerful kingdom that shall never fall. The Apostle John writes, "*For whatsoever is begotten of God overcomes the world: and this is the victory that has overcome the world, even our faith*" (1 John 5:4).

Questions over the book of Obadiah

1. What sin were the Edomites guilty of?

2. What five things did Edom put their trust in?

3. How many people of Edom shall escape God's judgments?

4. What did Edom do to Jacob?

5. Compare and contrast Obadiah 1:15 and Romans 12:19.

6. Will there be any that escape God's wrathful judgment?

7. How vast would the kingdom of God be in days of the "*saviors?*"

8. Application of the book of Obadiah: Give a brief history of the Edomites

9. What significance do you see in Obadiah's use of Jacob and Esau's names (see Obadiah)?

10. True or False: Edom will be brought low while Jacob (Zion) is exalted.

Jonah

Robertson's Notes

Bible Book 32 of 66

"They that regard lying vanities forsake their own mercy"

Jonah 2:8

Introduction

Some have considered the book of Jonah as a myth due to its fanciful story of a prophet being swallowed by a great fish and surviving. Many look at Bible events such as a world wide flood, parting the Red Sea, and the earth opening and swallowing up the family of Korah as fictional stories that cannot possibly be truth. Jesus' use of Jonah's experience at Matthew 12:39-41; however, stamps a factual approach to the book as one belonging to the canon of Old Testament scriptures. Jonah was a prophet of Israel during the days of Jeroboam II (2 Kings 14:23-25). The 2 Kings passage leaves us with the impression that Jonah's work was at the beginning of Jeroboam's reign and the middle of Amaziah's (i.e., the 15 or so year). The date of the book was around the year 790 to 780 BC. Historical evidences point out that Joash, the father of Jeroboam, had been paying tribute to the Assyrians (see ISBE volume 1 page 335). During the days of Jeroboam, Assyria was having internal problems yet continued, under king Adadnirai III, to conquer lands to the West and Southwest (i.e., Damascus, Tyre, and Sidon). The weakening of Syria, ruled by Ben-hadad, gave Israel a chance to recover much of its lost land (see 2 Kings 13:22-25). The historical facts regarding Assyria, a ruthless nation that was bent on conquest, forms the background for this study. Assyria worshipped a multitude of deities. The father of all Assyrian deities was known as Anu. Latter, Ashur became the national God of the Assyrians. Ashur eventually was given credit as the creator and god of Assyrian war that gave them victory (ISBE, volume 4, page 86-87).

Overview of the book of Jonah

The Story of Jonah is a very fascinating study. God gave his prophet a command yet the instructions were not followed. Jonah was told to go to Nineveh to preach because their wickedness had reached up into heaven. Jonah; however, goes the complete opposite direction. God's prophet would learn that those who disobey the Lord are subject to his chastening hand (see Psalms 32:4-5).

When one disobeys God their mind is not thinking correctly. God moves men to corrective thinking through tribulation. First, the Lord causes a great tempest in the Mediterranean Sea to toss the ship that the prophet had boarded trying to escape to Tarshish. When no relief of the storm was experienced the men of the ship cast Jonah into the sea. Immediately, a great fish swallows up the prophet and he spends the next three days and three nights its belly. Jonah experienced the terrifying depths of the ocean while in the fish's belly. He had water, sea weed, and no doubt many other horrible smelling things that were in the stomach of the great fish all around him. When he could bear his fish prison no more he cries out to God for help.

Jonah, in his three day ordeal, came to a conclusion. The prophet of God concluded that those that "*regard lying vanities forsake their own mercy*" (Jonah 2:8). Jonah knew that God was merciful only to those who obey his divine will (see Isaiah 55:1-5; Acts 13:34-39 and Romans 4:7-8). God's grace, mercy, and justification is not given to those who seek to do things their own ways (see Jeremiah 10:23). Jonah came to this conclusion after he had suffered the "*affliction*" of the tempestuous sea and spending three days and nights in the belly of a great fish (Jonah 2:2).

When the Pharisees of Jesus' day demanded to see the Lord perform a sign he said to them, "39 *An evil and adulterous generation seeks after a sign; and there shall no sign be given to it but the sign of Jonah the prophet:* 40 *for as Jonah was three days and three nights in the belly of the whale; so shall the Son of man be three days and three nights in the heart of the earth*" (Matthew 12:39-40). The unbelieving Pharisees would come to obey the commandments of God and attain mercy through not only hearing of the powerful gospel message but by great tribulation as Jonah experienced. Jesus too would experience tribulation at the hands of wicked men so that mercy may be extended to all.

When we are pressed and afflicted to the point of calling out to God we come to see our great need for his divine mercy. We also learn of God's desire for our obedience. May we all have the self control, spiritual desire, and fortitude to continue in this great lesson we learn. So many lessons are learned in the throws of pain yet when God relieves us we return to the wickedness he freed us from. We should all see and fear the mighty hand of God against wickedness and be moved to steer clear of sin.

God gives his prophet a second chance and reiterates his command to go to Nineveh and preach. Jonah complies with God's will and preaches to the great and wicked city. The people of Nineveh repent due to Jonah's preaching and God repents from his purpose of destroying them. While God is pleased with Nineveh Jonah is extremely angry. The prophet of

God has no desire to see the great city of sixty thousand plus people saved. Jonah would rather die than see the Gentiles saved (see Jonah 4:3, 9).

There is an obvious contrast considered between the mariners, the people of Nineveh, and Jonah. Both the mariners and people of Nineveh have a desire to live where as Jonah seeks death (Jonah 1:14 and 3:9). There was a battle taking place in the mind of Jonah. The prophet of God knew the Lord's will concerning Nineveh; however, his personal desire to see something different happen won over his mind. While the Mariners and people of Nineveh express their faith in God and willingness to do works worthy of repentance Jonah would rather die.

Jonah had previously concluded from his affliction, at the hands of God, that *"they that regard lying vanities forsake their own mercy"* (Jonah 2:8). Apparently there was a lying worthless doctrine circulating that taught that God and his people should want nothing good for the people of Nineveh seeing that they were idolaters and Gentiles. Nothing; however, could be further from the truth. The Lord had early on taught through Abraham that he intended for all nations to be blessed with mercy and forgiveness (see Genesis 12:1-4). Why then does Jonah want nothing good to happen to the people of Nineveh when God wants to save them?

What causes a man to reject the will of God? The answer to this question is the grand lesson of the book of Jonah. Jonah said that he would rather die than to live and see God have mercy on Nineveh. Interestingly, the prophet Hosea and Jesus had somewhat to say about such an attitude. Hosea said that the wicked people of Israel would rather die than turn and follow God's commandments. The people would "8 *say to the mountains, Cover us; and to the hills, Fall on us*" (see Hosea 10:8). Jesus quoted from Hosea when carrying his cross to Calvary. Women came weeping to him as he suffered immensely under the whip of the Romans and weight of the cross. Jesus tells them not to weep because the time comes when the wicked will say "30 *to the mountains, Cover us; and to the hills, Fall on us. 31 For if they do these things in the green tree, what shall be done in the dry?*" (Luke 23:30-31) The Lord's point is that as God chastises men for wickedness they would rather go to their grave in death than to turn to his divine will (see also the Apostle John's use of these words at Revelation 16:9). Jonah, at his present state of mind, was numbered with the hard hearted of the ages. He would rather die than see God's will complete for the people of Nineveh.

What causes a man to reject the will of God? The answer to the question is found in the book of Jonah. People reject God's will when their personal will is more to be desired. God's will is rejected because people place higher value on their personal opinions, judgments, convictions, and preconceived religious ideas. Jonah, like many today, do what pleases them rather than what pleases God (see Amos 4:4-5). The book of Jonah ends. God is seen dealing with Jonah with great patience. The Lord reasons with Jonah about his decisions to die rather than accept the divine will for Nineveh. We are not told if Jonah opened his eyes to his error yet the decision of all men to do so lays before us all (Colossians 3:17).

JONAH CHAPTER 1

Synopsis

God has his special men and women in every generation that rises to the occasion of his desires and fulfils his divine objectives. Jonah was to be God's man of the hour during the days of Nineveh's great wickedness. The Lord commands his prophet to go to Nineveh and preach to it so that they would have an opportunity to be saved. Jonah; however, goes the opposite direction. The prophet enters a ship bound for Tarshish to flee from the presence of God (Jonah 1:3). The right minded man of God would do all possible to be in the presence of God yet Jonah fled from the Lord (Jonah 1:10).

Jonah's fascinating journey that would bring him to understand obedience and mercy begins in the Mediterranean Sea. The ship he enters is caught in the grip of God as the Lord churns the seas in violence. The mariners fear for their lives yet Jonah sleeps. Jonah tells the mariners that in order to save their lives they must cast him into the sea. So the mariners cast Jonah into the sea and immediately a great fish swallows him up. Jonah spends three days and nights in the belly of the great fish.

Application

Chapter one reveals the consequences of not obeying God's laws. Secondly, we see character flaws in Jonah that we ought to not only note but learn from. Jonah appears to have a hatred for the Gentiles rather than desiring mercy for all men (more on this brought out in chapters 3 and 4). The bitterness of Jonah's mind was cause for his lack of love and concern for the eternal souls of others. Jonah was a man of deep convictions (see Jonah 1:9). Unfortunately, like so many today, he let his convictions get the better of him. To permit a personal conviction or opinion to supersede the word of God is the height of arrogant folly (see 2 Thessalonians 2:1-4). Though a man or woman may be very convicted of God they will erase their good standing with the Lord if they put their personal convictions and opinions above the laws of God. When we do things that we see fit to do rather than what God commands we sin.

Jonah 1

Jonah Rejects God's Instructions (1:1-3)

"**1** *Now the word of Jehovah came unto Jonah the son of Amittai, saying,* **2** *Arise, go to Nineveh, that great city, and cry against it; for their wickedness is come up before me*" **(1:1-2).**

Jehovah calls upon his prophet to perform a duty. Jonah is to go to Nineveh, the great city, and preach a message of repentance due to their wickedness that had "*come up before*" the Lord. Nineveh was a city located in the area of Mesopotamia on the banks of the Tigris River. The city was originally established by Nimrod, a mighty hunter that came from the land of Babylonia to Assyria and there built "Nineveh" (see ISBE volume 3 page 538). The city of Nineveh would eventually become the capital of Assyria. The etymology of the Hebrew word for the city indicates an association with a fish. The Mesopotamians worshipped the river goddess Nina that supposedly hailed from the Tigris River.

The "*wickedness*" of this great city was the cause of God sending Jonah. Later this book will reveal that the people of Nineveh were "*evil and violent*" (see Jonah 3:8). God's omniscience, universal sovereignty, and mercy are under consideration. Nineveh was a heavily populated city of Gentiles. Many souls were lost in sin. God desired to present the people with truth so that they may be saved (see 2 Peter 3:9). The Lord, as in the days of Sodom and Gomorrah, gives the righteous a chance to escape. The omniscience and universal sovereignty of God is seen in that God knew of their wickedness and expected no less from these Gentiles than he did the Jews.

"**3** *But Jonah rose up to flee unto Tarshish from the presence of Jehovah; and he went down to Joppa, and found a ship going to Tarshish: so he paid the fare thereof, and went down into it, to go with them unto Tarshish from the presence of Jehovah*" **(1:3).**

Jonah was from the town of Gath-hepher (see 2 Kings 14:25). Gath-hepher was located about ten miles due west of the Sea of Galilee. Rather than obeying God's word and traveling Northeastward toward Nineveh the prophet travels around fifty miles southwestward to Joppa (a coastal town of Philistia on the Mediterranean Sea). Jonah pays a fare to travel from Joppa to Tarshish (likely a city on the North African coast of the Mediterranean Sea).

At this point we are not told why Jonah ran from God and his divine command to go to Nineveh and preach. Was Jonah afraid of the violent people of Nineveh? Was Jonah convicted of God's kingdom and felt the people of Nineveh unworthy of the gospel? Why did Jonah run from God's command to preach to the people of Nineveh?

The Lord Captures Jonah with a Great Fish (1:4-17)

"**4** *But Jehovah sent out a great wind upon the sea, and there was a mighty tempest on the sea, so that the ship was like to be broken.* **5** *Then the mariners were afraid, and cried every man unto his god; and they cast forth the wares that were in the ship into the sea, to lighten it unto them. But Jonah was gone down into the innermost parts of the ship; and he lay, and was fast asleep*" **(1:4-5).**

Jonah was going in the opposite direction that God had commanded that he go. The souls of Nineveh were at stake yet God's prophet is running away from the "*presence of God*" (Jonah 1:3). The Lord visits his prophet while traveling in the sea. God causes a mighty tempest to rise and the ship was being tossed in a violent manner. The mariners began to pray to their gods and cast unnecessary items overboard to save the ship and their lives. While all this chaos is going on Jonah was below the deck of the ship "*fast asleep*." There appears to be no fear or anxiety on the part of Jonah for not doing the will of God.

"**6** *So the shipmaster came to him, and said unto him, What are you doing, O sleeper? Arise, call upon your God, if so be that God will think upon us, that we perish not*" **(1:6).**

The "*shipmaster*" would be an officer or captain in command of the ship. While all the ship workers (mariners) are doing all that they possibly can to save their lives Jonah is sleeping. The shipmaster is amazed and demands that Jonah call out to his God as all the others are doing. The case was one of dire conditions. How can one be so unengaged in life as to be asleep at such a time as this?

"**7** *And they said every one to his fellow, Come, and let us cast lots, that we may know for whose cause this evil is upon us. So they cast lots, and the lot fell upon Jonah.* **8** *Then said they unto him, Tell us, we pray, for whose cause this evil is upon us; what is your occupation? And where do you come from? What is your country? And of what people are you?*" **(1:7-8).**

Lots were often cast to determine many things in Bible days (see Joshua 18:10; 1 Chronicles 25:8; Luke 23:34 and Acts 1:26). Jonah received the short stick (i.e., some form of throwing stones or choosing sticks of various lengths) that identified him as the source of the trouble. The mariners of the ship now want to know everything about Jonah. Though they believed in a multitude of gods it was now clear that this great calamity was caused by the God of Jonah.

"**9** *And he said unto them, I am a Hebrew; and **I fear Jehovah**, the God of heaven, **who has made the sea and the dry land.** **10** Then were the men exceedingly afraid, and said unto him, What is this that you have done?*

For the men knew that he was fleeing from the presence of Jehovah, because he had told them" **(1:9-10).**

Jonah tells the mariners all about himself and Jehovah God (i.e., the creator of all things). News of a mere man angering such a powerful God as the creator of the sea and dry land caused the mariners to be "*exceedingly afraid*." The mariners are utterly astonished that Jonah would run in disobedience from such a powerful God. Jonah proclaims his "*fear*" of Jehovah God; however, his actions illustrated otherwise. While the pagan mariners could see Jonah's folly the man of God was hardened toward his error. Though God was the one Lord of heaven and creator of the sea and dry land Jonah was not doing what he commanded.

What is it about man that causes him to rebel against the Almighty God? We have all done this at some point or another. We see the might of God in creation and learn of his great authority through his revelation. Nonetheless, in moments of weakness or brazen ignorance, we all deny his divine requests. To reject the one who holds supreme authority in this world is indeed daring and foolish yet we have all done this (see Romans 3:23 and 2 Peter 2:10) (14d). Jonah will learn not only about God's mercy but also his divine demand for man to do as he commands.

Jonah is cast off the ship and swallowed by a great fish due to his disobedience to the Lord (1:11-17)

"**11** *Then said they unto him, What shall we do unto you, that the sea may be calm unto us? For the sea grew more and more tempestuous.* **12** *And he said unto them, Take me up, and cast me forth into the sea; so shall the sea be calm unto you: for I know that for my sake this great tempest is upon you*" **(1:11-12).**

Jonah is surprisingly willing to lose his life so that the pagans on the ship would be saved. This is an odd situation. The prophet of God does not want to go to Nineveh to preach to them so he runs. If his reason for running from God's command to go to Nineveh was a hatred of their pagan ways then he is not consistent in his convictions. One thing we do note is the prophet's accountability. He knows that the sea is in a great tempest because of his wrong doing. Jonah is not willing that the mariners perish for his error. The facts before us are that Jonah refused to obey God, he is asleep during the great tempest, and is willing to lose his life for the sake of the mariners.

"**13** *Nevertheless the men rowed hard to get them back to the land; but they could not: for the sea grew more and more tempestuous against them.* **14** *Wherefore they cried unto Jehovah, and said, We beseech you, O Jehovah, we beseech you, let us not perish for this man's life, and lay not upon us innocent blood; for you, O Jehovah, have done as it pleased you*" **(1:13-14)**.

Jonah appears to be willing to perish rather than praying out to God for mercy on the ship. The mariners were not God fearing men yet the tempest sea has made believers out of them. Though Jonah has advised them to cast him into the sea they would rather try to save this man's life. While the heathen valued Jonah it was the God fearing man of God that appears to have no concern over the lives of others.

The mariners go so far as to cry out to God for help rather than calling upon their own gods. The mariners pray that God would not permit them to die due to his anger with Jonah. Secondly, Jonah has requested that they throw him into the sea; however, the men knew that doing such would mean the death of the prophet. The mariners pray that God would not view such an act as murdering an innocent man. Notice the faith of the mariners in God that grows by the moment in this tempest ocean. All men are drawn to God in the tempest of life. Whether those same men remain faithful to God after they make their vows is up to the individual. Jonah; however, is not heard praying or calling out to God at this moment of desperation. He appears to be so angry about the salvation of the people of Nineveh and even the Mariners that he is willing to die in the sea rather than try to help them.

"**15** *So they took up Jonah, and cast him forth into the sea; and the sea ceased from its raging.* **16** *Then the men feared Jehovah exceedingly; and they offered a sacrifice unto Jehovah, and made vows.* **17** *And Jehovah prepared a great fish to swallow up Jonah; and Jonah was in the belly of the fish three days and three nights*" **(1:15-17).**

Once the men threw Jonah into the sea it *"ceased from its raging."* The creator of the ocean received what he was divinely after. The mariners, in a state of awe, feared God, sacrificed to him, and made vows determining to worship and recognize the God of Jonah. It is very likely that they saw the *"great fish"* that God prepared swallow Jonah. The prophet of God goes out of their sight and into the depths of the ocean where he would spend the next three days of his life. Jesus speaks about this event to the Pharisees at Matthew 12:40. To completely understand why Jesus used the incident of Jonah at Matthew 12 we must continue to the next chapter.

Questions over Jonah Chapter 1

1. Why did God send Jonah to Nineveh?

2. Why was Jonah cast into the sea?

3. What happened to Jonah when he fell into the sea?

4. How long was Jonah in the depths of the sea?

5. Read chapter one and list every characteristic about Jonah that you can find.

JONAH CHAPTER 2

Synopsis

The Lord squeezes Jonah in the depths of the ocean for his disobedience. The prophet is within the belly of a great fish with sea weed wrapped all around him. At the height of tribulation the prophet calls out to God for help. Jonah could see that the position he held toward Nineveh was wrong.

Application

Throughout our lives we will hear varying religious doctrines. To receive words that do not represent God's authoritative will is to err greatly. The trouble with receiving erring doctrines is that it puts us at odds with the very God that we are convicted to serve. The book of Jonah challenges us to not be enamored with doctrines that have a ring of goodness but do not represent the truth. Just because a doctrine appeals to a personal opinion or conviction of mine does not make it the truth. Jonah had apparently received the doctrine that the Gentiles of Nineveh were unworthy of God's mercy. Such teaching is identified as a *"lying vanity"* and Jonah was guilty of giving regard to it (Jonah 2:8).

The source of erring doctrines was traced out by Jesus at Matthew 12. Jesus is accused by the Pharisees of casting out demons from people by the power of Beelzebub the prince of demons. Jesus refutes their erring words and said, *"Blasphemy against the Spirit shall not be forgiven"* (Matthew 12:31). Jesus spoke divinely inspired words of the Spirit whereas the Pharisees spoke words of their own making that contradicted the words of the Spirit. Denominational church bodies dot the landscape of our country teaching the precepts and doctrines of man in contradiction to the Lord's commandments. Jesus said, "8 *this people honors me with their lips; but their heart is far from me. 9 But in vain do they worship me, Teaching as their doctrines the precepts of men*" (Matthew 15:8-9). It is the doctrines that originate in the mind of men that have the potential to overthrow the faith of many (see 2 Timothy 2:17-18).

These same Pharisees that were guilty of blasphemy demand to see a sign performed by Jesus. Jesus tells them that the only sign they will see is the "39 *sign of Jonah the prophet:* 40 *for as Jonah was three days and three nights in the belly of the whale; so shall the Son of man be three days and three nights in the heart of the earth*" (Matthew 12:39-40). Jonah came to reject the teachings, opinions, and personal convictions of others for the word of God by the tribulation he experienced in the great fish for three days and nights. After the affliction Jonah learned of God's truth and mercy. Jonah was brought to meekness and lowliness by the tribulation he experienced. God was not pleased with his actions brought on by erring teaching. The only way the erring Pharisees, who were guilty of blasphemy, would receive God's mercy would be to give way to truth and repent. Nothing but tribulation awaited these Pharisees as was the case with Jonah. Would they turn to God in repentance? Only God knows what happened with all the Pharisees of Jesus' day.

Jonah 2

Jonah comes to himself and Prays to God (2 all)

"**1** *Then Jonah prayed unto Jehovah his God out of the fish's belly*" **(2:1).**

Jonah has spent three days in the belly of a great fish. He has had plenty of time to think about the events that have brought him to this precarious situation in life. Jonah is not found praying about God's command to go to Nineveh and neither is he heard praying when the ship was being tossed about in the sea. The prophet of God now prays.

"**2** *And he said, I called by reason of mine **affliction** unto Jehovah, and he answered me; out of the belly of Sheol cried I, and you heard my voice.* **3** *For you did cast me into the depth, in the heart of the seas, and the flood was round about me; all your waves and billows passed over me*" **(2:2-3).**

Chapter two is careful to catalogue the great "*affliction*" that Jonah suffered before he calls out to God. Jonah knew that it was God that had commanded him to go preach to Nineveh (Jonah 1:2). Jonah also knew that it was God, the creator of the seas and dry land, that had caused the ship to be tossed in the tempest sea (Jonah 1:12). Jonah knew that it was God that had prepared the great fish to swallow him (Jonah 1:17). Jonah had been in the depths of the sea. He could feel the pressure of such depths and hear the waves and waters all around him. The prophet of God, no doubt in terror over the situation, contemplated the events and calls out to the Lord in the time of his "*affliction.*"

The Lord uniformly works throughout every generation in man's life. Those who reject his commandments have nothing but plagues and affliction to look forward to (see Psalms 32:4-5 and Revelation 16:8-11).

"**4** *And I said, I am cast out from before your eyes; Yet I will look again toward your holy temple.* **5** *The waters compassed me about, even to the soul; the deep was round about me; the weeds were wrapped about my head.* **6** *I went down to the bottoms of the mountains; the earth with its bars closed upon me for ever: yet have you brought up my life from the pit, O Jehovah my God*" **(2:4-6).**

Jonah was in a deadly situation. The great fish had swallowed him and taken him to the depths of the sea. The prophet of God has water and sea weed wrapped around him. He is helpless and doomed without God's help. Jonah sees his undone condition of being "*cast out from before your* (God's) *eyes*" due to his rebellion. The prophet of God knows that he will once again "*look toward your holy temple.*" He calls out to God from the depths of the sea and the Lord hears the prophet's words.

Jonah's prayer helps us get to know him better. Though the prophet had disobeyed God and showed no care or concern for the souls of men he did care and love God. Jonah was to learn that loving God meant loving all his created beings. The people of Nineveh were in danger of loosing their eternal souls. God was willing to save any and all who would call out to him (Joel 2:32 and 2 Peter 3:9). Jonah is also in great danger. The prophet calls out to God and the Lord is helping his prophet see that as he needs and prays for help even so there are people in Nineveh that need help. Jonah was no better or more deserving of God's mercy than are the people of Nineveh.

"**7** *When my soul fainted within me, I remembered Jehovah; and my prayer came in unto you, into your holy temple*" **(2:7).**

Jonah knew that his life would soon end in this perilous situation and it is at this dire moment that he "*remembered Jehovah*" and called out to him in prayer. We may all see or put ourselves into this situation. Jonah has been commanded, by God, to go to Nineveh and preach to them; however, he disobeyed and the Lord chastens him with the great fish experience. Jonah "*remembers*" or acknowledges God's divine interaction in his life. Though the prophet could not see the holy temple he by faith knew that it was associated with the presence of God and so he prays. It was at the moment of a fainting soul that Asaph prayed to God regarding his life long affliction (see Psalms 77:3). God brings a man to the breaking point before flesh and blood will finally open their eyes to their error and beg for God's mercy. Jonah's heart would be changed not by unchecked disobedience but through affliction, chastisement, and punishment.

"**8** *They that regard lying vanities forsake their own mercy*" **(2:8).**

Jonah cries out to God in his moment of great need and makes a simple statement. The prophet said, "*They that regard lying vanities forsake their own mercy.*" The Greek Septuagint helps us with the words "*vanities*" (Greek *mataia*) meaning "vain, empty, idle, trifling, frivolous or thoughtless" (LS 489) and "ineffective, groundless, or useless" (Moulton 250). The Greek *kai* is the conjunction "and" (Moulton 208). The Greek word *pseude* "*lying*" means "to speak falsely or deceitfully or to deceive by a lie" (Moulton 442) (LXX 1095). Jonah has concluded, by his experience in the angry sea and belly of the fish, that those who give "*regard*" (consideration) to idle or empty lying words "*forsake their own mercy.*" The inference is that there was some teaching that the Gentiles were unworthy of God's salvation. Jonah had received this erring doctrine to his own soul's demise.

God has purposed his mercy for all men. The prophet Isaiah speaks of God's mercies in light of the coming Christ who would forgive man of their sins (compare Isaiah 55:1-5 with Acts 13:34-39). God's mercy, the forgiveness of sins, belongs to those who are obedient to his everlasting covenant (law of Christ that instructs men to receive salvation) (see Isaiah 24:5). When man rejects the commandments of God he rejects God's merciful forgiveness. Jonah opened his eyes to his error of not going to Nineveh as God commanded and concluded that he had forsaken his own mercy.

Today, if I reject the covenant of God for my own personal desires, opinions, convictions, or conscience I will lose out on the mercy of God. If I accept the lying doctrines of another I forsake the mercy of God. God's mercy, the forgiveness of sins, is contingent upon my reception and obedience to truth. Peter, speaking of Jesus said, "12 *in none other is there salvation: for neither is there any other name under heaven, that is given among men wherein we must be saved*" (Acts 4:12). Every man and woman alive must come to give reverence and fear to the words of the God who created the seas and the earth. The Apostle Paul said, "17 *Whatsoever you do, in word or deed do all in the name of the Lord Jesus, giving thanks to God the Father through him*" (Colossians 3:17). Jesus, quoting from Isaiah, said that many worship God in vain because they "*teach the doctrines of men*" (Matthew 15:8-9). To put one's hope or trust in man's religious ideas or the things of this world is utter foolishness (9f). The story of Jonah teaches us to make a clear distinction between the erring doctrines, opinions, and convictions of men and divine truth.

"**9** *But I will sacrifice unto you with the voice of thanksgiving; I will pay that which I have vowed. Salvation is of Jehovah*" **(2:9).**

God's prophet has learned a valuable lesson while spending three days in the depths of the ocean wrapped up in sea weed. Jonah has tasted the might of God and the fierceness of his wrath against disobedience. He has learned that man's opinions and convictions are not to be put on par with God's laws. The prophet has been chastised in the depths of the ocean. Jonah sees the will of God for man. The Lord demands obedience from all. Jonah, like all of us at times, has found himself at odds with God because he has followed the commandments of men rather than the commandment of the Lord. The prophet of God vows that he will do better and he will sacrifice his offerings to God both for sins and thanksgiving. The prayer ends with a firm and confident "*Salvation is of Jehovah*" (as opposed to any man's doctrines).

"**10** *And Jehovah spoke unto the fish, and it vomited out Jonah upon the dry land*" **(2:10).**

Jonah's conclusion to his ordeal in the sea gave cause for God to save his prophet. The great fish vomits Jonah out of its belly on to the dry ground and he is saved alive. Jonah's disposition of humility and sorrow over his mistakes was gained only by the "*affliction*" in the great fish's belly.

It is fascinating that the Lord not only illustrates authority over the physical elements of the world (Matthew 8:25-27 and 14:26-27), demons (Matthew 8:30-32), sickness, diseases, and physical deformities (Matthew 9:20-21, 29-31 and 12:13-14), and life (Matthew 9:18-19) but he also commanded animals and they obeyed (Matthew 17:27 and Jonah 2:10). We too ought to obey the authoritative voice of God (9f).

Questions over Jonah Chapter 2

1. What caused Jonah to call out to God for help?

2. Why did God "*cast Jonah into the depths of the sea*?"

3. How serious was Jonah's situation within the great fish?

4. What did Jonah conclude as a result of his time in the belly of the great fish?

5. What do we learn about Jesus quoting from the events of Jonah in the great fish at Matthew 12:39-41?

6. How did Jonah get back to dry ground?

JONAH CHAPTER 3

Synopsis

Jonah was merely a vehicle that the gospel was to travel through. Nineveh was the target audience. When God's preacher delivered a divine message of repentance it was so powerful that the people had no option but to obey. Nineveh's works of obedience, their repentance, was exactly what God expected and desired of them. When they performed his divine will he changed his purpose of destroying them.

Application

Never diminish the power of the gospel of Jesus Christ. Though Nineveh was an exceedingly wicked city they nonetheless were changed by the preaching of God's servant. The Apostle Paul writes, "16 *I am not ashamed of the gospel for it is the power of God unto salvation to every one that believes to the Jew first and also to the Greek*" (Romans 1:16). Though cities such as Rome, Corinth, and Ephesus had churches that were deeply corrupted by prejudices and worldliness Paul nonetheless preached. The apostle's preaching changed lives. Paul could have easily said that there would be no way of changing the hearts of wicked people such as the Corinthians yet he methodically exposed all their dark deeds. The point being is that we, like Jonah and Paul, have a duty of preaching to perform. We must leave the results up to the power of God and his gospel (see 1 Corinthians 3:6).

Gospel preaching produces an awareness of man's personal responsibility to perform works of obedience. The Old and New Testaments teach God's expectations of man's faith and obedience. Nineveh's repentance is identified, by divine revelation, as "*works*" that are pleasing to God (Jonah 3:10). When the Apostle Peter commanded repentance and baptism for the forgiveness of sins, Acts 2:38, these actions were considered works of obedience (see Acts 2:38 compared with Ephesians 1:7 and 1 Peter 1:18-22). All who expect to be saved from God's wrath today must perform works worthy of repentance (see Matthew 3:8 and Acts 26:20).

Jonah 3

Jonah obeys God and preaches to Nineveh (3:1-4)

"**1** *And the word of Jehovah came unto Jonah the second time, saying,* **2** *Arise, go unto Nineveh, that great city, and preach unto it the preaching that I bid you*" **(3:1-2).**

There is great significance placed on the phrase "*word of Jehovah*" and "*preaching that I bid you*." The "*lying vanities*" of Jonah 2:8 are depicted as lies when compared to the standard of truth that comes from God. God gives Jonah the same command that he had originally given him; i.e., go preach God's words to Nineveh. The will of God had not changed even though Jonah, and apparently others, had received lying vanities.

"**3** *So Jonah arose, and went unto Nineveh according to the word of Jehovah. Now Nineveh was an exceeding great city, of three days journey.* **4** *And Jonah began to enter into the city a day's journey, and he cried, and said, Yet forty days, and Nineveh shall be overthrown*" **(3:3-4).**

It was a three day journey to Nineveh from wherever the fish had vomited Jonah out. Upon arrival, Jonah began to preach that the people must change their evil practices else the city shall be overthrown. God gives the people of Nineveh forty days until his judgment shall pass upon them.

Nineveh's Response to Jonah's Preaching (3:5-10)

"**5** *And the people of Nineveh believed God; and they proclaimed a fast, and put on sackcloth, from the greatest of them even to the least of them.* **6** *And the tidings reached the king of Nineveh, and he arose from his throne, and laid his robe from him, and covered him with sackcloth, and sat in ashes*" **(3:5-6)**.

We may all be astonished that Jonah's message was so readily received. We must remember that the name of Jehovah God demanded respect throughout the world (see Romans 9:17). The mariners were familiar with Jehovah God and were very fearful (Jonah 1:10). To hear that the God that created the heavens, earth, and seas was angry with them and threatened punishment was enough for their repentance. The people fast and put on sackcloth in a show of a broken heart filled with sorrow due to their sins. Even the king of Nineveh performed acts of repentance.

Once again we are caused to think about the lack of fear on Jonah's part (see discussion at Jonah 1:9-10). Nineveh did not have to be told by God twice to do something yet the man of God, who supposedly feared God, had to be moved to obedience with affliction. Humility and meekness are not characteristics that people are born with but rather traits that must be worked or established in the heart (see Isaiah 66:1-2). The people of God are not given such a heart but rather must make this a part of their being if they expect to be a part of the "*salvation of Jehovah*" (Jonah 2:10).

"**7** *And he made proclamation and published through Nineveh by the decree of the king and his nobles, saying, Let neither man nor beast, heard nor flock, taste anything; let them not feed, nor drink water;* **8** *but let them be covered with sackcloth, both man and beast, and* **let them cry mightily unto God**: *yea, let them turn every one from his evil way, and from the violence that is in his hands*" **(3:7-8)**.

The king of Nineveh is so convicted by the preaching of Jonah that he decrees a city wide time of mourning, fasting, and prayer due to the people's wickedness. Nineveh is said to be guilty of practicing *"evil ways and violence."* Preaching that comes from God's word has great affects on the heart of those who fearfully see the reality of eternity (Hebrews 4:12) (10e) (18f).

Again, we carefully note that the people of Nineveh cried out to God for mercy at the mere threat of affliction whereas it took great affliction for Jonah to come to this point. Jonah was put to shame by the Gentiles. The Gentiles showed a heart of meekness (compliance) toward God whereas the prophet of God had been subject to *"lying vanities."*

"**9** *Who knows whether God will not turn and repent, and turn away from his fierce anger, that we perish not?"* **(3:9)**

Fascinatingly, the people of Nineveh and the mariners did not want to *"perish"* at the hands of God (see also Jonah 1:14). Jonah; however, was willing to neglect God's command to preach to Nineveh and even be cast into the sea rather than to call out to God and obey him. There is an obvious contrast being made between the Gentile mariners, people of Nineveh, and Jonah.

Humanity shares a common interest in living as opposed to dying. When the disciples were on the tumultuous Sea of Galilee they cried out to Jesus saying, *"Save, Lord; we perish"* (see Matthew 8:23-27). The key to successful preaching of the gospel (i.e., having people believe and baptized for the remission of sins) is to depict their present lifestyles and decisions as a matter of life and death. People want to live now and forever. To sin is to die forever (Romans 6:23). Nineveh changed because they wanted to live. Many of those of Israel and Judah died because of their lack of displaying a will to live. Jesus said that many in the future will likewise die (see Matthew 12:38-41). Again, Jesus said, "3 *I tell you, Nay: but except you repent, you shall all in like manner* **perish**" (Luke 13:3) (19n).

"**10** And **God saw their works**, *that they turned from their evil way; and God repented of the evil which he said he would do unto them; and he did not*" **(3:10)**.

God saw their "*works*" and then changed his purpose of destroying the city. "*Works*" are important in gaining God's favor. Jonah's earlier works did not illustrate faith in God or love and mercy for the lives of his fellow man. The standard of truth has always been to reward the faithful and condemn the wicked. People manifest a true faith in God by their obedient works they perform (see Genesis 15:6; Acts 14:1-2; Romans 4:1-3; Hebrews 11 all and James 2:14ff) (11d). Nineveh's "*works*" was their repentance. Repentance is a work of obedience that God expects (see Acts 26:20)!

Questions over Jonah Chapter 3

1. What command did God give Jonah for the second time?

2. Did Jonah obey God's command?

3. What was Jonah's message to Nineveh?

4. How did the people of Nineveh respond to Jonah's message?

5. What did Nineveh's response to Jonah's preaching say about the power of the gospel?

6. How did God react to the people of Nineveh?

7. What do we learn about the relationship between works of obedience and faith by studying Jonah chapter 3?

JONAH CHAPTER 4

Synopsis

God saves Nineveh due to their meek and lowly disposition toward the will of God. While a major Gentile city is being compliant with God's will Jonah is pouting about God saving them. Jonah did not believe that Nineveh should be saved. If the people of Nineveh were to survive then Jonah feels no need to go on living. Jonah, in a sense, is putting God to the test. Jonah is demanding that God either kill all the people of Nineveh or take his life. The patience of God toward Job is incredible. The Lord reasons with his prophet by way of a gourd plant. If only Jonah could see that he was placing value in the wrong areas of life. The book of Jonah ends and we are not told what became of Jonah. Did Jonah repent as the meek people of Nineveh? We are not told; however, what really matters now is how you and I handle truth.

Application

Those who place their opinions, judgments, and convictions on par with God's divine will are in sore error. Jonah's will to die rather than comply with God's divine will is a disposition that has existed for ages. Unfortunately many people will go to their grave in hard hearted disagreement with the will of God. Those; however, who meekly serve God will enjoy an eternity of peace and joy. The lesson of Jonah is that we all comply with God's established and eternal will. I cannot possibly think that my current existence, opinions, judgments, and convictions have equal or greater weight than the eternal word of God. Rather than argue with God let us all humbly submit to his divine laws.

Jonah 4

Jonah Complains to God (4:1-3)

"**1** *But it displeased Jonah exceedingly, and he was angry*" **(4:1)**.

Jonah's true mind is exposed. The prophet of God desired something totally different for Nineveh than did the Almighty creator of heaven and earth. Jonah foolishly placed his personal opinions and convictions above the will of God.

"**2** *And he prayed unto Jehovah, and said, I pray, O Jehovah, was not this my saying, when I was yet in my country? Therefore I hasted to flee unto Tarshish; for I knew that you are a gracious God, and merciful, slow to anger, and abundant in lovinkindness, and you would repent of the evil*" **(4:2)**.

We are given information now that was not known at the beginning of the study. Jonah ran from the presence of God because he knew that the Lord is gracious, merciful, slow to anger, loving, and willing to turn his wrath away from those who obey him. Why did Jonah not want for Nineveh what God wanted for them? Jonah is now very angry that God is sparing the people of Nineveh. Jonah would rather see Nineveh destroyed by the hand of God for their wickedness.

There was a battle taking place in the mind of Jonah and wickedness had won. Jonah's mind had been polluted by "*lying vanities*" in relationship to the salvation of the people of Nineveh (Jonah 2:8). Some where some one had pass along a teaching that eternally condemned the Gentiles and Jonah believed it with all his being. At the same time; however, the prophet knew of God's character of grace, mercy, and love toward all. God's divine will is revealed regarding the salvation of the Gentiles (see Genesis 12:1-4 and many statements made by other prophets). Though the truth was known many, because of a hard heart of prejudice, refused to believe.

"**3** *Therefore now, O Jehovah, take, I beseech you, my life from me; for it is better for me to die than to live*" **(4:3).**

The value of human life and the eternity of the souls is the thrust of much of the book of Jonah. The mariners were afraid for their lives and did not want to perish (Jonah 1:14). The people of Nineveh did not want to perish either (Jonah 3:9). Jonah; however, was ready to let the mariners cast him into the sea and here he is ready to have God take his life from him due to his anger.

Jonah is angry because God has determined to save Nineveh. Jonah obviously does not want to see Nineveh saved. Jonah's personal desires and opinions about Nineveh have been placed above the divine will of God. The prophet is so angry that he asks God to take his life because, from his perspective, "*it is better for me to die than to live.*" Though Jonah is said to be a God fearing man of faith he nonetheless does not agree with God's will (see Jonah 1:9). The prophet would rather die than see God's will be done.

Hosea and Jesus had somewhat to say about Jonah's mindset. Hosea, speaking of the Northern nation of Israel, said that the people would rather die than to turn to God. As Israel watches the mighty hand of God at work they will "*say to the mountains, Cover us; and to the hills, Fall on us*" (see Hosea 10:8). Jesus made this same statement to the weeping women who cried and bewailed as he carried his cross to be crucified. Jesus turns to the women and said that people would soon say, "*cover us and to the hills, Fall on us*" and then he explains the words saying, "*For if they do these things in the green tree, what shall be done in the dry*?" (Luke 23:31). The Lord's point was that the people were wicked and without shame. While the object of punishment and chastisement is repentance many would rather die in the hardness of their hearts than repent (see Revelation 16:9). Furthermore we find the Apostle John making this statement at Revelation 6:16 in relationship to people choosing death rather than repenting at the behest of their wrathful and punishing God. Hosea, Jesus, and John's point is that many will choose death in this life rather than softening their hearts and acknowledging the error of their ways (17d). Jonah is numbered with the hard hearted of the ages that choose death over repentance and compliance with God's will. It is as though the hard hearted person is saying that if things cannot go their way they would rather die than live.

God Reasons with his Prophet (4:4-11)

"**4** *And Jehovah said, Do you well to be angry?* **5** *Then Jonah went out of the city, and sat on the east side of the city, and there made him a booth, and sat under it in the shade, till he might see what would become of the city*" **(4:3-5).**

The Lord hears the hard hearted prayer of Jonah and asks the prophet, "*Do you do well to be angry?*" God begins to reason with Jonah regarding his decision to die rather than except the salvation of the people of Nineveh. The prophet leaves the presence of God once again. He storms away to make a booth and to watch the city of Nineveh. It is as though he believed his fit of anger would cause God to turn against the great city of Nineveh that has repented. Jonah has lost sight of a great Biblical doctrine. God is merciful to those who are meek and lowly and turns against the proud and arrogant. The very God that Jonah claimed to love is not like him. It was up to Jonah to change his personality to fit God's will rather than God change his divine will that had been eternally established (see Romans 9:20).

"**6** *And Jehovah God prepared a gourd, and made it to come up over Jonah, that it might be a shade over his head, to deliver him from his evil case. So Jonah was exceedingly glad because of the gourd*" **(4:6).**

The intense heat had the potential of doing the prophet harm. God caused a gourd (Hebrew for "plant") to grow up over Jonah that he may be protected from the heat. Jonah was "*exceedingly glad because of the gourd*." The plant gave the prophet relief from the heat and a confident heart that God cared for him.

"**7** *But God prepared a worm when the mourning rose the next day, and it smote the gourd, that it withered.* **8** *And it came to pass, when the sun arose, that God prepared a sultry east wind; and the sun beat upon the head of Jonah, that he fainted, and requested for himself that he might die, and said, It is better for me to die than to live*" **(4:7-8)**.

Just as quickly as God caused the plant to grow and provide shade for Jonah it is likewise quickly taken away by a worm. The gourd was a blessing from God. Jonah should have realized the power and love of God through the gourd. The prophet of God ought to have cried out to God for help at his time of desperation. Jonah cries out to God but it is not for deliverance from his sin or plight in the heat. The prophet cries out to God requesting that his life be taken from him. To live would mean to give God glory and condescend to the Lord's will in submission and repentance. Jonah would rather die than to live with God saving Nineveh. The hardness of Jonah's heart is as legendary as the suffering of Job. The Apostle John told of a people whom God would chastise yet they would not repent due to the hardness of their hearts (see Revelation 16:8-11). God chastised Jonah with heat yet the prophet grew angry rather than repenting.

"**9** *And God said to Jonah, Do you do well to be angry for the gourd? And he said, I do well to be angry, even unto death*" **(4:9)**.

God had earlier asked Jonah if he did well to be angry because he saved the people of Nineveh but the prophet gave no answer (Jonah 4:4). God, once again, asks Jonah if it was good for him to be angry at the gourd seeing that it has died and he is under the duress of the hot sun. Jonah answers, "*I do well to be angry, even unto death*." Jonah was so hardened against God that he is willing to take death before changing his tone. This is again very interesting. The people of Nineveh were given the choice between life and death and they gladly chose life. Jonah; however, would rather die than exhibit a spirit of humility and asks the

Lord to forgive him for his lack of love for the souls of Nineveh (14f). While we may make many excuses for Jonah, in relationship to his hatred for the Assyrians, we cannot excuse his sinful behavior. Jonah's mind was nothing like God's mind of mercy and forbearance.

God had caused the gourd to live and die. God had the power of life and death over Nineveh and Jonah. Jonah would not give in to God's will because it did not fit his personal desires, opinions, and convictions.

"**10** *And Jehovah said, You have had regard for the gourd, for which you have not labored, neither made it grow; which came up in a night, and perished in a night:* **11** *and should not I have regard for Nineveh, that great city, wherein are more than six score thousand persons that cannot discern between their right hand and their left hand; and also much cattle?*" **(4:10-11).**

God's patience with Jonah is incredible. The Lord reasons with his prophet so that he may gain understanding and be saved. It is interesting to note that God said that Jonah has had "*regard for the gourd*." Jonah had previously had **regard** (give consideration to or view as valuable) for "*lying vanities*" in relationship to the Gentiles of Nineveh being saved (Jonah 2:8). Jonah considered the gourd to be of great value. The prophet did not labor or make it grow in any way. God gave it to Jonah because he saw the damage that the sun could do to him. While Jonah could see the value of the gourd as a blessing from God he could not or would not consider the value of the souls in Nineveh. If Jonah sees the value of the gourd to protect him from the heat could he not see the value of the sixty thousand plus souls in Nineveh along with a great deal of cattle?

We are not told of Jonah's response. Did the prophet finally see eye to eye with God? We have no answer to such a question yet you and I ought to learn to value the souls of all men. The story of Jonah is one of man pitting his own will against the will of God. The truly hard hearted will go to their grave in obstinacy while the meek will humbly comply with God's will. When the saved get to heaven they may asks the Lord about the outcome of Jonah's life. Did he continue in hardness of heart or did he humble himself before the Lord's will? What really matters now is how God evaluates my heart. Do I place my opinions and desires over the will of God? The truly meek of this earth will say, as did Jesus, "*Not my will by your will be done Lord*" (see Luke 22:42).

Questions over Jonah Chapter 4

1.   How did Jonah react to Nineveh's response to his preaching?

2.   Why did Jonah say, "*It is better for me to die than to live*?" (Jonah 4:8)

3.   Why did God asks Jonah, on two occasions, about the prophet's anger?

4.   Discuss God's reasoning with Jonah regarding saving the great city of Nineveh:

5.   Discuss the meaning of being meek in relationship to the character of Jonah.

6.   What became of Jonah? Did he learn God's intended lesson from the gourd plant? Did Jonah repent of his   latest outburst of anger?

Micah

Robertson's Notes

Bible Book 33 of 66

"He has showed you, O man, what is good; and what does Jehovah require of you, but to do justly, and to love kindness, and to walk humbly with your God"

Micah 6:8

Introduction

The days of Micah were evil times (Micah 2:3). There was scarcely a godly person to be found (Micah 7:2). Dependable and trustworthy people could not even be found among one's own family (Micah 7:5-6). The wicked spent their time devising sinful deeds against the impoverished people around them (Micah 2:1). The wealthy had no conscience when coveting, planning, and taking possession of another's field (Micah 2:2). God's people were guilty of idolatry (Micah 1:7), witchcraft (Micah 5:12), and possessing a haughty spirit (Micah 2:3). The people's "*desire*" and areas of "*diligence*" were not truthfulness and justice but rather "*evil ways*" (Micah 7:3). The "*sin of Jacob and the house of Israel*" were not limited to any one class of people (Micah 1:5). The rulers, heads, prophets, and priests were all guilty of coveting financial gain at the expense of others (Micah 3:1-11). Prophets who spoke negatively about the people's deeds were looked down upon (Micah 2:6).

The book of Micah reminds us of a court scene. Jehovah God calls all the earth to hear his testimony against Israel and Judah (Micah 1:2). The mountains and hills are like a jury that God calls Israel to in order to give their complaining testimony (Micah 6:1ff). Israel exemplifies their state of spiritual delusion when exclaiming their faithfulness to God while practicing unlawful deeds (Micah 3:11 and 7:4). The Lord explains to his people that it matters not whether they sacrifice thousands of rams and offer ten thousand rivers of oil he will always reject it so long as their hearts and deeds are far from Him (Micah 6:6-7). The Lord then states, "*8 He has showed you, O man, what is good; and what does Jehovah require of you, but to do justly, and to love kindness, and to walk humbly with your God*" (Micah 6:8). While Israel cheats the farmers, is unkind to the poor, and refuse to acknowledge their sins with a spirit of humility they remain impure and separate from God (Micah 6:11).

The hope that any may cling to, in these wicked days, was to be found in the coming Messiah from Bethlehem (Micah 5:2). He will reign in a kingdom (Micah 4 all) that is comprised of forgiven sinners (Micah 7:18-20). God will save a remnant who by faith walk in the steps of hope that they will one day be forgiven as God has promised (Micah 2:12; 5:7; 7:20).

The book of Micah teaches Christians living in the twenty first Century. The prophets that were before and those after Micah had the same basic message. Let man do justly, love kindness, and walk humbly with your God. To live in such a way is to display a spirit of faith and humble subjection to the will of God rather than my own personal will (Romans

8:1ff). God has created all things and even time itself. He has the sovereign right to measure man by his standard and expects that we will do as he pleases. Eternity is at the heart of books like Micah. We will not find within its pages a plan to get rich or to be successful in climbing the corporate ladder. What we find are instructions that will help us make it to heaven.

The Prophet Micah

Little is known about the prophet Micah. He is referred to as a "*Morashtite*" which indicates his home place of Moresheth-gath in Judah (Micah 1:1). The books of Jeremiah (see Jeremiah 26:18 / Micah 3:12) and Matthew (Matthew 2:6 / Micah 5:2) have quotes from Micah. These quotes indicate the authenticity of Micah in the cannon of scripture.

Date

Micah prophesied during the days of Jotham (740 – 732 BC), Ahaz (732 – 716 BC), and Hezekiah (716 -687 BC), kings of Judah (Micah 1:1). Samaria was destroyed by the Assyrians at 722 BC. Micah speaks of this event in the future tense at Micah 3:6. The book must have been written before 722 BC sometime during the days of Jotham.

MICAH CHAPTER 1

Synopsis

The omniscient God of all creation is watching and listening to the sinful events transpiring throughout the entire world. The Lord has special interest in the events transpiring in Samaria and Jerusalem. God would send his prophets one after another to Jacob yet they were often ignored and even killed (see Luke 11:47; Acts 7:52 and 1 Thessalonians 2:15). The Day of Judgment had arrived! The Lord would beat their idols and burn their prostitutes in judgment. The fierceness of God's wrath would be so severe that lamentation of wailing would be heard from far off. There would be no relief for the wicked.

Application

God sees and hears all that man does in every generation (see Jeremiah 23:23-25). There will consequentially be no viable excuse for the wicked when God judges mankind by his works (Romans 1:20 and Revelation 20:10-15). The wounds of idolatry and prostitution must be healed before spiritual healing can take place (Micah 1:9). Many today have incurable wounds of sin due to a stubborn and deluded mind. When man puts his personal desires, opinions, convictions, and conscience above the laws of God there is great trouble (see Jonah 2:8).

Micah 1

All Israel shall be punished for their Idolatry (1:1-7)

"**1** *The word of Jehovah that came to Micah the Morashtite in the days of Jotham, Ahaz, and Hezekiah, kings of Judah, which he saw concerning Samaria and Jerusalem*" **(1:1).**

God exposes the sins of both Samaria and Jerusalem during the days of king Jotham, Ahaz, and Hezekiah (see introduction for dates). Samaria was the capital city of Israel while Jerusalem was the capital of Judah. Micah was to be God's spokesman of the day. The prophet's task would be one of great condemnation and divine warnings against widespread wickedness.

"**2** *Hear, you peoples, all of you; hearken, O earth, and all that therein is: and let the Lord Jehovah be witness against you, the Lord from his holy temple.* **3** *For behold, Jehovah comes out of his place, and will come down, and tread upon the high places of the earth.* **4** *And the mountains shall be melted under him, and the valleys shall be cleft, as wax before the fire, as waters that are poured down a steep place*" **(1:2-4).**

God is depicted as sitting upon his throne in the heavens watching and listening to the wicked people not only of Samaria and Jerusalem of the entire earth. Israel, Judah, and the world of men were practicing idolatry in high places. God has only watched to this point yet now he is ready to act out in vengeance. The fierceness of God's wrath against wickedness is seen by a description of the mountains and valleys melting like wax and pouring out as water. The Day of Judgment comes upon a disobedient people and it will be intense.

"**5** *For the transgressions of Jacob is all this, and for the sins of the house of Israel. What is the transgression of Jacob? Is it not Samaria? And what are the high places of Judah? Are they not Jerusalem?*" **(1:5).**

The name "*Jacob*" is used throughout the Bible to represent the elect remnant of God for all times (see Isaiah 59:20-22; Amos 7:5 and Romans 11:26-27). To be identified as Israel or Jacob was to wear a highly royal and priest like name that set you apart as holy from the rest of the sinful world. Many in Samaria and Jerusalem; however, were not living up to their name and divine expectation. The Apostle Paul reveals a distinction between those who would lay claims to being of Israel and those who are the true Israel and Jacob at Romans chapters nine through eleven. Paul said, "*For they are not all Israel, that are of Israel*" (Romans 9:6). Many people of Samaria and Jerusalem had proved by their sinful actions that they were not of the true Israel and Jacob. Samaria and Jerusalem were filled with idols of other deities and God would melt them like wax. Many had lost their distinction as God's people and could not be distinguished from those of the whole earth.

"*6 Therefore I will make Samaria as a heap of the field, and as places for planting vineyards; and I will pour down the stones thereof into the valley, and I will uncover the foundations thereof. 7 And all her graven images shall be beaten to pieces, and all her hires shall be burned with fire, and all her idols will I lay desolate; for of the hire of a harlot has she gathered them, and unto the hire of a harlot shall they return*" **(1:6-7)**.

God had given strict warnings about idolatry when Israel came to Mount Sinai (see Exodus 20:1-6). God had also said that prostitution for hire was an abomination (see Deuteronomy 23:18). The time of judgment had come to Samaria and Jerusalem. God has watched from his throne the people's wickedness of idolatry and prostitution and his anger burns against them. The Lord will "*beat to pieces*" Israel's idols and burn her prostitutes with fire.

Micah's Lamentation (1:8-16)

"*8 For this will I lament and wail; I will go stripped and naked; I will make a wailing like the jackals, and a lamentation like the ostriches. 9 For **her wounds are incurable**; for it is come even unto Judah; it reaches unto the gate of my people, even to Jerusalem*" **(1:8-9)**.

The "*incurable wound*" of Samaria and Jerusalem was idolatry and prostitution. These two sins have spread like a disease from Israel to Judah. Micah considers the people's sins as a festering wound that will not heal. One can only imagine a terrible flesh wound that continues to be mashed into the ground and tormented every day so that it has no chance of healing. Sins that go on without shame are like a festering wound that one does not take care of. The natural thing to do would be to take care of the wound and get it healed. Those; however, that love sin will keep doing the very things that brought the wound on in the first place. Such a mind is so bent on sin that it loses sight of the health of the eternal soul.

Sin has a way of deluding the mind and causing man to not be aware or care for the consequences of their actions. Sinful man can only see the immediate gratification before their eyes. Such sins may continue a lifetime and at the end a man may look back on all the carnage he has caused not only in his own soul but the destroyed lives of others (14d).

"**10** *Tell it not in Gath, weep not at all: at Bethleaphrah have I rolled myself in the dust.* **11** *Pass away, O inhabitant of Shaphir, in nakedness and shame: the inhabitant of Zaanan is not come forth; the wailing of Bethezel shall take from you the stay thereof*" **(1:10-11).**

Micah 1:10-16 is somewhat difficult to interpret. It seems that Micah is making a play on the meaning of the names of these cities and applying the meaning to Israel's sin. We need to be familiar with the moral conditions of each of the cities named to understand why Micah spoke of them in such a way. There are ten cities in all examined or compared. Five cities are listed, and then Jerusalem and then five more cities are given. The prophet commands not to tell of Israel's impending destruction to **Gath** possibly so that the Philistines would have no cause for rejoicing. The Philistines were a long standing enemy of Israel and would no doubt rejoice over word of their fall.

Micah is said to have rolled himself in the dust of **Bethleaphrah** (a city whose name means dust town). The name of the city illustrates the condition of the prophet's heart. The city of **Shaphir** is known as the beautiful or fair city. Beauty and fairness will be turned to shame and nakedness. Not much is known of **Zaanan** but the etymology of the word indicates something far off. It may be that the lamentation of Israel is said to not stop at Bethezel but goes even afar off.

"**12** *For the inhabitant of Maroth waits anxiously for good, because evil is come down from Jehovah unto the gate of Jerusalem.* **13** *Bind the chariot to the swift steed, O inhabitant of Lachish: she was the beginning of sin to the daughter of Zion; for the transgressions of Israel were found in you*" **(1:12-13).**

Maroth (bitterness) is likely a place around **Jerusalem**. Maroth is depicted as waiting anxiously for something good yet sees only the harsh judgment of God (i.e., there will be no relief). **Lachish** is warned to prepare for battle due to Israel's sin having its beginning with her. We are not told how Israel's sins began with Lachish yet the all seeing and all knowing God identifies Jacob's sin as having its beginning here. Lachish, a city in Judah, would later become the headquarters of Sennacherib of Assyria as they assail Judah. Lachish is located very close to Philistia and likely was influenced before other cities in the area of idolatry and prostitution. The wound of sin was established here and never healed.

"**14** *Therefore shall you give a parting gift to Moreshethgath: the houses of Achzib shall be a deceitful thing unto the kings of Israel.* **15** *I will yet bring unto you, O inhabitant of Mareshah, him that shall possess you: the glory of Israel shall come even unto Adullam.* **16** *Make yourselves bald, and cut off your hair for the children of your delight: enlarge your baldness as the eagle; for they are gone into captivity from you*" **(1:14-16).**

Moreshethgath (the hometown of Micah) shall be taken as a gift by Israel's enemies. **Achzib** shall deceive the kings of Israel in some unrecorded way. **Mareshah** shall be taken and occupied by the Assyrians. **Adullam** shall be taken as well. Each of the cities represents parts of God's judgment against the sinful and un-repenting people of Judah and Israel. Micah recommends that the inhabitants of Israel and Judah begin to bald their heads now in shame and sorrow.

Questions over Micah Chapter 1

1. What people is Micah's prophecy concerned with?

2. What sins was Jacob guilty of?

3. Why would Micah lament and go stripped naked wailing?

4. What was the beginning of sin to the daughter of Zion?

MICAH CHAPTER 2

Synopsis

While the wicked of Jacob plot and plan to cheat innocent people out of their property God too is planning. The Lord has witnessed Jacob's gross sin and has determined to punish them. The words of punishment from prophets; however, was not received. The people loved the words of drunken prophets that foretold of smooth roads for Israel. The truth; however, was that the wicked would be greatly punished. There would be a remnant that survives as is always the case (Micah 2:12-13).

Application

Time and man's works expose true hearts. God has witnessed the great wickedness of the world and his own people. The story of every generation is that of many performing wickedness and few that remain righteous. There will be, in every generation, people who are considered God's remnant (Micah 2:12-13 and Romans 11:1-5). The remnant is comprised of people who will serve God in faithfulness no matter the events of life. Where do you and I fall in among humanities moral condition? Are we part of God's faithful remnant? Do we comprise the many that shall face the wrath of God? The object of these Old Testament prophecies is to instill fear within our minds so that we would not want to be standing on the wrong side of God now and forever.

Micah 2

Woe to greedy Oppressors (2 all)

"**1** *Woe to them that devise iniquity and work evil upon their beds! When the morning is light, they practice it, because it is in the power of their hand*" **(2:1).**

Micah has exposed the sins of Idolatry and prostitution in Samaria and Jerusalem. These two sins; however, were not the only thing spiritually amiss in Jacob. There were some who spent their nights planning to do some dark and sinful deed and when the morning came they performed the planned act. Shamelessly the sinners of Samaria and Jerusalem performed their sinful deeds in the day time because "*it was in the power of their hand.*" Seeing that the deed seemed appropriate and they would suffer no apparent consequences they did it. Recall that Solomon said, "25 *There is a way that seems right unto a man but the end thereof are the ways of death*" (Proverbs 16:25). Again, the wise king writes, "29 *Devise not evil against your neighbor seeing that he dwells securely by you*" (Proverbs 3:29).

God created man with a free will. Though all men are under divine law not all choose to fear God and keep his commandments. Solomon writes, "*For that they hated knowledge and did not* **choose** *the fear of God*" (Proverbs 1:29 - see also Psalms 81:12; Acts 7:42 and Romans 1:24, 26) (15l).

"**2** *And they covet fields and seize them; and houses, and take them away: and they oppress a man and his house, even a man and his heritage*" **(2:2).**

Many of the people of Israel and Judah were **covetous** to the point of cheating their fellow brethren (see Amos 8:4). They would stay up all night planning ways to cheat their brother out of his land, house, and his heritage. Samaria and Jerusalem were idolaters, guilty of prostitution, covetous, and willing to do anything to get gain from their own brethren.

"**3** *Therefore thus said Jehovah: Behold, against this family do I devise an evil, from which you shall not remove your necks, neither shall you walk haughtily; for it is an evil time*" **(2:3).**

Amos prophesied to the kings and land of Israel before Micah. Nothing had changed among the people regarding the times being "*evil*" (see also Amos 5:13). While the wicked of Samaria and Jerusalem have spent their nights devising evil plans and their days carrying them out God too is devising plans. God has watched the wickedness of Samaria and Jerusalem from his heavenly abode and he has seen and heard their sinful deeds. God has watched as his people practiced idolatry, participated in prostitution, acted out plans of covetousness, and cheated their own brethren out of their inheritance. The day that God's devised plans unfold will be a time when Israel is carried away captive by the Assyrians and Judah by the Babylonians.

These will be days of shame for these two nations and so they shall walk no more with a spirit of "*haughtiness*." Solomon tells us that there are seven things that are an abomination to God. The first abomination mentioned is "*Haughty eyes*" (see Proverbs 6:16-19 and 21:24). Pride and arrogance is a disease of the mind that surely leads to death. Again, Solomon writes, "13 *the fear of God is to hate evil: Pride, and arrogance, and the evil way, and the perverse mouth, do I hate*" (Proverbs 8:13). Samaria and Jerusalem lived in ways that angered God. **The people were nothing like their heavenly Father (see Leviticus 11:44).**

"**4** *In that day shall they take up a parable against you, and lament with a doleful lamentation, and say, We are utterly ruined: he changes the portion of my people: how does he remove it from me! To the rebellious he divides our fields.* **5** *Therefore you shall have none that shall cast the line by lot in the assembly of Jehovah*" **(2:4-5).**

"*They*" that take up a parable against Israel would be their enemies. With a mocking spirit they lament "*we are ruined, God has removed our portion, why oh why Lord? Our fields are divided and given to the enemy...*" The boundaries of the people's lands will been removed and marred. There will be no one left to redo the property lines. Truly all is lost.

"**6** *Prophesy not, thus they prophesy. They shall not prophesy to you: reproaches shall not depart*" **(2:6)**.

The English standard version reads, "*Do not preach--thus they preach-- one should not preach of such things; disgrace will not overtake us.*" The people of Samaria and Jerusalem grew weary of the condemning preaching of the prophets of God (see Isaiah 30:10 and Jeremiah chapters 27-28). When they devised their wicked plans and performed their wicked deeds God's prophets condemned them. The wicked were doing what they wanted rather than what God demanded of them. As long as they lacked humility, subjection, and meekness preaching that exposed their error would only inflame them. Nothing changes from generation to generation. The Apostle Paul warns of those who would have a desire to hear smooth and fair speeches rather than saving words of condemnation (see 2 Timothy 4:3).

"**7** *Shall it be said, O house of Jacob, Is the Spirit of Jehovah straitened? Are these his doings? Do not my words do good to him that walks uprightly*?" **(2:7)**

The ASV footnote reads "impatient" for "straitened." The Bible in Basic English reads, "*Is the Lord quickly made angry? Are these his doings? Do not his words do good to his people Israel*?" Micah illustrates the confused and deluded state of mind that the people had. Though they have practiced idolatry, prostitution, and great covetousness they could not see that God would condemn them because they were the "*house of Jacob.*" This "can do no wrong" attitude prevailed in the mind of the Jews from here to the days of Jesus and the apostles. The Apostle Paul spends much of the book of Romans proving the Jews sin though they saw no wrong that they had done (Romans 3:9). Many today have a faulty view of God's expectations, sin, and personal responsibility. To think that one is eternally safe from the wrath of God because of a one time confession statement is utter foolishness when laid along side the Word of God (29l).

Micah reminds Samaria and Jerusalem that God blesses the man that *"walks uprightly."* God has always impartially judged man not by who he is but what he does (see Revelation 20:10-15). God has given man his standard truths of righteousness and justice (Isaiah 28:17). All men are equally judged by this standard. God shows no partiality toward race, gender, or social background (see Acts 10:34).

*"**8** But of late my people are risen up as an enemy: you strip the robe from off the garment from them that pass by securely as men averse from war. **9** The women of my people you cast out from their pleasant houses; from their young children you take away my glory for ever"* **(2:8-9).**

Israel is its own worst enemy. The debtors strip the robe off the one in debt, cast women in the streets making them homeless, and separate the mother from child through human trafficking for debts. These cold acts of indecency caused the name of God to be blasphemed among the nations. As Gentile nations witnessed and heard of these actions they considered Samaria and Jerusalem in a light that God had never intended. Jacob was sending the wrong message to the world. Due to their demanding and impatient ways they took *"away the glory of God for ever."* God's name is glorified by the world as they witness his power, mercy, and patience among his people. Israel; however, painted God out to be a ruthless God concerned only for money (19p).

*"**10** Arise, and depart; for this is not your resting place; because of uncleanness that destroys, even with a grievous destruction. **11** If a man walking in a spirit of falsehood do lie, saying, I will prophesy unto you of wine and of strong drink; he shall even be the prophet of this people"* **(2:10-11).**

Micah calls upon the ungodly of Israel to *"arise and depart"* due to their wicked works of darkness. Israel's attentive ear is only to the prophet that speaks lies while for hire of wine and strong drink. As long as the erring prophet is paid he will tell the people what they want to hear. While we may be appalled by such a thought it none the less happens even in our society today. Preaching becomes a job to many evangelists. To maintain one's job they preach smooth words that do not condemn. These smooth words of positive preaching are often the key to staying in one place for many years (18a). The erring prophets had free reign in Samaria and Jerusalem because no one was testing the "*spirit*" he preached in with the word of God (see 1 John 4:1-4).

"**12** *I will surely assemble, O Jacob, all of you; I will surely gather* **the remnant of Israel**; *I will put them together as the sheep of Bozrah, as a flock in the midst of their pasture; they shall make great noise by reason of the multitude of men.* **13** *The breaker is gone up before them: they have broken forth and passed on to the gate, and are gone out; and their king is passed on before them, and Jehovah at the head of them*" **(2:12-13).**

While the prophets of God called out the idolaters, prostitutes, and covetous there was always a "*remnant of Israel*." As there will always be those who believe they can do no wrong there will also be those who actually try their best to do no wrong. The "*remnant of Israel*" is comprised of those who serve the Lord with all their heart. When they sin, and all do, their hearts are broken (Psalms 51 all; Isaiah 66:1-2 and Romans 3:23). Here are meek and lowly people who put God and his words first in their lives. There will always be these types of people in the world (Romans 11:1-5)! There will also always be those who choose sin over righteousness (Micah 2:1).

The "*breaker*" that goes before them is likely an allusion to the Messiah. Jesus would tear down the wall between sin and man by way of his blood sacrifice (Ephesians 2:14). Through the blood of Christ men would be forgiven of their sins (Matthew 26:26-28).

Questions over Micah Chapter 2

1. What was in the power of the hands of the people?

2. What parable or lamentation would be voiced in these days?

3. Who was the prophet of this people?

4. Who is God the head of?

MICAH CHAPTER 3

Synopsis

Micah calls upon the rulers, prophets, and priests of the house of Israel to remember their responsibility to uphold justice, righteousness, and equity in the land. A tragedy was occurring within the borders of Israel and Judah. Due to money motivated leaders their cities were being built and the economy was thriving. The great problem; however, was that all was going well for the greedy because they were taking from the poor and even having some killed for their property and inheritance. While the strong, intellectual, and unscrupulous people were thriving the poor were being taken advantage of. God was not pleased at the least bit.

Application

Those who hold positions of authority in God's kingdom have the divinely ordained responsibility to uphold truth and law. When elders, deacons, and preachers are received into the congregation there must be wisdom applied to the selection. Men with minds of worldliness will only do damage to the body of Christ. When we follow God's divinely recorded qualifications for these leaders things will have a great start (see 1 Timothy 3:1-14).

Micah 3

Judgments against the Rulers, Priests, and Prophets (3:1-4)

"**1** *And I said, Hear, I pray you, you heads of Jacob, and rulers of the house of Israel: **is it not for you to know justice?** **2** You who hate the good, and love the evil; who pluck off their skin from off them, and their flesh from off their bones;* **3** *who also eat the flesh of my people, and flay their skin from off them, and break their bones, and chop them in pieces, as for the pot, and as flesh within the caldron*" **(3:1-3).**

The "*heads of Jacob*" were the princes or rulers of the people (i.e., head or ruler over a tribe of people). These men had the responsibility of knowing and practicing "*justice.*" God's kingdom had a standard law that governed it. God's revealed law is identified as "*righteousness, justice, and equity*" (see Proverbs 1:3 and Isaiah 28:17). Righteousness and equity have to do with guiding people in an exact and rigid law. "*Justice*" (LXX *krima*) means "judgment, a sentence, administration of justice, execution of justice, or an administrative decree" (Moulton 241). It was the duty of the rulers to 'execute justice' (i.e., make administrative decisions based on God's exact and rigid laws). There would be cases of the common people that would come before them and they would need to base their judgments upon the instructions of God's laws.

Rather than practicing justice the rulers were unjust. These men "*hate good and love evil.*" The ruler's love of evil was so base that Micah depicted them as those who would chop people in pieces, eat the flesh, and break the bones of their countrymen (by taking their land and inheritance - see previous chapter). Greed and lust was the standard that motivated them.

"**4** *Then shall they cry unto Jehovah, but he will not answer them; yea, he will hide his face from them at that time, according as they have wrought evil in their doings*" **(3:4).**

Israel and Judah's "*wounds are incurable*" because they have chose to love evil and hate good (see Micah 1:9 and 2:1). They have practiced idolatry (Micah 1:7), participated in prostitution (Micah 1:7), devised evil (Micah 2:1), taken necessities of life from the poor out of their greed (Micah 2:8-10), and loved the lies of false prophets hired for strong drink

(Micah 2:11). Consequentially, God "*will not answer them*" but rather he will hide his face. Sin separates one from the Lord (14c). The Lord has nothing but judgment for the wicked because "*they have wrought evil in their doings.*" God does not answer the prayers of sinful people who do not acknowledge their error (Psalms 66:18; 109:7; Isaiah 1:11-15; Matthew 6:5-8; 7:7-11 and John 9:31). Solomon said, "29 *Jehovah is far from the wicked; But he hears the prayer of the righteous*" (Proverbs 15:29).

Judgment against the False Prophets among the People (3:5-8)

"**5** *Thus said Jehovah concerning the prophets that make my people to err; that bite with their teeth, and cry, Peace; and whoso puts not into their mouths, they even prepare war against him:* **6** *therefore it shall be night unto you, that you shall have no vision; and it shall be dark unto you, that you shall not divine; and the sun shall go down upon the prophets, and the day shall be black over them*" **(3:5-6).**

The prophets of Micah's day "*make my* (God's) *people to err*" in that they spoke lies rather than truth (see Micah 2:11). The false prophets spoke smooth and positive messages that made the people comfortable so long as the cash, alcohol, and food flow continued. Those who would not support the false prophets were told negative and harsh things. The determining factor for what was preached was the prophet's monetary gain. Many preachers today approach gospel preaching the same way. While the financial support is there smooth words are preached (18a).

"**7** *And the seers shall be put to shame, and the diviners confounded; yea, they shall all cover their lips; for there is no answer of God.* **8** *But as for me, I am full of power by the Spirit of Jehovah, and of judgment, and of might, to declare unto Jacob his transgression, and to Israel his sin*" **(3:7-8).**

Those who speak of their own accord shall have their mouths stopped. Micah; however, spoke from divine revelation. Micah claimed to be full of power, judgment, and might by the Spirit of Jehovah that he may declare the sin of Judah and Israel. The words of condemnation from the prophet were of divine origin (i.e., "*by the Spirit of Jehovah*"). To have the "*Spirit of Jehovah*" is to prophecy words of truth from the mind of God (see Numbers 11:26-30 and 12:6) (10l). Preaching truth was not something of Micah's day that would bring him support yet he had no choice but to proclaim God's unsearchable riches.

Israel's Priests, Prophets, Heads, and Rulers are Divinely Denounced (3:9-12)

"**9** *Hear this, I pray you, you heads of the house of Jacob, and rulers of the house of Israel, that abhor justice, and pervert all equity*" **(3:9)**.

The prophet earnestly calls upon the heads and rulers of Israel to consider their sinful ways. The heads and rulers "*abhor justice and pervert all equity.*" Their abhorrence of justice is found in their cheating, robbing, and lying to the common man. They perverted equity in that they rejected the direction or guidance of truth.

"**10** *They build up Zion with blood, and Jerusalem with iniquity*" **(3:10)**.

The heads and rulers bore the responsibility of murdered men who sought justice and equity only to find death. The heads and rulers caused Jerusalem to become wealthy by cheating, lying, and even killing innocent people for their property.

"**11** *The heads thereof judge for reward, and the priests thereof teach for hire, and the prophets thereof divine for money: yet they lean upon Jehovah, and say, Is not Jehovah in the midst of us? No evil shall come upon us*" **(3:11)**.

Micah gives specifics as to how Zion is built up on blood and iniquity. The motivation for the heads, priests, and prophets is money. Money will be the determining factor, rather than truth, for the direction of judgments and truth. The heads and priests, while committing crimes against God's laws, conclude that God is with them and no evil shall befall them. They have practice their sin for so long that it has become their standard of living rather than God's laws. Delusion often rules the hearts of men today. When we believe a practice or teaching is right we may convince ourselves of its validity simply by use of human reason (38).

"**12** *Therefore shall Zion for your sake be plowed as a field, and Jerusalem shall become heaps, and the mountain of the house as the high places of a forest*" **(3:12).**

Judah and Israel's spiritual delusion kept them in the comfort of their sins. Zion would be "*plowed as a field*" due to an unwillingness to acknowledge and repent of sinful deeds. The Lord God Almighty is certainly patient and merciful to those who will repent (see Jonah 4:1ff). God will not; however, overlook the sins of man. Those who will not change are destined to judgment. The only sin a man will not be forgiven of is the sin he refuses to repent of (see Numbers 15:30-31; Mark 3:28-30 and 1 John 5:16-17).

Questions over Micah Chapter 3

1. Who is guilty of hating good and loving evil?

2. What grotesque thing did Micah accuse the rulers of doing?

3. True or False: The prophets of Samaria and Jerusalem helped God's people find truth.

4. Who shall be put to shame and confounded when God shuts their mouths?

5. What motivated the prophets and priests in the days of Micah?

6. What do we learn about the responsibility of elders, deacons, and preachers of the NT church by studying Micah 3?

MICAH CHAPTER 4

Synopsis

Judah and Israel was led by wicked rulers and guided by false prophets. There was little to no justice and equity in the land. There will come a day in the future; however, when God would establish his kingdom and all its citizens would reign in righteousness. The seemingly lame, weak, and sickly people will be members of God's kingdom and shall serve God in obedience. While Jacob of Micah's day did not resemble the heavenly Father the Jacob of the "*latter days*" will be the mirror image of God (see Romans 8:29 and 1 Peter 1:15-17).

Application

Micah chapter 4 gives a precise time that the future kingdom of God, church, would be established. When we connect all the dots given in the Old Testament regarding the establishment of God's kingdom they all point to the day of Pentecost as revealed at Acts chapter 2. Men and women were baptized for the forgiveness of their sins and added to God's kingdom (Acts 2:38-42). Baptized members of the body of Christ love the Lord with all their heart. Members of the Lord's church purpose to live Godly in Christ Jesus no matter the consequences they face in life (2 Timothy 3:12).

Micah 4

The Establishment of Zion in the Latter Days (4:1-5)

"**1** *But in the latter days it shall come to pass, that the mountain of Jehovah's house shall be established on the top of the mountains, and it shall be exalted above the hills; and peoples shall flow unto it*" **(4:1).**

Micah 4:1-3 is found at Isaiah 2:2-4. Isaiah's time of prophecy began a few years earlier than Micah's but for the most part they were teaching at the same time. God spoke the same words of divine prophecy to both these prophets. The "*latter days*" point to a time when people would love God and keep his commandments rather than having wicked rulers and people that were idolatrous and worldly.

The "*latter days*" were spoken of in Daniel 2:28 approximately 150 years after Isaiah and Micah. What are the "*latter days*?" Nebuchadnezzar, king of Babylon, had a dream that is recorded at Daniel 2. A giant image was composed of four parts representing four world empires. The Chronology is given in Daniel 2 and Daniel 7. Babylon, Medo-Persian, Grecian and Roman Empires were represented by the image. Daniel said that it would be during the days of the Roman Empire (Daniel 2:44 / latter days of Daniel 2:28) that Jehovah God would establish his kingdom of righteousness and holiness. The Apostle Peter quotes from Joel 2:28ff at Acts 2:16-21 as he connects the current events of Acts 2 with the prophecy of the coming of the kingdom of God in the "*latter days.*" Furthermore, after the church was established at Acts 2 the apostle Peter said, "*Yea and all the prophets from Samuel and them that followed after, as many as have spoken, they also told of **these days***" (Acts 3:24) (12h).

During these "*latter days*" Micah said that "*the mountain of Jehovah's house shall be established*." The prophet Zechariah reveals to us what the "*mountain of Jehovah's house*" is. Zechariah writes, "*3 Thus said Jehovah: I am returned unto **Zion**, and will dwell in the midst of Jerusalem: and Jerusalem shall be called the city of truth; and **the mountain of Jehovah of hosts**, the holy mountain*" (Zechariah 8:3). Zion in Jerusalem was the sight of David's residence and was earlier known as "*the city of David*" (2 Samuel 5:7). Zion, the city of truth, the mountain of Jehovah, and the holy mountain were all synonymous names. The author of Hebrews gives the spiritual meaning of Zion saying, "*but you are come unto **mount Zion**, and unto **the city of the living God**, the heavenly Jerusalem, and to innumerable hosts of angels, to the general assembly and **church** of the firstborn who are enrolled in heaven, and to God the Judge of all, and to spirits of just men made perfect...*" (Heb. 12:22-23). Zion and the mountain of Jehovah's house is the future church.

Notice that Micah and Isaiah, as well as other prophets, speak of the church being a place that people naturally flowed to. The new kingdom of God (the Lord's church) will be so glorious and blessed that all nations shall desire its blessings. As men see the cause of their curse and plagues and witness the peace of the saints they will flow into the city of God, Jerusalem, Zion, kingdom of God, or church (see Zechariah 2:11; 3:10 and Revelation 21:24). The psalmist writes, "**11** *let Mount Zion be glad! Let the daughters of Judah rejoice because of your judgments!* **12** *Walk about Zion, go around her, number her towers,* **13** *consider well her ramparts, go through her citadels, that you may **tell the next generation** **14** that this is God, our God forever and ever. He will guide us forever*" (Psalms 48:11-14).

"**2** *And many nations shall go and say, Come, and let us go up to the mountain of Jehovah, and to the house of the God of Jacob; and he will teach us of his ways, and we will walk in his paths. For out of Zion shall go forth the law, and the word of Jehovah from Jerusalem*" **(4:2).**

The kingdom of God would be a place of salvation and peace for all peoples and nations (Genesis 12:1ff and Galatians 3:26-28). All nations will be drawn to the kingdom of God by divine "*teaching*" (Isaiah 2:3 and Micah 4:2). Jesus stated this same fact in John 6:44-45. The Apostle Paul also said that "*faith comes of hearing and hearing by the word of God*" (Romans 10:17). Citizens of the kingdom of God would be admitted as they subject themselves to the gospel message or teaching of Jesus (2 John 9-11). This "*teaching*" is referred to as "*the law*" (Isaiah 2:3). The gospel message is the law (compare Ephesians 1:13 to Galatians 6:1-2). The law went forth from Pentecost (Acts 2:38). The place was Jerusalem (Isaiah 2:3; Luke 24:44 and Acts 2:1ff). With all these Bible facts we can easily determine that the church was "*established*" on the day of Pentecost as recorded in Acts 2:38-44 (12h).

"*3 and he will judge between many peoples, and will decide concerning strong nations afar off: and they shall beat their swords into plowshares, and their spears into pruning-hooks; nations shall not lift up sword against nation, neither shall they learn war any more. 4 But they shall sit every man under his vine and under his fig-tree; and none shall make them afraid: for the mouth of Jehovah of hosts has spoken it. 5 For all the peoples walk every one in the name of his god; and we will walk in the name of Jehovah our God for ever and ever*" **(4:3-5).**

"*He*" is none other than God. The Lord shall judge between nations in that he shall set the gospel before mankind and note the direction they take. Paul wrote, "*16 know you not, that to whom you present yourselves as servants unto obedience, his servants you are whom you obey; whether of sin unto death, or of obedience unto righteousness?*" (Romans 6:16). Those who obey the law of God shall be one nation under the kingdom of God as opposed to being many nations with contrary languages, beliefs, and races (22a). This one nation under God shall be united in truth and have no interest in fighting each other due to their common stand in the hope of heaven through the forgiveness of sins. The future kingdom of God would not be a kingdom of war with swords, spear, and arrows but rather a spiritual kingdom of peace (John 18:36 and Romans 14:17) (12m). The prince of peace would rule over it (see Isaiah 9:6). The law would be a message of peace (see Ephesians 2:17). These nations shall "*walk in the name of Jehovah our God*" (i.e., by his divine authority) (see Ephesians 4:1-4 and Colossians 3:17).

The Glorious Reputation of God's Kingdom Returns (4:6-8)

*"**6** In that day, said Jehovah, will I assemble that which is lame, and I will gather that which is driven away, and that which I have afflicted; **7** and I will make that which was lame a remnant, and that which was cast far off a strong nations: and Jehovah will reign over them in mount Zion from henceforth even for ever"* **(4:6-7).**

When "*that day*" shall come (i.e., the kingdom of God or church established in Jerusalem) the Lord will assemble the lame and those who have been afflicted and cast out. The call to assemble will come from none other than the gospel message (2 Thessalonians 2:13-14). The seemingly week, feeble, downtrodden people will be those who comprise the kingdom of heaven (1 Corinthians 1:18-25). The appearance of Christians, from a worldly standpoint, is that of weakness, feeble, and lame. The world of men mistakes meekness and lowliness for sickness. It is the meek and lowly of the world that will have the humility to comply with God's words and admit their sins so that they may be forgiven (51). These lame people will be identified as God's "*remnant*" because he forgives their sins and they press forward in obedience all the days of their lives (see Micah 7:18 and Romans 11:1-5).

The rich, proud, powerful, and wise of the world will see no need for truth and reject it. God; however, will reign as king over his humble servants throughout eternity. The rich and powerful of this world who would not subject themselves to Christ's authority shall have their time and then forever end in pain and agony. There is a great contrast between the rulers, prophets and priest of Micah's day and those who would be part of God's kingdom in the latter days.

"***8** And you, O tower of the flock, the hill of the daughter of Zion, unto you shall it come, yea, the former dominion shall come, **the kingdom** of the daughter of Jerusalem*" **(4:8).**

Psalms 48:1-3 helps us give a clear identification to the "*tower of the flock*" as it relates to the mountain of Jehovah's house, house of God, Zion, Jerusalem, and strong nation (see Micah 4:1-7). The "*tower of the flock*" and "*hill of the daughter of Zion*" is equated to the "*holy mountain,*

Zion, and city of the great king" (Psalms 48:1-3). The tower that Micah speaks of is the church and now we find it equated to the "*kingdom*." The New Testament church is identified as the kingdom of God (see Matthew 3:2; 16:19; Mark 9:1; 1 Thessalonians 2:12; Colossians 1:13-14 and Hebrews 12:20-28).

"*The former dominion*" shall return to the kingdom of God. David's reign over Israel was a time of conquest and great national power. Israel was viewed as a mighty nation that could not be easily challenged. This former reputation and glory would return to God's people as they united in truth and formed a massive kingdom of baptized forgiven believers the world over (see Amos 9:11-12). The kingdom under Christ would not conquer nations but sin. The church would be indestructible and no man or Satan would have the power to prevail against it (see Matthew 16:18) (12bb).

The Victorious Kingdom of God (4:9-13)

"*9 Now why do you cry out aloud? Is there no king in you, is your counselor perished, that pangs have taken hold of you as a woman in travail? 10 Be in pain, and labor to bring forth, O daughter of Zion, like a woman in travail; for now shall you go forth out of the city, and shall dwell in the field, and shall come even unto Babylon: there shall you be rescued; there will Jehovah redeem you from the hand of your enemies*" **(4:9-10).**

Micah, while speaking of the future hope of a united kingdom under God, tells God's people that there is even nearer hope than this. Their current state is pain and anguish due to the news of their punishment. They will be cast into the field and taken to Babylon as captives. God will not forsake them in Babylon. The Lord shall redeem or rescue them from their enemies and cause them to return to Jerusalem (see Ezra and Nehemiah). Though the world may believe that they're a forsaken people they are not (see Psalms 22:1 and Matthew 27:46).

"**11** *And now many nations are assembled against you, that say, Let her be defiled, and let our eye see our desire upon Zion.* **12** *But they know not the thoughts of Jehovah, neither understand they his counsel; for he has gathered them as the sheaves to the threshing-floor.* **13** *Arise and thresh, O daughter of Zion; for I will make your horn iron, and I will make your hoofs brass; and you shall beat in pieces many peoples: and I will devote their gain unto Jehovah, and their substance unto the Lord of the whole earth*" **(4:11-13).**

Micah looks to the day of Israel and Judah's fall. "*Many nations are assembled against you.*" The surrounding nations have a desire to see Israel fall due to their jealousy and hatred for her. Edom is one nation who took pleasure and even plundered Judah as she fell to the Babylonians (see notes at Obadiah 1:10ff). Wicked nations such as Assyria and Edom have no understanding of the will of God and they will be threshed by the kingdom of God.

How will God's kingdom of saints thresh nations like Edom and Assyria if it is to be a spiritual kingdom that has put aside all the utensils of physical warfare? The answer is simple. Christ is the king of his kingdom of saints (i.e., the church). The scriptures depict Jesus as threshing the ungodly by way of agonizing punishment for their sins so that they may repent (see notes at Revelation 19:11-16). Though the masses of sinful humanity oppose the Christian they will never succeed against God's true elect remnant (Romans 11 and Revelation 20:7-9). The remnant of God's people will defeat the wicked by way of the blood of Jesus Christ. They will always have the purpose of doing right and when they fall they will pick themselves up and vow to do better in the future!

Questions over Micah Chapter 4

1. What other prophets spoke of "*the mountain of Jehovah's house*" (Micah 4:1-3)?

2. What is this mountain?

3. Where would God reign over the remnant forevermore?

4. Where would God's people be redeemed from the hand of their enemies?

5. Who would beat in pieces many peoples?

6. True or False: Micah chapter 3 helps us pin point the time that the New Testament Church was established.

MICAH CHAPTER 5

Synopsis

Micah takes us down a future road of great triumph. At the current day Israel and Judah suffer great pain as a woman giving birth to a child. When the child is delivered; however, he shall rule God's kingdom with eternal might. The remnant of Jacob shall serve their new king in his kingdom as God's saints. The true saints of God will be like lions in a forest of weaker beasts. The Christ will reign supreme over his kingdom and all things of this world that men trust in will be crushed.

Application

The Apostle Paul's depiction of God's remnant of believers at Romans chapter 11 is very significant to understanding this chapter. God has an elect class of people that he has foreknowledge of called the saints, elect, or remnant of Jacob. These true saints have purposed to serve God with all their heart. There will be no power of Satan too great to remove them from their faith because God will always protect them (Revelation 12). These Bible chapters do not teach that some people will never fall from grace because they're the elect of God as though it were impossible. It is possible that any and every man can fall from grace. The point is that God knows that there will always be people of strong faith that will serve him not matter the cost in this life (see Romans 11:4-5).

Micah 5

The ruler of Eternal Peace comes from Bethlehem and will Build a Strong Kingdom (5:1-9)

"**1** *Now shall you gather yourself in troops, O daughter of troops: he has laid siege against us; they shall smite the judge of Israel with a rod upon the cheek*" **(5:1).**

Though chapter four ends this verse no doubt belongs to its context. Assyria would certainly siege Israel and smite the king and they shall be led away as captives (see below at Micah 5:6). While defeat seems permanent God's true remnant will be eternally victorious. God is providentially permitting all these things to take place to accomplish his end of saving the elect remnant. God's sovereignty is to be seen in Assyria's rise to power, Israel's fall, Babylon's rise to power, and Judah's fall (see Daniel 2:21). The people of God; however, were never intended to forever fall to their enemies. God has an eternal spiritual kingdom that shall be greater than any nation that the earth has ever known in power and longevity.

"**2** *But you, Bethlehem Ephrathah, which is little to be among the thousands of Judah, out of you shall one come forth unto me that is to be ruler in Israel; whose goings forth are from old, from everlasting*" **(5:2).**

Micah sees dark and dreary days ahead for the wicked of Judah and Jerusalem; however, God has an eternal plan. Micah has revealed God's plan to establish an eternal powerful kingdom in the "*latter days*" (Micah 4). Now we see that this powerful kingdom would be ruled by one "*whose goings forth are from old and everlasting.*"

The new ruler of God's kingdom would be an eternal being as deity. People, during Jesus' day, considered this prophecy to be fulfilled by the Messiah (see Matthew 2:1-6). Contextually Matthew refers to Micah's revealed eternal ruler as the "*King*" of God's spiritual kingdom (see Matthew 2:1-2) (5b). When we read of Jesus' birth place at Bethlehem

Ephrathah (Matthew 1:5-6) and his eternal state of being (John 1:1-2, 14) we easily conclude that he is the king that Micah speaks of.

Jesus will come from Bethlehem, "*which is little to be among the thousands of Judah.*" It is fascinating to note God's choices in his king and people. Jesus would come from the little known place of Bethlehem and God's people would be the "*driven away, lame, and afflicted*" (Micah 4:6). The Apostle Paul writes, "*27 but God chose the foolish things of the world, that he might put to shame them that are wise; and God chose the weak things of the world that he might put to shame the things that are strong*" (1 Corinthians 1:27). Much of God's work in the world of sinners goes against the preconceived ideas of man. Jesus would be a lowly and meek king rather than a boisterous warlord (Matthew 11:29). Those in Christ's kingdom would be just like him in lowliness and meekness (Romans 8:29 and 1 Corinthians 11:1).

"*3 Therefore will he give them up, until the time that she who travels has brought forth: then the residue of his brethren shall return unto the children of Israel*" **(5:3).**

God gives up his people to captivity, pain and anguish for the sins they have committed against him. This shall last until his people have produced the ruler that is to be born in Bethlehem. At that time the "*residue of his brethren shall return*" to God through the ruler from Bethlehem. All men will have the opportunity of being forgiven of sins and restored to God's favor.

It is fascinating to follow the overall picture that is fully developed in the book of Revelation. Israel would suffer pain as a woman giving birth to a child while in Assyrian and Babylonian captivity. God would preserve his people as they figuratively give birth to his beloved Son who would reign as king over God's kingdom the church. Revelation chapter 12 gives details to Micah's words in relationship to the church that belongs to Jesus. Satan would cause great pain for Christ's church yet the remnant would survive by the help of God. The point is that there will always be men and women who will serve God no matter what happens in this life.

This elect remnant will never permit Satan to pull them away from the faith.

"**4** *And he shall stand, and shall feed his flock in the strength of Jehovah, in the majesty of the name of Jehovah his God: and they shall abide; for now shall he be great unto the ends of the earth*" **(5:4).**

Jesus, unlike the wicked shepherds of Israel and Judah, would feed his people "*in the strength of Jehovah.*" The "*strength of Jehovah*" is none other than justice, equity, and righteousness that the rulers of Micah's day discarded for their personal pleasures (see Romans 1:16). Jesus would latter say, "14 *I am the good shepherd; and I know mine own, and mine own know me...* 16 *and other sheep I have, which are not of this fold: them also I must bring, and they shall hear my voice: and they shall become one flock, one shepherd*" (John 10:14-16). As shepherd of the flock of sheep the Lord cares, tends, feeds, and supplies all the necessities of life for those under his care.

"**5** *And this man shall be our peace. When the Assyrian shall come into our land, and when he shall tread in our palaces, then shall we raise against him seven shepherds, and eight principal men.* **6** *And they shall waste the land of Assyria with the sword, and the land of Nimrod in the entrances thereof: and he shall deliver us from the Assyrian, when he comes into our land, and when he treads within our border*" **(5:5-6).**

"*This man*" is the Christ, ruler, and one who shall "*feed his flock.*" "*Peace*" between God and man through the forgiveness of sins will be possible through "*this man*" (Jeremiah 31:31-40 and Matthew 26:26).

There was no Assyrian threat during the days of the Christ. The Assyrian under consideration must be a figurative use of the nation to indicate all the enemies of God. The sword used by the people of God in his kingdom will be the word of God rather than carnal weapons against those we disagree with (compare Micah 4:3 to Ephesians 6:17). The kingdom of God, the true elect remnant of Jacob, would never be defeated (see Isaiah 33:20; Daniel 2:44-45; Zechariah 4:7; Matthew 16:18 and Revelation 20:7-10).

"**7** *And the remnant of Jacob shall be in the midst of many peoples as dew from Jehovah, as showers upon the grass, that tarry not for man, nor wait for the sons of men*" **(5:7).**

Those who comprise Zion (i.e., the kingdom of God / church) are now depicted as "*the remnant of Jacob.*" Micah speaks of the transgressions of Jacob at chapter 1:5. The name "*Jacob*" is used throughout the Bible to represent the elect remnant of God for all times (see Isaiah 59:20-22; Amos 7:5 and Romans 11:26-27). To be identified as Israel or Jacob was to wear a highly royal and priest like name that set you apart as holy from the rest of the sinful world. Many in Samaria and Jerusalem; however, were not living up to their name and divine expectation. God promises that a "*remnant*" would come out of Jacob that would serve him in faithfulness.

God's remnant people are compared to "*dew and showers upon the grass.*" The grass is sustained and grows by the water and even so the nations shall be spiritually sustained and grow by the waters of life that the disciple of Christ shall distribute through teaching (Matthew 28:18-20) (19n).

"**8** *And the remnant of Jacob shall be among the nations, in the midst of many peoples, as a lion among the beasts of the forest, as a young lion among the flocks of sheep; who, if he go through, treads down and tears in pieces, and there is none to deliver.* **9** *Let your hand be lifted up above your adversaries, and let all your enemies be cut off*" **(5:8-9).**

Micah, and other authors of both the Old and New Testaments, paint a picture of Christ's church being indestructible. There is no great mountain of persecution or afflictions that will have the power to take away the elect's faith or place in the kingdom of God (see Zechariah 4:7). Though the world of wicked men comes against the saints they will not prevail because God is with those who love him (see Revelation 20:7-10).

"*Jacob shall be among the nations*" as "***lions*** *among the beast of the forest.*" There is no beast (wicked man of the societies the saints live in) that has the power to spiritually kill the saints of God. Jesus said, "*28 and be not afraid of them that kill the body but are not able to kill the soul: but rather fear him who is able to destroy both soul and body in hell*" (Matthew 10:28). The picture is one of great power that the elect saints of God possess (15a). To know that no wicked man or even Satan himself has the power to destroy my soul is a source of great confidence. The Apostle Paul said, "*What then shall we say to these things? If God is for us, who can be against us?*" (Romans 8:31)

Vengeance against the Wicked (5:10-15)

"**10** *And it shall come to pass in that day, said Jehovah, that I will cut off your horses out of the midst of you, and will destroy your chariots:* **11** *and I will cut off the cities of your land, and will throw down all your strongholds*" **(5:10-11).**

Micah's attention is now turned to the wicked. David said, "*Some trust in chariots, and some in horses; But we will make mention of the name of Jehovah our God*" (Psalms 20:7). All things such as horses, chariots, cities, and strongholds that the people put their trust in would be cut off. "*That day*" is a time of a spiritual kingdom under the ruler from Bethlehem (Jesus and the church). Again, remember that the weapons of the people from the spiritual kingdom shall be spiritual rather than carnal (see also 2 Corinthians 10:4).

"**12** *And I will cut off witchcrafts out of your hand; and you shall have no more soothsayers:* **13** *and I will cut off your graven images and your pillars out of the midst of you; and you shall no more worship the work of your hands;* **14** *and I will pluck up your Asherim out of the midst of you; and I will destroy your cities.* **15** *And I will execute vengeance in anger and wrath upon the nations which hearkened not*" **(5:12-15).**

These verses indicate how deep Israel and Judah's rebellion to Jehovah God had gone. The land was occupied by those who practiced witchcraft and soothsaying (i.e., false prophets who claimed to be able to tell what was to happen in the future without the aid of God). The land had graven images and pillars (i.e., obelisks) erected within. The Asherim (i.e., an Assyrian goddess who was supposedly wife to the war god Asir, the national god of Assyria) was also found in the land. The people who claimed to belong to God even worshipped these images which were the "*work of their own hands*."

When the kingdom of God is established and the ruler from Bethlehem reigns supreme God will cut off all these wicked works of man's hands through vengeance, anger, and wrath. All such things affront the name of Jehovah God and are only representatives of people who will not hear and obey his ways. Again, the true elect of God in his kingdom will be impervious to these wicked vises because of their great love for the Lord.

One may read such verses and conclude that God desires his eternal kingdom to crush all who stand in its way. The crusaders took on the same mentality as the Muslims in this respect. But again, we must remember that the text clearly points to a spiritual kingdom. Micah's ruler born in Bethlehem that would be king over God's Zion kingdom is the Christ of Matthew 2:5-6. Jesus said that his kingdom was not of this world (John 18:36). The great battle under consideration is a spiritual battle. The book of Revelation explains this spiritual battle against Satan in great detail.

Man has the power, through Jesus Christ, to destroy the strongholds of sin within the mind and rid them forever through the blood of Jesus Christ (Ephesians 1:7). Unfortunately, the Jews of Jesus' day misunderstood the words of the prophets regarding Christ. Preconceived ideas of a physical kingdom with a war lord as king filled the minds of the ignorant as they waited for Rome to be destroyed (see Matthew 11:16-19 and 17:10-13) (11h).

Questions over Micah Chapter 5

1. Who would come from Bethlehem that has no origins?

2. What will this everlasting person do for Israel?

3. Who is the "*remnant of Jacob?*"

4. Discuss how the saints will be comprised of an indestructible kingdom?

5. What will God cut off and destroy?

MICAH CHAPTER 6

Synopsis

God calls the nations of Israel and Judah to a court room for trial. The Lord demands to know, after taking such good care of his people, why they would live in rebellion. The people respond with sarcasm. Israel does not believe that there is any pleasing God. The wicked people of God believed that even if they gave their first-born child God would want more. The people's hearts had grown weary with serving God and they do not give God much time or thought. God; however, would not give up on his people. The Lord struck them with a "*grievous wound*" that was designed to cause them to open their eyes to their sins (Micah 6:12). The Lord wanted his people to serve him because of a true love for their creator.

Application

The Apostle Paul said that it would be, "*through many tribulations we must enter into the kingdom of God*" (Acts 14:22). Man does not feel a great need to call out to God for help unless distress in his life. Often times God causes that distress by inflicting grievous wounds for our transgressions (Micah 6:12). When people feel the sting of their sin through trouble or great guilt they call out to God for help (Acts 2:21). It is at that point that people make vows to God so that their grievous wound of trouble would be relieved (Psalms 22:25; 50:14; 56:12; 65:1 etc) (19w). Though the time of chastisement is very grievous it yields peaceable fruit of righteousness (see Hebrews 12:11). God knows exactly what kind of spiritual medicine we all need so that we may "*do justly, love kindness, and walk humbly*" with him (Micah 6:8).

Micah 6

Israel is called upon to state their case against Jehovah (6:1-8)

"**1** *Hear now what Jehovah said: Arise, contend before the mountains, and let the hills hear your voice.* **2** *Hear, O you mountains, Jehovah's controversy, and you enduring foundations of the earth; for Jehovah has a controversy with his people, and he will contend with Israel*" **(6:1-2).**

Micah has examined the sinful condition of both Israel and Judah. He has prophetically revealed a day in the future when Christ's kingdom would be established and people would be righteous and just. The prophet of God now returns to his present day. Currently God has a "*controversy with his people*" (see also Hosea 4:1-6).

The Lord has presented a case against Israel in the previous chapters. Israel and Judah are guilty of practicing idolatry (Micah 1:7), participating in prostitution (Micah 1:7), devising evil (Micah 2:1), taking the necessities of life from the poor out of their greed (Micah 2:8-10), and loving the lies of false prophets hired for strong drink (Micah 2:11). Furthermore Israel and Judah's rulers, prophets, and priests did not seek out righteousness and justice (Micah chapter 3). The mountains stand as a jury to hear the accusations of God against Israel and now they are called upon to hear Israel's testimony against Jehovah.

"**3** *O my people, what have I done unto you? And wherein have I wearied you? Testify against me.* **4** *For I brought you up out of the land of Egypt, and redeemed you out of the house of bondage; and I sent before you Moses, Aaron, and Miriam*" **(6:3-4).**

The Lord asks his rebellious people questions regarding why they are disobedient to his laws. God has done so much for his people yet they repay him with disrespect and irreverent service. Was it so terrible to be taken such good care of that their relationship could be compared to a mother eagle taking care of her young (see Exodus 19:4)? Furthermore, when Israel was in Egyptian bondage God sent them a deliverer, Moses, to care for them in their time of great distress. Both Aaron and Miriam were sent by God to the Hebrews as well for their betterment. By God's great power he removed his people out of bondage and gave them laws at Sinai. Was this cause for their disobedience?

"**5** *O my people, remember now what Balak king of Moab devised, and what Balaam the son of Beor answered him; remember from Shittim unto Gilgal, that you may know the righteous acts of Jehovah*" **(6:5).**

The Lord makes requests that his people "*remember*" the days when Balak hired Balaam to curse Israel. By the providential care of God; however, Balaam actually blessed the nation (Numbers 22-24). The event of Balaam has greater significance to history than many may believe. We find Balaam's name associated with false teachers in the New Testament (see 2 Peter 2:15; Jude 1:11 and Revelation 2:14). God divinely protected his people from Balak and Balaam.

God calls upon his people to remember Shittim (the place of rest before crossing the Jordan and entering Canaan) "*unto Gilgal*" (the place they first camped after crossing the Jordan and entering Canaan). The "*righteous acts of Jehovah*" are to be remembered. God cared for Israel. He provided them safe passing through the Jordan River. He protected them and cared for them throughout all their journeys. God fulfilled his promises. How can a protected and cared for people act so violently against a loving Father?

Remembering those who do great good and those who do great harm to the church today would certainly be scriptural. To forget the deeds of a false teacher is to later accept his teachings. Micah has no problem calling out the names of those who tried to destroy the people of God in times past (24d).

"**6** *Wherewith shall I come before Jehovah, and bow myself before the high God? Shall I come before him with burnt-offerings, with calves a year old?* **7** *Will Jehovah be pleased with thousands of rams, or with ten thousands of rivers of oil? Shall I give my first-born for my transgression, the fruit of my body for the sin of my soul?*" **(6:6-7)**

The ungrateful nation that accuses Jehovah God of wearying them asks, "In what way shall we gain your favor God... have we not made your ordained sacrifices?" Furthermore the people sarcastically say, "*Shall I give my first-born for my sins*?" The people are responding to God's controversy by saying that there is no pleasing God. The greatest mistake any child can make is to perform duties for the sole sake of appeasing a parent. When there is no true love and concern for the ones who love you then acts of obedience will only be done because one "has to do them." When an individual does what he or she is told because they respect, honor, and love the lawgiver there is a healthier relationship. Israel's sacrifices were not done out of a spirit of love and adoration for God and his will but out of a spirit of ritualistic habit. Faith was not a part of their lives. Sacrifices were made because this is what they had always been taught to do by those who went on before them. Sacrifices were what they were supposed to do rather than what they wanted to do.

As long as a spirit of unbelief continued the Lord said that they could bow before him, offer thousands of rams, and thousands of rivers of oil yet he will not accept them. The Bible has many passages where these same concepts are taught (see 1 Samuel 15:22ff; Psalms 51:16-17; Hosea 6:5-6; Amos 5:4-6 and Matthew 22:37-38).

When David's sin with Bathsheba was exposed by Samuel the king acknowledged and confessed his great error. David writes a beautiful prayer about this situation at Psalms 51. The king shamefully acknowledges his error and pours his heart out to God in prayer. David writes, "**16** *for you will not delight in sacrifice, or I would give it; you will not be pleased with a burnt offering.* **17** *the sacrifices of God are a* broken spirit; a broken and contrite heart, O God, you will not despise" (Psalms 51:16-17). David knew exactly what God expected. There was no redo of the situation. There was no amount of animals to sacrifice upon the altar of burnt offering that would restore the life and family of Uriah and Bathsheba. God's request for all who violate his laws and ruin the lives of other people is to have a "*broken and contrite heart.*" "A contrite heart or spirit is one in which the natural pride and self-sufficiency have been completely humbled by the consciousness of guilt (see Isaiah 66:1-2 and Jeremiah 23:29)" (ISBE volume 1; page 767-768). The prophet Isaiah said, "15 *For thus said the high and lofty One that inhabits eternity, whose name is Holy: I dwell in the high and holy place, with him also that is of a contrite and humble spirit, to revive the spirit of the humble, and to revive the heart of the contrite*" (Isaiah 57:15). God's word has the power to humble the hardened hearts of sin (see Jeremiah 23:29 and 2 Corinthians 2:14-16). David's heart was truly broken over his sin. The Apostle Paul said, "10 *Godly sorrow works repentance unto a salvation that brings no regret*" (2 Corinthians 7:10) (19q). God wants people to do his divine will and have sorrow when they fail.

"**8** *He has showed you, O man, what is good; and what does God require of you, but to do justly, and to love kindness, and to walk humbly with your God*?" **(6:8).**

While Israel asks, "*wherewith shall I come before Jehovah...*" the Lord answers, "I have showed you in times past what I want but you have not listened." The more the people heard from the prophets the more they erroneously concluded that they could not please God.

What does God want to see from his people? God requires that his people, "*do justly, and to love kindness, and to walk humbly with your God*" (13b). God requires a "*just*" conduct toward all men. Israel had cheated and even taken what was not rightfully theirs from the poor (see Amos 2:6-7; 4:1; 5:11-12; 8:4 and Micah 6:11). Rather than loving "*kindness*" many of the people of God were downright ugly to their fellow man by murdering them and taking their inheritance. Their love was oppression rather than a spirit of kindness and willingness to help others (see Hosea 12:7). Lastly, God demands that his people "*walk humbly with your God.*" The Lord's will is that the Christian would walk in righteousness and justice because of a fear and love for him. Man ought to be humble rather than filled with a spirit that expresses itself by saying, "there is no pleasing God." We ought to all know our lowly place before the creator of heaven and earth.

The Lord has delivered a law that is intended to help people. When we submit ourselves to this law and ask the Lord to forgive us when we violate it we display a heavenly attitude that God desires (see Isaiah 57:15 and Matthew 5:1ff).

God's Charge against His People (6:9-16)

"*9 The voice of Jehovah cries unto the city, and the man of wisdom will see your name: hear the rod, and who has appointed it. 10 Are there yet treasures of wickedness in the house of the wicked, and a scant measure that is abominable? 11 Shall I be pure with wicked balances, and with a bag of deceitful weights?*" **(6:9-11)**

Micah calls upon the people to hear the words and accusations made against them because they are the words of Jehovah! Those who are "*of wisdom*" will certainly hear and heed. The wise thing for all humanity to do is to give ear and heed to the Lord's will. The child who has had the rod of correction upon him will certainly respond with humble and loving obedience (see Proverbs 29:15). The foolish; however, will grow harder the more he or she is stroked.

The injustice of God's people is thoroughly exposed! The wealthy gain their treasures by false balances and deceitful weights (see also Hosea 12:7 and Amos 8:5). The balance and weights of the swindlers was illegally calibrated to read less than the actual weight of grain that the poor brought to the market so that the merchant bought more than what he paid for. As long as people cheated others with deceitful balances they could not be "*pure*" (see also 1 Peter 1:22).

"**12** *For the rich men thereof are full of violence, and the inhabitants thereof have spoken lies, and their tongue is deceitful in their mouth.* **13** *Therefore I also have smitten you with **a grievous wound**; I have made you desolate because of your sins.* **14** *You shall eat, but not be satisfied; and your humiliation shall be in the midst of you: and you shall put away, but shall not save; and that which you save will I give up to the sword.* **15** *You shall sow, but shall not reap; you shall tread the olives, but shall not be anointed with oil; and the vintage, but shall not drink the wine.* **16** *For the statutes of Omri are kept, and all the works of the house of Ahab, and you walk in their counsels; that I may make you a desolation, and the inhabitants thereof a hissing: and you shall bear the reproach of my people*" **(6:12-16).**

The rich used balances of deceit to cheat the poor and needy out of their labor and produce. Their dishonest business is identified as "*violence and sin.*" God's judgment against the wicked cheaters of his people was to punish them with a "*grievous wound*" (i.e., exile to the Assyrians and captivity to Babylon). Micah had earlier revealed the people's "*incurable wound*" to be their sin that goes unrecognized and practiced without sorrow or shame (see Micah 1:8-9). God will turn the lives of the rich wicked upside down. They will eat but not be full. The wicked will try to save money yet the thief will take it by force. They will work hard for oil and wine yet they will have nothing. There are always consequences to sin in man's life. God's method of changing man's heart is to chastise them with great trouble so that they may be humble and repent.

God gives another reason for striking them with "*a grievous wound*" (i.e., chastisement for their error). Not only did Israel and Judah practice idolatry (Micah 1:7), participate in prostitution (Micah 1:7), devise evil (Micah 2:1), take the necessities of life from the poor out of their greed (Micah 2:8-10), and love the lies of false prophets hired for strong drink (Micah 2:11) but they also followed the laws of "*Omri and Ahab.*" Jeremiah had called out the names of the wicked and false prophets of his days as now does Micah (see Jeremiah 28:1-4). The apostles also called out the names of the troubling teachers of their days (1 Timothy

1:20 and 2 Timothy 2:17-18) (24d). The works of Omri are depicted as more wicked than any other king before him (1 Kings 16:25-26). Omri and his son Ahab did evil in that they cast off the Lord for Baal (see 1 Kings 16:29-33). The rulers of Israel and Judah were more faithful at following the statutes of idolatry than the laws of God. Such perversions of life are viewed by God's prophets as going backward rather than forward (see Jeremiah 7:24). The jealousy of the Lord was running high and the wicked were to pay a high price for their rebellion. Many today cast off the teachings of God for the teachings of one's own imagination and bring the same jealousy and anger of God into their lives.

Questions over Micah Chapter 6

1. Who has a controversy with the people of God?

2. How would God's people remember the righteous acts of God?

3. What does God require of his people?

4. Why has God struck his people with a grievous wound?

5. What will happen to all the people's labor?

6. What laws did God's people follow?

MICAH CHAPTER 7

Synopsis

Micah and the elect speak at chapter 7. God has laid his case against his people and they have responded in perplexity. While the unjust are perplexed the righteous say, "*Woe is me*" (Micah 7:1). While the wicked are sarcastic with God the righteous say, "*I will bear the indignation of Jehovah, because I have sinned against him*" (Micah 7:9). There is no perplexity on the part of God's elect because they know exactly what they have done wrong. As we compare the two minds of the elect and the wicked we see how that great trouble will come to each man's house (Micah 7:5-6 and Matthew 10:21, 35-36). God's truths will divide the wicked from the righteous and there will be trouble. The righteous will be wowed by God's truths and he will feed, correct, and guide them all the days of their lives (Micah 7:14).

Application

Micah chapter 7 is an explanation of Paul's words to the Romans at Romans 3 and 11. The Apostle Paul explains that all, even the elect of God, sin (Romans 3:23). Micah illustrates the difference; however, between the unspiritual minded sinner and the man that loves God yet falls in sin from time to time. The elect remnant of God will "*bear the indignation*" of the Lord by way of chastisement for their sins yet will he rise (Micah 7:9). God's true elect will see the "*marvelous things*" of God's truths and lay prostrate before God in humility (see Micah 7:15).

The merciful, kind, and loving heavenly Father will forgive the elect because they seek it with a contrite heart (see 1 John 1:8-10).

Micah 7

Lamentations over the woeful spiritual state of God's People (7:1-6)

"**1** *Woe is me! For I am as when they have gathered the summer fruits, as the grape gleanings of the vintage: there is no cluster to eat; my soul desires the first-ripe fig*" **(7:1).**

The one who says, "*Woe is me*" cannot be God due to the use of the pronoun "*I*" at Micah 7:7. It cannot be the people as a whole either due to their rejection of God. The speaker of chapter seven is Micah and the elect remnant of God.

2 *The godly man is perished out of the earth, and there is none upright among men: they all lie in wait for blood; they hunt every man his brother with a net.* **3** *Their hands are upon that which is evil to do it diligently; the prince asks, and the judge is ready for a reward; and the great man, he utters the evil desire of his soul: thus they weave it together*" **(7:2-3).**

The spiritual or godly man is said to be "*perished out of the earth.*" Every direction one looks there is nothing but cheaters, murderers, covetous, prostitutes, idolaters, and wicked men in general. The hands of all men appear to be very diligent at working evil. Not only are the common people in the kingdom wicked but all the rulers, judges, and princes are diligent to practice sin as well. The common man, great man, and rulers of the people weave their wickedness together as they plot and plan their sinful deeds to take advantage of others (see Micah 2:1-2 and Hosea 7:3).

The hands of men are "*diligently*" fixed on evil rather than righteousness. The prince and judge are motivated by covetous desires and the great man by the "*evil desire of his soul.*" Where is the diligence and desire to follow God's ways (Philippians 3:14; 2 Timothy 2:15 and Hebrews 11:6)?

"**4** *The best of them is as a briar; the most upright is worse than a thorn hedge: the day of your watchmen, even your visitation, is come; now shall be their perplexity*" **(7:4)**.

The watchmen of old had spiritual foresight and warned of a day when God's people would be visited with judgment due to their wicked deeds (see Ezekiel 3:17). When God looks upon his people he sees that the best of them "*is as a briar*" in that he wounds all those who come his way. The "*upright is worse than a thorn hedge.*" The people's sin of injustice and idolatry has caused them to be a threat to others physical and spiritual well being.

When God judges them by heavy chastisement the people would be "*perplexed.*" The people of God continued to make their sacrifices to God (see Micah 6:6-7 and Malachi 1:6-10). The people thought all was well with God (see Micah 3:11). When people get so far removed from loving and serving God they lose sight of truth and divine expectations (see Leviticus 11:44 and 1 Peter 1:15-16). People become delusional in that they think that performing a few religious acts gets them in good with God. The Lord demands that man give him their whole heart (Proverbs 23:26). Jesus tells us that many on the Day of Judgment will be just as perplexed because they did not follow all of God's will (Matthew 7:22) (Consider Jeremiah 2:22; 4:22; 13:22 and 16:10) (38).

"**5** *Trust not in a neighbor; put no confidence in a friend; keep the doors of your mouth from her that lies in your bosom.* **6** *For the son dishonors the father, the daughter rises up against her mother, the daughter-in-law against her mother-in-law; a man's enemies are the men of his own house*" **(7:5-6)**.

When family rises up against family the days are truly evil (see Micah 2:3 and Amos 5:13). Micah reveals the people's deep seated wickedness in that wives and husbands cannot trust each other and family members in general are turning against each other as enemies (see Matthew 10:21-23). It is God's word that causes the conflicts within a home. When truth is heard it causes different reactions in different people. While some love the truth and are brought to sorrow and repentance others are angered (see Revelation 16:8-11). The affects of the truth will often pit one family member against another and this was the work of Jesus so that the chaff would be separated from the wheat (see Matthew 10:34-39).

The Remnant Speaks (7:7-13)

"**7** *But as for me, I will look unto Jehovah; I will wait for the God of my salvation: my God will hear me*" **(7:7)**.

The general population of Israel and Judah is like briar and thorn bushes. They reap the rewards of a life of sin. There are others among the briars and thorns that are different. These people care nothing for idolatry, covetousness, prostitution, or listening and paying false prophets to speak lies to them. The people under consideration are the remnant of Jacob. These people; however, are not completely without blame. The difference between the remnant and the briar people is that the remnants recognizes their sins and are ashamed.

Micah chapter 7:7-13 gives a detailed picture of the life of those who would truly be God's remnant in Zion for evermore. God's remnant waits faithfully and confidently for the complete fulfillment of the Lord's promises. While waiting they make sinful mistakes yet they acknowledge those errors and vow to do better in the coming days (15a).

"**8** *Rejoice not against me, O my enemy: when I fall, I shall arise; when I sit in darkness, Jehovah will be a light unto me*" **(7:8)**.

The wicked witnesses the rise and fall of the righteous as they sin and are chastised. The admonition to those who would laugh at the hardships and tribulation of the righteous is to take care in what they do. The righteous is not like the wicked in that they will pick themselves up in Godly sorrow and repentance and be restored to full strength. David said, "**24** *though the righteous fall he shall not be utterly cast down; for Jehovah upholds him with his hand*" (Psalms 37:24).

"**9** *I will bear the indignation of Jehovah, because I have sinned against him, until he plead my cause, and execute judgment for me: he will bring me forth to the light, and I shall behold his righteousness.* **10** *Then mine enemy shall see it, and shame shall cover her who said unto me, Where is Jehovah your God? Mine eyes shall see my desire upon her; now shall she be trodden down as the mire of the streets*" **(7:9-10).**

The remnant of God "*bear the indignation of Jehovah*" when they sin. There are no excuses made for their folly only broken hearted sorrow. The chastising hand of God is heavy upon them yet their hearts are even more inclined to acknowledge their sins and repent (17d). David wrote, "*4 for day and night your hand was heavy upon me: my moisture was changed as with the drought of summer. 5 I acknowledged my sin unto you and mine iniquity did I not hide: I said, I will confess my transgressions unto Jehovah; and you forgave the iniquity of my sin*" (Psalms 32:4-5). When the contrite sinner makes such petitions to God he is forgiven and restored to the light of God's special care and promises. They are like the publican who beat his breast saying, "*Lord be merciful to me a sinner*" (Luke 18:13).

The enemies of righteousness draw the wrong conclusions when they witness the saints of God suffering. They conclude that God either doesn't exist or he doesn't care seeing that his people suffer. Those who draw such erroneous conclusions will be "*trodden down as the mire in the street.*" Micah had earlier spoken of this event at chapter 4:11-13. The remnant of God will thresh the wicked like lions in that they will soundly defeat all their wicked vices and temptations through the blood of Jesus Christ. Micah previously wrote, "*8 And the remnant of Jacob shall be among the nations, in the midst of many peoples, as a lion among the beasts of the forest, as a young lion among the flocks of sheep; who, if he go through, treads down and tears in pieces, and there is none to deliver*" (Micah 5:8).

"**11** *A day for building your walls! In that day shall the decree be far removed.* **12** *In that day shall they come unto you from Assyria and the* *cities of Egypt, and from Egypt even to the River, and from sea to sea, and from mountain to mountain.* **13** *Yet shall the land be desolate because of them that dwell therein, for the fruit of their doings"* **(7:11-13).**

There appears to be a double meaning here much like as found at 2 Samuel 7:12ff. God had promised David that through his seed his kingdom would be established for ever. This was obtained first through Solomon but later through the Christ. Likewise, God would bring back his people from Babylonian captivity under Zerubbabel to rebuild the walls around the city of Jerusalem. Spiritually speaking, God would be a *"wall of fire round about"* the elect to protect them from the wicked (Zechariah 2:5). Though the Babylonians had torn down the walls of Jerusalem God would be that spiritual wall that would never be destroyed (see 2 Chronicles 36:19 and Nehemiah 1:3). God is a powerful refuge to those who put their trust and faith in him. David said, *"Show your marvelous lovingkindness, O you that save by your right hand them that take refuge in you from those that rise up against them"* (Psalms 17:7) (3bb).

"In that day" is a time that refers to the Messianic age when men and women shall come to the kingdom of God from all parts of the world (see Zechariah 2:11; 3:10; 8:20-23 and Revelation 15:4 and 21:24). While the world of sinful men wallows in a land of desolation *"in that day"* the people of God shall be blessed.

The Faithful Remnant lift up their Voice in Prayer (7:14-20)

"**14** *Feed your people with your rod, the flock of your heritage, which dwell solitarily, in the forest in the midst of Carmel: let them feed in Bashan and Gilead, as in the days of old, as in the days of your coming forth out of the land of Egypt will I show unto them marvelous things"* **(7:14-15).**

God is the shepherd of his *"flock"* (i.e., the elect remnant of Jacob) (see also Psalms 80:1). The shepherd of the flock used a staff or rod to correct, protect, care, comfort, and guide the sheep. God's word is likened unto a shepherd's staff that comforts, corrects, and protects (see Psalms 2:9 and Revelation 2:27) (10e). The staff or rod of truth would guide the remnant of God's elect into the solitary forest away from the world of wickedness. God would show his flock of believers "*marvelous things*" from his divine revelation. The true people of God enjoy looking into the truths of the gospel and they are wowed by the things they see and learn. These awe inspiring sights came in the days of the Lord and his apostles by way of miracles and teaching (see Mark 10:24; Luke 2:47; 9:43 and Acts 2:7-12). When officers that were commanded to apprehend Jesus came back empty handed the chief priest and Pharisees asked what had happened. The officers said, "*Never man so spoke*" (John 7:46). We are all equally wowed as we study through the scriptures. We connect the dots of learning to find truths that bring us to our knees and at times we even tear up as our flaws are exposed. Truly the Word of God is wonderful!

"**16** *The nations shall see and be ashamed of all their might; they shall lay their hand upon their mouth; their ears shall be deaf.* **17** *They shall lick the dust like a serpent; like crawling things of the earth they shall come trembling out of their close places; they shall come with fear unto Jehovah our God, and shall be afraid because of you*" **(7:16-17)**.

David explains at Psalms 72:9 that remote tribes of men shall "*lick the dust*" of the future king of Zion. To "*lick the dust*" is "a symbolic expression of deep humiliation, abasement, or grief" (ISBE volume 1, page 998). The idiom illustrates a great degree of fear and subjection from one to another. David envisions the world of men bowing before the king of Zion in great fear rendering tribute and gifts as they worship and serve him (see also Isaiah 49:23). The right minded peoples of the world will come before the Lord God Almighty trembling at his very authorized words (see Isaiah 66:1-2). They will be "*ashamed*" of all their efforts to suppress his truths.

When Philip preached at Samaria and performed mighty works by the power of God all those who followed after Simon the sorcerer dropped what they were doing and followed God (Acts 8:6-10). God's power would be demonstrated in ways that no one could refute. When the power was displayed men obeyed the gospel message (see Mark 16:20).

"**18** *Who is a God like unto you, that pardons iniquity, and passes over the transgression of the remnant of his heritage? He retains not his anger for ever, because he delights in lovingkindness.* **19** *He will again have compassion upon us; he will tread our iniquities under foot; and you will cast all their sins into the depths of the sea*" **(7:18-19).**

Micah and the elect remnant of Jacob ask, "*Who is a God like you*?" God "*pardons*" the sins of the remnant because they humbly seek out his blessings (1 John 1:8-10). Though the remnant must bear the indignation of God through chastisement it will not last for ever (see Micah 7:9-10). The answer to the question regarding the identity of God is that there is no comparing him to anyone or thing (see Isaiah 46:9-10). God is slow to anger, kind, and compassionate. He forgives those who seek out forgiveness. The sins of the remnant are removed so far out of God's sight that they are likened unto being tossed to the bottom of the sea. Can anyone determine the distance between the east and west? The Psalmist tells us that "12 *As far as the east is from the west, So far has he removed our transgressions from us*" (Psalms 103:12). The idea is that forgiven sins are out of God's sight (Jeremiah 31:34).

"**20** *You will perform the truth to Jacob, and the lovingkindness to Abraham, which you have sworn unto our fathers from the days of old*" **(7:20).**

"*Jacob*" is the elect remnant that shall remain faithful to God throughout their lives (see notes at Micah 2:2; 4:2 and 5:7-8). "*The truth*" that shall be performed to "*Jacob*" will be forgiving their sins as though they were tossed to the bottom of the ocean (see above). To forgive people of their sins is identified as the "*lovingkindness to Abraham*." God had promised Abraham that through his seed would come a blessing to all nations. The New Testament book of Galatians identifies that promise as the forgiveness of sins through the blood of Jesus Christ (see Genesis 12:1-4 compared to Galatians 3:8, 16). God would fulfill his promises and illustrate his kindness by forgiving man's sins through his beloved son Jesus (see Isaiah 53).

Questions over Micah Chapter 7

1. Compare and contrast Micah 7:2 with Romans 3:9-23.

2. What is the "*best*" of the people compared to?

3. Compare and contrast Micah 7:6 to Matthew 10:34-36.

4. Why would Micah, and all others, bear the indignation of God?

5. What makes God so unique? (see Micah 7:18-20)

Nahum

Robertson's Notes

Bible Book 34 of 66

"Jehovah is a jealous God and avenges; Jehovah avenges and is full of wrath; Jehovah takes vengeance on his adversaries, and he reserves wrath for his enemies"

(Nahum 1:2)

Introduction

Assyria was once an oasis for merchants due to trade and commerce (Nahum 2:8). Those whom she conquered provided a rich storehouse of wealth (Nahum 2:9). There was not one nation that had not been touched by her cruelty (Nahum 3:19). God used the wicked nature of the Assyrians to accomplish his end of stroking Israel with the rod of correction (Isaiah 10:5). The time of Assyria's punishment, however, had now come (Isaiah 10:24-27). The once feared, wealthy, and strong nation was about to be reduced to trembling knees and pale faces for the fear they would now experience at the hands of Jehovah God (cf. Nahum 2:10).

The sovereignty of Jehovah God is depicted in Nahum. The Lord God Almighty has authority and power over all creation. The seas, storms, lush vegetative areas, mountains, "*yea the world and all that dwell therein*" are subject to his will (Nahum 1:3-5). Jehovah called upon Assyria to fortify her walls and build up her military might for the day of her judgment (cf. Nahum 1:12; 3:14). Though Assyria did all within her power to resist she was going to be reduced to ashes. The sovereignty of Jehovah would be directed at Assyria in the form of the Babylonians. Babylon would crush Assyria with the horrendous bloodshed that Assyria had used on her enemies. Nahum records, "2 *The noise of the whip, and the noise of the rattling of wheels, and prancing horses, and bounding chariots,* 3 *the horseman mounting, and the flashing sword, and the glittering spear, and a multitude of slain, and a great heap of corpses, and there is no end of the bodies; they stumble upon their bodies*" (Nahum 3:2-3). Jehovah would use Babylon as his "*battle axe*" (Jeremiah 51:20) to "*dash in pieces*" (Nahum 2:1) Assyria. When the Lord was finished with Babylon, he would punish her for her wickedness as well (see Jeremiah 51:24).

Those who do not bow their heads or knees to the sovereign will of God shall be eternally punished. Jehovah God is the Lord of all flesh (Jeremiah 32:27). All will one day bow their stubborn knees before him (Philippians 2:10). Jesus will judge each man and woman by his deeds he has done (Rev. 20:12-13). God's word will be the standard by which man is judged (John 12:48). Let all of humanity recognize the sovereign rule of Jehovah God and submit to his precepts before it is everlasting too late.

Nahum the Prophet

Nahum is known as the Elkoshite (one from Elkosh of which nothing is known). Nahum received a divine vision that revealed a condemning judgment against Nineveh and Assyria (Nahum 3:7, 18).

Date

Two points of interest help us date the book of Nahum. First is the fall of Noamon. Noamon was the sacred name for the great city of Thebes in Egypt. Isaiah had prophesied that the Egyptians would be carried away as captives by the Assyrians (Isaiah 20:3-4). Assurbanipal, king of Assyria, reigned from 669 to 627 BC. Assurbanipal gained control over Egypt during the year 667 BC (probably the date of Noamon's (Thebes) fall. Nineveh fell in 612 BC to Nabopolassar of Babylon. Nahum's prophecy describes the destruction and carrying away of the powerful Egyptian Thebes as a past event (Nahum 3:8ff) and the destruction of Nineveh as a future event (Nahum 1:1; 3:7). The date of the book is, therefore, between 667 and 612 BC.

Theme

Nineveh and the Assyrians will fall because of their wickedness. The spiritual whoredom of Assyria is defined by their devising evil against Jehovah (Nahum 1:11), giving wicked council (Nahum 1:11), worshipping graven images (Nahum 1:14), being vile (Nahum 1:14), being full of lies (Nahum 3:1), forcibly seizing and taking property that did not belong to them (Nahum 3:1), and practicing witchcraft (Nahum 3:4).

NAHUM CHAPTER 1

Synopsis

Assyria has served her purpose of chastising and punishing Israel (see Isaiah 10:5-6). Assyria, though used by God as a rod in his hand, would not escape the Lord's judgments. The universal and timeless sovereignty of God demands that he expect the same lawfulness in the lives of the people of Assyria as he does with the people of Israel (see Jeremiah 32:27). Nineveh has been examined by God and found to be *"vile"* (Nahum 1:14). Nothing but the wrath of God awaited these vile people. God promised to afflict his people no more with Assyria (Nahum 1:12). This was good news to Israel and cause for vows of repentance to be made (Nahum 1:15).

Application

God was angry with Assyria because she exchanged his divine glory for idols. The Assyrians walked by their own design rather than fearing God and obeying him. God's fierce wrath would be upon them and they would bother Israel no more. God continues to work the same way today. God chastens sinners so that they may be moved to repent through their vows. God is like a father to his people. A father is angered when his children err. The Lord punishes the children and they vow to do better. Likewise, Christians today are God's children (see Galatians 3:27-28). When we experience trouble due to our sins we vow, through repentance, to never perform those deeds again (see Luke 13:1-5).

Nahum 1

The Awesome Power of Jehovah (1:1-8)

"**1** *The burden of Nineveh. The book of the vision of Nahum the Elkoshite*" **(1:1).**

The word "*burden*" is also translated "oracle" in the ASV footnotes which means, "A command or revelation from God" (AHD 873). The LXX translates the Hebrew word to Greek as *lemma* meaning "anything received or income" (LS 471) (LXX 1106). Nahum divinely 'received' revelation regarding Nineveh that he refers to as a "*book of vision*." Ezekiel (Ezekiel 1:1), Daniel (Daniel 4:5), and Zechariah (Zechariah chapters 8-14) all saw divine visions too. Though God had regard for Nineveh during the days of Jonah he now prepares to unload his wrath for their sins. Jonah would have loved to have the duty of Nahum; however, it was a different time that proved to be a different test for the prophet of God.

"**2** *Jehovah is a jealous God and avenges; Jehovah avenges and is full of wrath; Jehovah takes vengeance on his adversaries, and he reserves wrath for his enemies*" **(1:2).**

The very mention of Nineveh conjures up the identity of Jehovah being a jealous, vengeful, and wrathful God who is against those whose deeds are wicked. The enemies of God will feel the full brunt of his divine anger. God is likened unto a husband to Israel. The enemy is likened unto one who is flirting with a husband's wife. Jehovah is jealous and thereby unleashes his wrath and vengeance upon the enemies.

"**3** *Jehovah is slow to anger, and great in power, and will by no means clear the guilty: Jehovah has his way in the whirlwind and in the storm, and the clouds are the dust of his feet*" **(1:3).**

God's true character is peace and patience. Nahum tells us that he is "*slow to anger.*" Once God's anger is stirred however it is intense. If an unruly people are feeling the brunt of his wrath it is because they have exhausted his patience and longsuffering characteristics. Those guilty of God's wrath will experience the power of divine condemnation and judgment. The guilty will by no means be cleared of their offences while in a state of rebellion.

"**4** *He rebukes the sea, and makes it dry, and dries up all the rivers: Bashan languishes and Carmel; and the flower of Lebanon languishes*" **(1:4).**

The power of God is revealed over nature itself. God has the power to rebuke the sea and rivers and they would be dry. Jesus at one time rebuked the stormy Sea of Galilee and it was calm (see Matthew 8:23-27). God exercised control over the animal kingdom as well (Numbers 22:21ff and Jonah 2:10) (3a).

Bashan, Carmel, and Lebanon were places where great soils and lush vegetation existed; however, they too were subject to God's universal sovereignty. Though the sea and rivers be places of water and Bashan, Carmel, and Lebanon places of lush vegetation they were all subject to God's indignation.

"**5** *The mountains quake at him, and the hills melt; and the earth is up heaved at his presence, yea, the world, and all that dwell therein*" **(1:5).**

The fierce power of God is depicted even in the inanimate objects of this earth such as the mountains, hills, and earth. If the lifeless things tremble at the thought of God's anger then the live things will certainly fear. Nahum tells us that at the presence of God the "*world and all that dwell therein*" trembles. God's fierce indignation against wickedness will come to be known and experienced by all. The wise shall take notice and act appropriately by acknowledging and repenting of their sins while the fool scoffs.

"**6** *Who can stand before his indignation? And who can abide in the fierceness of his anger? His wrath is poured out like fire, and the rocks are broken asunder by him*" **(1:6).**

Nahum challenges all creation to find one man that can successfully stand before Jehovah's wrath and not be affected. Shall the mountains, mighty rivers, or seas stand before God and not be affected? The answer is obvious. No man or part of nature can withstand the might of God. When God's fiery wrath is poured out not one shall stand.

"**7** *Jehovah is good, a stronghold in the day of trouble; and* **he knows them that take refuge in him**. **8** *But with an over-running flood he will make a full end of her place, and will pursue his enemies into darkness*" **(1:7-8).**

God is often viewed as a father figure throughout the scriptures (see Jeremiah 31:9-20 for an excellent illustration). One may read through the Old Testament and concluded that God was very often angry at his people. Fathers today are sometimes viewed as angry. Dads are very loving and they care much for their children; however, when rules are broken he is not happy. God loves and cares for his children yet he has very high expectations for them (see Psalms 82:6 and John 10:34).

Those who recognize the awesome power of God will run to him in subjection seeking refuge from the storms of life. Those who do recognize the power and sovereign rule of God are known by him. To be known of God is to be in good standing (Galatians 4:9). The Apostle Paul writes, "19 *Howbeit the firm foundation of God stands, having this seal, the Lord knows them that are his: and let every one that names the name of the Lord depart from unrighteousness*" (2 Timothy 2:19). There is an elect remnant that will serve the Lord come what may in this life and God knows who they are.

Those not known of God will not escape his wrath. Like a flood that runs through a town destroying everything in its path so Jehovah will end the place of the sinful. Isaiah speaks of a flood that shall wash away the wicked at chapter 28:17. One's approach to divine truth distinguishes the righteous from the unrighteous.

The Destruction of Assyria Foretold (1:9-13)

"*9 What do you devise against Jehovah? He will make a full end; affliction shall not rise up the second time. 10 For entangled like thorns, and drunken as with their drink, they are consumed utterly as dry stubble*" **(1:9-10).**

The oracle against Nineveh and Assyria is the subject of Nahum (see Nahum 1:1; 3:7, 18). The prophet poses a question to the Assyrians. "*What do you devise against Jehovah?*" There will be nothing the Assyrian can do to defeat Jehovah's purpose and wrath against them. They are mere men and he is God. Jehovah shall defeat them so soundly that they shall not rise up a second time.

God used the wicked ways of Assyria to accomplish the punishment of an evil Israel (Isaiah 10:5-6). When God's purpose was achieved; i.e., sinful Israel was soundly defeated and exiled by the Assyrians, then the Lord would thoroughly punish the wicked nation of Assyria (Isaiah 10:24ff). Again, not only does the sovereignty of God extend to the natural elements of the world but also the kingdoms of men (see Daniel 2:21). God is in complete control (3a).

Assyria was deluded with the wine of pride much like Judah (see Jeremiah 13:9-14), Edom (Jeremiah 49:16 and Obadiah 1:3), and the Babylonians (Habakkuk 2:5) (38). Assyria considered their fortresses and army to be as impenetrable as a thorny hedge.

"*11 There is one gone forth out of you, that devises evil against Jehovah, that counsels wickedness. 12 Thus said Jehovah: though they be in full strength, and likewise many, even so shall they be cut down, and he shall pass away. Though I have afflicted you, I will afflict you no more. 13 And now will I break his yoke from off you, and will burst your bonds in sunder*" **(1:11-13).**

The "*one gone forth out of you*" (i.e., Assyria) is either a king or the entire spirit of rebellion displayed on the part of the Assyrians toward God. The Lord would strike Assyria in their days of "*full strength*" and take them down. The flesh of men has no power to challenge the God of all creation. God has brought Assyria up to a mighty nation that he may "*afflicted*" Israel due to their sin. Assyria; however, will never rise again to afflict the people of God. Daniel tells us that God raises nations and brings them down to fit his sovereign design (Daniel 2:21).

God pronounces death to Assyria and thanksgiving for Judah (1:14-15)

"*14 And Jehovah has given commandment concerning you, that no more of your name be sown: out of the house of your gods will I cut off the graven image and the molten image; I will make your grave; for you are vile*" **(1:14).**

Ashur, the god of war, was the national god of the Assyrians. The Assyrians also worshiped Ishtar, the wife of Ashur and goddess of love, war, and protection. Other Assyrian deities were Nergal the god of war and plagues, Aruru the goddess and midwife of the gods, and Geshtue whose blood was supposedly used by the god Mami to create man. Jehovah God will prove these deities to be nothing more than a figment of man's imagination when he cuts their images and houses down with absolutely no resistance.

Assyria will have a grave prepared for them because they were "*vile.*" The word "*vile*" is a strong word of wickedness and depravity. The Assyrian's vile spirit is in association with their deities. The pagans worshipped their deities by way of erecting temples, sacrifice, prayer, and burning incense. These practices were an abomination to God because it gave credit of man's blessings to one other than the Lord.

The Apostle Paul, speaking about the Gentiles' idolatry, said that they "*23 **changed** the glory of the incorruptible God for the likeness of an image of corruptible man, and of birds, and four-footed beasts, and creeping things*" (Romans 1:23). Man exchanges the glory of God when he worships by any other means than what the Lord authorizes by his divine pattern. The word "*change*" (Greek *hellazan*) means "to change, altar, or transform" (Moulton 16). Liddell and Scott define the Greek word as "another, one besides, or any one else" (LS 38). When people look to the creation of this world and conclude that God is yet replace his divine glory and revelation for their own human opinions they are identified as idolaters. The prophet Samuel said, "23 *for rebellion is as the sin of witchcraft, and stubbornness is as idolatry and teraphim*" (1 Samuel 15:23). Those who rebel against the commandments of God act as though there is "another" god besides him. The "glory" of man is being created in the image of God and being directed by his divine will. We bring glory to God by obeying his commandments (John 15:1-11 and Revelation 14:7). If we follow our own religious opinions and teachings we have exchanged God's glory for another. To exchange this glory for another is a great perversion. Anyone who performs religions acts based upon their opinions, personal beliefs, or convictions and demands that others follow suit apart from the authorized words of God are due his divine wrath (55a).

"**15** *Behold, upon the mountains the feet of him that brings good tidings, that publishes peace! Keep your feasts, O Judah, perform your vows; for the wicked one shall no more pass through you; he is utterly cut off*" **(1:15).**

Nahum now addresses Judah (the Southern kingdom). Judah is to rejoice because Assyria is soundly defeated by Jehovah God. The Lord will soon send a messenger to the people of Judah to reveal this good news! Let Judah rejoice with feasts and vows of thanksgiving. Though the event has not taken place it is sure to come. One comes bringing glory to the name of God by preaching the good news that God gives him. Isaiah and the Apostle Paul use these same words to reveal that there is good news that comes from God and will relieve man of his sins (see Isaiah 52:7 and Romans 10:15). When people suffer for their sins they are moved to call out to God for help and relief (Acts 2:21). The good news is that God will relieve those who humble themselves to him in obedience.

God's chastisement by way of Assyria has had its desired affect upon Judah. The wicked and vile idolaters have made the lives of God's people miserable (see Nahum 2:9). God has chastened his people with his indignation (see Micah 7:9). The people, in their distress, call out to God for help and make their *"vows"* to him. Their vow is that they will not sin any longer due to the great trouble it has brought to their lives (Psalms 22:25; 50:14; 56:12; 65:1 etc) (19w).

The psalmist writes, "13 *I will come into your house with burnt offerings; I will perform my vows to you,* 14 *that which my lips uttered and my mouth promised when I was in trouble.* 15 *I will offer to you burnt offerings of fattened animals, with the smoke of the sacrifice of rams; I will make an offering of bulls and goats. Selah*" (Psalms 66:13-15). The psalmist acknowledges God's miraculous deliverance at a time of *"trouble."* Though the days were difficult, as men and circumstances appear to have the upper hand and all seemed to be lost, the psalmist remained faithful and God blessed him. God's deliverance is cause for great praise and sacrifices of burnt offerings. During the days of great trouble vows were made in relationship to deliverance. The psalmist, in the midst of his intense heart breaking ordeal, vowed to follow God's laws stringently if only he would deliver him out of this great trouble and calamity. God has delivered and the vows will now be performed.

There is a fascinating study in God's word regarding making vows to God at times of great calamity in life. There are many who find themselves in trouble, make great promises to God to turn their lives around and serve him in faithfulness if only he would deliver them, and yet seldom do many follow through with these vows. The smoker tells God that if only he can survive lung cancer he will stop smoking yet many often go right back to it after being healed. Far too many times Christians make similar vows to God yet fail to follow through with their promise to God.

All divine laws demand perfect obedience (see Galatians 3:10 and Romans 2:13). God's expectation for his people of every age is perfect obedience (Galatians 3:10; Matthew 5:48; 1 Peter 1:15-16; 1 John 4:17

etc.). The vow or oath made on these occasions was to follow God's laws. Christians today make a similar oath and vow at baptism (see Romans 6:1-11). We purpose to put as much distance as humanly possible between us and sin. We put to death the old man of sin and serve God with renewed interest of love and faith (Romans 6:1-11 and Colossians 3:5-11) (19w). As a punished child tells his parents that he is sorry for his wrong deed and will do better in the future even so God demands that we equally act through repentance. We must come to understand, like the child at home, that if God's laws are broken there will be consequences. When we come to this understanding there will be hope for our eternal justification.

Questions over Nahum Chapter 1

1. Who does Nahum write an oracle against?

2. What characteristic of God is under consideration at Nahum 1:1-8?

3. True or False: God's patience has run out with Nineveh.

4. Why did God intend to make a grave for the people of Nineveh?

5. Who brings glad tidings to Judah?

NAHUM CHAPTER 2

Synopsis

Assyria's power had run its designed course. She was to learn that she was just as subject to God's laws as every other nations of the world throughout history. Nineveh's wickedness would be judged and God would punish her by the strong arm of Babylon.

Application

No matter how strong and mighty a nation may get they pale in comparison to Jehovah God. No matter how wise a man may be he stands ignorant before God. No matter a man's wealth he stands impoverished before God. Nahum paints a picture of the universal and eternal sovereignty of Jehovah God in our minds. God raised Nineveh (Assyria) to great power to punish Israel and now he brings them down for their own wickedness. There is no powerful nation or wise people that will outwit or defeat God in battle. Jeremiah writes, "23 *Let not the wise man glory in his wisdom neither let the mighty man glory in his might, let not the rich man glory in his riches;* 24 *but let him that glories glory in this, that he has understanding, and knows me, that I am Jehovah who exercises lovingkindness, justice, and righteousness, in the earth: for in these things I delight, said the Lord*" (Jeremiah 9:23-24).

Nahum 2

The Destruction of Assyria and Nineveh (2:1-7)

"**1** *He that dashes in pieces is come up against you: keep the fortress, watch the way, make your loins strong, fortify your power mightily.* **2** *For Jehovah restores the excellence of Jacob, as the excellence of Israel; for the emptier has emptied them out, and destroyed their vine branches*" **(2:1-2).**

Nahum reveals the punishment to Assyria for her wickedness. "*He that dashes in pieces*" is none other than the Babylonians. The prophet Jeremiah wrote, "**7** *Babylon has been a golden cup in Jehovah's hand, that made all the earth drunken: the nations have drunk of her wine; therefore the nations are mad...* **20** *You are my battle-axe and weapons of war: and with you will I break in pieces the nations; and with you will I destroy kingdoms*" (Jeremiah 51:7, 20). God would use Babylon to destroy Assyria and there would be no amount of fortification that would stop them. Assyria had "*emptied*" out the land of Israel and now they were to be punished for their "*vile*" ways (see Nahum 1:14). The Lord would "*restore the excellence of Jacob*" by way of Babylon.

"**3** *The shield of his mighty men is made red, the valiant men are in scarlet: the chariots flash with steel in the day of his preparation, and the cypress spears are brandished.* **4** *The chariots rage in the streets; they rush to and fro in the broad ways: the appearance of them is like torches; they run like the lightnings*" **(2:3-4).**

Nahum speaks of Babylonian infantry and chariots as though they have already entered the city of Nineveh to destroy. The scene is one of chaos. Chariots are rushing in every direction as quick as lightning and the people of Nineveh are falling dead.

"**5** *He remembers his nobles: they stumble in their march; they make haste to the wall thereof, and the mantelet is prepared.* **6** *The gates of the rivers are opened, and the palace is dissolved.* **7** *And it is decreed: she is uncovered, she is carried away; and her handmaids moan as with the voice of doves, beating upon their breasts*" **(2:5-7).**

While Nineveh is under siege she remembers her noble fighters and summons them to the wall of the city. The men, likely out of terror, stumble to their positions on the wall. Meanwhile, the Babylonian "*mantelets*" are moving toward the city (i.e., towers that sat on four wheels used by a siege army to allow their men protection from arrows and a climbing device [or in some cases battering ram]) over the cities walls). Once the wall is breached a flood of Babylonian infantry men will engulf the city. The city is finished and the women moan in despair.

"**8** *But Nineveh has been from of old like a pool of water: yet they flee away. Stand, stand, they cry; but none looks back*" **(2:8).**

During days past Nineveh was like an oasis in the desert where men would gladly come. Now; however, people flee in terror. The military general commands that the men stay and fight yet the men of war flee and "*none looks back.*"

"**9** *Take the spoil of silver, take the spoil of gold; for there is no end of the store, the glory of all goodly furniture.* **10** *She is empty, and void, and waste; and the heart melts, and the knees smite together, and anguish is in all loins, and the faces of them all are waxed pale*" **(2:9-10).**

Fascinatingly, Assyria is identified as the "*wicked one*" at Nahum 1:15. The words "*wicked one*" is *Belial* in the Hebrew language meaning "worthlessness" (AG 139). The International Standard Bible Encyclopedia adds, "In Jewish apocalyptic writing (Book of Jubilees, Ascension of Isaiah, Sibylline Oracles) the name was used to describe Satan or the antichrist. Paul used the word in this sense in 2 Corinthians 6:15. The 'man of lawlessness' in 2 Thessalonians 2:3 is probably an equivalent of the 'man of Belial.'" (ISBE volume 1 page 454). Unger's Bible Dictionary adds, "Worthlessness or wickedness. Belial is often used in the KJV as if it were a proper name, but beyond question it should not be regarded in the OT as such, its meaning being 'worthlessness,' and hence 'recklessness, lawlessness.' The expression 'son' or 'man of Belial' must be understood as meaning simply a worthless, lawless fellow (Deuteronomy 13:13; KJV; Judges 19:22; 20:13). In the NT the term appears (in the best manuscripts) in the form of Belias, and not Belial, as given in the KJV. The term, as used in 2 Corinthians 6:15, is generally understood as applied to Satan, as the personification of all that is bad" (The New Unger's Bible Dictionary 154).

There is a principle established here that is brought out further in the book of Revelation. Assyria was a wicked force that fell as do all wicked men and nations throughout history (see Revelation 18:4). The wicked live their lives in pride and arrogance as though they fear nothing yet when God's heavy hand falls upon them they are terrified. The wicked are plundered of their treasures and brought very low (see Revelation 18:12-16). Nineveh's inhabitants, once strong and fierce, now are those whose knees knock together in fear and their faces are pale due to their terror (see Isaiah 29:22 and Revelation 6:8). The Babylonians have divinely arrived on the world scene and they are mightier than Assyria.

"**11** *Where is the den of the lions, and the feeding-place of the young lions, where the lion and the lioness walked, the lion's whelp, and none made them afraid?* **12** *The lion did tear in pieces enough for his whelps, and strangled for his lionesses, and filled his caves with prey, and his dens with ravin*" **(2:11-12).**

The Lord poses a question to the Assyrians. Where are all your mighty men who without conscience destroyed and devoured other nations as though they were lions in the forest? Where has the fear of your enemies gone? The Assyrians devoured and took captive many yet wherein is their strength now? The point is clear, yes they were and are mighty yet standing against the Lord they are melted away and exposed as nothing in comparison to the great God.

"**13** *Behold, I am against you, said Jehovah of hosts, and I will burn her chariots in the smoke, and the sword shall devour your young lions; and I will cut off your prey from the earth, and the voice of your messengers shall no more be heard*" **(2:13).**

The Assyrian was once the rod of correction in the hands of Jehovah God yet now they are reduced to a shaken, destroyed, and plundered nation. The psalmist speaks of the great warlike disposition of God when he wrote, "9 *He makes wars to cease unto the end of the earth; he breaks the bow, and cuts the spear in sunder; he burns the chariots in the fire*" (Psalms 46:9). Assyria hears the most fearsome words a man or nation could ever hear. God said, "*Behold, I am against you.*"

Questions over Nahum Chapter 2

1. Who would God use to destroy Assyria?

2. True or False: There would be no amount of fortification to save Assyria.

3. Describe the scene within the city of Nineveh as their enemies invade (Nahum 2:1-8).

4. Compare Nahum 2:9-10 with Revelation 18:4, 12-16.

NAHUM CHAPTER 3

Synopsis

The Lord makes a fearful statement to the people of Nineveh when he said, "Behold, I am against you" (Nahum 3:5). Nahum sees fearful visions of Nineveh being laid siege to and chariots roaring down the streets. The prophet of God sees dead bodies everywhere and the people of Nineveh fleeing for their lives. God calls upon Nineveh to make all the preparations they wanted for the coming siege. Nothing; however, would help them. God had determined to destroy her for the wickedness she practiced. The world will clap their hands in joy at the fall of this once fearsome and mighty nation.

Application

There is no hope when attempting to live the life of the rich, famous and mighty. People that seek the very things that God warns us against fight against God's divine will. There is no winning in such situations. The worldly man appears to have so much now yet it is God that has the final say so regarding man's eternal soul. May we never permit a few moments of pleasure on this earth take the place of our hope of eternal heaven with God (see Hebrews 11:24-26).

Nahum 3

The aftermath of Nineveh's Fall (3:1-7)

"**1** *Woe to the bloody city! It is all full of lies and rapine; the prey departs not*" **(3:1)**.

Nineveh was bloody due to its siege and destruction by Babylon. Babylon was divinely ordained to lay siege to the city because she was full of "*lies and rapine*" (i.e., Forcible seizure of another's property). Nineveh and Assyria were no different than anyone else when it came to being punished for sin.

"**2** *The noise of the whip, and the noise of the rattling of wheels, and prancing horses, and bounding chariots,* **3** *the horseman mounting, and the flashing sword, and the glittering spear, and a multitude of slain, and a great heap of corpses, and there is no end of the bodies; they stumble upon their bodies*" **(3:2-3)**.

Nahum gives a graphic vision of the aftermath of Babylon's invasion. The battle has been fought and the picture is one of complete destruction for Nineveh and its inhabitants. The Babylonians can scarcely walk or ride through the streets due to the amount of dead bodies.

"**4** *because of the multitude of the whoredoms of the well-favored harlot, the mistress of witchcrafts, that sells nations through her whoredoms, and families through her witchcrafts*" **(3:4)**.

Nahum, once again, explains that God is just in destroying Nineveh. There would be, as there are today, those who would see the destruction and claim that God must not be a loving and caring God to do such things. The prophet of God is careful to explain that Nineveh was getting her just reward for her "*multitude of whoredoms and witchcrafts.*" Nineveh gained the favor of many and then did them harm as a woman of whoredoms would do. She did harm not just to nations but to individual families as well (see Revelation 17:1-2 and 18:3).

The Old Testament reveals three cities designated as harlots. First, there is Nineveh (here Nahum 3:1, 4). Second, there is Tyre (Isaiah 23:15-17) and third there is Babylon (Isaiah 47:5ff). The world was enamored with all three of these cities due to their wealth, fame, and might. Though the world saw these wealthy, famous, and strong cities as honorable God saw their pride and arrogance (see Isaiah 23:8-9). The Apostle John similarly depicts the temptation of worldliness in the form of Babylon at Revelation 18. Though the whole world is enamored with riches, fame, and power such entities of this life fall every generation. The only lasting commodity for man to pursue in this life is faith in God.

"*5 Behold, I am against you said Jehovah of hosts, and I will uncover your skirts upon your face; and I will show the nations your nakedness, and the kingdoms your shame. 6 And I will cast abominable filth upon you, and make you vile, and will set you as a gazing-stock. 7 And it shall come to pass, that all they that look upon you shall flee, and say, Nineveh is laid waste: who will bemoan her? Whence shall I seek comforters for you?*" **(3:5-7).**

"*Nakedness*" is always associated with "*shame*" and embarrassment throughout the scriptures (see Isaiah 47:3; Ezekiel 16:35ff; 22:6-12; 23:11; 23:28ff; Lamentations 1:4-9; Jeremiah 1:4-9; 1 Timothy 2:8-10 and Revelation 16:15) (25j). Babylon's thrashing of Assyria is depicted as shameful and embarrassing to them as would be the case if they were to walk about with their thighs uncovered.

The Lord would cause Assyria to be viewed as a filthy and vile people after they are defeated. No one will mourn over her fall. All the nations that were cruelly treated by her would now rejoice over her fall.

Nineveh's Doom (3:8-19)

"*8 Are you better than Noamon, that was situated among the rivers, that had the waters round about her; whose rampart was the sea, and her wall was of the sea? 9 Ethiopia and Egypt were her strength, and it was infinite; Put and Lubim were your helpers. 10 Yet was she carried away, she went into captivity; her young children also were dashed in pieces at the head of all the streets; and the cast lots for her honorable men, and all her great men were bound in chains*" **(3:8-10).**

Noamon was the sacred name for the great city of Thebes in Egypt. Isaiah had prophesied that the Egyptians would be carried away as captives by the Assyrians (Isaiah 20:3-4). Assurbanipal, king of Assyria, reigned from 669 to 627 BC. Assurbanipal gained control over Egypt during the year 667 BC (probably the date of Noamon's {Thebes} fall). Nineveh fell in 612 BC to Nabopolassar of Babylon.

A city that appeared to the world to be impenetrable was brought low. Surely pride comes before the fall (Proverbs 16:18). If Noamon did not stand against Jehovah then Nineveh surely will not. God is no respecter of persons. The sinner is condemned no matter if he is yellow, brown, black or white (consider Romans 3:9ff).

"**11** *You also shall be drunken; you shall be hid; you also shall seek a stronghold because of the enemy.* **12** *All your fortresses shall be like fig-trees with the first-ripe figs: if they be shaken, they fall into the mouth of the eater*" **(3:11-12).**

Nineveh shall drink the full cup of God's wrath and be drunk in destruction (see Isaiah 49:26 and Jeremiah 25:27). Though she seeks the help of others and fortifies her walls she will be shaken and devoured like a fig tree with ripe fruit.

"**13** *Behold, your people in the midst of you are women; the gates of your land are set wide open unto your enemies: the fire has devoured your bars*" **(3:13).**

Nineveh's defense would not be able to stand against the strong enemy because they will be as weak women. Jeremiah used this idea too (see Jeremiah 50:37 and 51:30). Their efforts to fortify the city amounted to having gates wide open for the enemy to devour them. There was no stopping God's wrath and no protecting themselves successfully. God is the Almighty and has no challengers!

"**14** *Draw water for the siege; strengthen your fortresses; go into the clay, and tread the mortar; make strong the brick-kiln.* **15** *There shall the* *fire devour you; the sword shall cut you off; it shall devour you like the canker-worm: make yourself many as the canker-worm; make yourself many as the locust"* **(3:14-15).**

Nahum calls upon Nineveh to do their vain work of gathering water and fortifying the walls of the city. Nineveh is called upon to gather up all the fighting men they can accumulate. No matter the preparations and accumulations their demise and destruction is inevitable. God has decreed their destruction and they will have no success fighting against him.

"**16** *You have multiplied your merchants above the stars of heaven: the canker-worm ravages and flees away.* **17** *Your princes are as the locusts, and your marshals as the swarms of grasshoppers, which encamp in the hedges in the cold day, but when the sun arises they flee away, and their place is not known where they are"* **(3:16-17).**

Though merchants gained wealth from Nineveh they are no where to be found in the time of her trouble. They have taken from the city and now leave it devoured. The governing and military leaders (i.e., princes and marshals) are numerous; however, they too flee the city due to fear (see Revelation 18:11-17).

"**18** *Your shepherds slumber, O king of Assyria; your nobles are at rest; your people are scattered upon the mountains, and there is none to gather them.* **19** *There is no assuaging of your hurt; your wound is grievous: all that hear the report of you clap their hands over you; for upon whom has not your wickedness passed continually?"* **(3:18-19).**

The political and military leaders are slumbering in death. The line of Assyrian kings is ended. The general people are scattered and there is no returning for them. The deep wound of Babylon is incurable. God chastises and punishes not only his own people for their sins but the nations of men. Micah spoke of God's chastening hand against a sinful Judah saying, "13 *Therefore I also have smitten you with* **a grievous wound**; *I have made you desolate because of your sins*" (Micah 6:13).

There would be no "*assuaging*" (i.e., to make less painful) Assyria's wound because of her sins. They will certainly die painful deaths!

The world had felt the cruel might of Assyria at one point or another. The nations that experienced the cruel and inhumane methods of war will not mourn over her death. Assyria exiled, impaled upon poles, flayed and made walls of their cities out of the skin of their enemies. These same subjects of Assyria's cruelty now rejoice over her fall.

Questions over Nahum Chapter 3

1. Describe, once again, the scene within the city of Nineveh from Nahum 3:1-3.

2. Compare and contrast Nahum 3:4 with Revelation 17:1-2 and 18:3-4.

3. What will people do when they look upon Nineveh?

4. Was there any hope for Assyria?

5. How do the nations respond to the fall of Assyria?

Habakkuk

Robertson's Notes

Bible Book 35 of 66

"The righteous shall live by his faith"

(Habakkuk 2:4)

Introduction

Habakkuk is a recorded conversation and prayer between the prophet and Jehovah God. Habakkuk does not understand why God has seemingly ignored his complaint against Judah (Habakkuk 1:2-3). The prophet complains that Judah continues in their violence, perversion, and causing the law to cease to exist (i.e., law is slacked) through a lack of use and knowledge and God seems to be indifferent (Habakkuk 1:4).

The Lord answers Habakkuk's complaint by revealing his universal sovereignty over all creation and the kingdoms of men. God will punish Judah by *"rising up the Chaldeans"* to great power (Habakkuk 1:6). The

Babylonians will be bitter, terrible, and dreadful (Habakkuk 1:6-7). Judah will not get away with her sin. Habakkuk is not completely satisfied with the answer God gives and has another complaint (Habakkuk 2:1). Habakkuk does not understand how a just and righteous God could use such a perverted nation as Babylon to accomplish his will. The Chaldeans were filled with pride (Habakkuk 1:9-11; 2:4 and Jeremiah 50:29-31) and worshipped the god of might (Habakkuk 1:10-11). Babylon killed, conquered, and plundered other nations for "*evil gain*" (Habakkuk 2:9). The prophet understands that God has "*established him* (Babylon) *for correction*" and "*ordained him for judgment*" (cf. Habakkuk 2:12). What remains a myth to Habakkuk is how a just God could look upon the perverseness of nations such as Babylon and actually use them to accomplish his ends. God answers the prophet by explaining his sovereign rein is over not only animals, rocks, and people but also the kingdoms of men. All things are at God's disposal to punish the wicked and reward the faithful. Babylon was not chosen by God to punish his people because they were good or evil but because of their place as a mighty nation. Babylon was no different than a river that God would use to chastise the wicked (see Habakkuk 3:7-9).

The Prophet and Date of Letter

The name Habakkuk means "embrace or embracer" (ISBE volume 2, page 583). There is absolutely no information about the background or person of Habakkuk recorded. A general date may be determined by readings such as Habakkuk 1:5-11. God would raise the Babylonians (Chaldeans) to great power. The language appears as though Babylon had already been involved in great warfare, conquering nations, and dreaded as Assyria once was. Nineveh, the great city of Assyria, was conquered by Babylon during the year 612 BC. Babylon's "rise" to power began at this point. Judah would not feel the actual brunt of Babylon until 605 BC (the year the Egyptians were defeated at Carchemish by Nebuchadnezzar - see Jeremiah 46:2; Daniel 1:1ff and 2 Chronicles 36:6ff). Though the Lord had pronounced the end of Judah during the days of Manasseh (i.e., 695 – 645 BC) it would not take place for another

40 years. An exact date is impossible to conclude from the facts that are given. The Date of Habakkuk is likely between the fall of Nineveh (i.e., 612 BC) and first attack on Judah (605 BC). Josiah would have been at the end of his reign as king of Judah (640 to 609 BC.). Judah experienced great peace and achieved many religious reforms under Josiah by the year 621 BC (2 Kings 22:1-23:25). Nebuchadnezzar's determination to put Egypt in subjugation eventually meant taking Judah. Habakkuk appears to be a contemporary with Zephaniah and Jeremiah.

The Righteous shall live by Faith

The final chapter of Habakkuk is a prayer on behalf of the prophet to his God. Habakkuk's conversation with God has proved beneficial. He now understands the sovereignty of God and prays a fervent prayer. He recognizes that God's will is to destroy the wicked of Judah with a nation of greater wickedness than they. His conclusion is one of the greatest statements of faith found in the Bible. Considering the sure calamity that is coming upon the people of God the prophet writes, "*Yet I will rejoice in Jehovah, I will joy in the God of my salvation. Jehovah, the Lord, is my strength; and he makes my feet like hinds feet, and will make me to walk upon my high places*" (Habakkuk 3:18-19). Faith in God and his promises is the very thing that keeps Christians today afloat in this wicked and godless society that we live in. Let the righteous today "*live by his faith*" and look to the eternal promises of God (Habakkuk 2:4 and Philippians 4:13). Forgiveness of sins will be our ticket into the eternal heavens with the Lord.

HABAKKUK CHAPTER 1

Synopsis

Habakkuk begins his oracle with an open discussion between the prophet and the Lord. Habakkuk has seen the violence and wickedness in Judah and wants to know why God does not act. The Lord answers his prophet explaining that he has seen and heard the wicked cries of Judah and has prepared the Chaldeans to violently punish them. Habakkuk then replies with confusion. The prophet wants to know how God can use such a wicked nation as Babylon to accomplish his objectives.

Application

A great lesson revealed is that Christians should be confident that God knows and sees all things that are occurring in this world. The Lord cares about his people and does not want to see any of them perish (see 2 Peter 3:9). The Lord will violently punish the wicked if necessary to move them to repentance. It is far better to suffer punishment now then to suffer it for all eternity.

Habakkuk 1

Habakkuk's Complaint (1:1-4)

"**1** *The burden which Habakkuk the prophet did see*" **(1:1)**

The book of Habakkuk begins much like Nahum. Nahum's vision was in relation to Nineveh and the fall of Assyria (see Nahum 1:1 and 3:18). The word "*burden*" is translated "oracle" in the ASV footnotes which means, "A command or revelation from God" (AHD 873). The LXX translates the Hebrew word to Greek as *lemma* meaning "anything received or income" (LS 471) (LXX 1106). Habakkuk divinely 'received' revelation regarding the destruction of Judah, Jerusalem, and Babylon.

"**2** *O Jehovah, how long shall I cry, and you will not hear? I cry out unto you of violence, and you will not save.* **3** *Why do you show me iniquity, and look upon perverseness? For destruction and violence are before me; and there is strife, and contention rises up*" **(1:2-3)**.

The prophet of God has been given divine revelation regarding the people of Judah. He has seen the violence, sin, and perverseness within the walls of Jerusalem. Habakkuk has seen the impending destruction and violence for the city and nation while strife and contention among fellow citizens goes on. People seem to be oblivious to the impending terror. Habakkuk calls out to God in deep anguish knowing what comes yet God is silent. The prophet sees the visions of terror and yet God does not communicate otherwise. Habakkuk is fearful that God has turned away from the people in apathy and there is no hope forevermore.

"**4** *Therefore the law is slacked, and justice does never go forth; for the wicked does compass about the righteous; therefore justice goes forth perverted*" **(1:4)**.

Habakkuk believes that God's silence is cause for the people's unlawfulness. God remains silent while sin, perversions of the flesh, cheating of the poor, and a lack of justice takes place in the city. Judah turned to their own ways in the days of God's silence and forgot his divine laws (see Jeremiah 7:24; 8:6 and 18:15). Seeing that they prospered and faced no immediate consequences they pressed forward in their sin.

God's Response to the prophet's Complaint (1:5-11)

"**5** *Behold you among the nations, and look, and wander marvelously; for I am working a work in your days, which you will not believe though it be told you.* **6** *For, lo, I raise up the Chaldeans, that bitter and hasty nation, that march through the breadth of the earth, to possess dwelling places that are not theirs*" **(1:5-6)**.

The Lord breaks his silence. He has not ignored the perversions and lawlessness of Judah or any other nation. God has potentially dealt with Judah as a father yet she would not turn to the Lord (see Jonah 4:2 and Nahum 1:3). While God is the Lord of patience, longsuffering, and kindness he is also the Lord of wrath (see Nahum 1:2ff). God is preparing to unleash his divine wrath in such a violent manner that even if told to people before it happened they would not believe it.

The Lord explains his plans to punish the wicked of Judah by way of the "*Chaldeans*" (see Jeremiah 51:20). The Chaldeans would "*rise*" to power by the sovereign will of God (see Daniel 2:20-21). There will be no success in resistance because God has raised the Babylonians to power for a divine mission (see Jeremiah 27:12). Babylon would move swiftly against her enemies and with a spirit of great bitterness and cruelty they will conquer nations.

"**7** *They are terrible and dreadful; their judgment and their dignity proceed from themselves.* **8** *Their horses also are swifter than leopards, and are more fierce than the evening wolves; and their horsemen press proudly on: yea, their horsemen come from far; they fly as an eagle that hastens to devour*" **(1:7-8)**.

Habakkuk reveals the fearsome might of Babylon. The dread of the Chaldeans will rest upon the world of wicked men. Pride moves their armies forward as they move like leopards and wolves across the land. These fierce men will swoop down like eagles and take their prey. The sound of their coming will strike terror in the hearts of all those who stand before them.

"**9** *They come all of them for violence; the set of their faces is forwards; and they gather captives as the sand.* **10** *Yea, he scoffs at kings, and princes are a derision unto him; he derides every stronghold; for he heaps up dust, and takes it.* **11** *Then shall he sweep by as a wind, and shall pass over, and be guilty, even he whose might is his god*" **(1:9-11)**.

The Chaldeans are a people of purpose. Their objective is to conquer lands by means of "*violence.*" Their pride and arrogance is depicted in their view of other nations, kings, and princes. Jeremiah wrote of Babylon saying, "*29 call together the archers against Babylon... for she has been proud against Jehovah, against the Holy One of Israel... Behold, I am against you, O you proud one, said the Lord, Jehovah of hosts...*" (Jeremiah 50:29-31). Babylon scoffs at all who would dare stand against them. They shall come throughout the world and make captives "*as the sand.*" The Chaldeans will leave devastation behind them as a terrible tornado or hurricane force wind. The Chaldeans are a people of war and their "*might is his god.*" Daniel said the same thing about the future Roman Empire (see Daniel 11:38).

Though the Lord raised them up by his sovereign will to accomplish punishment upon the wicked of Judah he will certainly not hold them guiltless (Jeremiah 51:7, 20-22). Babylon shall feel the full wrath of God when they are punished for their wicked ways (Jeremiah 25:12; 50:14 and 51:11). One may asks, "How can God raise up a nation to perform such wicked acts against other wicked people and then punish them?" Remember that God raised Pharaoh up the same way. The Lord never makes anyone do evil things (James 1:12ff). The Lord simply uses the hardened hearts and wicked character of men to accomplish his divine objectives (see Romans 9:17-24). The divine objective of the Chaldeans was to punish Judah for her grotesque sins.

Nothing but **violence** at the hands of a wrathful God awaited the hard hearted people of Judah (see Jeremiah 6:7; 13:22; 20:8; 51:35, 46 and Lamentations 2:6). God brings the Babylonians upon Judah like a plague. Those who would not seek truth (Jeremiah 5:1), obey (Jeremiah 6:16;

7:21-24; 13:10, 17 and 26:13), repent of their sins (Jeremiah 18:8 and 25:5), and amend their ways (Jeremiah 18:11 and 26:13) were doomed to death by sword, pestilence, and famine (Jeremiah 29:18). Judah's experience with the extreme violence of Babylon causes many to say, "16 *Woe unto us! For we have sinned*" (Lamentations 5:16).

Habakkuk Responds to God's Words of Violence at the hands of the Chaldeans (1:12-17)

"**12** *Are you not from everlasting, O Jehovah my God, my Holy One? We shall not die. O Jehovah, you have ordained him for judgment; and you, O Rock, have established him for correction*" **(1:12)**.

The prophet of God hears of the Lord's fierce anger and readiness to deal with Judah in extreme violence. Habakkuk addresses the Almighty God of heaven and earth with tones of great respect. Habakkuk's previous complaint was that God seemed to be apathetic to the wickedness that was transpiring in Judah. The Lord responds by telling the prophet that the Chaldeans who are a terrible, violent, and fierce enemy will devour them. Habakkuk now knows that God has "*ordained*" and "*established*" Babylon to judge and correct his people.

"**13** *You that are of purer eyes than to behold evil, and that can not look on perverseness, why then do you look at them that deal treacherously, and hold your peace when the wicked swallow up the man that is more righteous than he;* **14** *and make men as the fishes of the sea, as the creeping things, that have no ruler over them?*" **(1:13-14)**.

The book of Habakkuk reads as one having a conversation with God. The prophet has an honest question for God. Seeing that God is holy and cannot look upon evil and perverseness how is it that he can look and empower the wicked Chaldeans? How can God "*hold his peace*" while the Chaldeans unleash their cruel violence upon Judah and Jerusalem?

The Prophet's original petition was that God would not be passive about the wickedness in Judah. Jehovah answers saying that he will punish with one more wicked than Judah. Habakkuk understands that Judah's wickedness must be punished but the prophet does not understand how that God could punish the wicked with one more wicked than they are. How is it that God can deal and use such people and remain a just and righteous God?

"**15** *He takes up all of them with the angle, he catches them in his net, and gathers them in his drag: therefore he rejoices and is glad.* **16** *Therefore he sacrifices unto his net, and burns incense unto his drag; because by them his portion is fat, and his food plenteous.* **17** *Shall he therefore empty his net, and spare not to slay the nations continually?*" **(1:15-17).**

Habakkuk does not understand how God can raise such a terrible nation to punish and even destroy his own people. The prophet of God considers the heinous and violent work of the Chaldeans. They are like fishermen with nets that captures all that are before them and none escape (see also Jeremiah 16:16-17). Will the Lord walk with the wicked to vent his rage against his people in Judah and Jerusalem?

Questions over Habakkuk Chapter 1

1. What stood before the eyes of Habakkuk?

2. Who would God raise and ordain for correction?

3. How does Habakkuk describe this mighty nation that God raises to power?

4. Who is this mighty nation's god and what do they sacrifice to it?

5. What is so perplexing to Habakkuk?

HABAKKUK CHAPTER 2

Synopsis

Habakkuk receives his longed for answer regarding how God can use the wicked to accomplish his divine objectives. There is no overlap of the righteous and the wicked. God clearly outlines the character of those who would live in sin and those who will live by their faith. The Lord's use of the wicked to accomplish his objectives does not make those same wicked people acceptable in his sight. The wicked will be judged and by God's laws just as the righteous.

Application

The Apostle Paul writes, "19 *Howbeit the firm foundation of God stands having this seal, the Lord knows them that are his: and, Let every one that names the name of the Lord depart from unrighteousness*" (2 Timothy 2:19). God knows exactly who his elect people are and he knows the wicked. A wicked man would be a fool if he thought that just because God used him to accomplish a spiritual task that he may escape the judgment of the Lord. Likewise a righteous man is foolish to think that his current standing with God will provide an ever open door to heaven with no efforts. God's prophet is showed, by revelation, that God is no respecter of persons. Secondly, Habakkuk sees that God's use of the wicked does not justify them. Thirdly, Habakkuk sees that God knows his truly righteous and they're distinctly different than the ungodly of this world. The righteous will live by faith no matter the things they face in this life and God knows them.

Habakkuk 2

The Lord Clears up Habakkuk's Confusion (2:1-4)

"**1** *I will stand upon my watch, and set me upon the tower, and will look forth to see what he will speak with me, and what I shall answer concerning my complaint*" **(2:1).**

Habakkuk's complaint is that God seeks to correct his own people by the hands of the proud and wicked. The prophet wants to know how that a just and holy God can work through the wicked to achieve his divine objectives. Habakkuk determines to stand watch on the wall of the city for God to come with an answer to his complain and question.

"**2** *And Jehovah answered me, and said, Write the vision, and make it plain upon tablets, that he may run that reads it.* **3** *For the vision is yet for the appointed time, and it hastens toward the end, and shall not lie: though it tarry, wait for it; because it will surely come, it will not delay*" **(2:2-3).**

The Lord does not disappoint Habakkuk. He answers the prophet by telling him to write the revelation upon tables so that there may be a record of the news and so that they who read may run. The readers are running from the terror that was to befall Judah. God would use the violent Chaldeans to punish his own people. The prophecy is sure and will not fail.

"**4** *Behold, his soul is puffed up, it is not upright in him; but the righteous shall live by his faith*" **(2:4).**

The Lord acknowledges Habakkuk's complaint about the wickedness of the Chaldeans. The Lord knows of the proud and arrogant spirit of Babylon. The Lord also knows what constitutes the "*righteous.*" There is a distinct difference between the proud and righteous. The Apostle Paul quotes from Habakkuk 2:4 at Romans 1:17 and Galatians 3:11. Speaking of the gospel message Paul writes, "**17** *for therein is revealed a righteousness of God from faith unto faith: as it is written, But the righteous shall live by faith*" (Romans 1:17). The laws of God are designed to not only bring man to faith in the Lord but to "*live*" (obey) those laws. The "*righteous*" will do this very thing. "*Righteousness*" (Greek *dikaiosune*) is "regular, exact, rigid, right, lawful, just... real, genuine, or true" (LS 202). The gospel exposes the rigid, exact, right, and lawful ways of God for man to live (see Ephesians 4:1-4 and 1 Peter 1:15-16). One is considered righteous (right and lawful) when receiving the forgiveness of sins through their obedience of hearing, learning, gaining knowledge, repenting and being baptized. "*Living*" by faith infers obedience. Notice that "*living by faith*" is equivalent to "*faith unto faith*." The gospel reveals the rigid, exact, and lawful ways of God and man's part is to live it.

God knows that the righteous will live by faith whereas his divine laws are scoffed at by Babylon and many in Judah. Habakkuk wants to know how God can use the ungodly to punish his wicked people and God begins his answer to the prophet by examining the difference between the two. The author of Hebrews also quotes from Habakkuk 2:3-4 at 10:37-38. The Hebrew Christians were being treated terrible by the wicked as well yet God commanded them to hold on to their faith because it would not be long before Jesus would come into the world and their reward be realized. Likewise, the Chaldeans would surely come to the world of Judah and crush her. No matter what takes place; however, the "*righteous will live by faith*." This is a direct identity of the elect of God on this earth. God knows those who are truly his because no matter if the Chaldeans come to punish them or if it is the Assyrians these people will remain faithful to God (see 2 Timothy 2:19).

"**5** *Yea, moreover, wine is treacherous, a haughty man, that keeps not at home; who enlarges his desire as Sheol, and he is as death, and cannot be satisfied, but gathers unto him all nations, and heaps unto him all peoples.* **6** *Shall not all these take up a parable against him, and a* *taunting proverb against him, and say, Woe to him that increases that which is not his! How long? And that lades himself with pledges!* **7** *Shall they not rise up suddenly that shall bite you, and awake that shall vex you, and you shall be for booty unto them?* **8** *Because you have plundered many nations, all the remnant of the peoples shall plunder you, because of men's blood, and for the violence done to the land, to the city and to all that dwell therein"* **(2:5-8).**

The footnote of the ASV reads, "And also because his wine he is a haughty man." This speaks of the Chaldeans' drunkenness not with literal wine but pride. They have become dulled of reason by means of their pride gained through victory against the nations. Their *"might"* is their god and the greater they display their might the greater their faithfulness to their god. They are intoxicated with battle. They cannot stay at home and be satisfied with their solid state. The Chaldeans' power must be flexed and the world feel its dread. There is; however, only so much the world will take of this abuse. The nations will come up with a taunt or song that reveals the eventual downfall of Babylon. These conquered nations will soon rise and bite Babylon and take great spoil.

Before any or all lose heart in utter discouragement the Lord foretells of the end days of Chaldean oppression just as he foretold of the beginning. As God dealt with the erring Assyrians (Isaiah 10:24ff) even so will he deals in vengeance against the violence of the Chaldeans (see Jeremiah 25:12). Though Judah will be defeated and spend 70 years in captivity there will be a day when the Babylonian Empire, by the hands of the Medes and Persians, will *"end."*

"**9** *Woe to him that gets an evil gain for his house, that he may set his nest on high, that he may be delivered from the hand of evil!* **10** *You have devised shame to your house, by cutting off many peoples, and have sinned against your soul.* **11** *For the stone shall cry out of the wall, and the beam out of the timber shall answer it"* **(2:9-11).**

The second of five woes is pronounced upon Babylon. Babylon had gained great wealth by *"evil gain."* They were guilty of taking that which did not belong to them. Their imaginary god of might flexed its muscles and plundered nations for no just cause other than a greedy quest for world dominance. Before plundering took place; however, many innocent people died at the hands of the greedy and violent Chaldeans. The stones and timbers upon the mighty wall around the city of Babylon would cry out in anguish. This figuratively indicated the wicked way in which the wall was financed and built. *"The wall"* around Babylon was historic. Babylon's walls were approximately 60' thick, it had over 100 towers, and outside the wall was a moat that connected to the Euphrates River. God has not overlooked the Chaldeans' sinfulness but rather pronounces woes upon them.

"**12** *Woe to him that builds a town with blood, and establishes a city by iniquity!* **13** *Behold, is it not of Jehovah of hosts that the peoples labor for the fire, and the nations weary themselves for vanity?* **14** *For the earth shall be filled with the knowledge of the glory of Jehovah, as the waters cover the sea*" **(2:12-14)**.

This third woe is against those who would build towns with blood and establish cities by iniquity. When Babylon conquered lands there was much bloodshed. Their sin was compounded when they unlawfully took the people's lands. The conquered people would be enslaved to do the work of building cities and walls for the Babylonian Empire. The real purpose of life proves that such gains as property, slaves, and riches will help no one in the realm of eternity. Habakkuk writes, "*The nations weary themselves for vanity*" (25h). Jesus similarly said, "**26** *for what profit has a man, if he gets all the world with the loss of his life? Or what will a man give in exchange for his life?*" (Matthew 16:26 - Bible in Basic English). Too many today weary themselves for vanity as they seek desperately to attain this world's goods.

God says that when one's purpose is to gain riches by wicked means it is a vain exercise. The reason for that is because, "*the earth shall be filled with the knowledge of the glory of Jehovah...*" God's purpose for man is not to live violently in greed gaining from the world its goods but rather filling the earth with his knowledge. The prophets Isaiah and Zechariah made this same statement in relationship to the establishment of the Lord's church (see Isaiah 11:9 and Zechariah 14:8-9). The objective of the church of Jesus Christ will be to spread the gospel message throughout the whole world (see Matthew 28:18-20 and Ephesians 3:10) (12d).

"*15 Woe unto him that gives his neighbor drink, to you that adds venom, and makes him drunken also, that you may look on their nakedness! 16 You are filled with shame, and not glory: drink also, and be as one uncircumcised; the cup of Jehovah's right hand shall come round unto you, and foul shame shall be upon your glory. 17 For the violence done to Lebanon shall cover you, and the destruction of the beasts, which made them afraid; because of men's blood, and for the violence done to the land, to the city and to all that dwell therein*" **(2:15-17).**

The forth woe is pronounced against Babylon due to her spreading seeds of greed and empty promises of wealth. The wine of greed and power is hard for the mind of the world to reject. Jeremiah said that Babylon had given the nations her intoxicating wine and made them as mad as they (Jeremiah 51:7). Once the nations partook of the wine of greed their shame, as nakedness, was exposed for all to see. Another way of saying we see their true shameful colors.

The Lord reveals to Habakkuk Babylon's usurpation of the Lord's sovereignty over all creation (i.e., nature and kingdoms). Babylon had no second thoughts about changing the course of nature, kingdoms, and animals to fit their bidding. The Chaldeans murdered man and beast to set up their governments as they so desired.

"*18 What does the graven image profit, that the maker thereof has graven it; the molten image, even the* **teacher of lies**, *that he that fashions its form trusts therein, to make dumb idols? 19 Woe unto him that said to the wood, Awake; to the dumb stone, Arise!* **Shall this**

***teach?** Behold, it is overlaid with gold and silver, and there is no breath at all in the midst of it.* **20** *But Jehovah is in his holy temple: let all the earth keep silence before him"* **(2:18-20).**

The fifth and final woe is pronounced against Babylon due to her idolatrous ways (see also Jeremiah 50:38). Babylon's skilled craftsmen have made graven or molten images of wood overlaid with silver and gold. Though the image is lifeless it is a *"teacher of lies."* The worshipper believes and trusts in the *"dumb idol"* that has been made with hands. The reality of the matter is that the wood, silver, and gold cannot speak (i.e., it is dumb). The idol cannot really teach because there is no breath in it. People; however, treat these man made objects as though they were alive (see Isaiah 44:9-20).

Many today treat teachers of lies as though they were honorable and respectable men. Teachers of lies are no different than the dumb idol without a brain and those who listen and follow them are just as guilty as the foolish idolater of these OT times (24a). When the false teacher proclaims his opinions, personal convictions, and or conscience as truth they set themselves up as gods (see 2 Thessalonians 2:4). The grave error of this is that man, rocks, wood, and metal has created nothing and is not qualified to make up moral laws for man to follow. People may say that it is foolish to worship a piece of wood or stone; however, they are just as foolish for receiving the teachers of error today (55a).

Contrary to the dumb non-existent idol is Jehovah God. God is alive and well in his holy temple. All of earth (man, kingdoms, animals, rocks, mountains, trees, rivers and seas) are to be silent and reverence his holy and awesome authority (Zechariah 2:13). The measuring line has been set at meekness, righteousness, and truth (Isaiah 28:17). God alone has the authority to set the established pattern and he did so before the foundation of the world was made (Ephesians 1:3-7). Man is advised to *"silence"* his opinions, convictions, and preconceived ideas of religious service. All are advised to *"silence"* their wicked scattering of good people through wicked influences. Sinful behavior and language is commanded to cease! Only those who conform to the eternal image of Christ are permitted into the holy city of God.

Questions over Habakkuk Chapter 2

1. Why does the Apostle Paul quote from Habakkuk 2:4 at Romans 1:17?

2. List and discuss the five woes that God speaks against Babylon.

3. How would you define modern day idolatry?

HABAKKUK CHAPTER 3

Synopsis

The prophet of God has expressed his bewilderment over the Lord's use of the wicked to accomplish his holy objectives. Babylon would treat Judah violently as a means of punishment for their sins. Habakkuk expresses his concerns about this matter and waits for God's reply. The Lord gives his prophet a reply at chapter 2. Habakkuk is told that there is a clear distinction between the righteous and the wicked (Habakkuk 2:4). The wicked are known of God and nothing but woe awaits them. The answer is complete and we now read the prophet's response to God's words through this prayer. Habakkuk is amazed at the enlightenment of God's universal and sovereign authority over all nations of men.

Application

Habakkuk's prayer helps us understand God's universal authority and sovereignty over the nations and creation. God has at his disposal both the physical elements of this world and the nations of men to accomplish his will. Habakkuk sees God sitting upon his divine throne policing the world of men. God is not apathetic to man's works but rather acts in his own time to punish, chastise, and correct. God is depicted as having bolts of lightning and rays shooting from his hands and feet to correct the wicked. Those who live in sin have nothing but the divine wrath of God to look forward to. Trouble and fear is in store for the wayward. Knowing that God sees and hears all that we do is motivation to not sin.

Habakkuk 3

Habakkuk's Prayer (3 all)

"**1** *A prayer of Habakkuk the prophet, set to Shigionoth*" **(3:1).**

Habakkuk's prayer is "*set to Shigionoth*." The word "*Shiggaion*" is "A technical term of uncertain meaning occurring in the superscriptions to Psalms 7 and Habakkuk's prayer (plural at Habakkuk 3:1). Probably indicates a lamentation psalm of a special character or for a particular purpose and perhaps therefore accompanied by special ceremonies... a poem characterized by wild emotions and irregular construction" (ISBE volume 4, page 476). God's answer to Habakkuk's questions and his knowledge of Judah and Babylon's fall gives cause for a very emotional response to the Lord in prayer.

2 *O Jehovah, I have heard the report of you, and am afraid: O Jehovah, revive your work in the midst of the years; in the midst of the years make it known; in wrath remember mercy*" **(3:2).**

Job made a similar remark when he came to his senses and recognized the fearful might of Jehovah God (see Job 42:5-6). Jeremiah said that all nations should fear the awesome name of God because their wise men are brutish before him (Jeremiah 10:7). The ancient "*work*" of God has been driving out the nations that hate Israel with his own hand and punishing the wicked of all peoples (see Psalms 44:1-2). Habakkuk prays that God would remember his mercy in the day of his great wrath against sinners. The Psalmist writes, "19 *your righteousness also, O God, is very high; you who have done great things, O God, who is like unto you? 20 You, who have showed us many and sore troubles, will quickened us again and will bring us up again from the depths of the earth*" (Psalms 71:19-20).

"**3** *God came from Teman, and the Holy One from mount Paran. His glory covered the heavens, and the earth was full of his praise,* **4** *and his* *brightness was as the light; he had rays coming forth from his hand; and there was the hiding of his power*" **(3:3-4).**

Teman and Paran are mountainous regions in and around Edom. The scriptures speak of God's wrath being unleashed upon Teman or Edom for their refusal to give him glory (see Jeremiah 49:7; Amos 1:12 and Obadiah 9). There is no nation out of his glorious sight. God is depicted as sitting in the heavens with his glory above the entire earth (see Psalms 113:4 and 148:13-14). The Lord's glorious reputation as creator, the righteous one, his divine wrath, and mercy to those who love him has spread throughout the earth. The Psalmist writes "1 *Bless Jehovah, O my soul. O Jehovah my God, you are very great; your are clothed with honor and majesty:* 2 *Who covers yourself with* **light** *as with a garment; who stretches out the heavens like a curtain*" (Psalms 104:1-2). The bright light of God's glory appears to be a description of not only his holiness but his supreme authority among the nations no matter the time or place (see Daniel 7:9-10).

Habakkuk sees the glory of Jehovah God with "*rays coming from his hands*" or horns at his side (ASV footnotes). The "*power*" of God is found in these rays or horns. The reference for God's hidden power points us to Job 26:14 where Job writes, "*But the thunder of his power who can understand?*" God is from everlasting, his authority is universal and eternal, he has displayed his great glory and might throughout the generations as he raises nations for his purpose and brings them down (Daniel 2:21).

"**5** *Before him went the pestilence, and fiery bolts went forth at his feet*" **(3:5).**

The Almighty Jehovah God is depicted as being gloriously and fearfully above the earth and all nations. The Lord watches over all mankind. His great power and might are seen in "*pestilence and fiery bolts*" that came from his feet. One memorable example of God's pestilence bolting from his feet was the case of Israel murmuring against God's decision to destroy Korah and his household. Korah had attempted to usurp the authority of God by taking Moses and Aaron's place. The Lord reacts swiftly and aggressively with a crippling plague that kills 14,700 people before it is ended by the offering of Aaron (see Numbers 16:41-50).

"**6** *He stood, and measured the earth; he beheld, and drove asunder the nations; and the eternal mountains were scattered; the everlasting hills did bow; his goings were as of old*" **(3:6).**

Another word for "*measure*" is "shook." King David knew of God's power to drive out the wicked from among his people. The king prays, "5 *Let them be as chaff before the wind and the angel of Jehovah driving them on*" (Psalms 35:5). God is depicted as sloshing the physical elements of creation such as the mountains, sea, and rivers at Psalms 114. God is able to shake creation to accomplish his objectives as he did during the days of Israel's deliverance from Egypt. Habakkuk sees the eternal powerful God as one whose "*goings were as of old*" (see also Habakkuk 1:12 and Micah 5:2).

"**7** *I saw the tents of Cushan in affliction; the curtains of the land of Midian did tremble.* **8** *Was Jehovah displeased with the rivers? Was your anger against the rivers, or your wrath against the sea, that you did ride upon your horses, upon your chariots of salvation?* **9** *Your bow was made quite bare; the oaths to the tribes were a sure word. You did cleave the earth with rivers*" **(3:7-9).**

Habakkuk turns to an example of God gloriously sitting above the earth watching over the nations. When God sees the wicked acts of men and nations he acts as though fiery bolts of plagues come from his feet and rays from his hands. The land of Cush (Ethiopia) and Midian were the enemies of God and they suffered "*affliction*" for their wickedness.

God shook the earth using the rivers and seas to plague the wicked by way of punishment. God was not angry with the rivers or seas; however, he used them to accomplish his divine objective of punishing the wicked. Likewise God's use of Babylon to punish Judah was not a matter of their right or wrong actions. God's use of Babylon was a display of his fiery bolts and rays from his hands. Babylon was no different than the river or seas that God used to accomplish his punishment.

God is depicted as riding upon horses as though he moves in a military fashion against the wicked by way of shaking the earth and its elements in a nation's life or path. The book of Revelation similarly depicts horse riders bringing the plagues of God upon the wicked as God shakes the earth and skies trying to cause men to see their sin and repent (see Revelation 6 all and 9:9).

"**10** *The mountains saw you, and were afraid; the tempest of waters passed by; the deep uttered its voice, and lifted up its hands on high.* **11** *The sun and moon stood still in their habitation, at the light of your arrows as they went, at the shining of your glittering spear*" **(3:10-11)**.

Habakkuk's prayer considers the fear of God's great, glorious, eternal, and universal sovereignty. Those who break his divine laws are heard and saw by the long arm of God's omniscient mind, eyes, and ears (see Jeremiah 23:23-25). God is depicted as policing the earth from all eternity, finding, and rooting out wickedness by way of plagues. So fearful is the sight of God's glorious might and policing force that the mountains, depths of the oceans, sun and moon are depicted as quaking in dread. The prayer of Habakkuk is very revealing in that it should cause us all to take note of God's eyes that are upon his creation. This world belongs to God and he demands that everyone submit to his laws. Those who do not submit to God will suffer as he rides his horse casting pestilence and plagues from his hands and feet as fiery arrows or "*glittering spear*" (17d) (14e).

"**12** *You did march through the land in indignation; you did thresh the nations in anger.* **13** *You went forth for the salvation of your people, for the salvation of your anointed; you wounded the head out of the house of the wicked man, laying bare the foundation even unto the neck*" **(3:12-13)**.

God threshed the Egyptians, the Assyrians, those of the Northern (Israel) and Southern (Judah) kingdoms, and he will soon thresh the Babylonians. Why was God's indignation so hot? Men walked in sin against his divine and glorious laws. The only way to turn the wicked to the ways of "*salvation*" was to chastise them with plagues (see Deuteronomy 28:58-62; 29:22-25; Hebrews 12:6-13 and Revelation 16:8-11).

God's "*anointed*" (Greek *christos*) (LXX 1108) would soon come and provide the promised blessings of salvation through the forgiveness of sins. The Greek Septuagint's *christos* is defined as "anointed, the Christ, the Anointed One, or the Messiah" (Moulton 439). The idea of the "*anointed*" one is depicted at Isaiah 45:1. Cyrus is identified as the "*anointed*" (Hebrew *mashiyach* / Messiah or Greek *christos* / Christ) of God. Here the word simply means one consecrated (i.e., "to dedicate to a given goal or service... to have a sacred purpose" [AHD 312]). The divine service or sacred purpose given to Cyrus by God was to have them return to Jerusalem to rebuild the city, temple, and its walls. The divine service or sacred purpose given to Jesus, the Messiah prophesied of in the OT, was to set men free from the bondage of sin (see Jeremiah 31:31ff). God "*anointed*" Christ with the Holy Spirit and power to accomplish this divine objective (see Acts 10:38).

God had wounded the deadly wicked Zedekiah of Judah and he will certainly do the same to all those (such as Nebuchadnezzar of Babylon) who oppose his sovereign rule (see Ezekiel 21:21-27). Habakkuk fearfully sees the indignation of God against Judah in the form of Babylon as her king is exposed and taken by the enemy.

"*14 You did pierce with his own staves the head of his warriors: they came as a whirlwind to scatter me; their rejoicing was as to devour the poor secretly. 15 You did tread the sea with your horses, the heap of mighty waters*" **(3:14-15).**

The days of old were filled with times where the Lord turned the enemies' swords upon their own selves to give Israel victory. Those who came out against the poor and unprotected were threshed upon like a chariot that runs through a river.

"**16** *I heard, and my body trembled, my lips quivered at the voice; rottenness enters into my bones, and I tremble in my place; because I must wait quietly for the day of trouble, for the coming up of the people that invade us*" **(3:16)**.

Habakkuk sees, by divine vision, the great and glorious God as he acts out in indignation against the wicked the world over. Judah will be no different. God is no respecter of persons. The prophet of God knows and sees what comes and he trembles and his voice quivers within him. There is nothing to do but quietly wait for "*the day of trouble*." There was no complaining prayer to God that would stop his divine indignation. The world of wicked men must face God's plagues lest they be forever and hopelessly lost in sin. The "*people that invade us*" is none other than the Babylonian Empire led by Nebuchadnezzar and his captain Nebuzaradan.

"**17** *For though the fig-tree shall not flourish, Neither shall fruit be in the vines; The labor of the olive shall fail, and the fields shall yield no food; The flock shall be cut off from the fold, and there shall be no herd in the stalls:* **18** *Yet I will rejoice in Jehovah, I will joy in the God of my salvation.* **19** *Jehovah, the Lord, is my strength; and he makes my feet like hinds feet, and will make me to walk upon my high places*" **(3:17-19)**.

Habakkuk knows by faith that Jehovah's divine vision of the invading Chaldeans who shall thresh Judah is sure. A day comes when all figs, olives, and flocks will be no more. What shall the people do? The prophets have revealed the dreaded judgment of God and it is sure. Again, what shall they do? The prophet tells us what he shall do. "*Yet I will rejoice in Jehovah, I will joy in the God of my salvation.*" Such wonderful words of faith ought to motivate us all to such a lofty state of obedience unto the Lord. We too must see and come to know the ways of God. The Lord sits above the earth policing it so that man would live lawfully and eternally in peace. Those who live in sin have nothing but "*trouble*" to look forward to (Habakkuk 3:16).

There comes a day in our future when God will judge mankind one last time (Romans 2:3ff). What should we all do in the meantime? What manner of man ought I to be in this present world? Shall I lay up treasures in this earth? Shall I cheat and steal to achieve my objectives in business? Shall I try to elevate myself in the eyes of fellow laborers? Shall I give up a life of godliness because of another brother's discouraging remarks? Shall I give up my faith for the world's goods, pleasures, and pride? Let us all say as Habakkuk (and others who have faithfully gone on before us - Hebrews 11:1ff), "*Yet will I rejoice in Jehovah, I will joy in the God of my salvation.*" The glorified saints shall walk upon the high places of God in heaven.

Questions over Habakkuk Chapter 3

1. What is Habakkuk afraid of?

2. What does Habakkuk see coming from God's hands and feet?

3. What does God actually shoot with his bow and arrows at men?

4. What did Habakkuk determine to do as the "*people that invade us*" approach?

5. What would Habakkuk do during and after the Babylonians destroy Judah?

Zephaniah

Robertson's Notes

Bible Book 36 of 66

"Woe to her that is rebellious and polluted!"

Zephaniah 3:1

Introduction

Zephaniah's primary objective is to awaken Judah out of spiritual slumber. Judah was guilty of sin and due God's condemning judgment of fierce anger and wrath (Zephaniah 1:17). Zephaniah refers to this time as the "*Great Day of Judgment*" (Zephaniah 1:14-16; 2:2 and 3:8). The prophet of God draws a stark contrast between God true remnant and the wicked of the world (Zephaniah 3:5). The wicked are nothing like God whereas the righteous emulate the Lord in their lives. Those who will live in a meek and lowly fashion shall have true hope in this life (see Zephaniah 3:13).

Prophet and Date of Writing

Zephaniah was of a kingly bloodline. He begins his prophecy by tracing his heritage back to Hezekiah king of Judah. The date of Zephaniah's prophecy is given as *"in the days of Josiah the son of Amon, king of Judah"* (Zephaniah 1:1). Josiah reigned from 639 to 608 BC. Josiah came to power in Judah at the age of 8 and at the age of 16 he began to seek after God (2 Chronicles 34:1-3). During Josiah's day the prophets Jeremiah, Nahum, Habakkuk, and Zephaniah spoke divinely inspired words against Judah. Josiah saw to it that many religious reforms took place; however, nothing could detour God's purpose of punishing his wicked people for their sins (see 2 Kings 21:10-15).

Judah's Sin

To look upon Judah was to look upon the world of heathens. Judah was clothed with *"foreign apparel"* and the Lord could not distinguish them from other sinful peoples (Zephaniah 1:8). Judah practiced idolatry (Zephaniah 1:4), was rebellious, polluted, disobedient, and would not receive correction (Zephaniah 3:1). Judah had no shame in committing sin (Zephaniah 2:1). Every aspect of society was perverted. The **general populace** had a divided allegiance between their king, wealth, and God (Zephaniah 1:5, 13). The people were ignorantly content in their ungodliness all the while thinking that God would not do them harm or good (Zephaniah 1:12). **Servants** displayed disrespect toward their masters (Zephaniah 1:9). Judah's **princes, judges, prophets**, and **priests** were perverted as well (Zephaniah 3:3-4). Isaiah, describing the moral condition of Judah, said that they were corrupt from head to toe (see Isaiah 1:5).

The Remedy for Judah and the Ungodly of all Times

God's desired character in his people is spiritual meekness (Zephaniah 2:3). Meek people will fear God and receive the correction he administers (Zephaniah 3:7). Those who wait (trust) in Jehovah will not be disappointed (Zephaniah 3:8). The Lord requires nothing less today. God desires his disciples to be meek (Matthew 5:5), God fearing (1 Peter 2:17), to emulate his words and deeds (Romans 8:29), and be willing to receive the Lord's correction (Hebrews 12:9). So many today, like those of Judah, are corrected by God's word only to rebel and reject all his divine help.

What is at Stake?

There is much at stake when contemplating rebellion or acting with a spirit of humility and meekness when sin occurs in one's life. Zephaniah reveals forgiveness of sins as the first thing at stake (Zephaniah 3:11). To live with the guilt of sin is more that the human soul can bear. When we sin against God it generally bothers us a great deal. Our hands may hang low in a disheartened state (Zephaniah 3:16-18). The second thing that Zephaniah reveals to be at stake is one's level of happiness and contentment. Real happiness and rejoicing ought to come from experiencing the forgiveness of our sins (Zephaniah 3:14). The rebellious can fabricate happiness, through ignorance of sin and its consequences, yet true happiness is found in the Lord (Zephaniah 1:12).

The Christian today has the word of God that exposes sin (Romans 3:20 and 7:7). The expected outcome of sin, in the Christian's life, is great sorrow and shame within the heart (2 Corinthians 7:10). The remedy for the Christian's sin and guilt is humble repentance (Acts 17:30) and prayer (Acts 8:22 and 1 John 1:9). God continues to supply our every spiritual need!

ZEPHANIAH CHAPTER 1

Synopsis

Zephaniah reveals the fierce anger of God against Judah and Jerusalem. The Lord would cut off all life. Even those idols that had no life would be cut off and destroyed. All those that were clothed with foreign apparel would be punished because they lost their spiritual sanctification. Zephaniah summarily tells us that Judah would be crushed in God's anger by Babylon "*because they have sinned*" (Zephaniah 1:17). No amount of treasures on this earth would be able to buy back their souls.

Application

Zephaniah helps us see the value of self examination. God is depicted as watching on the watchtowers of life so that those who violate his commandments would be punished and moved to repentance. If only people of all generations would consider the spiritual state of their souls they may save their eternal lives. We must all see that there is nothing but "*punishment*" that awaits the wicked (Zephaniah 1:8, 12). No amount of treasures we may amass on this earth will have the power to save the erring.

Zephaniah 1

All Creation is Affected by God's Judgment against the Wicked (1:1-6)

"**1** *The word of Jehovah which came unto Zephaniah the son of Cushi, the son of Gedaliah, the son of Amariah, the son of Hezekiah, in the days of Josiah the son of Amon, king of Judah*" **(1:1)**.

Zephaniah was the great great grandson of Hezekiah king of Judah. The "*word of Jehovah*" comes to Zephaniah during the days of King Josiah. God may have spoken to Zephaniah through a dream (Daniel 7:1 and Joel 2:28), vision (Obadiah 1:1; Joel 2:28ff and Amos 1:1), or direct communication (Numbers 7:89).

"**2** *I will utterly consume all things from off the face of the ground, said Jehovah.* **3** *I will consume man and beast; I will consume the birds of the heavens, and the fishes of the sea, and the stumbling blocks with the wicked; and I will cut off man from off the face of the ground, said Jehovah*" **(1:2-3)**.

Habakkuk revealed in his prayer that God gloriously watches over the earth so that his laws may be followed by all (Habakkuk chapter 3). The Lord sees and hears all things that man does (Jeremiah 23:23-25). Before God comes in indignation shaking the earth, mountains and rivers he sends words of warnings through his prophets (see Habakkuk 3). Likewise, God's gospel message is given to man today before the great and terrible day of final judgment.

Zephaniah waste no time introducing his work but rather gets right to his message of fierce judgment upon the entirety of creation for the wickedness of Judah. The condemning judgment is against man, beasts, birds, fishes, and the stumbling-blocks with the wicked (i.e., things that cause sin such as idols and false prophets along with those who accept these things). All of creation will be consumed with the wicked. The sinfulness of man will affect the rivers, mountains, beasts, birds, fish, and even kingdoms of man in that God uses these parts of nature to punish man's wickedness.

"**4** *And I will stretch out my hand upon Judah, and upon all the inhabitants of Jerusalem; and I will cut off the remnant of Baal from this* *place, and the name of the Chemarim with the priests;* **5** *and them that worship the host of heaven upon the housetops; and them that worship, that swear to Jehovah and swear by Malcam;* **6** *and them that are turned back from following Jehovah; and those that have not sought Jehovah, nor inquired after him"* **(1:4-6).**

A specific prophecy is levied against Jerusalem and Judah. The worship of Baal (the Canaanite god) had taken a prominent place in the minds of God's people. Baal worshippers were led by the *"Chemarim"* (i.e., idolatrous priests - see 2 Kings 23:5). All those who worshipped Baal would have the wrathful hand of God stretched out over them. Worshippers of the skies would also be judged. God's wrath would be stretched out against those who swear to *"Malcam"* while swearing to Jehovah. Malcam could be one of two things. The ISBE tells us that Malcam was a Hebrew word meaning "their king" but also it identified "the national deity of Ammon, usually called Molech or Milcom" (ISBE volume 3, pages 228-229). God's hand would be against those who left off following him and those who never did follow him. No one who rejects the totality of God's word will escape his condemning punishment.

The Lord would have no part of divided allegiance (see Matthew 12:30). Many of God's people wanted to have part in the popular idolatrous worship of the surrounding heathen nations while claiming a belief in God.

The Foolish and Unsuspecting will be caught off guard by the Lord's Day of Judgment (1:7-13)

*"***7** *Hold your peace at the presence of the Lord Jehovah; for the day of Jehovah is at hand: for Jehovah has prepared a sacrifice, he has consecrated his guests.* **8** *And it shall come to pass in the day of Jehovah's sacrifice, that I will punish the princes, and the king's sons, and all such as are clothed with foreign apparel"* **(1:7-8).**

Habakkuk similarly writes, "20 *let all the earth keep silence before him*" (Habakkuk 2:20). All of creation is to fear and give reverence to God due to his great power and sovereign rule over earth. Religious ideology, apart from divine revelation, was to be silenced (9f). Zephaniah now tells the creation to "*Hold your peace at the presence of the Lord Jehovah.*" The reason for the silence and holding of one's thoughts is that "*the day of Jehovah is at hand.*" The day that would see all of God's warnings upon the wicked fulfilled. If ever there was a time to silence one's religious opinions, convictions, and conscience it is now.

The Day of Judgment is depicted as a day of sacrifice where guests are invited to come and partake of the flesh. The guest called to the sacrifice can be none other than the Chaldeans of Habakkuk 1:6. The Day of Judgment will see Jerusalem and Judah's princes and king's sons punished because they clothed themselves with "foreign apparel." To look upon Judah and Jerusalem was to look upon the foreign nations. They had taken on the practices of the heathen from the clothes that they wore to the deities they worshiped. God's people are to be sanctified from the interest of the world (i.e., success, riches, the glory of men, and the lust of the flesh) (see 1 John 2:16-17). There should be a distinct difference in not only the clothes Christians wear, but also their language and worship (19h).

God's people today need to make the distinction between sin and righteousness. The way I approach many things in this life tells the Lord what my disposition to the world is. Those whose regard in this life is for the glory of this world will not have the glory of God for eternity. Why not seek to bring glory to God by keeping his commandments (see John 15:1-10)? Christians can involve themselves in many events of the world such as camping, fishing, competing in various sporting events and still bring God glory. The moment; however, these events become the focus of my life I have clothed myself "*with foreign apparel.*" While the world looks to achievement in this life the Christian ought to have his or her sight fixed on eternity (25s). Jesus said, "24 *No man can serve two masters; for either he will hate the one, and love the other; or else he will hold to one, and despise the other. You cannot serve God and mammon"* (Matthew 6:24).

"**9** *And in that day I will punish all those that leap over the threshold that fill their master's house with violence and deceit.* **10** *And in that day said Jehovah, there shall be the noise of a cry from the fish gate, and a wailing from the second quarter, and a great crashing from the hills.* **11** *Wail, you inhabitants of Maktesh; for all the people of Canaan are undone; all they that were laden with silver are cut off"* **(1:9-11).**

Further signs of Judah and Jerusalem's wickedness are revealed. God gloriously sat above the earth watching and listening. God saw that Judah's servants were not loyal to their masters (see also Ephesians 6:5-8 and Colossians 3:22-25). Servants deceived their masters and acted in violent ways. Servants may have robbed and even killed their masters. The second class of people of Judah and Jerusalem were the merchants that used deceitful balances and received gain by ways of cheating (Hosea 12:7 and Amos 8:5). The gate areas of Jerusalem where trade and commerce took place would hear wails of anguish due to the horrific punishment that comes to the cheaters and those who despise justice.

"**12** *And it shall come to pass at that time, that I will search Jerusalem with lamps; and I will punish the men that are settled on their lees, that say in their heart, Jehovah will not do good, neither will he do evil.* **13** *And their wealth shall become a spoil, and their houses a desolation: yea, they shall build houses, but shall not inhabit them; and they shall plant vineyards, but shall not drink the wine thereof"* **(1:12-13).**

The sovereign God of creation will send his searching light throughout the city of Jerusalem that he may find "*the men that are settled on their lees.*" The "*lees*" of wine was the pulp and other unstrained parts such as skin and seeds that are a byproduct of wine production. When grapes were squeezed they were generally separated from the "*lees*" for drinking purposes. Wine left on the lees was unstrained. To be "*settled on lees*" would be wine that sat in an unstrained state. Zephaniah equates being settled on lees with a hear that says, "*Jehovah will not do good, neither will he do evil."* To be *"settled on lees"* is an expression that reveals one's lack of fear for wrong doing. It is the life that is unstrained from sin. There were obvious warnings from the prophets during Josiah's days; however, some people simply ignored them saying, "God will not do anything these negative prophets are saying" (see Isaiah 30:10). Judah was ignorantly content to continue in their ungodliness while their souls were lost. They did not see that God would condemn them (38).

Part of the reason many of Jerusalem were indifferent and did not think anything bad was going to happen was their current wealth. They had beautiful homes, vineyards, and servants and considered it a blessing that meant God's approval. Let us learn the valuable lesson here. Just because we have homes, automobiles, plenty of food, and drink does not mean that God's favor is with us. Look to the money giants of our society and trace out their lifestyles. Can we say that God is with these rich and famous people? Those that are minded to be rich shall surely suffer earthly and eternal pain (1 Timothy 6:9-10).

The Great day of the Lord will Distress Judah and Jerusalem (1:14-18)

"14 *The great day of Jehovah is near, it is near and hastens greatly, even the voice of the day of Jehovah; the mighty man cries there bitterly"* **(1:14).**

While many cannot see that God would possibly do such horrible things to Judah and Jerusalem the prophet Zephaniah proclaims that the day draws very near. The *"mighty man cries bitterly"* on this horrid day because all of his valiant efforts are vanity. No matter how hard he fights he shall not prevail against Jehovah. Jeremiah said that it was useless to resist Babylon (Jeremiah 38:2) because it is God fighting against them (Jeremiah 21:5).

"15 *That day is a day of wrath, a day of trouble and distress, a day of waste and desolation, a day of darkness and gloominess, a day of clouds* *and thick darkness, a day of the trumpet and alarm, against the fortified cities, and against the high battlements"* **(1:15-16).**

A vivid picture of the siege of Jerusalem and utter defeat is given. God's wrath shall be poured out upon Jerusalem and the city will be laid waste. Upon this day there will be darkness, clouds of smoke from the burning of the walls and city, and trumpets sounding out alarms. The fortified city with its high battlements (i.e., the corner towers) is no match for the invading Chaldeans. Jeremiah writes, "15 *The Lord has trodden as in a winepress the virgin daughter of Judah*" (Lamentations 1:15b). Again, the prophet writes, "10 *the hands of the pitiful women have boiled their own children; they were their food in the destruction of the daughter of my people. 11 Jehovah has accomplished his wrath, he has poured out his fierce anger...*" (Lamentations 4:10-11).

"**17** *And I will bring distress upon men that they shall walk like blind men,* **because they have sinned** *against Jehovah; and their blood shall be poured out as dust, and their flesh as dung.* **18** *Neither their silver nor their gold shall be able to deliver them in the day of Jehovah's wrath; but the whole land shall be devoured by the fire of his jealousy: for he will make an end, yea, a terrible end, of all them that dwell in the land*" **(1:17-18).**

The "*distress*" that accompanies the "*great day of Jehovah*" is due to man's sin. The people's sin brings "*grievous deaths*" to all of Jerusalem (see Jeremiah 16:4). There end will be "*terrible.*" Jeremiah records the terribleness of Jerusalem's siege when he said, "9 *And I will cause them to eat the flesh of their sons and the flesh of their daughters; and they shall eat every one the flesh of his friend, in the siege and in the distress, wherewith their enemies, and they that seek their life, shall distress them*" (Jeremiah 19:9). The people of Jerusalem will find no savior in their riches when God's wrath is poured out over Jerusalem (25h).

Questions over Zephaniah Chapter 1

1. What would God consume?

2. What would God do to Baal and Chemarim?

3. Who would God "*punish?*"

4. How does Zephaniah describe the "*great day of Jehovah*?"

5. Why would God punish people on this great day?

6. True or False: Some in Judah would be able to use their gold and silver to relieve their punishment.

ZEPHANIAH CHAPTER 2

Synopsis

The Lord calls upon Babylon, the nation that has no shame, to battle against the wicked of the world. Zephaniah writes oracle judgments against the Philistines, Moab, Ammon, and Egypt. These nations rejoiced in the fall of Judah while committing the same gross immorality. The sovereign God of all creation will not let such behavior go unpunished.

Application

The universal sovereignty of God is depicted in this chapter. God's expectation for all mankind is that of meekness and righteousness (Zephaniah 2:3). When a person or nation reject the commandments of God there is nothing but punishment that waits. Not one of us today will get away with any one sin that we have committed. Those who are meek will not only acknowledge their sin but they will pray fervently to God for forgiveness.

Zephaniah 2

The Universality of Jehovah's wrath against the Ungodly (2 all)

"**1** Gather yourselves together, yea, gather together, O nation that has no shame; **2** before the decree bring forth, before the day pass as the chaff, before the fierce anger of Jehovah come upon you, before the day of Jehovah's anger come upon you" **(2:1-2).**

"*Punishment*" for the sins of idolatry and a lack of "*shame*" awaits Judah and Jerusalem (see Zephaniah 1:8, 12 and Jeremiah 6:15). Nahum wrote, "*6 who can stand before his indignation? And who can abide in the fierceness of his anger? His wrath is poured out like fire, and the rocks are broken asunder by him*" (Nahum 1:6). Sin is no laughing matter (Jeremiah 15:17-18). God is very angry because his people have forsaken him.

The "*day of Jehovah*" is a day in which the power of God will be unleashed in such a way that he will be seen as actually fighting against Judah (see Jeremiah 21:5). There will be plagues and pestilence that are fired like lightning bolts from his hands and feet at the wicked (see Habakkuk 3:3-5).

"*3 Seek Jehovah, all you meek of the earth, that have kept his ordinances; seek righteousness, seek meekness: it may be that you will be hid in the day of Jehovah's anger*" **(2:3).**

The prophet gives instructions to the Lord's elect remnant at a time in which his fierce anger is about to be unleashed. Those who are the "*meek of the earth*" are identified as those that have "*kept his ordinances*." The word "*meek*" (LXX *tapeinoi*) means "to exhibit humility and contrition (remorse for sins)" (Moulton 397). The word meek shares synonyms in the English language such as being humble, submissive, or compliant. The New Testament uses the Greek *praus* translated meek meaning "meek, gentle, kind, or forgiving" (Moulton 340). Liddell and Scott add "Mild, soft, gentle, or meek" (LS 666). The meek have the uncanny ability to recognize the heinous nature of sin. They acknowledge their own sin and weakness of the flesh and beg God to forgive them. The meek have deep sorrow over their sins. Overall the meek are humbled by the human experience of sin. Such a one is meek in the sense that he or she is brought low by their sin. Such a one realizes that all sin and have a gentle and kind disposition toward others. Humanity has a common plight and that is that we sin. The meek have a proper disposition or spirit in this experience (see Psalms 25) (20b).

Zephaniah tells the meek of this world that if they will continue on the path of righteousness it may be that God's fierce anger will not touch them.

"**4** *For Gaza shall be forsaken, and Ashkelon a desolation; they shall drive out Ashdod at noonday and Ekron shall be rooted up.* **5** *Woe unto the inhabitants of the sea-coast, the nation of the Cherethites! The word of Jehovah is against you, O Canaan, the land of the Philistines; I will destroy you, that there shall be no inhabitant.* **6** *And the sea-coast shall be pastures, with cottages for shepherds and folds for flocks.* **7** *And the coast shall be for the remnant of the house of Judah; they shall feed their flocks thereupon; in the houses of Ashkelon shall they lie down in the evening; for Jehovah their God will visit them, and bring back their captivity*" **(2:4-7).**

Zephaniah delivers a prophecy against the **Philistines**. The inhabitants of Philistia will not escape the fierce wrath of God. The four principle cities of Philistia are named with the exclusion of Gath (see Amos 1:6-8). Their land shall be taken and given to the captives of Judah who return under Zerubbabel. Zephaniah mentions the "*Cherethites*." The *Cherethites* were a Philistine clan whose territory was adjacent to southern Judah... The name is related to the name of Crete, from which island at least part of the Philistines had come" (ISBE volume 1, page 641).

Ezekiel speaks of God's wrath against the Philistines in similar language saying, "**15** *Thus said the Lord Jehovah: Because the Philistines have dealt by revenge, and have taken vengeance with despite of soul to destroy with perpetual enmity;*" (see Ezekiel 25:15). While Ammon, Moab, and Edom all rejoiced over the fall of Judah, the Philistines are depicted by Ezekiel as a people who have in some unrevealed way, "*taken vengeance with despite of soul*" to destroy God's people. The Philistines are marked by their spirit of "*revenge*." Isaiah explains that God's anger was directed against the Philistines because they rejoiced at the fall of Egypt (see Isaiah 14:28-32). People today ought to take care not to rejoice over the fall of nations and wicked men. Recently Hugo Chavez, the Venezuelan president, died and many were laughing and rejoicing. The Lord has no pleasure in the death of the wicked and neither should we as his people (see Ezekiel 33:11). Jeremiah devotes an entire chapter to an oracle against the Philistines; however, it is only seven verses long and focuses on the idolatry of the nation (see Jeremiah 47).

"**8** *I have heard the reproach of Moab, and the reviling of the children of Ammon, wherewith they have reproached my people, and magnified themselves against their border.* **9** *Therefore as I live, said Jehovah of hosts, the God of Israel, Surely Moab shall be as Sodom, and the children of Ammon as Gomorrah, a possession of nettles, and salt pits, and a perpetual desolation: the residue of my people shall make a prey of them, and the remnant of my nations shall inherit them.* **10** *This shall they have for their pride, because they have reproached and magnified themselves against the people of Jehovah of hosts.* **11** *Jehovah will be terrible unto them; for he will famish all the gods of the earth; and men shall worship him, every one from his place, even all the isles of the nations*" **(2:8-11).**

Zephaniah has denounced the Philistines for their part in Judah's demise. The prophet of God now turns his attention to Moab and Ammon.

Moab lay on the eastern side of the Dead Sea. The people of Moab were descendants of Lot by one of his own daughters (Genesis 19:30-38). Moab was not a favored nation. God referred to them as the pot in which one washes feet (Psalms 60:8). Israel had defeated Sihon, king of the Amorites, and settled in the land of Moab. The tribes of Gad, Reuben, and half of Manasseh remained in Moab rather than going into Canaan. Moab was known as the "*people of Chemosh*" rather than the "*people of Jehovah*" (see Numbers 21:29 and Jeremiah 48:7-8, 45ff). Chemosh was Moab's national deity. Solomon erroneously erected an altar for Chemosh worship during the days of the United Kingdom (see 1 Kings 11:7). Moab had developed feelings of contempt for Israel and Judah through the years that was likely due to jealousy and being in subjection to them (see Ezekiel 25:8-10).

The Moabites have a history of angering Jehovah. The Moabites, under king Balak and the prophet Balaam, seduced the people of God to commit fornication and idolatry. The Lord was very angry with Moab (see Numbers 22). Jeremiah reveals more of Moab's sins at Jeremiah chapter 48. Moab had rejoiced over the fall of Judah as did Ammon and Edom (Jeremiah 40:14 and Ezekiel 25). Jeremiah and Zephaniah record the sin of **pride** being a primary issue with Moab (see Jeremiah 48:26-30). The oracle of Isaiah against Moab explains that this sinful nation would not go unpunished (Isaiah 15-16).

The people of **Ammon** were descendants of Lot by one of his own daughters as was Moab (see Genesis 19:30-38). Ammon, like Moab, does not have a favorable history with Israel. Ammon oppressed Israel for eighteen years during the days of the judges (see Judges 10). Later they would unite with the Syrians to war with Israel, however, Joab defeats them (2 Samuel 10-12). Ammon paired up with their brother nation Moab and invaded Judah during the days of Jehoshaphat (2 Chronicles 20). When Hazael and the Syrians pressed the people of God it was the Ammonites who took advantage of Israel in their weakened state and practiced acts of cruelty against them (see Amos 1:13-15). Tiglath-pileser of Assyria would eventually conqueror Israel to the east of the Jordan River leaving Gad, Reuben, and half the tribe of Manasseh devastated. The Ammonites took this opportunity to claim the broken people's land (see 2 Kings 15:29 and 1 Chronicles 5:26).

The prophet Amos had this illegal land possession in mind when he condemned them at Amos 1:13-15. The land belonged to Gad yet Ammon took the land at a time of Israel's weakness. Ammon is called "*Malcam*." Malcam was the "national deity of Ammon, usually called Molech or Milcom" (ISBE volume 3, page 229). "The rabbinic writers described a bronze statue, human in form but with an ox's head, hollow within and heated from below. Children were placed inside this structure and immolated while drums drowned out their cries" (ISBE volume 3, page 401).

"**12** *You **Ethiopians** also, you shall be slain by my sword.* **13** *And he will stretch out his hand against the north, and destroy **Assyria**, and will make Nineveh a desolation, and dry like the wilderness.* **14** *And heards shall lie down in the midst of her, all the beasts of the nations: both the pelican and the porcupine shall lodge in the capitals thereof; their voice shall sing in the windows; desolation shall be in the thresholds: for he has laid bare the cedar-work.* **15** *This is the joyous city that dwelt carelessly, that said in her heart, I am, am there is none besides me: how is she become a desolation, a place for beasts to lie down in? Every one that passes by her shall hiss, and wag his hand*" **(2:12-15)**.

God would put his sword of victory into the hands of the Babylonians and they would utterly destroy the Ethiopians and or **Egypt**. Pharaoh Necho reigned in Egypt from 566 - 550 BC (other historians place the date at 611 to 595 BC). Josiah's last year as king of Judah (565 BC) was ended when he went out to meet the Egyptians in battle and died. Egypt's aim was world conquest. The Jews in Judah placed Jehoahaz on the throne in place of Josiah. Jehoahaz ruled three months and was captured and sent to Egypt. Pharaoh of Egypt placed Jehoiakim as a vassal king over Judah. It was in the fourth year of the vassal reign of Jehoiakim that Nebuchadnezzar came up against Egypt (561 BC). The Egyptian armies had marched through Palestine northward to Syria. The Egyptians advanced to Carchemish with the intentions of exterminating the Assyrians and met an unexpected foe in the Babylonians (2 Kings 23:29-24:1-4).

Jeremiah's prophecy regarding the demise of Egypt at chapter 46 was in relation to the battle at Carchemish. Two world powers, Egypt and Babylon, would battle for supremacy. The Egyptians were called to war by Jehovah God. Their horsemen and foot soldiers were told to make ready for the battle. The Egyptians seemed invincible; however, the Lord was fighting with the Babylonians. The sight of the advancing Chaldeans struck terror in the hearts of the Egyptians. Many Egyptians begin to retreat while others were slaughtered.

During the days of Josiah **Assyria** had not yet been defeated by the Babylonians. Those who heard the prophecy that Nineveh and Assyria would fall by the hands of the Babylonians were in disbelief. To the world's utter surprise the great city of Nineveh would fall. The Lord depicts Nineveh's defeat so thoroughly that it will only be a place for wild animals to dwell.

Questions over Zephaniah Chapter 2

1. What characteristic, if found in a man, would cause him to possibly be hid in the "*day of Jehovah's anger?*"

2. Who is the "*remnant of the house of Judah?*"

3. Why would God be "*terrible*" to Moab and Ammon?

4. Who would be destroyed by the sword of God?

5. Who foolishly said, "*I am and there is none besides me?*"

ZEPHANIAH CHAPTER 3

Synopsis

Zephaniah draws a contrast between God and all of humanity. Many wicked men of Judah stand in stark contrast to God. The people of Judah did not obey or trust in God. Judah would not receive correction and refused to draw near to the Lord. The princes, prophets, judges and priests were corrupt. God, on the other hand, would never perform acts of iniquity. There would be a remnant; however, that would receive correction and forgiveness. These people would be forever blessed.

Application

People of all ages would do well to give heed to the words of Zechariah. God forbid that we would live in such hardened rebellion that we would eventually be destroyed. God chastens or punishes his created people because he loves them. Those who receive correction will meekly acknowledge their sins and call out to God for forgiveness. The good news, gospel, is that forgiveness is to be found in Christ Jesus. Zephaniah is preaching the most basic principles of the gospel in this final chapter. When students of God's word get to the New Testament they find that it corresponds perfectly with the instructions of the Old Testament. I read and understand in both testaments that if I call out to God for help at times of my sin he will listen and answer.

Zephaniah 3

The Righteous and Rebellious Examined (3:1-13)

"**1** *Woe to her that is rebellious and polluted! To the oppressing city!* **2** *She obeyed not the voice; she received not correction; she trusted not in Jehovah; she drew not near to her God*" **(3:1-2).**

The object of the meek is to avoid the fierce anger of God by seeking out righteousness (see Zephaniah 2:3). Zephaniah lists all the characteristics that define the meek and lowly elect remnant of God in these two verses. Meekness and acceptability of man to God is based upon one's obedience, the ability to receive correction, trust in God, and draw near to him. Those who will not do these things are identified as "*rebellious and polluted*." To be rebellious is to be an unbeliever (see Numbers 20:10-12). Zephaniah equates rebellion to being morally polluted.

Judah was like a stubborn heifer (Hosea 4:16) that would not obey God (Hosea 7:11). The Lord corrected her stubborn and rebellious ways by using Babylon. Though Babylon threatens annihilation the wicked remain wicked. God's chastisement had no effect on the hardened of heart.

"**3** Her princes in the midst of her are roaring lions; her judges are evening wolves; they leave nothing till the morrow. **4** Her prophets are light and treacherous persons; her priests have profaned the sanctuary they have done violence to the law" **(3:3-4).**

The **princes** of the people (i.e., heads of the families) devoured the poor and weak like a lion her prey (see Amos 4:1). The **judges** of Judah are likened unto the evening wolves that devour sheep in that they loved not justice (Micah 3:9). The **prophets** of Judah are "*light and treacherous*" in that they teach false doctrines and do so for financial gain (see Micah 3:5, 11). The **priests** have profaned the sanctuary of the Lord and have done violence to the law in that they "*teach for hire*" (see Micah 3:11).

"**5** *Jehovah in the midst of her is righteous; he will not do iniquity; every morning does he bring his justice to light, he fails not; but the unjust know no shame*" **(3:5).**

Zephaniah draws a steep contrast that exists between the sinful people of Judah and the God they claim to know and serve. The people are actually nothing like God (see Leviticus 11:44). The characteristics of "*righteousness*" and "*justice*" belong to God. "*Righteousness*" (LXX *dikaiosunen*) means "regular, exact, rigid, to speak quite exactly, right, lawful, just, or real and genuine" (LS 202). "*Justice*" (LXX *krima*) means "judgment, a sentence, administration of justice, execution of justice, or an administrative decree" (Moulton 241). The Apostle Paul explains to the Romans that Christians are to be conformed to the image of Jesus Christ (Romans 8:29). The Apostle Peter tells us that we are to be just as holy as God is (1 Peter 1:15-16 and 2 Peter 1:4). Jesus said that we are to be perfect as God is perfect (Matthew 5:48). The Apostle John said that we are to be as God in this world that we live in (1 John 4:17). When man sins and feels no shame for that sin he is nothing like God (23).

The people of Judah and Jerusalem are not right and just but rather "*unjust*" and know "*no shame.*" Any executions of actions or works that are not exact, rigid, and lawful are shameful. The problem with Judah was that they did not feel the sting of shame for their sin as they should have. Shame is a barometer within a Christian's mind that excuses or accuses the conscience of sin (see 1 Timothy 2:9). When sin occurs in my life it is shame that moves me to repentance (2 Corinthians 7:10-11). Those who feel no shame have had their conscience seared with a hot iron so that they become comfortable rather than ashamed. The Apostle Paul wrote, "2 *through the hypocrisy of men that speak lies, branded in their own conscience as with a hot iron*" (1 Timothy 4:2).

"**6** *I have cut off nations; their battlements are desolate; I have made their streets waste, so that none passes by; their cities are destroyed, so that there is no man, so that there is no inhabitant.* **7** *I said, Only fear me;* **receive correction**; *so her dwelling shall not be cut off, according to* *all that I have appointed concerning her: but they rose early and corrupted all their doings"* **(3:6-7).**

God has thoroughly instructed his people. The Lord has revealed his divine expectations and desires for all men by way of his prophets. Zephaniah calls upon Judah to *"fear God"* and *"receive correction."* Other prophets have instructed Judah to acknowledge their sins (Jeremiah 3:13-14 and Hosea 5:15), seek God (Amos 5:4), do justly, love kindness, and walk humbly with the Lord (Micah 6:8).

The *"correction"* is given as cutting off nations so that they are desolate. Will Judah open her eyes to God's corrective measures and repent of their wickedness or will she too be cut off? God will accept nothing less that genuine *"fear."* God gives all men the choice in life to fear him or to rebel (see Proverbs 1:29). *"Fear"* (LXX *fobos*) means "panic fear such as causes flight, terror, properly of the outward show of fear, or to strike terror into one" (LS 867). Solomon gives a solid definition to the doctrine of fearing God throughout the book of Proverbs.

First, Solomon defines the fear of God as having a meek or humble spirit (see Proverbs 22:4). Secondly, Solomon gives a precise definition of fearing God at chapter eight by saying that it is to hate evil, pride, arrogance, and a perverse mouth (see Proverbs 8:13). All sin and rebellion brings great trouble to people's lives as God chastens and punishes the wicked. Man ought to be fearful of the mighty hand of a wrathful God who hates sin (see Hebrews 10:31). David wrote, "4 *for day and night your hand was heavy upon me: my moisture was changed as with the drought of summer. 5 I acknowledged my sin unto you and my iniquity did I not hide: I said, I will confess my transgressions unto Jehovah; and you forgave the iniquity of my sin*" (Psalms 32:4-5). God plagues, chastises, and or punishes the sinner so that he will be moved to repentance (see Amos 4:6-11; Hebrews 12:5-13 and Revelation 16:8-11). When I begin to see the terror of the Lord **before** I perform an act of sin I am gaining wisdom and knowledge (see Proverbs 1:7). The

Apostle Paul wrote, "*knowing therefore the fear* (or terror) *of the Lord we persuade men*" (2 Corinthians 5:11) (36).

"*8 Therefore wait for me, said Jehovah, until the day that I rise up to the prey; for my determination is to gather the nations, that I may assemble the kingdoms, to pour upon them mine indignation, even all my fierce anger; for all the earth shall be devoured with the fire of my jealousy*" **(3:8).**

The idea of waiting upon God is to put all of one's trust in the Lord. The judgments of God are true and the meek will continue in faith until and through the dreaded Day of Judgment (see Isaiah 64:4). When the Great Day of Judgment comes it will be an outpouring of God's indignation, anger, and fire of his jealousy. The wicked will be plagued and given pestilence. God will use rivers, mountains, and other nations to accomplish his work of wrath. God gathers the wicked for punishment in every generation (see also Revelation 20:7-9).

"*9 For then will I turn to the peoples a pure language, that they may all call upon the name of Jehovah, to serve him with one consent. 10 From beyond the rivers of Ethiopia my suppliants, even the daughter of my dispersed, shall bring mine offering. 11 In that day you shall not be put to shame for all your doings, wherein you have transgressed against me; for then I will take away out of the midst of you your proudly exulting ones, and you shall no more be haughty in my holy mountain*" **(3:9-11).**

At the time of God's fierce wrath against wickedness being poured out upon the nations of men he will consequentially "*turn the peoples to a pure language.*" The "*pure language*" is the "*calling upon the name of Jehovah.*" Throughout the New Testament we find the teaching that God's chastening (Hebrews 12:5-13 and Revelation 3:19), man's shame over his sins (Luke 18:13 and 2 Corinthians 7:10), fear of God's condemning judgments (Proverbs 8:13 and Romans 2:4-10), and one's own family history of going through these things (see Zechariah 1:5-6) moves people to call out to God for help. The good news is that there is help! The gospel of Jesus Christ is defined as "good news."

Zephaniah sees a day in the future when Christ would be a sacrifice for sins and man given the opportunity of forgiveness. The meek will be ashamed of their transgressions and moved to call out to God in repentance. Those days will see a separation of the righteous and the unrighteous. Those who call out to God in humility, shame, and meekness will come to the "*holy mountain*" of God which is his church (see Isaiah 2:1-4 and Hebrews 12:18-24).

"**12** *But I will leave in the midst of you an afflicted and poor people, and they shall take refuge in the name of Jehovah.* **13** *The remnant of Israel shall not do iniquity, nor speak lies; neither shall a deceitful tongue be found in their mouth; for they shall feed and lie down, and none shall make them afraid*" **(3:12-13).**

Those who come to the "*holy mountain*" will receive forgiveness. These forgiven people will be known as the "*remnant of Israel*" and they will not sin, speak lies, or speak words of deceit (see 1 John 3:9-10). The remnant, or God's elect, have purposed in their hearts not to sin (see Romans 11:1-7). God's elect love and cherish his divine truths and are filled with shame and sorrow when they sin. Though their spirits be lowly due to their sins they shall not fear man knowing that God is on their side (see Luke 15:5).

A Time of Great Rejoicing (3:14-20)

"**14** *Sing, O daughter of Zion; shout, O Israel; be glad and rejoice with all the heart, O daughter of Jerusalem.* **15** *Jehovah has taken away your judgments, he has cast out your enemy: the King of Israel, even Jehovah, is in the midst of you; you shall not fear evil any more*" **(3:14-15).**

The fierce wrath of God is unleashed upon the wicked in the form of plagues and pestilence. There will rise out of the dust cloud of God's fierce anger a remnant (the "*daughter of Zion*") that will call out to God for help. God will answer their cries and cleanse them of their sins as they are added to his divine kingdom. The remnant will be like God and so he will dwell in the midst of them as their king. The righteous will not fear the wicked for God is on their side.

"**16** *In that day it shall be said to Jerusalem, Do not fear; O Zion, let not your hands be slack.* **17** *Jehovah your God is in the midst of you, a mighty one who will save; he will rejoice over you with joy; he will rest in his love; he will joy over you with singing.* **18** *I will gather them that sorrow for the solemn assembly, who were of you; to whom the burden upon her was a reproach*" **(3:16-18).**

Hands that hang down are hands that indicate an exasperated and downtrodden heart. The God fearing people who are saved from the judgments of sins through the Messiah are called upon to lift up these hanging hands and rejoice in their salvation. The Lord shall assemble the meek of the earth that fear him and they shall sing in joy for their burden of sin has been removed.

Great sorrow is produced within the heart of the meek and they that fear God. When I sin I not only disappoint God but my self and others. The guilt of sin has a way of making a man's hands hang down in discouragement. Thanks be to God that he will forgive those who faithfully wait for him (Romans 7:24-25).

"**19** *Behold, at that time I will deal with all them that afflict you; and I will save that which is lame, and gather that which was driven away; and I will make them a praise and a name, whose shame has been in all the earth.* **20** *At that time will I bring you in, and at that time will I gather you; for I will make you a name and a praise among all the peoples of the earth, when I bring back your captivity before your eyes, said Jehovah*" **(3:19-20).**

Zephaniah has a dual meaning to his words like many of the other prophet's writings. First, God will miraculously release his remnant people from Babylonian captivity and they shall be marveled at among the nations. Secondly, God would fulfill his promise to release his remnant from sin so that they fear no evil and hope in God.

HAGGAI

Robertson's Notes

Bible Books 37 of 66

"Go up to the mountain, and bring wood, and build the house; and I will take pleasure in it, and I will be glorified, said the Lord"

Haggai 1:8

Introduction

Haggai was a prophet of God that prophesied to the Jews who had returned to Jerusalem from Babylon during the year 536 BC (i.e., the first year of Cyrus over Babylon / see Ezra 1:1-2). The returning Jews were led back to Jerusalem to rebuild the temple of God that had been destroyed by the Babylonians. Seventy years had been spent in Babylonian captivity as foretold by Jeremiah (Jeremiah 25:11). God had **promised** that the captives would be released and that they would be able to reconstruct Jerusalem, the temple, and the city walls. God's promises; however, always have a part for man to do in order to receive his blessings. The Lord not only promises that a new temple would be built but **commanded** that the returning Jews do the work (Ezra 1:1-2 and 6:14). The Jews were to learn that the grand significance of God's temple is that it would be a figure of the holy and eternal temple, or kingdom of God, to come during the days of Christ (see book of Zechariah first six chapters).

Zerubbabel returns to Jerusalem with 50,000 people to build the temple under the authority of Cyrus (Ezra 1:1-2 / see also Isaiah 44:28). A strong and zealous start by the people results in the completion of the foundation of the temple after two years of being in Jerusalem (Ezra 3:8ff). The adversaries (Samaritans); however, discourage the Jews from building. The Samaritans *"weakened the hands of the people of Judah"* and *"frustrated their purpose all the days of Cyrus king of Persia, even until the reign of Darius king of Persia"* (Ezra 4:4-5, 24). The next 15 years pass with no work being done on the temple of God (compare Ezra 4:24 to 6:1ff). The people failed to keep God's command to build the temple and were consequentially in sin. The objective of God's prophet Haggai was to motivate the people to get back to the work of rebuilding the temple. They were to learn that with the help of God no mountain of a barrier would ever stand in the way of the Lord's eternal temple (see Zechariah 4:7).

Date of Haggai

Haggai comes on the scene to work among the delinquent people of Judah on the first day of the sixth month in the second year of Darius (Ezra 5:1-2). The prophet's first address to the people, regarding their delinquency, made a great impression on Zerubbabel, Joshua, and the people. They return to their work of constructing the temple as early as the twenty-fourth day of the same month (compare Haggai 1:1 and 14-15). Four years later (total of 21 years) the temple is completed (six total years of actual construction) (compare Ezra 1:1; 3:8 and 6:15). This dates the book to the second year of Darius the king (i.e., 519 BC) (note that the 17 years in Jerusalem minus 536 BC equals 519 BC).

First of four Oracles: Get Busy

Haggai reveals God's displeasure in the people's 15 year period of disobedience (Haggai 1:4). Once again the Lord commands, through Haggai, that the people get to work on the temple (Haggai 1:8). Haggai calls upon the people in Jerusalem to reason with God. Haggai asks them to **consider** why they are in the current distress of drought (Haggai 1:11), little harvest (Haggai 2:16), mildew and hail (Haggai 2:17). Why all the distress? *"Because of my house that lies waste, while you run every man to his own house"* (Haggai 1:9). The sovereign God of creation has called upon nature to correct his people. Throughout the scriptures we learn that God created this world to follow his laws and regulations. Those who refuse obedience always suffer consequences (see Psalms 32:4-5 and Hebrews 12:5-13). God's people today ought to be concerned and *"consider"* why we suffer the things we do. Like Job and David of old we must figure out if we are suffering because God is testing us (Job 23:10) or are we suffering because we have sinned (Psalms 32:4-5). Too many today are so hardened in sin that they do not consider the suffering they go through. Like mindless zombies they trudge through life never attempting to change their lives so that blessings would come (see Revelation 16:9-11).

After Haggai's *"stirring"* words (see Haggai 1:14) the Jews *"consider"* these things and respond with obedience and fear (Haggai 1:12). The people begin working 24 days after Haggai delivers the first oracle (Haggai 1:15). The great lesson learned is that God's blessings are contingent upon Israel's obedience (compare Haggai 1:7-9 with Haggai 2:19). When God promised to bless all nations through his Son Jesus he intended for man to do their part to be saved. The scriptures are replete with examples of people only receiving the blessings of God if they comply with his laws (Isaiah 54:3; Jeremiah 31:31-34 and Acts 13:33-39) (13b). Noah (Genesis 6:8-22 and Hebrews 11:17), Abraham (Hebrews 11:8), Joshua (Joshua 6:1-5 and Hebrews 11:30), Namaan (2 Kings 5), The blind man of John 9:7, and three thousand people in Jerusalem on the Day of Pentecost (Acts 2:37-44) all received God's gracious promises by complying with his commandments. Likewise, the people of Judah would only receive God's blessings of rain and crops if they obeyed his commandment to build the temple (see Zechariah 7:12-15).

Second of four Oracles: Encouragement

Haggai delivers his second revelation to the people of Jerusalem three and a half weeks after the people begin working on the temple. Once again discouragement settled in among the builders. This time it was not the Samaritans but rather their view of the current temple. Ezra tells us that after the foundation was laid many mourned due to the little stature of the temple in comparison to Solomon's (Ezra 3:12 and Haggai 2:3). The book of Zechariah helps us to have greater understanding here. An angel asks Zechariah a question at Zechariah 4:10 saying, "*Who has despised the day of small things?*" Though the foundation of the temple may seem small and insignificant to some it truly was not. This is a very significant statement regarding the spiritual nature and significance of the church. The Lord admonishes them, through his prophets Haggai and Zechariah, so that they would understand that God is not in the physical temple but the spiritual (see Acts 17:24). He will be a wall of fire around this spiritual temple and dwell with them (see Zechariah 2:5). The Lord is building his church through the seed of Zerubbabel, Christ, and it will not be insignificant. People will be forgiven of their sins (see Zechariah 3:3-5, 9 and 4:7)! The object of the book of Zechariah is to enlighten the returning Jews concerning the grand significance that they represent at this point of history. God's eternal temple and kingdom is soon to come. Now was the time to put their faith and trust in God and build with the hope of the coming Christ and his kingdom.

Haggai encourages the people by telling them to **be strong** because God is with them in their efforts (Haggai 2:4). While the Samaritans and discouragement weakened them God commands them to be strong (see Ezra 4:4-5, 24). There is no time or place for weakness that leads to disobedience through neglect, apathy, or lethargic disinterest. God accepts no excuses. There is too much at stake! His divine expectations for his people are that they be strong and work. He equips us (Ephesians 6:10ff and 1 Peter 4:11).

Third of Four Oracles: A Call for Repentance

Haggai delivers the third revelation to the people of Jerusalem three months after the work on the temple had started. Though the people had obeyed through fear (Haggai 1:12) and begun to rebuild the temple (Haggai 1:14) they were still considered "*unclean*" (Haggai 2:14). Haggai calls upon the people to consider their sinful ways and turn to God that they may receive the blessings of Jehovah (Haggai 2:15-18). The book of Zechariah will bear out the fact that even though they began to build the temple God's blessings continued to be withheld from them due to their disobedience (Zechariah 8:9-13). The lesson to be learned is that God expects his people to be holy and perfect as he is holy and perfect (see Matthew 5:48; 1 Peter 1:15-17 and 1 John 4:17).

Four of Four Oracles: The Hope of the Anointed Christ

Haggai delivers this last oracle the same day that he received and delivered the third (i.e., three months after the work of the temple had begun). Zerubbabel is told that the Lord has chosen him to bring about his anointed one. Through Christ, all eternal blessings will be found to those who turn their hearts to him. Haggai's prophetic solution to all the returnees' issues, and man's today, is Jesus Christ. Christ will strengthen our hands with his promises of forgiveness and blood that was shed for our redemption (see Ephesians 1:7). The Apostle Paul said, "*I can do all things through him* (Christ) *that strengthens me*" (Philippians 4:13). The Christian's strength comes from the confidence that God will fulfill all his promises. Motivation to live holy and perfectly in line with God's laws is discovered in the promises of God. Haggai knew this and so he preached. Zechariah would take the baton of preaching Christ and his kingdom from Haggai and give us greater details.

Consider the kings of Persia

Cyrus (559 [536 over Babylon] – 530 BC) – Allowed Jews to return to Jerusalem, under the leadership of Zerubbabel, to rebuild the temple (Ezra 1:1-2). The Jews efforts were frustrated all the days of Cyrus (Ezra 4:5).

Cambyses (530 - 522 BC) (the Ahasuerus or Xerxes of Ezra 4:6-23) – Killed his brother Smerdis to secure his position as King of Persia. Cambyses received letters from the Samaritans in relation to the construction of the temple. He authorized a decree to cease the work on the temple due to the history of Jewish rebellion in Jerusalem (Ezra 4:19-21).

Gomates (Pseudo-Smerdis) (521 BC) – Laid claims to being the murdered brother of Cambyses and usurped the throne of Cambyses while he was away in Egypt. Gomates was killed by a Persian officer and thus his rule lasts for only a few months.

Darius the Great (521 - 486 BC) – During the second year of Darius (i.e., 519 BC) Haggai and Zechariah prophesied unto the Jews in Judah and Jerusalem and encouraged them to return to the work of the temple (Ezra 4:24-5:1). Tattenai (the governor beyond the River / Ezra 5:3) questioned the validity of their work. The governor wrote a letter to Darius requesting a search to be made in the Persian archives as to whether or not Cyrus ever gave a decree that the temple be constructed (Ezra 5:17). Darius found that Cyrus did give such a decree (Ezra 6:3) and consequentially gave authority to Zerubbabel and the Jews to continue the work (Ezra 6:14). Four years latter, the sixth year of Darius, the temple was completed (Ezra 6:15).

HAGGAI CHAPTER 1

Synopsis

The returning Jews were to learn very valuable lessons in life. Their eternal abode depended upon how they handled the current situation. They had sinned against God by not building his temple as he had commanded. Their reason for the current rebellion was not excused or accepted by God. The Samaritans and size of the temple had been sources of great discouragement that moved them to sin. The Lord caused a drought to occur so that his people would see their need for repentance.

Application

The Christian is to learn that no man ought to ever have the power to take your faith away. Haggai's instructions to God's people are that they move past the ignorance of other men and the weakness of discouragement and get to doing the work he demands.

Another lesson seen in this first chapter of Haggai is that we must all come to understand why we suffer at times. When we are going through hardships we ought to "*consider*" them and ask "*why*" (Haggai 1:7-9). The "*why*" is not a 'woe is me' type of question but rather the interrogation of our inner spiritual standing with God. I should examine my life to see if my suffering is due to my own sin (see 2 Corinthians 13:5).

Haggai challenges the people of God to do this very thing. God chastens those he loves yet if we do not consider what is happening to us then the punishment will not have its desired affects (see Hebrews 12:5ff). Children that are spanked may experience pain yet if the parent is not successful in helping the child know why he is being punished then it does no good (33d). God, as a parent, is helping the delinquent Jews understand why they are being punished.

Haggai 1

The Bleak state of Judah is a reflection of their Failing to Build the Temple of God (Haggai's First Message to Judah) (1:1-11)

"**1** *In the second year of Darius the king, in the sixth month, in the first day of the month, came the word of Jehovah by Haggai the prophet unto Zerubbabel the son of Shealtiel, governor of Judah, and to Joshua the son of Jehozadak, the high priest, saying*" **(1:1)**.

The second year of Darius was the year 519 BC. The temple of God had lain dormant for 15 years. God had commanded that his temple be built yet the people permitted the Samaritans and the size of the temple foundation to discourage them to the point of disobeying God's command to build (Ezra 6:14). The Lord responds to the people neglectfulness by sending his prophets Haggai and Zechariah that they may be encouraged to resume the construction process.

"**2** *Thus speaks Jehovah of hosts, saying, this people say, it is not the time for us to come, the time for Jehovah's house to be built.* **3** *Then came the word of Jehovah by Haggai the prophet, saying,* **4** *Is it a time for you yourselves to dwell in your ceiled houses, while this house lies waste?*" **(1:2-4)**.

Some believe that the Jews were looking to Jeremiah's prophecy regarding spending 70 years in captivity and concluding that their time had not yet been completed. Some may have counted the captivity from the second or third wave of captives rather than the first wherein Daniel was taken (i.e. 605 BC - see Daniel 1:1, 21). Ezekiel, along with 10,000 others, was taken in the second deportation out of Jerusalem at 597 BC (2 Kings 24:14ff; Jeremiah 29:1 and Ezekiel 1:1-2). The final invasion of Babylon into Palestine occurred during the reign of Zedekiah (590 BC). If their Babylonian captivity was counted from the time of Ezekiel's capture rather than Daniel's then the people would have a point; however, it is clear that the captivity began with Daniel and that now, 70 years latter, God has fulfilled his promise to return the remnant to Judah.

Haggai sarcastically says, 'if you say that it is not time to build God's house are you justified in saying that it is time to build luxurious homes for yourselves while God's house lies in ruins?' (50) The prophet reasons with the people. If the captivity is not complete is it ok to let God's house lay wasted and for people to spend all their time, energies, and monies in building their own homes?

A "*ceiled*" home is one that no expense had been spared in its construction. Most Bible translations render the word "paneled." It may very well be that those who returned with Zerubbabel 15 years earlier had used all the cedar wood provided by Cyrus for their own homes rather than on the temple. The point is that they had left off doing God's will so that they could selfishly fulfill their own personal desires. They wanted nice houses rather than a completed temple. Their desires were in conflict with God's divine commands. Haggai's job was to realign the Jews desires with God's commandments.

"*5 Now therefore thus said Jehovah of hosts: consider your ways. 6 You have sown much, and bring in little; you eat, but you have not enough; you drink, but you are not filled with drink; you clothe you, but there is none warm; and he that earns wages earns wages to put it into a bag with holes*" **(1:5-6)**.

The prophet, by divine decree, calls upon the Jews to "*consider their ways.*" This phrase is used four times throughout this book. Fifteen years have past and the house of God lays waste. What have you been doing for these years? This would certainly be a good question for any

Christian who has neglected spiritual growth, repentance, worship, or any other spiritual aspect of life.

The prophet gives the Jews a panoramic view of their toil over the past fifteen years. They have worked hard yet brought in little. The blessings of harvest and the fruit of the vine appear to have been very little. Due to the desperate times clothing was insufficient and they were cold in the winter. Their money did not go very far due to times of want. Can they not see that something is wrong? God has withheld these blessings from them due to their disobedience. The prophet of God is challenging the people to think about why things are going as they are. People today ought to stop and ponder why they are suffering the things that they suffer. Job wanted to know why he was suffering and he concluded that it was because God was testing him (Job 23:10). David also wanted to know why he was suffering (see Psalms 30:6 and 42:9). David figured out that the reason he suffered, on many occasions, was because he had sinned and God was chastening him (see Psalms 30:1-5). If we suffer calamity and do not "consider" why these things are happening we will continue in our ignorance and sin. The people were being challenged to figure out why they had been suffering through these years. God was divinely punishing them for their wickedness because he loved them and wanted to see them get back to the work of building the temple as he commanded (17a).

"**7** *Thus said Jehovah of hosts:* **Consider** *your ways.* **8** *Go up to the mountain, and bring wood, and build the house; and I will take pleasure in it, and I will be glorified, said Jehovah.* **9** *You looked for much, and lo, it came to little; and when you brought it home, I did blow upon it.* **Why?** *Said Jehovah of hosts.* **Because** *of my house that lies waste, while you run every man to his own house"* **(1:7-9).**

Once again the Lord asks Judah to "*consider your ways.*" Judah is called upon to consider the current hardships and its relation to avoiding the command of God to build the temple. All the hardships of Judah are attributed to the house of God lying waste, "*while you run every man to his own house*." Their interest had taken another rout over these 15 years and God is not pleased. When the people get busy God's blessings will return to them.

No doubt their negligence to God's commands expanded over time. At first, they may have waited for some word that would permit them to rebuild. As time went on and no authorization to build was given they seemed to forget their primary objective. Sometimes people today can get so wrapped up in trying to make it through difficult times that they forget to put time into serving God. God uses natural resources to afflict his people that they may correct their ways (Hebrews 12:7ff) (17d).

"**10 Therefore** *for your sake the heavens withhold the dew, and the earth withholds its fruit.* **11** *And I called for a drought upon the land, and upon the mountains, and upon the grain, and upon the new wine, and upon the oil, and upon that which the ground brings forth, and upon men, and upon cattle, and upon all the labor of the hands*" **(1:10-11).**

Haggai was challenging the people to "*consider*" why they had suffered all these things. Years were going by in disobedience and God was correcting them yet they had not considered this. I have highlighted significant words in the verses above such as "*why*," "*because*," and "*Therefore*" to mark the reasons God withheld his blessings from the Jews (see also Jeremiah 2:17; 9:12-15; etc.). No rain meant smaller harvest of grain, new wine, and cattle. No rain means reduced labor forces. God, through Haggai, clears up the people's perplexity. They were in a terrible drought **because** they had forsaken God's commandment to build the temple. God was punishing them. The Lord has fulfilled his promise to bring them back to Jerusalem and now they needed to keep his charge (Deuteronomy 30:1-5 and Jeremiah 29:8-10).

The People give Heed to Haggai's charge and get back to Work on the Temple (1:12-15)

"**12** *Then Zerubbabel the son of Shealtiel, and Joshua the son of Jehozadak, the high priest, with all the remnant of the people,* **obeyed** *the voice of Jehovah their God, and the words of Haggai the prophet, as Jehovah their God had sent him; and the **people did fear** before Jehovah"* **(1:12).**

Upon hearing the words of Haggai the people were convicted of their sin of leaving off building the temple. They were ashamed of themselves and quickly got back to work. They had honestly *"considered their ways"* and found themselves to be in sin. They discovered that the reason for the lack of rain and harvest was their sin. God's chastisement had achieved its intended objective.

The word of God states that they now, *"obeyed the voice of Jehovah their God."* It was time for them to get back to building the temple. Not building the temple was a matter of disobedience. They had rebelled against God's commands long enough. Notice that the people's *"fear"* of God is equated to their *"obedience."* Those who do not fear God (i.e., have respect and reverence for) will not obey. The child who does not fear his father will not obey his father (36).

*"**13** Then spoke Haggai Jehovah's messenger in Jehovah's message unto the people, saying, I am with you, said Jehovah. **14** And Jehovah stirred up the spirit of Zerubbabel the son of Shealtiel, governor of Judah, and the spirit of Joshua the son of Jehozadak, the high priest, and the spirit of all the remnant of the people; and they came and did work on the house of Jehovah of hosts, their God, **15** in the four and twentieth day of the month, in the sixth month, in the second year of Darius the king"* **(1:13-15).**

Twenty four days after hearing Haggai's words of divine revelation they get back to work. They had considered the blessings of the land being withheld, how hard their toil was for seemingly nothing, the fact that they had left off building when they should have been working on the temple, and that God had given them a command and they had not fulfilled it. The preaching of Haggai, by divine revelation, *"stirred up the spirit"* of the governor, the high priests, and all the people. Gospel preaching that does not *"stir the spirit"* to do right is not gospel preaching (18c). Again, those who's spirits are not stirred or agitated by truth have little to no true love of truth or concern for eternity.

Questions over Haggai Chapter 1

1. Why did God send Haggai to the Jews in Jerusalem?

2. How many times does Haggai address the people?

3. What was the cause of the Jews' disobedience to build God's temple?

4. What were the people of Israel saying about the construction of God's house?

5. Why were the people in Jerusalem experiencing a drought, mildew, hail, and small harvests?

6. Does God continue to do similar things to the disobedient today?

7. How many times does Haggai say, "*Consider your ways*?"

8. How did the people respond to Haggai's words?

HAGGAI CHAPTER 2

Synopsis

God continues to mold the thinking of his people. Discouragement over the size of the temple was not to be entertained in the mind (see Zechariah 4:9-10). The temple of God was only a representation of the promises that were soon to come through Jesus Christ. The people's discouragement was superficial in that it took into consideration physical things. God moves his people to think on a spiritual level through the words of Haggai.

Application

Spiritual thinking will move one to meekness. The meek will not only identify one area of sin but all areas. The lesson of this chapter is holiness and sanctification. God's expectation of his people is total holiness and perfection. Though we may correct one area in life we are not accepted by God until we correct all our errors. Though the Jews had corrected the error of not building they remained in sin. God continued to punish them with no rain and little harvest until they could see their other unclean ways. Total correction and repentance is demanded of God.

Haggai 2

The Lord's Prophet delivers words of Encouragement (Haggai's Second Message to Judah) (2:1-9)

> "**1** *In the seventh month, in the one and twentieth day of the month, came the word of Jehovah by Haggai the prophet saying,* **2** *Speak now to Zerubbabel the son of Shealtiel, governor of Judah, and to Joshua the son of Jehozadak, the high priest, and to the remnant of the people, saying,* **3** *Who is left among you that saw this house in its former glory? And how do you see it now? Is it not in your eyes as nothing*?" **(2:1-3).**

Haggai addresses the people of God a second time two months after the first address. The seventh month in the Hebrew calendar was Tishri. Tishri was an important month to the Jews. The Day of Atonement was on the tenth day of this month. The fifteenth to the twenty second days of Tishri are the Feast of Tabernacles or booths. This was a seven day period of sacrificing and marked the conclusion of the harvest season. The twenty third of Tishri was a day of holy convocation (see Leviticus 23).

Near the end of the feast of Tabernacles the Lord tells Haggai to speak words of divine revelation to Zerubbabel and Joshua the high priest. The people had now been building the temple for about three and one half weeks (Haggai 1:15). Haggai is to pose a question. Who among the living has actually seen the former temple that Solomon built? What comparisons do you now make between Solomon's and the one you are now working on? Fifteen years earlier the foundation of the new temple was laid. Many elderly people looked upon the foundation and discern that it would not come close to meeting the glorious state of Solomon's temple (Ezra 3:12). We are given another clue as to why the people stopped working on the temple for so long. Not only had they been discouraged by the Samaritans but also they were discouraged by the size of the temple. Haggai's objective was to strengthen the minds of the discouraged (18c).

Zechariah reveals the spiritual significance of building the temple of God. While the people looked on the foundation of the temple and considered it small and seemingly less significant than Solomon's they were sorely mistaken. Zechariah teaches the people that the degree of significance to the temple can hardly be measured. The temple of Zerubbabel would prefigure the spiritual Zion to come (see Zechariah 4:9-10).

"**4** *Yet now* **be strong***, O Zerubbabel, said Jehovah; and be strong, O Joshua, son of Jehozadak, the high priest; and be strong, all you people of the land, said Jehovah,* **and work***: for* **I am with you***, said Jehovah of hosts,* **5** *according to the word that I covenanted with you when you came up out of Egypt, and my Spirit abode among you: fear you not*" **(2:4-5).**

God has given a command; i.e., build my temple (see Ezra 6:14 and Haggai 1:8). The people begin the work; however, the forces of discouragement have crushed their desire to fulfill God's will. The Samaritans and the size of the temple have discouraged them. Jehovah's purpose, through Haggai, was to encourage the people to do that which they knew he wanted them to do; i.e., build.

Haggai's encouraging message was "*be strong and work: for I am with you said Jehovah of host.*" The Christian today can be encouraged to do the work of God because he is with us and will strengthen us through his word (see Ephesians 3:16; Colossians 1:11 and 2 Timothy 2:1). When fear of man and discouragement come it does not find its origins in God. God had always promised Israel that He would be with them and fight for them if they would put their whole hearted trust in him (see Exodus 14:14 and 19:4-6).

There are many things at Satan's disposal that has the power to weaken the hands of God's people (2 Corinthians 2:11). Satan weakens the hands of God's people by discouragement, worldliness, and false doctrines of men. God's people were to learn that their true hope was not to be in a physical temple but in the Christ who dwell within them and forgive them of their sins.

"**6** *For thus said Jehovah of hosts: yet once, it is a little while, and I will shake the heavens, and the earth, and the sea, and the dry land;* **7** *and I* *will shake all nations; and the precious things of all nations shall come; and I will fill this house with glory, said Jehovah of hosts.* **8** *The silver is mine, and the gold is mine, said Jehovah of hosts.* **9** *The latter glory of this house shall be greater than the former, said Jehovah of hosts; and in this place will I give peace, said Jehovah of hosts"* **(2:6-9).**

The wording of these verses parallels that of Haggai 2:20-23 in relation to God's promise to establish his new kingdom and place his son Jesus on the throne. The point is obvious. The people were loosing sight of the big spiritual picture by getting discouraged about a small temple. They must go back to the prophecies of Ezekiel regarding God's future spiritual temple (see last 12 chapters of Ezekiel). The Lord promised to build his church with Christ as its head and king. God would fill this new kingdom with his Spirit and they would be greatly blessed with salvation. The current temple was only a stepping stone to get the people to the eternal and indestructible temple of God.

Haggai is looking to a day when the God of all creation shall cause kingdoms such as the Medes, Persians, Grecians, and Romans to rise and fall yet his glorious kingdom shall remain (see Daniel 2:44-45). The house of Jehovah God would be more glorious in the future. God's kingdom shall be the focal point of the entire world (i.e., the place where forgiveness of Jew and Gentile is found). There was absolutely no reason to be discouraged over this current temple. The Apostle Paul would latter say; "24 *The God that made the world and all things therein, he, being Lord of heaven and earth, dwells not in temples made with hands*" (Acts 17:24). Bit by bit and piece by piece of information was being trickled to the Jews through prophecy regarding God's kingdom and the people's eternal blessings. They had great things to look forward to in the future. Now is not the time to get discouraged because of the size of a temple. There is no time for discouragement in our lives when we think of the eternal blessings in Christ Jesus.

Haggai's Third Message to Judah: The Lord wants the Sinners to Acknowledge their sin before he returns his Blessings upon Them (2:10-19)

"**10** *In the four and twentieth day of the ninth month, in the second year of Darius, came the word of Jehovah by Haggai the prophet, saying,* **11** *Thus said Jehovah of hosts: ask now the priests concerning the law, saying,* **12** *If one bear holy flesh in the skirt of his garment, and with his skirt do touch bread, or pottage, or wine, or oil, or any food, shall it become holy? And the priests answered and said, No*" **(2:10-12)**.

The Lord gives Haggai another prophecy for Judah exactly three months after the work had been started (see Haggai 1:15). The priests of God were the ones who made a distinction between clean and unclean things and in so doing taught the people (see Leviticus 10:8ff). The "*holy flesh*" was no doubt the flesh of animals that had been offered as burnt offerings to Jehovah God. Haggai poses a question to the priests. If they bear holy flesh in the skirt of their garment will their garment, if it touches something like bread, wine, oil, or any food, cause the food to become holy? The priest rightly answered no because holiness is not transferred through one's garments.

"**13** *Then said Haggai, If one that is unclean by reason of a dead body touch any of these, shall it be unclean? And the priests answered and said, it shall be unclean*" **(2:13)**.

Another question is posed to the priests. If one has contact with a dead body will things he touches become unclean? The priests answered yes (see Numbers 19:22). Haggai's point is that holy things cannot be transferred to other things as holy; however, unclean things can be transferred. This was God's sovereign law.

"**14** *Then answered Haggai and said, So is this people, and so is this nation before me, said Jehovah; and so is every work of their hands; and that which they offer there is unclean*" **(2:14)**.

God had not yet restored his blessings of rain and fruitfulness of the land even though they had began to build the temple. The people did not understand. They had now begun the work as he had commanded and were even offering sacrifices to him on the altar. The nation; however, remained unclean and everything they touched was unclean. Work on their farms and the temple was unfruitful and unacceptable due to their unclean moral condition.

Zechariah reveals things about the state of God's people in Judea at this time that Haggai leaves out. Five months after the people had begun the work on the temple of God (compare Zechariah 1:7 with Haggai 1:15) Zechariah is pleading with them to "*return from your evil ways*" (Zechariah 1:4). The prophet of God labeled the people as "*wicked*" (Zechariah 5:5-7). Their problems ran much deeper than being simply discouraged from building the temple of God. Everything seemed to spiritually fall apart for the Jews once they stopped working on the temple. Their worship was said to be mundane, mechanical, ritualistic or habitual religious practices (Zechariah 7:1-7). God reveals that their hearts were as hard as an "*adamant stone*" though they thought all was well (Zechariah 7:12). The people devised evil against their own brethren (Zechariah 7:8ff), were "*unclean*" (Hag. 2:14), and placed their trust in false prophets (Zechariah 10:2). The message to the people was that if they wanted God's blessings they would have to not only build the temple but speak truth, execute truthful judgment, leave off evil devising, turn away from false oaths, and stop doing all the things that Jehovah hates (Zechariah 8:16-18).

Just because one is going through the motions of God's worship does not mean that the Lord accepts it. Jesus reveals this fact at Matthew 15:9. Isaiah and Amos warned the people of simply going through the motions of worshipping God without truly turning to him too (see Isaiah 1:11ff and Amos 5:21ff). The events surrounding the captives of Babylon returning to Jerusalem teaches us that God demands absolute holiness in man's life (see Matthew 5:48 and 1 Peter 1:15-17). Secondly, these Old Testament books teach us about the power of Satan. Through time,

Satan had caused the people to be disobedient to God's command to build the temple. The further down the road of discouragement and uncleanness they went the further from God they were. When one is far removed from God's commands it becomes very difficult for this person to see all their faults (14f).

"**15** And now, I pray you, **consider** from this day and backward, before a stone was laid upon a stone in the temple of God. **16** Through all that time, when one came to a heap of twenty measures there were but ten; when one came to the winevat to draw out fifty vessels, there were but twenty. **17** I smote you with blasting and with mildew and with hail in all the work of your hands; yet you **turned** not to me, said Jehovah" **(2:15-17)**.

Zerubbabel and the people had considered their negligence toward building God's temple and discovered ONE of the reasons God had withheld his blessings from them. Now, they have corrected their negligence to build yet their other works continued to be defiled and unpleasing to God.

Haggai tells the people to "*consider from **this day** and backward...*" To this day (and going back before one stone was laid in the building process of the temple / i.e., 15 years ago) they do not receive God's blessings. When they go to the field and expect a great harvest of wheat they only find fifty percent of what should have been expected. Likewise there was even less than fifty percent of expected wine production. Their harvest was affected due to God blasting the crops with mildew and hail. The work of the people's hands was frustrated by God because of their sins.

God was chastising them with a heavy hand and they did not even consider it. A fascinating part of David and Job's lives was that they spent a considerable amount of time trying to figure out why they were suffering. Job knew that he had not sinned against God so he concluded that he was being put to the test (see Job 23:10). David often figured out that God was chastising him for his sinful behavior (see Psalms 32:4-5).

The people of God during the days of Zerubbabel had considered their negligence to God's command to build the temple yet they had not considered their other sins. Those hardened in sin will often continue in their transgressions even though God chastises them with great hardships. Their minds are deluded (see 2 Thessalonians 2:11-12). They are being challenged to look at every aspect of their lives that they may be perfect and holy in every way.

"**18** *Consider, I pray you, from this day and backward, from the twenty fourth day of the ninth month, since the day that the foundation of Jehovah's temple was laid, consider it.* **19** *Is the seed yet in the barn? Yea, the vine, and the fig-tree, and the pomegranate, and the olive-tree have not brought forth; from this day will I bless you*" **(2:18-19).**

Nothing had changed in the production of the land. God has control over all things of this creation (even the crops of the field) (3a). The twenty fourth day of the ninth month would mark the beginnings of a change in the people's state of blessing. The inference is that they have learned their lesson, made their sacrifices, and changed their ways. They now understand that God's blessings are contingent upon a total change of heart that goes from rebellion to whole hearted service to him. Let the Christian know today that even though we may repent of our evil doings and begin obeying God's commands there is more that we must do to maintain our fellowship with the Lord. We must not only acknowledge our sin but humble ourselves before Jehovah God and pray that He would forgive us of our trespasses. Meekness is the ability to see not one or two sins but all one's sins.

Haggai's Fourth Message to Judah (2:20-23)

"**20** *And the word of Jehovah came the second time unto Haggai in the four and twentieth day of the month, saying,* **21** *Speak to Zerubbabel, governor of Judah, saying, I will shake the heavens and the earth;* **22** *and I will overthrow the throne of kingdoms; and I will destroy the strength of the kingdoms of the nations; and I will overthrow the chariots, and those* *that ride in them; and the horses and their riders shall come down, every one by the sword of his brother*" **(2:20-22).**

Haggai receives a second message on the same day that he receives the one discussed above. The same God that chastises Judah will likewise shake the world of nations. There is no kingdom that will ever rise against the kingdom of God and destroy it. God will raise kingdoms of men, use them for his divine glory, and discard them as he has done in old times (see Haggai 2:7; Daniel 2:21, 22, 44, and 45).

"**23** *In that day, said Jehovah of hosts, will I take you, O Zerubbabel, my servant, the son of Shealtiel, said Jehovah, and will make you as a signet; for I have chosen you, said Jehovah of host*" **(2:23).**

The "*day*" that God would destroy the kingdoms of men was the day that he made Zerubbabel a chosen "*signet*." The signet was an imprint on a ring or letter that signified authentication or authorization of one in a supreme position of authority or ownership. God chose Zerubbabel "*as a signet*." Zerubbabel would be a living symbol of authentication of God's promise to bring down the nations of men through his own divine kingdom.

Through veiled language the prophet reveals that Zerubbabel is God's choice for the lineage of the Messiah to continue. The promise that God made to Abraham and latter to David is renewed in Zerubbabel (see Genesis 12:1ff and 2 Samuel 7:11-14). Matthew's genealogies reveal Zerubbabel to be in the lineage of Jesus Christ (see Matthew 1:12, 16). The message is that people of all generations are to look for the conditional spiritual blessings in Jesus Christ. Those who do not completely conform their lives to the image of Jesus Christ will be chastised and caused to consider why they suffer the things they suffer.

Questions over Haggai Chapter 2

1. **True or False:** the size of the new temple did not really bother anyone.

2. Why does Haggai tell the people that the size of the physical temple doesn't really matter?

3. **True or False:** The people were considered clean and joyous as they began building God's temple again.

4. What role would Zerubbabel eventually play in man's salvation?

ZECHARIAH

Robertson's Notes

Bible book 38 of 66

"Thus said Jehovah of hosts: Let your hands be strong, you that hear in these days these words from the mouth of the prophets that were in the day the foundation of the house of Jehovah of hosts was laid, even the temple, that it might be built"

Zechariah 8:9

Introduction

To understand the message of Zechariah we must first lay the groundwork of historical events that lead up to the words of this prophet of God. God brought sword, pestilence, famine, and wild beast to Judah due to her rebellious ways yet she refused to lay these things to heart (Isaiah 42:25). During the reign of Zedekiah over Judah God brought the Babylonian Empire upon his own people to punish them for their persistent disobedience. Those who did not die in the siege of Jerusalem were taken captive to Babylon for seventy years as Jeremiah had foretold. The people of God were to be corrected and punished for her persistent sin (Jeremiah 25:11; 30:12 and 31:17-20). During these seventy years they were to experience the chastening of the Lord (Jeremiah 30:23-24). They would come to be "*ashamed*" of their rebellious ways (Jeremiah 31:19). Their shame would lead them to "*repent*" and call upon the Lord in prayer and praise (Jeremiah 31:19).

The Lord promised the captives that after seventy years were accomplished in Babylon he would bring them back to Jerusalem (see Jeremiah 29:10). Though the days of captivity were very unpleasant there were greater days to look forward to (Isaiah 44:1-8). God would bring his people back to Judah and they would be restored. Isaiah writes, "*28 That said of Cyrus, he is my shepherd, and shall perform all my pleasure, even saying of Jerusalem, she shall be built; and of the **temple**, your foundations shall be laid*" (Isaiah 44:28). Isaiah had a dual prophecy in mind that is brought out by the books of Ezra, Haggai, and Zechariah. God would cause his people to return to Judah and rebuild Jerusalem and the temple that was destroyed by Babylon. The spiritual side of the prophecy was that God would eventually establish his divine city, Zion or Jerusalem, in the New Testament days under Christ as its king.

The book of Ezra confirms the validity of God's promise to restore his people to their land (see 2 Chronicles 36:19-21 and Ezra 1:1ff). The captives that initially return with Zerubbabel were fully restored and they understood their divine mission to rebuild the city of Jerusalem and the temple (see Ezekiel 36:32-36 and Ezra chapter 3). Their hearts were purposed to do all that God had commanded them (see Ezra 3:2-4). The Lord had commanded them to build the temple and so they were eager to do his divine will (see Ezra 6:14). Two years after coming to Jerusalem they began work on the temple and laid the foundation (Ezra 3:8-10). When the people saw the foundation of the temple many wept due to the size compared to Solomon's temple (see Ezra 3:12). Zechariah would latter chastise the people for their ill informed sorrow. The people were to learn, by the work of Zechariah, that God intended much larger spiritual things for them than this immediate physical temple (see Zechariah 4:9-10).

The Jews were nonetheless excited about the temple of God. When the Samaritans came to offer help Zerubbabel rejected them as those who have no part in spiritual matters with the people of God (Ezra 4:1-3). The Samaritans did all within their power to frustrate and discourage God's people from building the temple seeing that they were not permitted to be involved in it (Ezra 4:4ff). The Samaritans *"weakened the hands of the people of Judah"* and *"frustrated their purpose all the days of Cyrus king of Persia, even until the reign of Darius king of Persia"* (Ezra 4:4-5, 24). The next fifteen years would go by without any work being done on the temple as God had commanded (compare Ezra 3:4 and 4:24 to Haggai 1:1, 15 and Zechariah 1:1). God's people had permitted a faulty view of the temple's size and discouragement at the hands of the Samaritans to cause them to disobey the Lord's command to build.

The book of Ezra tells us that God sent the prophets Haggai and Zechariah to the people to motivate them to get back to working on the temple (Ezra 5:1-2; Zechariah 6:15 and 8:9). Haggai's duty was to cause the Jews to *"consider their ways"* (Haggai 1:7). God had plagued the people of Judah with a drought and they were not even considering the cause of their discomfort (see Haggai 1:8-11). Haggai's words were received and the people obeyed God and went back to work (Haggai 1:12, 14). Zechariah's duty was to open the people's eyes to what laid ahead of them regarding the Lord's church and their future glorification.

Zechariah tells us that even after the people are motivated by Haggai to build they continued to experience drought and a lack of God's blessings (Zechariah 5:1-4 and 14:17). Two months after they had returned to the work on the temple Zechariah is still calling for their repentance of wicked works (compare Haggai 1:15 to Zechariah 1:1ff). Zechariah is pleading with them to *"return now from your evil ways"* (Zechariah 1:4) which he latter identifies as their *"wickedness"* (Zechariah 5:5-7). The people's "*wickedness*" came in the form of thievery and false witnessing (Zechariah 5:3-4), mundane, mechanical, ritualistic or habitual religious practices (Zechariah 7:1-7), and having a passion to acquire the riches and fame offered by the world (Zechariah 9:1ff). God reveals that their hearts were as hard as an "*adamant stone*" (Zechariah 7:12). The people devised evil against their own brethren (Zechariah 7:8ff) and they were "*unclean*" (Haggai 2:14). They had also lost sight of the spiritual significance of the temple by viewing it as small (Zechariah 4:9-10). The people of God had fallen back to the ways that caused them to go into captivity in the first place (see Zechariah 11:4-6; Amos 2:6 and 8:4-6). The objective of the drought was to drive the people to repentance yet rather than turning to God they turned to idols (see Zechariah 10:1-2). The message to the people was that if they wanted God's blessings they would not only have to build the temple but speak truth, execute truthful judgment, leave off evil devising, turn away from false oaths, and stop doing all the things that Jehovah hates (Zechariah 8:16-18). Total reformation was the only acceptable way to God.

Zechariah delivers eight divine visions and two oracles to the people over fourteen chapters. The object of the visions and oracles is to turn the people's hearts back to God. The people were to learn that God's blessings are contingent upon man's obedience from the heart (Zechariah 8:9-13). Zechariah takes his audience down a future road of a day and time when the Branch or Messiah would reign as king supreme over God's kingdom (Zechariah 3:6-8 and 9:9). This King shall provide a "*fountain*" (Zechariah 13:1) from his "*pierced*" body (Zechariah 12:10) that God's people may be cleansed of their sins (Zechariah 13:1). These "*living waters*" (Zechariah 14:8) shall ever be supplied by the "*King over all the earth*" (Zechariah 14:9). These facts are the foundation of the temple and rebuilding of Jerusalem that Isaiah spoke of at chapter 44:28.

Zechariah

Zechariah was a prophet of a priestly lineage who had returned to Jerusalem with Zerubbabel to rebuild the temple of God (Nehemiah

12:1-4, 16). Zechariah was an existing prophet of the day with Haggai and shared the same general purpose of motivating the delinquent Jews to get busy and build the temple (Ezra 5:1; Haggai 1:8 and Zechariah 4:9; 8:9). Some have referred to Matthew as the prophet of the kingdom of God in the New Testament. Zechariah would certainly be the prophet to take that title in the Old Testament though it would be a tight race with Ezekiel.

Date of Zechariah

God sends the prophets Haggai and Zechariah to his people to motivate them to return to the work of building the temple (Ezra 5:1ff). Fifteen years would pass before any additional work on God's temple would resume (Compare Ezra 4:24 to 6:1ff). Ezra 5:1-2 reveals that Haggai entered upon his work on the first day of the sixth month, in the second year of Darius. Zechariah began his work two months after Haggai (compare Haggai 1:1 and Zechariah 1:1). This dates the book to the second year of Darius the king (i.e., 519 BC). The last oracle of Haggai to God's people is dated the ninth month of the second year of Darius (i.e., 519 BC) whereas Zechariah went on another two years to reveal the visions and oracles of God to the people (Zechariah 7:1).

Application of the Book of Zechariah

The hope of Israel, going back to the days of Abraham, had always been to experience God's blessings of forgiveness (see Genesis 12:1-4 as fulfilled in Jesus Christ as Paul states at Galatians 3:10ff). Nothing has changed from testament to testament in relationship to God's requirements to receive his blessings. If the people in the days of Zerubbabel, Haggai, and Zechariah expected to see the curse of drought removed they needed to obey the commandments of God. Likewise, those today who would like the blessings of salvation through Christ must abide in the commandments of God. Those who obey God will not experience his divine curse (Zechariah 14:11). The Lord will protect, defend, and be a wall of protection for his true saints in Zion (see Zechariah 2:5; 9:8, and 15).

There are at least 20 cross references between Zechariah and Revelation (see introduction to this study). These references explain God's dealings in the lives of men even today. There is a great warfare taking place between the forces of good and evil. Satan's objective is to wash away the world in a flood of ungodliness by means of worldliness, temptation, persecution, and false teachers (see Zechariah 3:1-4 compared Revelation 12:13-17). During the days of Zerubbabel, Haggai, and Zechariah God's people were persecuted by the Samaritans (Ezra 4:1ff), tempted by the ways of the world (Zechariah 9:1ff), and lead in erroneous directions by false prophets (Zechariah 10:1ff). They had failed at keeping their original purpose to obey all that God had commanded them (see Ezra 3:1-4). God's people today often have desire to live righteously; however, the cares of the world, persecution, and false teaching are strong to pull us from our initial Christian objective (Matthew 13:10ff - parable of the sower). If not careful the Christian, like the Galatians, can fall from grace (see Galatians 5:4).

God is the Lord of love and mercy. The Lord is not willing that any should perish in their sins (2 Peter 3:9). The Lord has his divine ways to move sinful men to repentance. During the days of Zerubbabel, Haggai, and Zechariah God brought a plague of drought upon the people to cause them to turn back to him in obedience (Haggai 1:7-11 and Zechariah 8:9-13). Zechariah reveals to the people that this is God's modus operandi when man sins. God brings curses in the form of plagues to motivate people to repent (see Zechariah 5:1-4; 14:11; Deuteronomy 28:58-63; 29:20, 22-25; Revelation 15:8; 16:9-11 and 22:3). Those few who see the big picture and conclude that their suffering is a result of God's chastening hand will be plucked out of the fiery suffering unscathed (see Zechariah 3:1-4 and Jude 22-23).

The message of the prophet is that God's blessings are contingent upon man's obedience. The prophet solidifies this idea with the use of the word *"rain"* at Zechariah 14:17. Those who obey God will worship him in hope of receiving the fountain (Zechariah 13:1) of living waters (Zechariah 14:8) that cleans man of sins (Zechariah 13:1). The blessing of forgiveness is compared to the blessings of rain. When the people's hearts were right and they built the temple out of a spirit of faith then the rains would return (Zechariah 10:1). Likewise, today, when man obeys from a heart of faith they will receive God's blessing of the forgiveness of sins (Ephesians 1:3-7 as compared to Acts 2:38). Such a blessing can scarcely be overlooked by man. We need the forgiveness of sins far more than rain, food, lodging, money, entertainment, and emotional well being. No possible price can be placed upon the forgiveness of sins. Zechariah teaches us the value of God's blessings and the mode in which I am to obtain them. God wants us to obey him out of a heart of love and spirit of gratefulness. We too ought to build out of a spirit of obedience; however, let us never forget that if our actions of obedience are not motivated by faith and gratefulness then God does not accept it (Zechariah 7:11-14).

Zechariah spends a considerable amount of space identifying the kingdom of God and its inhabitants after his eight visions (chapters 8-14). Zechariah identifies the future kingdom of God as the Lord's church in the same manner as Ezekiel in his final nine chapters. The language is prophetically veiled yet with context and cross references at our side we see the truth. Zechariah's objective is to isolate the saints of God from the world not only on paper but in application within each person's life (see Zechariah 9:1-9). We must all conform our lives to the image of Jesus Christ in obedience else be faced with an eternity of punishment in hell (Revelation 20:10-15). God, through Zechariah, is reminding his people of his ways and how he achieves his will in the lives of men. Those who are humble and obedient will have no curse to move them to repentance but they will be in God's kingdom, protected, and defended from the flood of Satan's wickedness (Isaiah 28:17; Matthew 24:39; Luke 6:48 and Revelation 12:13-17).

Comparisons between Zechariah and Revelation

A red horseman is ready to take peace from the earth (Zechariah 1:8 / Revelation 6:4).

The horns of a beast infect Zion with sin (Zechariah 1:18-19 / Daniel 7 and Revelation 11).

Zechariah sees a man measuring Jerusalem (Zechariah 2:1-2 / Ezekiel 40:1-4 and Revelation 21:16).

The Christ or stone has seven eyes that go to and fro in the earth (Zechariah 3:9 and 4:10b compared to Revelation 5:6).

The prophet sees seven golden candlesticks (Zechariah 4:2 and Revelation 1:12-16).

The prophet sees two olive trees or branches (Zechariah 4:3, 11-13 and Revelation 11:1-4).

Satan attempts to destroy church in every generation yet he fails miserably (Zechariah 3:1-2; Acts 5:28-31 and Revelation 12:13-17).

The **curse** of plagues given to those who sin (Zechariah 5:1-4; Deuteronomy 28:58-63; 29:20, 22-25; Revelation 15:8; 16:9-11 and 22:3).

Wicked woman of Zechariah 5:5-8 and the Babylon harlot of Revelation 17:3-5.

Satan (wicked woman) bound in a jar or abyss (Zechariah 5:9-11 and Revelation 20:1-3).

Four colored horses bring the gospel and plagues that are designed to produce repentance (Zechariah 6:1-8 and Revelation 6 and 7).

The beauty, peace, glory, and salvation found in Zion, God's kingdom and church, shall be noticed by the nations of men and they shall flow into it (Zechariah 2:11; 3:10; 8:20-23 and Revelation 15:4 and 21:24).

Tyre stands as a representative of a harlot (Isaiah 23:15-17). She caused the nations to fall in sin due to their marveling at her fame and riches. She falls in every generation as does Babylon (see Zechariah 9:3-4 and Revelation 18:9-20).

God knows and protects his true kingdom (i.e., those that love truth and walk in meekness, righteousness, and justice) - (Zechariah 2:5; 8:7-8, 19; 9:8, 15 and Revelation 3:8; 7:2-3; 13:16; 21:14 and 22:18-19).

God calls upon his people to come out of the wickedness of the world (Zechariah 9:11-13 and Revelation 18:4).

The warfare between the Christian and the ideology of the world (Zechariah 10:3-7 and Revelation 17:14; 19:19-21 and 20:7ff).

Zechariah and John see Christians victoriously passing through the fiery sea of affliction (Zechariah 10:10-12 and Revelation 4:6 and 15:2). These trials are intended to perfect the saints (Zechariah 13:9 and Revelation 7:13-17).

Two thirds of the earth will be killed because they refuse repentance. God will plague, punish, and test men yet these two thirds will reject his divine pattern (Zechariah 13:7-8 and Revelation 7:1-4; 8:8-11 and 9:13-21). The one third left will continue to be put to the test and perfected by God (Zechariah 13:9; 1 Peter 1:6-7 and Revelation 7:13-17).

No additions or subtractions may be made to God's authorized divine revelation (Zechariah 13:3 and Revelation 22:18-19).

God will gather the nations of ungodly to fight against the saints in every generation (Zechariah 14:1-2 and Revelation 12:15-17 and 20:7-9).

ZECHARAIH CHAPTER 1

Synopsis

Zechariah's objective is to cause God's people to see what the world does not see. They are to know that chastisement comes to the ungodly by way of the red horseman with his great sword of calamity. They are to know that God's kingdom is eternal and indestructible. They are to know that though the world may appear fun, exciting, and entertaining its end is death.

Application

Christians today are not to permit the horn of Satan's tools to lure (or scatter) them away from truth, righteousness, and a meek spirit. David said that these three things are the cornerstone of God's kingdom (see Psalms 45:1-6). Isaiah said that righteousness and justice is the line that all are judged by (Isaiah 28:17). The world; however, is opposed to these character traits (see 1 John 2:15-17). The world seeks it own and so it shall suffer at the hands of God now and forevermore.

Zechariah, like Haggai, is challenging the people to open their eyes and to be inquisitive regarding all that is going on in their lives. They are to know that God is behind all their blessings and misery (see Haggai 1:7-11). The lesson is that God demands man's whole heart in obedience (see Leviticus 11:44 and 1 Peter 1:15-17).

Zechariah 1

A Call to the Disobedient to take Assessment of their current State (1:1-6)

"**1** *In the eighth month, in the second year of Darius, came the word of Jehovah unto Zechariah the son of Berechiah, the son of Iddo, the prophet, saying,* **2** *Jehovah was sore displeased with your fathers.* **3** *Therefore say unto them, Thus said Jehovah of hosts:* **Return** *unto me, said Jehovah of hosts, and I will return unto you, said Jehovah of hosts.* **4** *Be not as your fathers, unto whom the former prophets cried, saying, Thus said Jehovah hosts, Return now from your evil ways, and from your evil doings: but they did not hear, nor hearken unto me, said Jehovah*" **(1:1-4).**

The date and priestly heritage of Zechariah is discussed in the introduction. Consider a review of the words of Haggai so that the words of Zechariah will be understood:

a. The 50,000 returning captives under Zerubbabel were commanded to rebuild the temple of Jehovah (Ezra 6:14).

b. The Samaritans and size of the temple; however, discourage the people and for 15 years the temple lays waste (Compare Ezra 4:24 to 6:1ff and Haggai 1:3).

c. During this work stoppage the Lord has caused drought (Haggai 1:11), mildew, and hail (Haggai 2:17). All the work of the Jews hands failed because they were in sin (Haggai 1:9 and 2:14).

d. God sends Haggai and Zechariah (519 BC).

e. Haggai comes to the people first (Haggai 1:1). Twenty three days after his first prophetic words to the people they begin to work on the temple (Haggai 1:14 – 2:1). When Zechariah comes on the scene the people had begun working on the temple; however, they had not as yet turned their whole hearts to God. Consequentially, they continued to suffer drought, hail, and mildew (a failure of crops). Let us remember that Haggai had "*stirred*" the people to fear and obedience with his preaching during the sixth month and twenty fourth day (Haggai 1:12-15). Two months later Zechariah is calling upon them to "*return unto me, said Jehovah of hosts, and I will return unto you...*"

God's blessings continued to be withheld because they had not turned their whole hearts to God. Building the temple was but one thing that God desired from them. To receive his blessings they would have to turn their whole hearts to him (Leviticus 11:44 and 1 Peter 1:15-17). Zechariah begins his message to the Jews by reminding them of the horrible ordeal their fathers went through due to their unwillingness to turn their whole hearts to God. The people are called upon not to forget why they are in the current situation they are in. The temple of God, city of Jerusalem, and the city's walls lay in ruins because of their father's disobedience. They could not afford to let the lesson of Babylon and the consequences of disobedience escape them so quickly.

"**5** *Your fathers, where are they? And the prophets, do they live for ever?* **6** *But my words and my statutes, which I commanded my servants the prophets, did they not overtake your fathers? And they turned and said, Like as Jehovah of hosts thought to do unto us, according to our ways, and according to our doings, so has he dealt with us*" **(1:5-6).**

Each generation of people must develop faith and understanding of their own (16c). Success of such endeavors can be obtained by examining history and learning from our predecessors mistakes. Zechariah makes a strong appeal to history for the unfaithful in Jerusalem that were supposed to be building the Lord's temple.

The prophet calls upon them to look to their father's past. Jehovah had sent prophets such as Jeremiah, Nahum, Habakkuk, and Zephaniah to prophecy against Judah. The wicked people; however, would not listen to these men and so they were conquered and exiled. While these prophets and their father's all died the word of God remained.

Zechariah calls upon the people to look around them. Their city and God's temple was in ruins, the wall of Jerusalem had fallen, and their fathers have died in Babylon. Furthermore the rains had been withheld and they had little to eat. Should this not be enough to cause the current generation of disobedient to see the value of taking God's commandments seriously? All that God had said through the prophets that would take place has been so (consider Isaiah 46:8-11). Zechariah, like Haggai, challenges the people to open their eyes to the obvious (see Haggai 1:7-11).

God's word had not perished even though the people's fathers had died along with the prophets that warned them. A great lesson is learned here regarding established patterns. Though men may pervert the law of God, the church be in a state of disarray, and the godly are scarcely found the word of God abides forever (see Proverbs 8:22-26). Truth remains truth no matter what you or I may do to it. Jesus said that the word of God abides for ever (Matthew 24:35) (10e) (12bb). So God establishes an eternal and indestructible kingdom with an eternal and indestructible law (see Daniel 2:44-45).

Zechariah reveals the first of eight divine Visions (1:7-17)

"**7** *Upon the four and twentieth day of the eleventh month, which is the month Shebat, in the second year of Darius, came the word of Jehovah unto Zechariah the son of Berechiah, the son of Iddo, the prophet, saying,* **8** *I saw in the night, and, behold, a man riding upon a red horse, and he stood among the myrtle-trees that were in the bottom; and behind him were horses, red, sorrel, and white*" **(1:7-8).**

Before we look into the meaning of these visions we must take into consideration the context. The Jews had been shown their error and returned to working on the temple of God. God had punished them with drought and lack of crops to help them see their error (Haggai 1:7-11). The Lord has also sent his prophet Haggai to enlighten them to their true issues. They have acknowledged part of their error (i.e., not building the temple) but not all their error of uncleanness. The plague of drought continues due to their sin.

Three months after Zechariah's first address to the Jews in Jerusalem the prophet delivers the first of eight divine visions. Prophets of God saw divine visions and dreams wherein God disclosed to the world his plans (see Daniel 7:1; Obadiah 1:1 and Amos 1:1). John and Ezekiel were "*in the Spirit*" when they were shown apocalyptic visions (Revelation 1:10 and Ezekiel 37:1). Daniel, as here in Zechariah, also received revelation from God in the form of visions (Zechariah 1:7ff; Daniel 7:1; 8:1; etc.). Nehemiah writes, "*30 Yet many years did you bear with them, and testified against them **by your Spirit** through your prophets*" (Nehemiah 9:30; see also Ezekiel 1:3 and 11:4-7). The Apostle Peter tells us that God "*moved*" men to speak divine revelation by the Holy Spirit (2 Peter 1:21). The Holy Spirit "*entered into*" (Ezekiel 2:1-2) and "*fell upon*" (Ezekiel 11:5) men causing them to know and speak the mysteries of God. The Lord's objective is obvious. God wants man to hear and understand truth (10d).

Zechariah sees a night time vision of a man riding a red horse standing in the myrtle-trees in a bottom land area. Behind this horseman stood other horses of red, sorrel (red-brown), and white.

"**9** *Then said I, O my lord, what are these? And the angel that talked with me said unto me, I will show you what these are.* **10** *And the man that stood among the myrtle trees answered and said, These are they whom Jehovah has sent to walk to and fro through the earth.* **11** *And they answered the angel of Jehovah that stood among the myrtle-trees, and said, We have walked to and fro through the earth, and, behold, all the earth sits still, and is at rest*" **(1:9-11).**

The angel speaking with Zechariah explains the vision. The rider of the red horse and other angelic riders had a duty to go to and fro throughout the earth to see how the nations faired. Satan does the same thing (see Job 1:6-7). The report was that "*all the earth sits still, and is at rest.*" Things were to soon change due to the wickedness of man.

The Apostle John also saw a "*red horse*" whose duty was to "*4 take peace from the earth, and that they should slay one another: and there was given unto him a great sword*" (Revelation 6:4). As the horseman goes to and fro in the earth they find peace yet it is about to be removed. Man cannot dwell in peace while living in sin. The objective of the red horse, with his great sword, is to bring great calamity to the lives of men that they may repent (see context of Revelation 6:4 as well as Revelation 15:1 and 16:8-11). The people living in their sealed houses and morally unclean while the Lord's temple lay in ruins was cause for the rider of the red horse to wield his sword in their direction that God may chastise them and move them to repentance.

"**12** *Then the angel of Jehovah answered and said, O Jehovah of hosts, how long will you not have mercy on Jerusalem and on the cities of Judah, against which you have had indignation these seventy years?* **13** *And Jehovah answered the angel that talked with me with good words, even comfortable words.* **14** *So the angel that talked with me said unto me, Cry, saying, Thus said Jehovah of hosts: I am jealous for Jerusalem and for Zion with a great jealousy.* **15** *And I am very sore displeased with the nations that are at ease; for I was but a little displeased, and they helped forward the affliction*" **(1:12-15).**

The angel that revealed the red horse to Zechariah now asks God a question. "How long will you not show mercy on Jerusalem and the cities of Judah?" The angel reminds the Lord of the 70 years that they have spent in captivity. Jehovah answers the angel and the angel imparts the "*comforting*" information to Zechariah to distribute to the people as a prophet. Zechariah does not hear the reply of God but rather the angel of God tells him what God said.

The first thing that the Lord says is that he is "*jealous*" for Jerusalem and Zion yet displeased with all nations because they are at ease. The Bible in Common English translates Zechariah 1:12 as, "*I care passionately about Jerusalem and Zion*." The comforting words were that God sees and cares about what is going on with his people (Jerusalem and Zion) yet he is moved to anger over the idle world of sinners. Sinful people of the world do not consider their ways and neither do they consider the consequences of such wicked actions. The meek of God; however, consider their sin and repent. The question Zechariah was to pose to the people is "Who do you represent? Are you part of the wicked world or Zion?" The wicked "*help forward the affliction*" of their trespasses (i.e., bring God's chastening hand upon their own selves).

"**16** *Therefore thus said Jehovah: I am returned to Jerusalem with* **mercies**; *my house shall be built in it, said Jehovah of hosts, and* **a line** *shall be stretched forth over Jerusalem.* **17** *Cry yet again, saying, Thus said Jehovah of hosts: My cities shall yet overflow with prosperity; and Jehovah shall yet comfort Zion, and shall yet choose Jerusalem*" **(1:16-17).**

Like most prophetic writing we find dual meanings in the revelations. God would certainly be merciful to his people and permit them to rebuild his temple in Jerusalem; however, the main objective of these words is spiritual. We read of God's mercy and grace that would come in the form of the Christ as the Apostle Paul quotes from Isaiah 55:3 at Acts 13:34-39. By the mercy and grace of God he would forgive man of their sins though they did not deserve it (see Ezekiel 39:25-29). The results of forgiveness in Zion would be great comfort.

A measuring "*line*" would be stretched over this New Jerusalem (see notes at Zechariah 2:1). This line represents God's precise laws and expectations of man. Those who do not measure up to the line of truth, righteousness, and meekness have no part in God's grace and mercy. The prophet Isaiah writes, "17 *I will make justice the line, and righteousness the plummet; and the hail shall sweep away the refuge of lies, and the waters shall overflow the hiding place*" (Isaiah 28:17).

Zechariah's Second Vision (1:18-21)

"**18** *And I lifted up mine eyes, and saw, and, behold, four horns.* **19** *And I said unto the angel that talked with me, what are these? And he* *answered me, These are the horns which have **scattered** Judah, Israel, and Jerusalem*" **(1:18-19).**

Zechariah reveals his second vision to the delinquent Jewish who were responsible for building the temple. Zechariah sees four horns responsible for **scattering** Judah, Israel, and Jerusalem. Horns are Biblical symbols for power (see Daniel 7:7-8 and Amos 6:13). Four great powers are responsible for Israel and Judah's collapse (we are not told what four nations) (likely Assyria, Egypt, Babylon and one other). Again, a lesson learned from Haggai was that though there may be outside causes of one's disobedience the individual is responsible to obey.

"**20** *And Jehovah showed me four **smiths**.* **21** *Then said I, What come these to do? And he spoke, saying, These are the horns which scattered Judah, so that no man did lift up his head; but these are come to terrify them, to cast down the horns of the nations, which lifted up their horn against the land of Judah to scatter it*" **(1:20-21).**

The Bible in Basic English reads, "20 *Then the LORD showed me four metalworkers.* 21 *I said, 'What are they coming to do?' And he said, 'These are the horns that scattered Judah so that no one could raise his head. The metalworkers have come to terrify them and to destroy the horns of the nations, those who were attacking the land of Judah with their horns to scatter it.'*"

There are four "*smiths*" (metalworkers) seen by Zechariah that correspond to the four horns that scattered Judah and Israel. These four smiths are sent to "*terrify them, to cast down the horns of the nations...*" Though the nations that destroyed Judah and Israel may feel filled with power and might it is Jehovah that shall bring a terrifying nation against them. Time and time again Jeremiah warned Babylon of the consequences of her sinful actions. Jehovah God used Babylon to afflict the sinful people of Judah and then they too (i.e., the Babylonians) were punished for their sinful works (see Jeremiah 25:12; 50-51 and 50:14).

What purpose would it be to reveal these thoughts to the returned captives responsible for building the temple? The people of God needed to know that the Lord was the sovereign God of all creation and that he alone is responsible for their standing on the ruins of Judah at that very moment. He had taken them full circle. God's people had sinned with no regard for repentance. The Lord sent the Assyrians to Israel (Isaiah 10:6ff) and the Babylonians upon Judah (Jeremiah 51:20). As God caused these world empires to rise he also caused them to fall (see Daniel 2:21). Truly God is in control of all environments of creation. If only his people would now obey him with their true hearts he would certainly bless them (see Psalms 46).

There are fascinating equivalences between the book of Zechariah and Revelation. The horns that "*scatter*" Judah do so by causing her to sin. Judah came to be enamored with the horns of the nations and all that they stood for (i.e., lust, luxury, fame, and power). Judah was "scattered" by the lure of those of the world. Daniel chapter 7 and Revelation 11 speak of National beast with horns that affect the people of God. The message is that Christians are not to be swayed by the world's power, prestige, luxury, and lust. Let us be satisfied with God's unchanging law and know that his kingdom is eternal and indestructible. The Lord, not the nations of men, is in complete sovereign control of this world.

Questions over Zechariah Chapter 1

1. How long after Haggai began preaching did Zechariah begin his work?

2. What condition did God place upon the people in order for them to enjoy his blessings?

3. What does Zechariah say about the longevity of God's word?

4. Zechariah sees a series of eight visions from chapter 1:7 to 6:8. What did he see in the first vision (Zechariah 1:7-17)?

5. What did God's prophet see in the second vision (Zechariah 1:18-21)?

6. How do Zechariah's visions help us to have a greater understanding of the book of Revelation?

ZECHARIAH CHAPTER 2

Synopsis

Zechariah sees a man measuring the city of Jerusalem in his third vision.

Application

The people of the days of Zechariah are no different than people of any generation. God's laws have been eternally established as an unbreakable pattern for man to be molded to (see Isaiah 28:17; Zechariah 1:6, 16; 2:1 and Ephesians 1:3-7). All are commanded to conform their lives to the image of Jesus Christ (see Romans 8:29). Those who rebel against the pattern of righteousness will be reproved by God (see Revelation 3:19). As the world of men watch and observe God's chastening hand upon the disobedient they shall come to know that he alone is God. Through the ages men have seen the consequences of sinful behavior yet many refuse repentance till the day they die (see Revelation 16:8-11). Zechariah's duty is to open the eyes of God's people so that they see the obvious and repent before its everlasting too late.

Zechariah 2

Zechariah's Third Divine Vision (2 all)

"*1 And I lifted up mine eyes, and saw, and, behold, a man with a measuring line in his hand. 2 Then said I, Where are you going? And he said unto me, To measure Jerusalem, to see what is the breadth thereof, and what is the length thereof"* **(2:1-2).**

Once again, we consider the events and people as we look into Zechariah's visions. The people of God had disobeyed his command to build the temple. They permitted the world to sway them away from their divine directive. They had also grown further from God through hardness of heart and uncleanness. The visions of Zechariah are intended to help these specific people.

Zechariah now sees a third vision. A man is measuring the length and width of the city (see Zechariah 1:16 and Isaiah 28:17 - the line represents a standard or pattern of righteousness). The scriptures reveal other times when a man was measuring Jerusalem. Ezekiel is brought to see visions of a man measuring the city of Jerusalem at Ezekiel 40:1-4 in relationship to the new kingdom of God (church) with its new law and worship. The Apostle John also sees a man measuring Jerusalem at Revelation 21:16. The city at Revelation 21:16 is the *"bride, the wife of the Lamb"* or redeemed church of all time (see Revelation 21:9-10 and 19:6-9).

The references to a man measuring the city of Jerusalem reveal the exact and prescribed character of the true saints of God (see verse 4 below). While the Jews under Zerubbabel's watch have left off following God's will **the pattern** for the true saints remains pre-measured by God (see Zechariah 1:6, 16 and Ephesians 1:3-7). The point is that it matters not who transgresses the exact laws of God they nonetheless remain in affect and demand the same from all (9k).

"**3** *And, behold, the angel that talked with me went forth, and another angel went out to meet him,* **4** *and said unto him, Run, speak to this young man, saying, Jerusalem shall be inhabited as villages without walls, by reason of the multitude of men and cattle therein.* **5** *For I, said Jehovah, will be unto her* **a wall of fire** *round about, and I will be the glory in the midst of her"* **(2:3-5).**

The city of "*Jerusalem*" has been measured. The parameters of meekness, righteousness, and truth are the standards that those who enter this city must meet. It matters not if one is a Gentile or Jew the exact measurements are given and those who meet those measurements may enter (see Genesis 12:3). Jesus similarly gave the parable of the wedding feast at Matthew 22:1-14. Those who are not dressed in wedding garments of righteousness are excluded. The message is that those who do not measure up to Christ's standards of righteousness are cast into outer darkness. The Apostle John said that the clothing of the bride of Christ is "*the righteous acts of the saints*" (Revelation 19:8). Such statements illustrate the exclusive nature of the Lord's church (city of Jerusalem). Those who do not meet its measurements are out of fellowship with God (see Isaiah 59:1-2) (12cc).

The righteous are in God's kingdom and he is a "*wall of fire round about*." Though the Babylonians had torn down the walls of Jerusalem God would be that spiritual wall that would never be destroyed (see 2 Chronicles 36:19 and Nehemiah 1:3). God is a powerful refuge to those who put their trust and faith in him. David said, "7 *Show your marvelous lovingkindness, O you that save by your right hand them that take refuge in you from those that rise up against them*" (Psalms 17:7) (3bb).

"**6** *Ho, ho, flee from the land of the north, said Jehovah; for I have spread you abroad as the four winds of the heavens, said Jehovah.* **7** *Ho Zion, escape, you that dwell with the daughter of Babylon.* **8** *For thus said Jehovah of hosts: After glory has he sent me unto the nations which plundered you; for he that touches you touches* **the apple of his eye**" **(2:6-8).**

The Apostle John heard an angel of great authority saying, "2 *Fallen, fallen is Babylon the great, and is become a habitation of demons...* 4 *Come forth, my people, out of her, that you have no fellowship with her sins, and that you receive not her plagues:* 5 *for her sins have reached even unto heaven, and God has remembered her iniquities*" (Revelation 18:2, 4-5). The Babylon of Revelation represents sin in the form of lust of the flesh, pride of life, vain glory, power, and fame. The call is that all God's people would come out of her and be separate (see 2 Corinthians 6:17). The sanctified of God are distinctly different from the world because God has **drawn a line of righteousness** between them and those of the world (Zechariah 1:16; 2:1 and Isaiah 28:17).

Though Babylon was located to the east of Jerusalem they are always referred to as those of the north (Jeremiah 50:3). The sinful Jews that continue to suffer the ill effects of drought and no harvest are commanded to come out of the wicked spiritual state of Babylon. Stop sinning and live in meekness, righteousness, and truth. The Babylon of sin falls in every generation of mankind. The admonition to the saints is to not permit the wicked of Babylon to cause them to be cursed of God. The saints are the "*apple of his* (God's) *eye*" (see Deuteronomy 32:10 and Psalms 17:8). Those who would cause one of God's children to fall in sin are in deep trouble. Jesus said, "*6 But whoever causes one of these little ones who believe in me to sin, it would be better for him to have a great millstone fastened around his neck and to be drowned in the depth of the sea*" (Matthew 18:6 - ESV see also Romans 14:15 and 20). God greatly cares for his beloved saints (1 Peter 5:7).

"*9 For, behold, I will shake my hand over them, and they shall be a spoil to those that served them; and* **you shall know** *that Jehovah of hosts has sent me. 10 Sing and rejoice, O daughter of Zion; for lo, I come, and I will dwell in the midst of you, said Jehovah. 11 And many nations shall join themselves to Jehovah in that day, and shall be my people; and I will dwell in the midst of you, and you shall know that Jehovah of hosts has sent me unto you*" **(2:9-11).**

Those whom God "*shakes his hand over*" are those who would attempt to harm the "*apple*" of his eye (i.e., his beloved saints) (see 2 Thessalonians 1:6ff). The wicked will be sorely plagued for their wickedness yet in many cases they shall refuse repentance (see Revelation 16:8-11). As God brings violent calamity to the lives of the wicked all shall come to know that he alone is God (see Lamentations

2:5-7 and Ezekiel 11:10). The righteous will see God's chastisement in lives of the wicked and be comforted in the righteous lives they live.

Zion, the people of God who meet the measurements of Jerusalem, is called upon to rejoice. The Lord will dwell in the midst of them (see Ezekiel 43:1-5). The promise made to Abraham will see its fulfillment in Jesus Christ and his church (see Genesis 12:3-4 and Galatians 3:8). When the wise are sore troubled with God's heavy hand of punishment they will repent and know that God is Lord of all (see Psalms 32:4-5).

The new kingdom of God (his church) will be so glorious and blessed that all nations shall desire its blessings. As men see the cause of their curse and plagues and witness the peace of the saints they will flow into the city of God, Jerusalem, Zion, kingdom of God, or church (see Zechariah 2:11; 3:10 and Revelation 21:24). The psalmist writes, "*11 let Mount Zion be glad! Let the daughters of Judah rejoice because of your judgments!* 12 *Walk about Zion, go around her, number her towers,* 13 *consider well her ramparts, go through her citadels, that you may tell the next generation* 14 *that this is God, our God forever and ever. He will guide us forever*" (Psalms 48:11-14).

"**12** *And Jehovah shall inherit Judah as his portion in the holy land, and shall yet choose Jerusalem.* **13** *Be silent, all flesh, before Jehovah; for he is waked up out of his holy habitation*" **(2:12-13).**

This new spiritual Zion (kingdom of God / church) would be God's portion or inheritance (Isaiah 2:2ff). Ezekiel and the Apostle John speak of the inheritance of the saints being God himself yet here we see that the saints are God's inheritance (see Ezekiel 44:28 and Revelation 21:7). There is a fellowship developed between God and his people so that they both possess each other in unity and spirit (see John 17:16-21).

The natural observation for Jehovah God now is that all flesh "*be silent before the Lord.*" The nations of men have sinned and even caused some of the saints of God to stumble. God has woken out of his holy habitation and sent his red horse with plagues upon the wicked of the world. He will "*shake his hand*" over the wicked (see above at verse 9).

The measuring line has been set at meekness, righteousness, and truth (Isaiah 28:17). God alone has the authority to set the established pattern and he did so before the foundation of the world was made (again, note Ephesians 1:3-7). Man is advised to "*silence*" his opinions, convictions, and preconceived ideas of religious service. All are advised to "*silence*" their wicked scattering of good people through wicked influences. Sinful behavior and language is commanded to cease! Only those who conformed to the eternal image of Christ are permitted into the holy city of God. The lessons of this chapter have grand significance to all generations. The Jews needed to leave off their lust, pride, vain glory, and desires for fame and fortune on this earth if they desired God's blessings of rain to continue.

Questions over Zechariah Chapter 2

1. What did Zechariah see in the third vision (Zechariah chapter 2)?

2. What does the "*line*" represent?

3. Who is the "*apple of God's eye?*"

4. How would the people know that God had sent Zechariah as a prophet?

5. **True or False:** God continues to chasten the wicked today.

6. What significance is there to the statement, "*Be silent all flesh before Jehovah; for he is waked up out of his holy habitation?*"

ZECHARAIAH CHAPTER 3

Synopsis

The Lord has established a strict standard line of righteousness that the world must meet. Those out of line with righteousness are in sin. God would remove the sins of the world by his servant the branch. The Lord would be a wall of fire around forgiven sinners as a refuge for the homeless. Though God's people had been clothed in unrighteousness he would clean them and give them an entrance to his house.

Application

There is hope for the Christian. The elect remnant of God will always confess their sins to the Lord and seek his mercy and forgiveness. The Lord will save all who seek his salvation!

Zechariah 3

Zechariah's Fourth Divine Vision (3 all)

"**1** *And he showed me Joshua the high priest standing before the angel of Jehovah, and Satan standing at his right hand to be his adversary.* **2** *And Jehovah said unto Satan, Jehovah rebuke you, O Satan; yea, Jehovah that has chosen Jerusalem rebuke you: is not this a brand plucked out of the fire*?" **(3:1-2)**

Let us keep the context of these visions before our mind before looking into the meanings. The Jews have failed to build the temple of God and were suffering drought and food shortages. Haggai was successful in opening the eyes of the Jews; however, the blessings of rain and harvest have continued to be withheld. Sin continued to plague the lives of men. Zechariah's duty was to bring out true holiness in God's people.

The man with the measuring line of Zechariah chapter 2 continues to speak with the prophet of God. He has shown Zechariah the line of righteousness that God measures a man by (Zechariah 2:1), a glimpse of the future church (Zechariah 2:2-5, 10-12), chastisement of the wicked (Zechariah 2:9), and a call to his saints to be separate from the sinful of the world (Zechariah 3:13).

The man now shows Zechariah a vision of Joshua the high priest standing before the angel of the Lord. Joshua is not alone. Satan is at his right hand *"to be his adversary."* Satan's objective is to cause God's priesthood as much grief as he possibly can. He has been behind the sins of these priests and caused their holy garments to be soiled. The duty of the priests was to make a distinction between clean and unclean things; however, Satan had succeeded in perverting their minds so that they were ignorant of these things (see Leviticus 10:10 compared to Ezekiel 22:26). Hosea tells us that God's priests had forgotten the Lord's laws and caused other people to do the same (Hosea 4:6). Furthermore the priests of God were greedy and so perverted the law for money (Micah 3:11).

A defiled priesthood resulted in a defiled people. Satan has affectively scattered God's priests far from truth. The Lord; however, reminds Satan that these people were *"a brand plucked out of fire."* Through the fiery trials of Assyria, Babylon, and the Samaritans God's people were being sifted. The righteous were attaining better understanding about the sovereign authority of Jehovah God. The result was fear and obedience. The Apostle Peter said, "6 *Wherein you greatly rejoice, though now for a little while, if need be, you have been put to grief in manifold trials,* 7 *that the proof of your faith, being more precious than gold that perishes through it is proved by fire, may be found unto praise and glory and honor at the revelation of Jesus Christ*" (1 Peter 1:6-7). It is through the fiery trials of life that we learn to be more Christ like. One opens their eyes to character flaws and sin by closely examining current and past trials of life. The admonition is to see where you need to make changes rather than suffering with a dull and hardened mind of stupidity (3e).

"*3 Now Joshua was clothed with filthy garments, and was standing before the angel. 4 And he answered and spoke unto those that stood before him, saying, Take the filthy garments from off him. And unto him he said, Behold, I have caused your iniquity to pass from you, and I will clothe you with rich apparel. 5 And I said, Let them set a clean miter upon his head, and clothed him with garments; and the angel of Jehovah was standing by*" **(3:3-5)**.

Joshua, as high priest of God's people, is a representation of all the priesthood and people. His garments are filthy with the sins of pride, cheating, murder, idolatry, and general rebellion. We read of all the wickedness of Judah throughout the book of Jeremiah, Nahum, Zephaniah, and Habakkuk. All the people's sins are summarized by Joshua standing before the Lord being judged for their filth. Satan has succeeded in scattering God's people in sin yet he is not eternally victorious.

The Lord commands that the filthy garments be taken off of Joshua. This action symbolizes the Lord's power and willingness to forgive or "*cause your iniquity to pass from you.*" While we see this as a clear display of God's grace it is also abundantly clear that God's blessings are ever conditioned upon man turning in repentance and obedience to his will (see Zechariah 1:1-4) (13b). The man has shown Zechariah the future church and its citizens as forgiven sinners. The clean garments are those of righteousness and justice (see Matthew 22:1-14 and Revelation 19:8) (19g).

"*6 And the angel of Jehovah protested unto Joshua, saying, Thus said Jehovah of hosts: if you will walk in my ways, and if you will keep my charge, then you also shall judge my house, and shall also keep my courts, and I will give you a place of access among these that stand by"* **(3:6-7).**

The Bible in Common English reads, *"Then the LORD's messenger admonished Joshua."* God's people would need to straighten up to receive the forgiveness of their sins. *"If"* they would walk in the holy ways of God and keep his laws then they would find a place in God's *"house"* or church (see Ezekiel 44:7 in the context of God's future church as well as Hebrews 3:6 and 10:21). There have ever been conditions to meet in order to be in fellowship with God and in his house (see 1 Corinthians 15:1-2 and Colossians 1:21-23).

To *"judge"* God's house and *"keep my courts"* is to fulfill the work of the priest according to all God's ordinances. The work of God's people is to make sure that the unchanging truths of God's house are upheld by all the saints (see Isaiah 28:17; Zechariah 1:6, 16 and Ephesians 1:3-7) (19m). Doing this work would grant them access unto the Holy God of heaven. Works have ever been God's expectation of his people (see Revelation 20:12-13).

*"***8** *Hear now, O Joshua the high priest, you and your fellows that sit before you; for they are men that are a sign: for, behold, I will bring forth my servant the Branch "* **(3:8).**

God has promised, by his grace, to forgive the people of their sins if they would turn to him in obedience. Joshua and the priests would be a *"sign"* to the world that God forgives through his branch. When men were forgiven of their sins, on the Day of Pentecost, all knew that the words of the prophets were truth (see Acts 2:38).

The Lord now explains how he will forgive people of their sins. God would *"bring forth my servant the **Branch**."* Zechariah latter refers to the *"Branch"* as one who would rule on the throne of God's kingdom (Zechariah 6:12ff). The prophet Isaiah 11:1ff depicts this Branch or shoot as coming from the house or stump of Jesse, David's father, and so fulfilling God's promise made to David at 2 Samuel 7:12-16 and Isaiah

1:9. Jeremiah tells us that this "*Branch*" would be of the seed of David, reign as king, and he shall be called Jehovah our righteousness (Jeremiah 23:5-6). There is no doubt that the Branch under consideration is the Christ.

9 *For, behold, the stone that I have set before Joshua; upon one stone are seven eyes: behold, I will engrave the graving thereof, said Jehovah of hosts, and I will remove the iniquity of that land in one day.* **10** *In that day, said Jehovah of hosts, shall* **you invite** *every man his neighbor under the vine and under the fig-tree"* **(3:9-10).**

The Common English Bible reads for verse 9, "*See this stone that I have put before Joshua. Upon one stone, there are seven facets. I am about to engrave an inscription on it, says the LORD of heavenly forces. I will remove the guilt of that land in one day.*" The Lord had instructed Moses to engrave the names of the twelve tribes of Israel on two stones that were placed on the ephod worn by the high priest (see Exodus 28:6-11). At Revelation 2:17 the Lord promises a new name engraved upon a white stone to all who overcome sin in this life. The saints of God are connected to Christ in that they wear his name upon their foreheads (see Revelation 14:1). Through this engraved stone God would remove man's sins "*in one day.*"

The "*stone*" set before Joshua is the Branch or Christ. The scriptures identify Christ as a stone that many stumble over due to his laws or line of righteousness (see Isaiah 28:16; Matthew 21:42; Acts 4:11; Romans 9:33 and 1 Peter 2:4-7). The stone, Christ, has "*seven eyes*" as is also depicted at Revelation 5:6. The "*seven eyes*" are representative of Jesus' perfect all seeing and all knowing characteristics. Zechariah will reveal in the next chapter that "*these are the eyes of Jehovah, which run to and fro through the whole earth*" (Zechariah 4:10b). There is a close connection between the eyes of God, Christ, and the horsemen who go to and fro throughout the earth examining mankind (see Zechariah 1:8 and Revelation 6).

The Almighty would, in one day, remove the sins of the land that associates with his line. When Christ was crucified on the cross and established his kingdom peoples of all nations flowed to it as the prophet said. Christians would invite every man to come to this beautiful city of forgiveness and comfort. All who measure up to the line of righteousness and justice will be permitted to enter. The words of the prophet indicate an automatic reaction to truth and the house of God. The saints *"will invite every man his neighbor"* to the kingdom of God or his house. The Lord's saints will preach the gospel of the branch (Christ) and invite the sinful of the world to enter in if only they too would put on works worthy of repentance (19n).

Questions over Zechariah Chapter 3

1. Why is Satan standing at the right hand of Joshua the high priest?

2. What happened to Joshua and his filthy garments?

3. What is the high priest commanded to do in order to gain God's favor?

4. Who is the "*Branch*?"

5. Compare and contrast Zechariah 3:9 and 4:10 with Revelation 1:4-6 and 5:6.

6. What verse explains the Christian's responsibility to preach to the lost of the world?

ZECHARIAH CHAPTER 4

Synopsis

The fifth vision of Zechariah's is somewhat of a rebuke. The people of God had "*despised the day of small things*" by looking at the foundation of the temple and thinking little of it (see Zechariah 4:9-10). The angel reveals the surety and nature of God's later temple, house, kingdom, or church. God would build his house through the seed of Zerubbabel and no mountain of sin would have the power to stop it from being built or destroyed.

Application

Jesus, prophets, and preachers would present the gospel message to the world and those who obey that message would be forgiven of their sins and added to the kingdom of God. Building the temple of God was not a small matter! The eternal well being of all men's souls was under consideration.

Zechariah 4

Zechariah's Fifth Divine Vision (4 all)

"**1** *And the angel that talked with me came again, and waked me, as a man that is wakened out of his sleep.* **2** *And he said unto me, What do you see? And I said, I have seen, and, behold, a candlestick all of gold, with its bowl upon the top of it, and its seven lamps thereon; there are* *seven pipes to each of the lamps, which are upon the top thereof;* **3** *and two olive-trees by it, one upon the right side of the bowl, and the other upon the left side thereof.* **4** *And I answered and spoke to the angel that talked with me, saying, What are these, my Lord?"* **(4:1-4).**

Let us keep the context of these visions before our mind before looking into the meanings. The Jews have failed to build the temple of God and were suffering drought and food shortages. Haggai was successful in opening the eyes of the Jews to their error and they returned to work. God's blessings of rain and harvest; however, have continued to be withheld. Sin continued to plague the lives of men. Zechariah's duty was to bring out true holiness in God's people. The major problem of the people was that they were not looking to the future spiritual kingdom of God but rather to the earthly temple for hope.

The word "*again*" indicates that this is not the first time the prophet has been awaken this night and showed a vision. The angel asks Zechariah, "*What do you see?*" Zechariah saw a candlestick holder of gold that occupied seven lamps (i.e., candles). Each of the lamps had seven pipes coming out of them. At the top of this candlestick holder and seven lamps was a bowl. One olive tree was planted on both the right and left sides of the candlestick holder providing oil for the fuel. The holy place of the Mosaic tabernacle contained a single candlestick holder with seven lamps or candlesticks. The function appears to be illumination of the holy place. When Solomon built God's temple there were ten of these candlestick holders in the holy place (see 1 Kings 7:49ff and 2 Chronicles 4:7, 20).

As Zechariah views the vision he asks the angel, "*What are these, my Lord?*"

"**5** *Then the angel that talked with me answered and said unto me, Do you not know what these are? And I said, No, my lord.* **6** *Then he answered and spoke unto me, saying, This is the word of Jehovah unto Zerubbabel, saying, Not by might, nor by power, but by my Spirit, said Jehovah of hosts*" **(4:5-6).**

The angel seems somewhat surprised that Zechariah did not understand the vision. The angel then explains to the prophet that the vision is a message to Zerubbabel that the temple would not be built by might or power of men but rather by the Spirit of Jehovah. It seems that Zerubbabel had become discouraged and the Lord is giving him words of encouragement through the prophet. The temple God speaks of is both the earthly temple that Zerubbabel would build in Jerusalem and the spiritual temple his seed would build in the latter days of Jesus.

Zechariah really doesn't get an answer to his question at this point. All he knows is that the vision has to do with Zerubbabel's success in finishing the house of God in Jerusalem. God is telling the governor of the people that he will complete this temple by his divine help. More importantly; however, the spiritual house of God (church) would be established through the seed of Zerubbabel. Zechariah was to see this in the candlestick holder with its perpetual oil and olive trees.

"**7** *Who are you, O great mountain? Before Zerubbabel you shall become a plain; and he shall bring forth the top stone with shoutings of Grace, grace, unto it*" **(4:7)**.

Zerubbabel is to be assured that all mountains of deterrents to the building process would be removed. The discouraged hearts, due to the seemingly smallness of the foundation, lack of materials, surrounding nations such as the Samaritans, and any other "*great mountain*" of discouragement shall be removed and Zerubbabel will bring forth the final stone to complete the building process and shouts of joy or grace will be sung. To see such a project come to completion will give confidence to God's people (see Philippians 4:13). The saints are encouraged to be "*strong*" rather than permitting the wicked forces of Satan to knock us down (see Haggai 2:4 and Zechariah 8:13-15) (60).

What they needed to be looking to; however, was a temple not made with hands wherein God would dwell in righteousness (Hebrews 9:11, 24). No great mountain of sin would be able to prevent the spiritual sanctuary of God from being built and the Christian from entering into

God's house (12bb). No single man, nation, god, or false doctrine today has even the least bit of power to destroy God's kingdom (Psalms 48:8; Isaiah 40:17; 41:24 and Daniel 2:44-45). The kingdom of God would be built and it would stand for all eternity. Those who conform their lives to Christ and seek out forgiveness are recipients of God's grace. The "*top stone*" is no doubt another allusion to Christ (see previous chapter). Jesus would be the stone of grace that would reign in this eternal temple (see Isaiah 54:3 compared to Acts 13:33-39) (13a).

"**8** *Moreover the word of Jehovah came unto me, saying,* **9** *The hands of Zerubbabel have laid the foundation of this house; his hands shall also finish it; and you shall know that Jehovah of hosts has sent me unto you*" **(4:8-9).**

A prophetic statement regarding the completion of the temple of Jehovah God is made. The angel says that the vision of the seven golden candlesticks means that the temple will be completed by Zerubbabel. When the temple is complete all will know that the source of this prophecy was indeed divine (Isaiah 46:9ff). What this ought to teach us is that when the same Lord foretold of Zerubbabel's part in the latter spiritual house (i.e., the church through Jesus Christ) that it too would indeed (and it has) come to pass. When Zerubbabel heard these words he would certainly be infused with great confidence.

"**10** *For who has despised the day of small things? For* **these seven** *shall rejoice, and shall see* **the plummet** *in the hand of Zerubbabel; these are the eyes of Jehovah, which run to and fro through the whole earth*" **(4:10).**

The angel asks a question, "*Who has despised the day of small things?*" The foundation of the temple is under consideration (see previous verse). Many of the Jews had cried when they saw the small foundation of the new temple because they thought it was small and insignificant (see Ezra 3:12 and Haggai 2:3). Though the foundation of the temple may seem small and insignificant to some it truly was not. The importance of God's spiritual temple, in regards the man's soul, is eternally significant. God's temple would be spiritual in nature. The Lord admonishes the Jews, through his prophets Haggai and Zechariah, so that they would understand that God is not in the physical temple but the spiritual. He will be a wall of fire around this spiritual temple and dwell with them (see Zechariah 2:5).

There is a correlation between the seven lamps on the candlestick ("*these seven*") and the "*plummet*" that Zerubbabel figuratively represents and holds (see Zechariah 4:2). The Hebrew word for "*plummet*" (*eben habb dil*) is somewhat obscure but is translated by most Bibles as "plumb-line" or "weighted measuring line." "A plummet is a weight made of stone or metal which, when suspended by a cord, produces a plumb line. The plumb line is used to measure a straight vertical plane" (ISBE volume 3, page 295). Earlier the prophet of God had written "16 *Therefore thus said Jehovah: I am returned to Jerusalem with **mercies**; my house shall be built in it, said Jehovah of hosts, and **a line** shall be stretched forth over Jerusalem*" (Zechariah 1:16 see also 1:6 and 2:1). We have examined the meaning of this line at Zechariah 1:6 and 16 and firmly concluded that it is the line of righteousness that Isaiah speaks of at chapter 28:17.

God measures a man by this line and those who do not fit are rejected. Zerubbabel is seen to be holding this line in his right hand by the seven eyes of Christ (see Zechariah 4:10 as compared to Zechariah 3:9) (see also Ezekiel 1:15-21). David has written, "7 *Show your marvelous lovingkindness, O you that save by your **right hand** them that take refuge in you from those that rise up against them*" (Psalms 17:7). The right hand of God held "*righteousness*" (see Psalms 48:10).

God would build his temple through Zerubbabel and truth would be the standard by which all are measured. The eyes of Christ would rejoice as the church was established and truth preached (Acts 2).

"**11** *Then answered I, and said unto him, What are these two olive-trees upon the right side of the candlestick and upon the left side thereof?* **12** *And I answered the second time, and said unto him, What are these two* *olive-branches, which are beside the two golden spouts, that empty the golden oil out of themselves?* **13** *And he answered me and said, Do you not know what these are? And I said, No, my lord.* **14** *Then said he, These are the two anointed ones, that stand by the Lord of the whole earth"* **(4:11-14).**

Zechariah has now asked the angel three times about the meaning of the candlesticks and olive trees (see Zechariah 4:4, 11-12). More details of the initial vision are now given. Zechariah has seen branches of the olive trees extending to the bowl atop of the candlestick in which a perpetual source of golden oil is being supplied for light (apparently 49 pipes come out of the main bowl and in groups of seven they are extend to each candlestick providing fuel). Zechariah asks the angel the significance of these trees and branches and once again the angel seems to be surprised that Zechariah does not know.

The angel tells Zechariah that the two olive trees that are supplying the perpetual golden oil for the lamps are "*two anointed ones, that stand by the Lord of the whole earth.*" The Apostle John sees a mirror image of what Zechariah is now seeing at Revelation 11. John saw a vision of the church being persecuted for 42 months and his two faithful witnesses preaching for 1260 days. John then writes, "**4** *These are the two olive trees and the two candlesticks, standing before the Lord of the earth*" (Revelation 11:4 see also Revelation 1:12-16 and 4:5). What two people do we find standing "*before the Lord of the earth?*" Again, we may ask, who is it that represents a perpetual light to the world? Jesus was both priest and king (see Hebrews 6:20-7:1) (10q). The priests of God carry out God's immediate purpose of building the temple. So Christ and divinely inspired men preached the word of God that his eternal purpose may be achieved (Ephesians 3:8-12). It is the word of God that serves as a bright light in this perverted world (see Matthew 5:14-16). God's kingdom church would come to be built by those who teach and uphold the truth as a bright shining light (2 Corinthians 4:4 and 2 Timothy 1:10).

The two anointed ones mentioned here in Zechariah can be no other than Joshua the high priest and Zerubbabel the governing authority among the Jews in Judea. The high priest and king (ruler of the people) stand by the Lord of the whole earth. These two, i.e., Zerubbabel and Joshua, are types of the Christ and completed word of God to come. They carry out God's immediate purpose of building the temple and Christ, as the priestly king, would carry out Jehovah's eternal purpose.

The spiritual temple of God would not be built by the might of man but by the light of the gospel of Jesus Christ (see back at Zechariah 4:6). No mountain known to heaven and earth would have the power to stop this progress (Zechariah 4:7). All nations would be invited to enter into it (Genesis 12:1-3 and Zechariah 3:10). The book of Acts tells this most fascinating story of God fulfilling his promise to build an eternal kingdom that would never be destroyed. Once God's church was established it kept growing even until this day (see Acts 2:41; 4:4; 5:14; 6:1 etc.). Though Satan attempts to destroy the church in every generation of man he fails miserably (see Zechariah 3:1-2; Acts 5:28-31 and Revelation 12:13-17) (12bb).

Questions over Zechariah Chapter 4

1. What did Zechariah see in the fifth vision?

2. Where else in the Old Testament do we read of a candlestick holder with seven lamps and what was its function?

3. Compare and contrast Zechariah 4:6 and 4:14.

4. What is the "great mountain" that stood between the temple being built and God's people?

5. What are the "*small things*" that some have despised?

6. What are the two olive trees that stand on the right and left of the candlestick?

7. Compare and contrast Zechariah 4:11-14 with Revelation 11:1-6 and explain what Zechariah is seeing.

ZECHARIAH CHAPTER 5

Synopsis

Zechariah sees two additional visions in this chapter. First, the prophet sees the reality of God's curses upon the wicked of the world by way of plagues. Those who refuse to be aligned with God's word will be plagued in every generation. Secondly, the prophet sees a wicked woman contained in a ten gallon vessel. She represents Satan and his evil works. All who fellowship her sins are separated from the saints and taken to her own place.

Application

God's people needed to see the big picture before their eyes. They were in sin and consequentially plagued. They were contained in the ten gallon container with Satan because they fellowshipped his sin. The turmoil, discomfort, anguish, and agitation prefigures the hell they would experience for all eternity if they did not repent and change their lives. Peace and comfort now and forevermore lies in the balance of man's everyday decisions to live right as opposed to wrong.

Zechariah 5

Zechariah's Sixth Divine Vision (5:1-4)

"**1** *Then again I lifted up my eyes, and saw, and, behold, a flying roll.* **2** *And he said unto me, What do you see? And I answered, I see a flying* *roll; the length thereof is twenty cubits, and the breadth thereof ten cubits"* **(5:1-2).**

Again, let us keep the context of these visions before our mind before looking into the meanings. The Jews have failed to build the temple of God and were suffering drought and food shortages (Haggai 1:6-11). Haggai was successful in opening the eyes of the Jews to their error and they returned to work. God's blessings of rain and harvest; however, have continued to be withheld. Sin continued to plague the lives of men and until they opened their eyes it would continue. Zechariah's duty was to bring out true holiness in God's people. The major problem of the people was that they were not looking to the future spiritual kingdom of God but rather to the earthly temple for hope (Haggai 2:3-4 and Zechariah 4:9-10). The driving force of these early chapters has been on the future temple of God (house, kingdom, or church). The people needed to see the great significance in the temple of their day as well as the spiritual temple (church) of the future. Through Christ, and his kingdom, men would be forgiven of their sins (Haggai 1:11; Zechariah 3:4).

People of this day and age wrote letters and manuscripts upon rolls of various writing surfaces that were attached to two sticks and rolled upon them (a roll). Zechariah sees one of these rolls as it is completely unraveled and it is flying through the air. The measurements were 20 cubits in length by ten cubits in width (approximately 30' long by 15' wide) (a rather large roll of writing). Interestingly, Solomon's porch was measured the same (1 Kings 6:3). Jesus and his disciples would latter teach from this porch (see John 10:23; Acts 3:11 and 5:12).

*"**3** Then said he unto me, This is the **curse** that goes forth over the face of the whole land: for every one that **steals** shall be cut off on the one side according to it; and every one that swears shall be cut off on the other side according to it. **4** I will cause it to go forth, said Jehovah of hosts, and it shall enter into the house of the thief, and into the house of him that **swears falsely** by my name; and it shall abide in the midst of his*

house, and shall consume it with the timber thereof and the stones thereof" **(5:3-4).**

Zechariah's visions have had to do with God's **plague of drought** being unleashed upon the wicked so that they may repent of their dark and sinful deeds (see Haggai 1:11; Zechariah 1:7-8 and 2:9, 13). The flying roll is identified as the *"**curse** that goes forth over the face of the whole land."* Moses spoke of the man that would reject the authority of God saying, *"Jehovah will not pardon him, but the **anger of Jehovah and his jealousy will smoke** against that man, and all **the curse** that is written in this book shall lie upon him, and Jehovah will blot out his name from under heaven"* (Deuteronomy 29:20). The Apostle John, speaking of the **plagues** that come upon man to cause them to repent, said, *"8 and the temple was filled with smoke from the glory of God, and from his power; and none was able to enter into the temple, till the seven **plagues** of the seven angels should be finished"* (Revelation 15:8). The **curse** (flying roll) is the **plagues** that come upon the thief and false prophet. People suffer consequences of plagues when they sin so that they may repent (see Deuteronomy 28:58-63; 29:22-25 and Revelation 16:9-11). The returned Jews suffered through drought and little and diseased harvest because of their transgressions. The drought was intended to grab their attention and cause them to change.

Zechariah sees the seventh divine Vision (5:5-11)

*"**5** Then the angel that talked with me went forth, and said unto me, Lift up now your eyes, and see what is this that goes forth. **6** And I said, What is it? And he said, This is the ephah that goes forth. He said moreover, This is **their** appearance in all the land"* **(5:5-6).**

Zechariah has seen a flying scroll and now he sees a container that *"goes forth."* The angel tells Zechariah to look and see the large container that could hold an *"ephah"* (approximately 40 quarts or 10 gallons). The container with its contents symbolized *"their appearance in all the land."* We must keep reading to identify the antecedent of the plural pronoun *"their."* *"Their"* appearance was as 10 gallons going forth.

"**7** *(and, behold, there was lifted up a talent of lead); and this is a woman sitting in the midst of the ephah.* **8** *And he said,* **This is Wickedness**: *and he cast her down into the midst of the ephah; and he cast the weight of the lead upon the mouth thereof*" **(5:7-8).**

The subjects under consideration of verse six are now revealed to be a woman called "*Wickedness.*" Zechariah watches as a lead lid was lifted off of the ten gallon container and he could see this wicked woman within the ephah vessel. Once Zechariah has seen her the angel cast her back down into the vessel and sealed the top again with the lead lid.

The Apostle John also saw a woman who personified wickedness at Revelation 17:3-5. John sees a woman who had her name written on her forehead. The name reads, "*Mystery, Babylon the Great, the mother of the harlots and of the abominations of the earth*" (Revelation 17:5). Babylon of Revelation stands for wickedness the world over and the power thereof. People of the world and even many of the saints had been seduced by her (see Zechariah 2:7). Zechariah is shown a clear vision of this world wickedness that "*scattered*" God's people yet not beyond eternal repair (see Zechariah 1:21 and 3:3-9). The inference is that this "*Wicked*" woman was a personification of Satan's power of worldliness that the sinful people of Judah had fallen to. While they ought to have been busy building the temple of God and living by the line of righteousness they were fellowshipping the world of wickedness. These wicked people had lost their sanctification among the saints of God and so they were due his divine wrath through plagues (Haggai 2:14).

"**9** *Then lifted I up mine eyes, and saw, and, behold, there came forth two women, and the wind was in their wings; now they had wings like the wings of a stork; and they lifted up the ephah between earth and heaven*" **(5:9).**

Zechariah has witnessed the "*Wicked*" woman being sealed within a ten gallon container (ephah) with a lead lid. God has clearly contained her and does not permit her to leave her prison ephah. The prophet of God now sees two women with wings like a stork take hold of the ephah and carries it "*between earth and heaven.*" The scene is very similar to what John saw at Revelation 20:1-3. This wicked woman of sin is a representation of Satan who works within the generational lives of men. God permits him to be loosed and God restricts him by sealing him in a jar or abyss.

10 *Then said I to the angel that talked with me, Where do these bear the ephah?* **11** *And he said unto me, To build her a house in the land of Shinar: and when it is prepared, she shall be set there in her own place*" **(5:10-11).**

Zechariah asks the angel where the two women are taking the wicked women in the ephah. The angel responds by saying that they are taking her to the land of Shinar to build a permanent dwelling place for her. The land of Shinar was the place that Nimrod (a mighty hunter before Jehovah) established a kingdom. Nimrod's kingdom was opposed to Jehovah's principles and authority (see Babel and Nineveh) (Genesis 10:6-11:9). The angel, by way of this vision, is revealing to Zechariah that wickedness is to be separated from God's kingdom. Those who live in sin are contained within the ephah and reserved for plagues and chastisement. These wicked people are separate from the church of the Lord (12cc) (19h).

People of all generations are challenged by God to make a choice as to where they will pitch the tents of their minds and actions. Will we choose to live a life of sin and be contained in the ephah? Will we be identified with the woman called "*Wickedness*?" God's will is that his saints would come out of this Wicked woman "4 *that you have no fellowship with her sins, and that you receive not her plagues*" (Revelation 18:4). The people of God that had returned home from Babylonian captivity needed to make up their minds as to who they would serve. Would they live lives of cursedness now and forevermore through God's plagues (Revelation 7:1-4) or would they live in peace and comfort through obedience? The decision was theirs as it is ours today.

Questions over Zechariah Chapter 5

1. What did Zechariah see in his sixth vision?

2. What is the curse of Zechariah 5:3?

3. How does God's curse continue to work in the lives of men today?

4. Consider the affects of God's curse upon the disobedient. Why do you suppose people of all generations harden their hearts against God's laws and the affects of his curses?

5. Do you see any similarities between the woman called wickedness at Zechariah 5:5-8 and the Babylon harlot of Revelation 17:3-5?

6. What similarities do you see between Zechariah 5:5-11 and Revelation 20:1-3?

ZECHARIAH CHAPTER 6

Synopsis

More details of God's future kingdom and curses that rest in the house of the wicked are given. A great contrast exist between the curse and plagues that come with disobedience and the peace of God's kingdom that come with obedience (see Zechariah 6:13-15).

Application

The disobedient can expect lives of turmoil, trouble, anguish, pain, discontent, and punishment now and forevermore in hell. The obedient shall be ruled by the prince of peace and experience tranquility, contentment, and glory now and forevermore in heaven. The Lord continues to reveal his long rang plans to the returned Jews. They had lost sight of God's promises and the Lord is reminding them of the great significance of his future kingdom and their future existence.

Zechariah 6

Zechariah's Eighth Divine Vision (6:1-8)

"***1** And again I lifted up mine eyes, and saw, and, behold, there came four chariots out from between two mountains; and the mountains were mountains of brass. **2** In the first chariot were **red horses**; and in the second chariot **black horses**; **3** and in the third chariot **white horses**; and* *in the forth chariot **grizzled strong horses**. 4 Then I answered and said unto the angel that talked with me, What are these, my lord?"* **(6:1-4).**

Again, let us keep the context of these visions before our mind before looking into the meanings. The Jews have failed to build the temple of God and were suffering drought and food shortages. Haggai was successful in opening the eyes of the Jews to their error and they returned to work. God's blessings of rain and harvest; however, have continued to be withheld. Sin continued to plague the lives of men and until they opened their eyes it would continue. Zechariah's duty was to bring out true holiness in God's people. The major problem of the people was that they were not looking to the future spiritual kingdom of God but rather to the earthly temple for hope. The driving force of these early chapters has been on the future temple of God (house, kingdom, or church). The people needed to see the great significance in the temple of their day as well as the spiritual temple (church) of the future. Through Christ, and his kingdom, men would be forgiven of their sins.

Zechariah is shown the last of eight visions. Four chariots have appeared from between two mountains of brass (or copper). These two mountains of brass are related to the brass kingdom of Daniel 2:45 and or the mountain that the kingdom of God would be forged out of. See further notes below at verse 5-8.

The colors of the horses are given; i.e., red, black, white, and grizzled. We read of these exact colored four horses at Revelation 6:1-8. Jesus is the rider of the **white horse** and depicted as a warrior who conquers sin and death with his divine word (see also Revelation 1:5; 3:14 and 19:13). The Lord's divine objective is man's repentance. The **red horse** represented plagues upon the wicked that dwelled in peace (see Zechariah 1:8 and Revelation 6:3-4). The **black horse** brought famine (Revelation 6:5-6). Lastly, the pale or grizzled horse brought death in the form of *"sword, famine, pestilence, and wild beasts of the earth"* (Revelation 6:7-8). Zechariah has no idea what this vision means and so, once again, he asks the angel to help him understand.

"**5** *And the angel answered and said unto me, These are the **four winds of heaven**, which go forth from standing before the Lord of all the earth.* **6** *The chariot wherein are the black horses goes forth toward the north country; and the white went forth after them; and the grizzled went forth toward the south country.* **7** *And the strong went forth, and ought to go that they might walk to and fro through the earth: and he said, Get you hence, walk to and fro through the earth. So they walked to and fro through the earth.* **8** *Then cried he to me, and spoke unto me, saying, Behold, they that go toward the north country have **quieted my spirit** in the north country*" **(6:5-8).**

The angel explains to Zechariah that the four chariots are **four winds** that accomplish Jehovah's purpose in all the earth. We also read of **four winds** that were to plague the wicked at Revelation 7:1. Clearly the prophet of God is seeing the curse or plagues of God going forth upon the wicked for their dark deeds.

The strong grizzled horse would plague and kill the wicked of the world by four methods. Those methods were sword, famine, pestilence, and wild beast. Interestingly, both Jeremiah and Ezekiel said that these four methods of death faced the wicked of Jerusalem and Judah for their sins to move them to repentance (see Jeremiah 15:2 and Ezekiel 14:21). At this point, all the nations of the earth "*sits still and are at rest*" (Zechariah 1:12). This was not something that pleased God. Zechariah, in his first vision, records the words of God saying, "*I am very sore displeased with the nations that are at ease...*" (Zechariah 1:15). The wicked nations surrounding Palestine were destined to be shaken by Jehovah for their wickedness (Haggai 2:7 and Zechariah 2:9). A drought had locked up the people and was cause of their great misery (see Haggai 1:11). Interestingly Jeremiah wrote of a drought that was compared to the plagues of sword, famine, and pestilence (Jeremiah 14:1-12).

Daniel also saw "*four winds*" out of the sea and there appeared four beasts (Daniel 7:1ff). Daniel's four beasts parallel the one beast of

Revelation 13:1. The message is the same in both books. God permits Satan to rise, in the form of kingdoms of men and worldliness, in every generation. They have their one hour to tempt the world to sin and then they are conquered (see Revelation 17:10-14). The *"four winds"* are clearly judgments of God upon the world of man. The *"four winds"* under consideration in Zechariah 5 are equivalent to both the gospel and judgments of plagues upon the wicked so that they may repent as is indicated at Revelation 6 and 7.

Joshua the high priest crowned as king and responsible for building the house of God as Christ the Church (6:9-15)

"**9** *And the word of Jehovah came unto me, saying,* **10** *Take of them of the captivity, even of Heldai, of Tobijah, and of Jedaiah; and come the same day, and go into the house of Josiah the son of Zephaniah, whither they are come from Babylon;* **11** *yea, take of them silver and gold, and make crowns, and set them upon the head of Joshua the son of Jehozadak, the high priest;* **12** *and speak unto him, saying, Thus speaks Jehovah of hosts, saying, Behold,* **the man** *whose name is* **the Branch***: and he shall* **grow up** *out of his place; and* **he shall build the temple of Jehovah***;* **13** *even he shall build the temple of Jehovah; and* **he shall bear the glory***, and shall sit and rule upon* **his throne***; and he shall be a priest upon his throne; and the counsel of* **peace** *shall be between them both*" **(6:9-13).**

Three men; i.e., Heldai, Tobiajah, and of Jedaiah who were staying at the house of Zephaniah, were to be asked of their silver and gold offerings they brought from Babylon to construct a crown. The crown was to be placed upon the head of Joshua the high priest to signify his place as prophet and king of Palestine. Once the crown was placed upon Joshua's head Zechariah was to speak to him and say that a man named *"Branch"* would likewise rule as priest and king over God's future spiritual kingdom. We had earlier examined this man named *"Branch"* at Zechariah 3:8 and determined that the scriptures clearly reveal him to be the Christ (see notes at 3:8).

As sure as Joshua would see to it that God's house be built in Jerusalem even so Christ would build his spiritual house in spiritual Zion. Jesus would build his kingdom upon the fact that he was the Christ come to save men from their sins (Matthew 16:16ff.). The book of Zechariah continues to reveal details about God's future temple, kingdom, or church. Though the word "kingdom" is not used it is implied by the word "*throne*" at Zechariah 6:13.

There are seven attributes of the Branch given here (5b):

a. First, he is the Branch.

b. Secondly, the Branch would "*grow out of his place*" as a tree root or branch from the family of Jesse and David (Jeremiah 33:15).

c. Thirdly, the Branch would build the spiritual temple of Jehovah; i.e., his church (see Matthew 16:16ff). It would be an indestructible kingdom that will conquer all others who stand opposed to it (see Daniel 2:44-45).

d. Fourthly, the Branch would bear glory as king of God's spiritual kingdom (see Colossians 1:13).

e. Fifth, the Branch would rule his kingdom upon his throne. Though the word "kingdom" has not been used it is implied by the word "*throne*." Kings sit upon thrones of kingdoms.

f. Sixthly, the Branch would be priest of his kingdom (see Hebrews 7:1-3).

g. Lastly, the Branch's council would be that of peace (see Isaiah 9:6-7). This is a fascinating aspect of Christ and his church. Those who live by the standard line of righteousness shall experience peace rather than the curses and plagues of disobedience (see Zechariah 1:6, 16 and 5:3).

"*14 And the crowns shall be to Helem, and to Tobijah, and to Jedaiah, and to Hen the son of Zephaniah, for a **memorial** in the temple of*

Jehovah. ***15*** *And they that are far off shall come and build in the temple of Jehovah; and* **you shall know that Jehovah of hosts has sent me unto you***. And this shall come to pass, if you will diligently obey the voice of Jehovah your God"* **(6:14-15).**

The physical crown designed and made for Joshua the high priest would serve as a memorial to the three men who brought the precious gifts from Babylon and voluntarily gave them up for the Lord's purpose.

Finally, Zechariah is given revelation wherein it is revealed that the spiritual temple of Jehovah's would be built by not only Jews but peoples of all nations. When this multi-nationality kingdom is established then all would know that God's words were spoken through the prophet Zechariah. Salvation through the temple built by the Branch would come to pass for each person *"*if *you will diligently obey the voice of Jehovah your God"* (see 1 Corinthians 15:1-2 and Colossians 1:2-23). The issue is not that the temple's coming is contingent upon a person's obedience. The kingdom of Christ would come no matter one's disposition toward it. Christ's kingdom, or temple, however would only come to be within the lives of each individual who would "*obey the voice of Jehovah your God*" (13b). The prophet of God continues to instruct the minds of the people that their lives must be lived in holiness to avoid God's curses and enjoy the Branch's peace (see Isaiah 28:17 and Zechariah 1:16; 2:1; 4:10).

Questions over Zechariah Chapter 6

1. What does Zechariah see in the eighth and final vision?

2. How does this eighth vision relate to the horsemen at Zechariah 1:8 and Revelation 6?

3. Who was asked to make a crown for Joshua?

4. What did this crown represent?

5. Who would build the temple of Jehovah?

6. How would the people know that the Lord is God?

7. List seven characteristics of the "*Branch.*"

8. How do you suppose the temple of the days of Zerubbabel, Haggai, Zechariah, and Joshua the high priest is related and significant to the temple that the Branch would build?

9. What requirement did God put on the people?

10. There is an interesting contrast between the woman called wickedness that is filled with God's curses (Zechariah 5:8) and the Branch who rules a kingdom of peace (Zechariah 6:13). Discuss the differences of lives and experiences for both types of people who choose either wickedness or the branch.

ZECHARIAH CHAPTER 7

Synopsis

Consider the following events and dates:

Second year of Cyrus would be 537 BC and work on the temple of God begins (see Ezra 3:8)

Work comes to a halt after laying the foundation of the temple (Ezra 4:24)

Work on the temple resumes after the admonition of Haggai and Zechariah (Haggai 1:15). The year is 522 BC (second year of Darius, son of Hystaspes, King of Persia). The Jews had left off building the temple of God for approximately 15 years.

The temple is completed in the sixth year of Darius (four years latter) (518 BC).

Total time for construction is nineteen to twenty years.

The Jews sole purpose for leaving Babylon was to rebuild the temple in Jerusalem. Fifteen years pass; however, without any work after the foundation had been laid. The little work that they had done brought reactions of discouragement due to the small stature of the temple. The people were proving that they had lost sight of God's spiritual blessings and plans by building their own homes and being discouraged over the size of the new temple. The casual approach to fasting is another example of their loosing sight of spiritual matters.

Application

Throughout the history of God's people those who have suffered have done so, for the most part, due to forgetting God's words. People often get so bogged down with living life that they forget the most significant issues of life. Making it to heaven and living God should be the number one priority in life yet in most peoples' lives it is not. Zechariah's duty is to put the people back on track to considering the eternity of their souls.

Zechariah 7

God is sought after for an answer regarding Fasting (7 all)

"**1** *And it came to pass in the fourth year of king Darius, that the word of Jehovah came unto Zechariah in the fourth day of the ninth month, even in Chislev*" **(7:1).**

Two years and one month after Zechariah received 8 visions he records more of his work (see Zechariah 1:7). The people of God would not complete the temple construction for another two years (see Ezra 6:15). The current year would have been about 520 BC

"**2** *Now they of Bethel had sent Sharezer and Regem-melech, and their men, to entreat the favor of Jehovah,* **3** *and to speak unto the priests of the house of Jehovah of hosts, and to the prophets, saying, Should I weep in the fifth month, separating myself, as I have done these so many years?*" **(7:2-3).**

Bethel was the city that Jeroboam had begun calf worship long ago. When the captives of Babylon came back to Palestine many went to Bethel and rebuilt a small city there. There was an annual fast observed throughout the days of the people's captivity that reminded them of Nebuchadnezzar's attack and destruction of the temple (see Jeremiah 52:12). Now that the temple is being reconstructed the people want to know if they needed to continue this fast. Should they continue to buffet their bodies by withholding food from it so that they may remember their days of sorrow in Babylon?

David, while being held captive by enemies, once said "*3 my tears have been my food day and night, while they say to me all the day long, 'Where is your God?*'" (Psalms 42:3). The underlying principle of a fast is depicted in these verses. The tears of the king were the only food he had both day and night. David would not eat food while in the throws of guilt and sorrows. The human body is not much in the mood to eat when sorrows so deep fill the heart to the point of weeping. The object of a fast is to cause one to remember the times of sorrow and guilt produced by one's sins or various tests. These were times when food was not wanted. To fast is to put oneself back into the moment of great sorrow and distress. The exercise keeps the affects of sin, sorrows, and the patience obtained in times of tests before our mind. We are reminded of the consequences of sin and the lessons learned through tests so that we will be careful not to do things that will bring these sorrows to our lives (see 1 Peter 2:19-22) (19t).

"*4 Then came the word of Jehovah of hosts unto me, saying, 5 Speak unto all the people of the land, and to the priests, saying, When you fasted and mourned in the fifth and in the seventh month, even these seventy years, did you at all fast unto me, even to me?*" **(7:4-5).**

The fifth month fast commemorated the siege, destruction of Jerusalem and its temple, as well as the people's captivity. God had not commanded such a fast yet there was certainly nothing wrong with doing such things (see Acts 13:1-3 and 1 Corinthians 8:8). Moses; however, had commanded that all Israel fast on the seventh month of the year which was the Day of Atonement (see Leviticus 23:27-32). The people were to "*afflict their soul*" for twenty four hours (i.e., from the evening of the ninth day of the month to the evening of the tenth day).

The Lord does not answer their question regarding fasting directly but rather asks a question of his own. The people were very scrupulous about keeping the fifth and seventh month fasts for seventy years. God's question; however, is "*did you at all fast unto me?*" The inference is that the people did not keep the fasts unto God but rather unto themselves. Their service to God was merely an outward show of what was not really in the heart.

"*6 And when you eat, and when you drink, do not you eat for yourselves, and drink for yourselves? 7 Should you not hear the words which Jehovah cried by the former prophets, when Jerusalem was inhabited and in prosperity, and the cities thereof round about her, and the South and the lowland were inhabited?*" **(7:6-7).**

The Complete Jewish Bible reads, "*Rather, when you eat and drink, it's just to please yourselves, isn't it?*" When the people put themselves through a fast it served only their own selfish purpose. Like the Pharisees of the New Testament people were giving the appearance of piety and holiness by fasting while their hearts were corrupt (see Matthew 6:16-18 and Luke 18:9-14). When the people feasted it too served their own selfish purposes. Where was God in their fasting and feasting? The people had lost sight of God's promises and his divine expectations. They had blended in with the world around them and came to be concerned with things of this world. Though they continued to worship God through fasts their hearts were not with him.

If only Jerusalem would have listened to prophets such as Micah and Jeremiah they would not have experienced the great curse of Babylon. The message remains the same for these captives that have returned to Jerusalem to revive God's promise of a future kingdom and king (see Ezekiel 40-48). They were going back to the old ways that caused Judah to suffer such great curses. The drought was only a reminder yet it was not having its complete affects upon the people. Zechariah, like Haggai, is trying to get the people to ask why they are going through the drought. If the people would consider the drought and their sin they would learn the valuable lesson of repentance (see Haggai 1:7-11 and Revelation 16:8-11).

"**8** *And the word of Jehovah came unto Zechariah, saying,* **9** *Thus has Jehovah of hosts spoken, saying, Execute true judgment, and show kindness and compassion every man to his brother;* **10** *and oppress not the widow, nor the fatherless, the sojourner, nor the poor; and let none of you devise evil against his brother in your heart*" **(7:8-10)**.

The prophet exposes their dark deeds to bend their minds back to the line of righteousness (18c). These simple instructions and or commandments had been given to Israel and Judah before these current days. They rejected these commandments and so found themselves destroyed and taken captive. Nothing had changed as far as what God expected of his people. The inference is clear. The current people of God (returned captives) were falling into the same transgressions of those who preceded them even though they were warned by Jeremiah, Micah, Nahum, and Zephaniah.

"**11** *But they refused to listen, and pulled away the shoulder, and stopped their ears, that they might not hear.* **12** *Yea, they made their hearts as an adamant stone, lest they should hear the law, and the words which Jehovah of hosts had sent by his Spirit by the former prophets:* **therefore there came great wrath from Jehovah of hosts**" **(7:11-12)**.

The hard adamant stone heart of the people was revealed as Jehovah sent prophets with his words yet they "*stopped their ears*" to the "*words which Jehovah of hosts had sent by his Spirit by the former prophets.*" A hard heart is defined as one that **hears** God's word yet **will not act** upon it (14f). A great lesson is learned by studying the books of Ezra, Haggai, and Zechariah. The people of God were doing what they wanted to do rather than God's will. God's will was that his plan to redeem man through his Branch (Christ) and kingdom would be fresh upon the minds of his people and that they would work toward that great day. The people; however, were more concerned about building their own homes (see Haggai 1:3), gaining the goods of this world (Zechariah 5:4), and feasting (Zechariah 7:6).

The people's ways were "*unclean*" (Haggai 2:14) and their hearts as hard stone (Zechariah 7:12). It is very interesting to note that while the people have asked God about fasting for his sake he has given them a scathing rebuke. God knows the hearts of man. Many today may have an exterior image of good, generous, and loving yet their hearts are blackened with wickedness. God plagues and curses the wicked with his "*great wrath*" because he knows their hearts and demands their repentance (3h).

"*13 And it is come to pass that, as he cried, and they would not hear, so they shall cry, and I will not hear, said Jehovah of hosts; 14 but I will scatter them with a whirlwind among all the nations which they have not known. Thus the land was desolate after them, so that no man passed through nor returned: for they laid the pleasant land desolate*" **(7:13-14)**.

The curse of God's divine plague was in full force and they felt the mind bending trouble, pain, anguish, and turmoil that it brought to their lives. As the Lord's wrath was poured upon the wicked, because they refused repentance, they cried out to him in anguish. God; however, closed his ears to their cries just as they had closed their ears to his cries through the prophets for their repentance. When one follows another's will, such as self or a false prophet, how can that person possibly think that God will answer them in such a state of mind (61b)? Will He support such a one in their false ways? Is this how grace works? No! God's grace belongs to those who submit to his will rather than another. The responsibility of all hardships and desolation that they had experienced and will experience is self inflicted. When I violate the law it is I who am the cause of my trouble not the law itself. God will not hear the prayers of the wicked (see Proverbs 15:8-9, 29; Isaiah 1:11ff; Amos 5:21-23; John 9:31 etc.). Rather than praying to God for food, relief of pain and trouble, and protection from enemies the people of God ought to have prayed first for forgiveness.

Questions over Zechariah Chapter 7

1. How long had it been since Zechariah had his eight visions?

2. **True or False:** God was pleased with the people's fasting over the past seventy years.

3. Why did the captives in Babylon participate in fasts and feasts?

4. What instructions of God did the people not want to hear?

5. Why doesn't God hear the prayers of sinful men?

ZECHARIAH CHAPTER 8

Synopsis

The prophet of God encourages the Jews of Judah and Jerusalem to be strong and build the temple as God had commanded (see Zechariah 8:9). There were greater things at stake than a physical temple.

Application

Zechariah reveals three things that should motivate God's people to return to the work of building the temple. First, God will establish his eternal kingdom in the future. The current physical temple was only a stepping stone of obedience that would lead the people to the more significant kingdom where people would be forgiven of their sins. Secondly, this new kingdom would represent peace and joy as opposed to the trouble and calamity that comes with disobedience. Now was the time to review their past and the experience of their forefathers. They needed to be reminded of the trouble and calamity they experienced when living in disobedience so that they would get back to work. Thirdly, salvation was at stake. The people would be saved by God if only they would obey now. Entrance into God's kingdom now and in the future is contingent upon their obedience to the Lord's commandments.

Zechariah 8

God will once again dwell in Zion (8:1-8)

"**1** *And the word of Jehovah of hosts came to me, saying,* **2** *Thus said Jehovah of hosts: I am jealous for Zion with great jealousy, and I am jealous for her with great wrath*" **(8:1-2).**

The term "*Jehovah of hosts*" is used when contemplating God's wrath against the ungodly in the form of plagues and curses (see Zechariah 7:12). The Lord continues to give answer to Zechariah regarding the question of fasting from those of Bethel (see Zechariah 7:1-4). The Lord knows all things and looks into the hearts of men. The Lord's people had only fasted because it soothed their conscience regarding God's laws. While they fasted to keep one part of the law they violated many other parts. They were self condemned and did not even recognize it. The Lord reminds the people that he had warned their forefathers, through his prophets, of the consequences of such delusion. Yet their "*hearts were as an adamant stone...*" (Zechariah 7:12). The more law they heard the harder their hearts were against it because it was not what they wanted to do. Likewise, the fasting of Zechariah's day was not due to God's laws but because the people saw something in it for themselves (Zechariah 7:6). It seems odd how that bits and pieces of religious service to God can appease the conscience of one who violates so many other laws of God.

We may compare the people's scrupulous keeping of these fast with many denominational bodies today who celebrate holidays such as Easter and Christmas. These holidays are viewed as religious days to commemorate the birth and resurrection of Jesus. One will search in vain to find a commandment, inference, or example of Christmas or Easter being observed. Yet many today shall asks the Lord... "Shall we continue to keep Christmas and Easter as a sacred day of the year" while they live in contradiction to his divine laws (61c). The once or twice religious assembly per year appeases their weak conscience and they believe they have done their service to God for the year.

God had a rival when it came to keeping the people's hearts in tune to his laws. The rival was worldliness, false prophets, and selfish ambition.

Zion's interest was in God's rival and so they hardened their hearts against God and caused him to be "*jealous*" to the point of "*great wrath*." God, like a husband or father whose children or wife left him for another, is filled with jealousy and anger (3t).

"**3** *Thus said Jehovah: I am returned unto Zion, and will dwell in the midst of Jerusalem: and Jerusalem shall be called* **the city of truth**; *and the mountain of Jehovah of hosts, The holy mountain*" **(8:3).**

The Lord turns his attention to a future day when he would return to Zion, the city of truth, and the mountain of Jehovah of hosts, the holy mountain and dwell in the midst. These terms are synonymous with the future kingdom of God or **church** of Jesus Christ (see Isaiah 2:1-4 and Hebrews 12:22ff). The presence of God will indicate a purging of the unlawful practices of idolatry, injustice, and devising evil within the heart. God's dwelling place will be pure and undefiled. The people had pushed these grand spiritual thoughts of their redemption far from their minds and God had come to be very jealous. God's prophet continues to put the future spiritual kingdom before the minds of a people. They had forgotten the Lord's long range plans for their salvation and the Lord would not stand by idly while they lost their eternal souls (see Psalms 50:3, 21).

"**4** *Thus said Jehovah of hosts: there shall yet old men and old women dwell in the streets of Jerusalem, every man with his staff in his hand for very age.* **5** *And the streets of the city shall be full of boys and girls playing in the streets thereof.* **6** *Thus said Jehovah of hosts: if it be marvelous in the eyes of the remnant of this people in those days, should it also be marvelous in mine eyes? Said Jehovah of hosts*" **(8:4-6).**

The wicked had nothing but drought and God's plagues of a cursed life. The righteous; however, had peace to look forward to. Once again we see the contrast between the anguish of wickedness and the peacefulness of righteousness (see Zechariah 6:13). Both God and the true remnant of faithful see the coming kingdom as "*marvelous.*" While the wicked have a life of misery and mental anguish the righteous have "*marvelous*" lives. Their lives are marvelous because they are in a marvelous kingdom. It is marvelous because their sins are forgiven and they are happy, content, joyous, and filled with hope.

"**7** *Thus said Jehovah of hosts: Behold, I will save my people from the east country, and from the west country;* **8** *and I will bring them, and they shall dwell in the midst of Jerusalem; and they shall be my people, and I will be their God, in truth and righteousness*" **(8:7-8)**.

The east and west countries indicates whole world (see Isaiah 11:11-12). Worldliness and self interest will not be the ruin of God's elect in his kingdom. God's kingdom is indestructible and it will come to pass with Jesus reigning as king. No amount of wickedness has the power to stop its progress. The people of Zechariah's day were like Saul of Tarsus when Jesus appeared to him on the road to Damascus. Jesus said, "*Why are you kicking against the goad.*" Saul's battle against God's eternal kingdom plan was futile (see Acts 26:14).

Those whose lives are molded to the image of Jesus Christ in truth and righteousness will be brought into "*the midst of Jerusalem*" (i.e., the Kingdom and church of Christ). Jesus would later say that he is the "*the way, and the truth, and the life: no one cometh unto the Father, but by me*" (John 14:6). Zechariah has revealed the entrance into God's kingdom to be contingent upon one's stand and conduct toward the line of righteousness (see Zechariah 1:16 and 6:15). The relationship between God and man is contingent upon one's position toward "*truth and righteousness.*" Those willing to submit to God's laws in obedience will enter into the gates of the city of God and be protected by walls of salvation and righteousness (see Zechariah 2:5 and Isaiah 26:1-3). This will be a place of peace rather than the troubles and calamity that come with living lives of disobedience (see Zechariah 6:15) (11d) (10b).

God's Curse for the People's Laziness and Disobedient would be Lifted if only they would Love and Obey His Words (8:9-13)

"**9** *Thus said Jehovah of hosts:* **Let your hands be strong**, *you that hear in these days these words from the mouth of the prophets that were in the day that the foundation of the house of Jehovah of hosts was laid, even the temple,* **that it might be built**" **(8:9).**

Haggai acknowledged the people's world view of the temple and also encouraged them to be strong (see Haggai 2:3-4). The people had a faulty view and expectation of the temple and new kingdom of God. **Haggai and Zechariah's job has been to remind the people of the spiritual and eternal significance of the temple and kingdom of God (Zechariah 4:8-10).** When the people acknowledge this it would be a source of motivation and strength to their hands to do the work that is before them. There are greater and more eternal things at stake with building this temple.

The people are encouraged to get busy and build the temple. The blessings of peace that come with obedience and the curses in the form of plagues for disobedience is at stake. Moreover the people's reaction to truth and righteousness will determine how their lives would be lived out. Those who are disobedient to God's words would suffer his plagues now and forevermore if they don't repent. Those who are obedient would experience peace and glory now and forevermore as they remain obedient.

The Christian today can be strengthened to do the work of God through his word and because he is with us (see Ephesians 3:16; Colossians 1:11 and 2 Timothy 2:1). When fear of man and discouragement come it does not find its origins in God (2 Timothy 1:7). God had always promised Israel that he would be with them and fight for them if they would put their whole hearted trust in him (see Exodus 14:14 and 19:4-6). There are many things at Satan's disposal that has the power to weaken the hands of God's people (2 Corinthians 2:11). Satan weakens the hands of God's people by discouragement, worldliness, and false doctrines of men. Though these things may have the appearance of "*great mountains*" of discouragement the true saints of God will overcome them with the help of God (see Zechariah 4:7 and Philippians 4:13) (60). God's people were to learn that their true hope was not to be in a physical temple but in the Christ who dwell within them and forgive them of their sins.

The admonition is to be "*strong*" and "*build*" the house of God. The prophet Haggai also said, "*Yet now be strong, O Zerubbabel, said Jehovah; and be strong, O Joshua, son of Jehozadak, the high priest; and be strong, all you people of the land, said Jehovah, and work: for I am with you, said Jehovah of hosts*" (Haggai 2:4). God has given a command; i.e., build my temple (see Ezra 6:14 and Haggai 1:8). The people begin the work; however, the forces of discouragement and worldliness have crushed their desire to fulfill God's command. The Samaritans and the size of the temple have discouraged them. Jehovah's purpose, through Haggai and Zechariah, was to encourage the people to do that which they knew he wanted them to do; i.e., build. **Building the physical temple would be an important stepping stone of obedience in order for them to reach the eternal spiritual temple of God's kingdom, the church, and eventually heaven itself.**

"**10** *For before those days there was no hire for man, nor any hire for beast; neither was there any peace to him that went out or came in, because of the adversary: for I set all men every one against his neighbor.* **11** *But now I will not be unto the remnant of this people as in the former days, said Jehovah of hosts*" **(8:10-11).**

"*Those days*" were the days that the foundation of the temple was built and many were discouraged due to a worldly view of God's kingdom (see verse 9 above). The time of the people's lesson had run its course in the mind of God. He had withheld the rain, caused their crops to fail, and brought adversaries upon them that they may learn that all God's blessings are contingent upon a heart of love and obedience toward him (Haggai 1:9 and Zechariah 6:15).

"**12** *For there shall be the seed of **peace**; the vine shall give its fruit, and the ground shall give its increase, and the heavens shall give their dew;*

and I will cause the remnant of this people to inherit all these things. **13** *And it shall come to pass that, as you were a* **curse** *among the nations, O house of Judah and house of Israel, so will I save you, and you shall be a blessing. Fear not, but* **let your hands be strong**" **(8:12-13)**.

The Lord assures his people that the rains would return, peace between neighbors would be restored, they would have plenteous harvest, and eventually the grand blessings of forgiveness would be theirs in his kingdom. God's people had been looked upon by the surrounding peoples as a nation cursed for all the seemingly "bad luck" they experienced. Like the Hindus today the nations believed Judah's suffering to be karma or destiny. Nothing could be further from the truth. They suffered because of their own sinful actions. The Lord assures them saying, "*I will save you... Fear not, but let your hands be strong.*" The conditions of God graciously removing the curse from them was that they work hard with their hands and build the temple. The motivation for building was the blessings of God to look forward to. Temple building was not the only thing God was looking for in his people. Consider the next few verses.

The Conditions for removing the Curst (8:14-17)

"**14** *For thus said Jehovah of hosts: as I thought to do evil unto you, when your fathers provoked me to wrath, said Jehovah of hosts, and I repented not;* **15** *so again have I thought in these days to do good unto Jerusalem and to the house of Judah:* **fear not**" **(8:14-15)**.

When the evil deeds of Israel and Judah ("*your fathers*") came up unto the Lord his wrath was kindled and he determined to bring Assyria and Babylon upon them. Though kings such as Josiah did much religious reforms it was not enough to cause God to repent of his intentions for the people. Now, the Lord has once again thought about his people. Rather than bringing nations against them and withholding the blessings of rain and crops he has determined to bless them. Those willing to repent and seek out righteousness are encouraged to not "*fear.*" God will bless them with great peace in his kingdom. The people were to be strong and not fear because God's blessings with be with those who love him. The Apostle Paul said, "*God gave us not a spirit of fear but of power and love and discipline*" (2 Timothy 1:7).

"**16** *These are the things that you shall do: Speak every man the truth with his neighbor; execute the judgment of truth and peace in your gates;* **17** *and let none of you devise evil in your hearts against his neighbor; and love no false oath: for all these are things that I hate, said Jehovah*" **(8:16-17).**

Here are tangible commands that the people could grasp and do in order to avoid God's wrath. Fasting was not enough! If they were strong and feared not doing these commands great blessings awaited. What "*good,*" as opposed to cursing the disobedient with famine, pestilence, wild beasts, and sword did God plan to do for his people? The object of this book has been to illustrate the grand and marvelous significance of the coming kingdom of God ruled by the Branch. The "*good*" that God would do for his remnant would be to forgive their sins and place them in his kingdom the church (see Zechariah 8:15 above). To achieve these grand and marvelous blessings people needed to speak the truth and make truthful judgments. Furthermore those who expected to receive God's marvelous blessings were to not plan evil things against a neighbor and neither were they to love false oaths. God has ever conditioned his blessings for man on one's obedience (see Ephesians 1:3-7 compared to Acts 2:38).

The Blessings of Obedience will be Noticed and Desired by other Strong Nations (8:18-23)

"**18** *And the word of Jehovah of hosts came unto me, saying,* **19** *Thus said Jehovah of hosts: the fast of the fourth month, and the fast of the fifth, and the fast of the seventh, and the fast of the tenth, shall be to the house of Judah joy and gladness, and cheerful feasts; therefore* **love truth and peace**" **(8:18-19).**

The designated fasts would be a joy and gladness to the people when they "*love truth and peace*" as opposed to greed, worldliness, and false prophecies. Truth is God's laws or divine revelation. When one loves truth they obey truth (see John 14:15). The Apostle Paul writes, "*Wherefore, putting away falsehood, speak truth each one with his neighbor: for we are members one of another*" (Ephesians 4:25). Peace is experienced when a total transformation of one's thinking takes place (see Romans 12:1-2). Until this transformation of the mind takes place there is nothing but God's wrath in the form of curses and plagues (16c).

"**20** *Thus said Jehovah of hosts: it shall yet come to pass, that there shall come peoples, and the inhabitants of many cities;* **21** *and the inhabitants of one city shall go to another, saying, Let us go speedily to entreat the favor of Jehovah, and to seek Jehovah of hosts: I will go also.* **22** *Yea many peoples and strong nations shall come to seek Jehovah of hosts in Jerusalem, and to entreat the favor of Jehovah.* **23** *Thus said Jehovah of hosts: in those days it shall come to pass, that ten men shall take hold, out of all the languages of the nations, they shall take hold of the skirt of him that is a Jew, saying, We will go with you, for we have heard that God is with you*" **(8:20-23).**

What will turn wicked men and nations to God? As men see the cause of their curse and plagues and witness the peace of the saints they will flow into the city of God, Jerusalem, Zion, kingdom of God, or church (see Zechariah 2:11; 3:10; Revelation 15:4 and 21:24). The psalmist writes, "**11** *let Mount Zion be glad! Let the daughters of Judah rejoice because of your judgments!* **12** *Walk about Zion, go around her, number her towers,* **13** *consider well her ramparts, go through her citadels, that you may* **tell the next generation** **14** *that this is God, our God forever and ever. He will guide us forever*" (Psalms 48:11-14).

This should be what people see in the Lord's church today. The Lord's church is composed of people experiencing blessings from Jehovah, great peace, joy, happiness, and contentment in this life. Such a lifestyle of obedience from the heart ought to appeal to the peoples round about us and make them want to have a part in us (19n). The world is watching the Christian. It is of great importance that we live according to truth so that God's kingdom may grow through the godliness and peace of our lives (19e).

Questions over Zechariah Chapter 8

1. What will Jerusalem come to be called?

2. How would the temple be built?

3. Why does God tell the people to not fear?

4. What did God expect out of his people (Zechariah 8:16-17)?

5. What should people love?

6. Why would people of the nations take hold of the Jews skirt and say, "*We will go with you*?

ZECHARIAH CHAPTER 9

Synopsis

Zechariah reveals two burdens or oracles from chapters 9 through 14. The first oracle (chapters 9-11) is a judgment against the nations who put their trust in things other than God. The second oracle is directed toward Israel (chapters 12 through 14).

The prophet of God looks at the distinguishing characteristics of God's kingdom as opposed to the kingdoms of men. The kingdoms of men, such as Tyre and Philistia, place their trust in temporary things such as wealth, physical strength, national power, and pride. God's kingdom; however, looks to eternal hope in such things as righteousness, meekness, and justice. God had watched his people be destroyed by these temporary nations in times past because of their sin. When the Lord's spiritual kingdom is established; however, God will not sit back idly and watch his people be conquered. The Lord's kingdom will be comprised strictly of the righteous, just, and meek. He will know his people and they will be protected by his divine care (see 2 Timothy 2:19).

Application

An interesting study over the relationship between Old Testament and New Testament people of God is considered in this chapter. God was not always with his people in the Old Testament due to their sins. The nations of Israel and Judah were conquered due to sin. Prophecies regarding the kingdom of God in the New Testament indicate an impervious and indestructible power protected by God. The more we look into this the better acquainted we become with God's future kingdom, the church, and the more we gain understanding of the responsibilities the New Testament Christians have. God will always protect and guard those who live lives of meekness, righteousness, and justice. The humble, rather than the boisterous power and wealth seeker, will submit to God's commandments. The obedient child of God may be killed by the wicked yet their ultimate victory is depicted not on this earth but eternally in heaven (see Matthew 10:28). This is the primary lesson of Zechariah. The returned Jews needed to be directed to look to a future kingdom where eternal blessings would be experienced.

Zechariah 9

The Nations of Wicked men shall be Punished (9:1-7)

"**1** *The burden of the word of Jehovah upon the land of Hadrach, and Damascus shall be its resting place (for the eye of man and of all the tribes of Israel is toward Jehovah);* **2** *and Hamath, also, which borders thereon; Tyre and Sidon, because they are very wise.* **3** *And Tyre did build herself a stronghold, and heaped up silver as the dust, and fine gold as the mire of the streets*" **(9:1-3)**.

The word "*burden*" is also translated "oracle" in the ASV footnotes. Zechariah, like Isaiah, Jeremiah, Ezekiel, and Nahum, is delivering an oracle or judgment of God against the nations for their disobedience. The judgment concerns the nations of Hadrach (of Syria), Damascus, Hamath, Tyre, and Sidon. These nations put their trust in their might and wealth rather than God.

"**4** *Behold, the Lord will dispossess her, and he will smite her power in the sea; and she shall be* **devoured with fire**. **5** *Ashkelon shall see it, and fear; Gaza also, and shall be sore pained; and Ekron, for her expectation shall be put to shame; and the king shall perish from Gaza, and Ashkelon shall not be inhabited.* **6** *And a bastard shall dwell in Ashdod, and I will cut off the pride of the Philistines.* **7** *And I will take away his blood out of* *his mouth, and his abominations from between his teeth; and he also shall be a remnant for our God; and he shall be as a chieftain in Judah, and Ekron as a Jebusite*" **(9:4-7).**

The city of Tyre is located about 35 miles to the north of Mount Carmel (between Sidon and Acco). The name "Tyre" means rock (or a rocky island). Ezekiel 26:4-14 refers to Tyre as "*a bare rock, a place for the spreading of nets.*" "Today Tyre is joined to the mainland by a sandy isthmus (an accumulation on the mole built by Alexander the Great in the siege of 332 BC)" (ISBE v. 4, pp. 932). Tyre had long been known for commerce and trade. Isaiah told the traveling ships to "*howl*" because she was about to fall (Isaiah 23:1). Interestingly, the OT reveals three cities designated as harlots. Those cities are Nineveh (Nahum 3:1, 4), Tyre (Isaiah 23:15-17) and Babylon (Isaiah 47:5ff). Tyre had caused the world to run after her because of her fame and riches yet she, like all the harlots of history, fall in defeat to Jehovah God (see also Revelation 18:1-20).

The world saw Tyre as "*honorable*" (Isaiah 23:8) yet God saw their pride and arrogance (Isaiah 23:9 and Ezekiel 28:1-2). Isaiah said, "*8 For my thoughts are not your thoughts, neither are your ways my ways, said Jehovah*" (Isaiah 55:8). While the world views sinful things as fun and exciting God has different views.

There would be no escape for the arrogant city (Isaiah 23:10-12). Tyre had been before untouched, like a virgin; yet now was depicted as a virgin woman who had been sexually abused and defiled (Isaiah 23:12). Tyre would lie dormant for the period of seventy years or the period of one world power such as Babylon. Tyre would then be restored but go right back to prostituting herself out like a harlot (Isaiah 23:17). Though rebellious, Tyre would play a part in achieving God's purpose; "*for her merchandise shall be for them that dwell before Jehovah, to eat sufficiently, and for durable clothing*" (Isaiah 23:18). This statement appears to be referring to the time after the seventy years of captivity in

Babylon when God's people were permitted to go back to Jerusalem and rebuild the temple by the help of Tyre (see Ezekiel 3:7).

Tyre's fourfold sin consisted of exercising malicious joy over the fall of Jerusalem (Ezekiel 26:2), viewing themselves as God (Ezekiel 28:2), being filled with pride (Isaiah 23:9), and putting their trust in the things of this world. Tyre's trust had been set in their riches gained from world wide trade (Ezekiel 26:12 and 27:27), their army (Ezekiel 27:11) and the city's walls and towers (Ezekiel 26:4; 27:11). Such success, in the eyes of the world, caused Tyre to suffer great delusion of grandeur and proclaim, "*I am a god*" (Ezekiel 28:2). They directed their own steps through confidence of the flesh. Jeremiah had said, "*O Jehovah, I know that the way of man is not in himself: it is not in man that walks to direct his steps*" (Jeremiah 10:23). Tyre considered themselves deity due to their high state of riches and worldly wisdom. They displayed their unlawful ways by proclaiming their king to be deity and following his sinful ways (Ezekiel 28:16).

The primary lesson we learn from the cities of Tyre and Sidon is that riches will not save a man (25h). Tyre had trusted in her riches yet Jehovah destroyed the city. Where were those riches when the king of Tyre, who in a state of delusion, proclaimed his deity and was slaughtered by another man in war (Ezekiel 28:9)? Secondly, we learn that "*pride comes before the fall*" (Proverbs 16:18). All of Tyre's hopes, trust, and security rest in their riches and world renown trade market. When one places their hopes in things other than the Lord they are doomed and truly without hope and security. Solomon wrote, "*There is a way which seems right unto a man; but the end thereof are the ways of death*" (Proverbs 14:12).

Zechariah moves from Tyre and Sidon to the chief cities of the Philistines (i.e., Ashkelon, Gaza, Ekron, and Ashdod). The fall of Tyre and its commerce affects the whole of the coast from Sidon to Egypt (Isaiah 23:2-7). These Philistine cities would see the fall of Sidon and Tyre and fear for their own safety. The Philistines' pride and idolatry would be taken from them as they are humbled by Jehovah. Some; however, the Lord would save as a remnant and they would be numbered with the people of God in the strong city of Zion.

Days of Hope await the true Israel (9:8-10)

"*8 And I will encamp about **my house** against the army, that none pass through or return; and no oppressor shall pass through them any more: for now have I seen with mine eyes*" **(9:8).**

We must note the context of the phrase, "*my house*." The house of God is both the immediate temple that is to be finished (Zechariah 7:2-3 and 8:9, 13) and the future kingdom or church (see Zechariah 1:16; 6:12-13 and 8:1-3; see also Ezekiel 44:7 in the context of God's future kingdom and church and Hebrews 3:6; 10:21 and 12:21-28). Throughout the history of God's house the Lord had sit back only to watch his people be defeated for their wicked deeds. No longer would God sit back and watch his house be destroyed. The house would change and would be comprised of those who walk the line of righteousness and justice (see Zechariah 1:6 and 16 as well as Isaiah 28:17). The Lord's kingdom people would be impervious to ruin at the hands of the wicked. No plan or power of man would have the power to overthrow God's kingdom (see Zechariah 4:7) (12bb). This new house of God would be protected by the Lord with walls of fire and salvation and gates that would permit no wicked man to enter (see Zechariah 2:5 and Isaiah 26:1-3). The wicked will remain subject to God's wrath yet those within have peace.

There is a clear distinction between the house of God during Old Testament days and the house of God ruled by Christ in the New Testament days. God could only watch his kingdom in Old Testament times be destroyed by other nations because of their sins. The new kingdom of God will not be comprised of sinners. The Lord, who knows the hearts of men, will make a clear delineation between the wicked and righteous. The righteous will choose to remain obedient to God's laws through his Son Jesus. The kingdom of God that Zechariah, and the prophets of old, speaks of is a kingdom that is comprised of only the meek, righteous, and just. It will not be a physical kingdom with some good and some evil like the days of the Old Testament kings and kingdoms. God's kingdom will be spiritual and the Lord will know who belongs to him and he will care for them (12a). The Lord certainly knows who belong to him today. Though there are building that bear his name across our landscape the Lord knows who are truly his. The Apostle Paul said, "*19 Howbeit the firm foundation of God stands, having this seal, the Lord knows them that are his: and, let every one that names the name of the Lord depart from unrighteousness*" (2 Timothy 2:19 and Revelation 7:2-3; 13:16).

"*9 Rejoice greatly, O daughter of Zion; shout, O daughter of Jerusalem: behold, your **king** comes unto you; he is **just**, and **having salvation**; **lowly**, and riding upon an ass, even upon a colt the foal of an ass. 10 And I will cut off the chariot from Ephraim, and the horse from Jerusalem; and the battle bow shall be cut off; and he shall speak **peace** unto the nations: and **his dominion** shall be from sea to sea, and from the River to the ends of the earth*" **(9:9-10).**

Zion, the house of God and future Church of Jesus Christ, is called upon to rejoice because of the indestructible nature of the kingdom. God is with them and he is their protector. The surety of the matter is further fixed in the minds of God's people by the prophet making a bold prediction. The king of God's kingdom will soon come with justice and salvation (Zechariah 2:5; 8:7; Isaiah 26:1-3; Matthew 1:21 and 26:26-28). He will be a lowly man who does not ride upon a war horse but rather upon "*a colt the foal of an ass.*" The humble nature of God's kingdom and king is depicted here. Matthew reveals the fulfillment of Zechariah's prophecy at Matthew 21:5-8. Matthew translates the word "*lowly*" as "*meek*" (Greek *praus*) meaning, "mild, soft, gentle, and meek ("showing patience and humility; gentle... Easily imposed upon; submissive" – AHD 782) (LS 666). A synonym for the word meek is "**compliant**." Jesus is a man who is compliant with law.

The character of Jesus would oppose all things that world empires and powers would stand for (i.e., wealth, pride, and worldly ambition to conquer and divide) (19h). While kingdoms like Tyre put their trust in riches and physical might Christ's kingdom would trust in Jehovah God (see Zechariah 9:3-4). While kingdoms like the Philistines were filled with pride Christ's kingdom would be for the meek and lowly. There is a distinct difference in the kingdoms of men and the kingdom of God! The wealth, power, fame, strength, and pride of men comes to an end in every generation yet Christ's kingdom of trust and meekness is eternal (see Revelation 18:2, 9-20). The Psalmist said, "6 *They that trust in their wealth, and boast themselves in the multitude of their riches; 7 none of them can by any means redeem his brother, nor give to God a ransom for him... 10 Wise men die, the fool and the brutish alike perish, and leave their wealth to others*" (Psalms 49:6-10). Notice the distinct difference between the lowly meek Jesus and the kingdoms of men. Our world is filled with people interested in money, power, and fame. Jesus was concerned with none of this. The true Zion will be just like Christ (see Romans 8:29). These lowly Christ like people will be protected forevermore by the Lord.

The rule of Christ would not be by carnal weapons of bows, chariots, and horses but he would rather rule his kingdom with peace. Carnal weapons will have no power against the kingdom of God and his saints. Though the world of sinful men may kill our bodies our souls remain in the care of God (see Matthew 10:28). The glorious kingdom of God will have no boundaries. Zechariah said that its borders will be from "*sea to sea and from the River to the ends of the earth*" (see Psalms 72:8). Luke writes, "*31 and behold, you shall conceive in your womb, and bring forth a son, and shall call his name Jesus. 32 He shall be great, and shall be called the Son of the Most High: and the Lord God shall give unto him the throne of his father David: 33 and he shall reign over the house of Jacob for ever; and of his kingdom there shall be no end*" (Luke 1:31-33). There is no time frame that limits Christ's kingdom and neither is there a geographic location that he does not have authority over. This is the everlasting kingdom that Daniel told of that is the greatest of all kingdoms (see Daniel 2:44-45). The message of the king will be "*peace.*" Peace with God, rather than a curse of plagues, is available to all who would call upon the name of the Lord in faith and trust. All nations of men will see this peace and desire this kingdom (see Zechariah 8:20-23).

The Lord addresses Zion (9:11-17)

"**11** *As for you also, because of the blood of your covenant I have set free your prisoners from the pit wherein is no water.* **12** *Turn you to the stronghold, you prisoners of hope: even to-day do I declare that I will render double unto you.* **13** *For I have bent Judah for me, I have filled the bow with Ephraim; and I will stir up your sons, O Zion, against your sons, O Greece, and will make you as the sword of a mighty man*" **(9:11-13)**.

The psalmist said, "*Gather my saints together unto me, those that have made a covenant with me by sacrifice*" (Psalms 50:5). The future blood of Jesus Christ would serve as a blood sacrifice that would remove men from the prison and pit of sin to freedom and glory by forgiveness (see John 8:31-36 and 1 Peter 3:19). Zion people would be a nation of "*hope.*" God is calling upon these people of hope to cast off the religious ideology brought about by the Macedonians (Grecians under Alexander the Great) and return to the Zion of hope. The entire scene is very similar to what we read of at Revelation 18:1-4.

"**14** *And Jehovah shall be seen over them; and his arrow shall go forth as the lightning; and the Lord Jehovah will blow the trumpet, and will go with whirlwinds of the south.* **15** *Jehovah of hosts will* **defend** *them; and they shall devour, and shall tread down the sling-stones; and they shall drink, and make a noise as through wine; and they shall be filled like bowls, like the corners of the altar*" **(9:14-15).**

Over and over Zechariah depicts Zion as a nation or kingdom that is impervious to the pit falls of other nations. The Lord "*defends*" (Zechariah 9:15), protects (Zechariah 9:8 and Isaiah 31:4-5), and is a wall of fire and salvation with gates that would permit no wicked man to enter (see Zechariah 2:5 and Isaiah 26:1-3). This means divine help in the future kingdom for the saints in Zion or the church. God's divine help comes in two forms. First, God helps and protects man from pride, glory, and worldliness of nations through his truths (Romans 1:16). The Lord's truths give divine direction and strength to his saints (2 Timothy 3:16-17). Secondly, God defends, protects, and is a wall of fire and salvation to his church by way of the blood sacrifice of Jesus Christ (see Matthew 26:26). Though the saints may sin from time to time they will be forgiven as they meekly admit their faults before God (see 1 John 1:8-9).

"**16** *And Jehovah their God will save them in that day as the flock of his people; for they shall be as the stones of a crown, lifted on high over his land.* **17** *For how great is his goodness, and how great is his beauty! Grain shall make the young men flourish, and new wine the virgins*" **(9:16-17).**

God, "*in that day,*" would cause Greece to rise to world prominence to accomplish his divine purposes (see Zechariah 9:13 above; Daniel 2:21 and 8:20-21). After the Medes and Persian rule, that they were currently under, the Grecians would rise to prominence just as Daniel had foretold. This world empire would cause many to go astray yet the true saints of God would be protected by the Lord.

Lest one get the wrong impression of these passages of scriptures we must remind the reader of the overall objective of Zechariah. Zechariah is not examining the irresistible grace of God that some speak of today when they talk of "once saved always saved." The people of God, in Zechariah's day, had been disobedient in performing the Lord's command to build the temple (see Haggai 1:1-11; Zechariah 4:9-10 and 8:9). God was motivating the people to get back to works of obedience so that they may be a part of the Zion church of the future (see Zechariah 6:15). Zion people performed obedient works of meekness, righteous, and justice (see Zechariah 8:16-17 and 9:9-10). God's kingdom people are not centrally localized but rather known of God throughout the world by their works of obedience (see 2 Timothy 2:19).

Questions over Zechariah Chapter 9

1. Why will God smite Tyre and Sidon?

2. Why would God "*cut off the pride of the Philistines?*"

3. Read Zechariah 9:9 and compare that to Matthew 21:5-8. What does this say about the differences between the kingdoms of men and the kingdom of God?

4. How far would the king of Zion's dominion reach?

5. Zechariah depicts Zion as a victorious kingdom. What significance do you see for the church today when reading Zechariah 9:11-17?

6. How does God know who are truly his people today?

ZECHARIAH CHAPTER 10

Synopsis

Zechariah reveals the end results of living lives of unfaithfulness and faithfulness.

Application

The power, strength, and confidence of the saints is depicted in Zechariah chapter 10. God's promise to the meek and lowly Zion is that he will protect and defend them. Throughout their lives they will walk through a fiery sea of tribulation yet God will be with them and they will be victorious with his divine help.

Zechariah 10

Properly Placed Trust (10:1-7)

"**1** *Ask of Jehovah rain in the time of the latter rain, even of Jehovah that makes lightnings; and he will give them showers of rain, to every one grass in the field.* **2** *For the teraphim have spoken vanity, and the diviners have seen a lie; and they have told false dreams, they comfort in vain: therefore they go their way like sheep, they are afflicted, because there is no shepherd*" **(10:1-2).**

The Jews had gone 15 years without working on the temple of God. The Lord plagued them with a drought and poor crops to move them to ask for divine relief through repentance (Haggai 1:7-11). We gain greater incite into the error of the Jews here. Zechariah reveals that rather than turning to God in repentance the people sought a quick fix to their problems by seeking comfort in the teraphim. Teraphim were a "type of idol or image, often associated with divination. The exact appearance and function of teraphim are unknown. Nebuchadnezzar restored the consultation of teraphim as a divinatory technique according to Ezekiel 21:21. It seems safest to conclude that teraphim were small idols kept in private households and consulted in divination (foretelling) (see Genesis 31:19)" (ISBE volume 4, page 793).

The inference is that many of God's people had turned to these teraphim gods for consultation regarding the future of their drought condition. Jeremiah tells us that these gods offer nothing but false hope and comfort (see Jeremiah 23:13-14). If only those who claim to be part of Zion would turn to God in full obedience and asks of him regarding rain he would make lightening and showers of rain come and the grass of the field would be green.

What is so attractive about false gods, prophets, and teachers? Why do so many in our world turn to these things rather than to God and his divine revelation? First, people are attracted to false gods, prophets, and teachers because most of the world leans in a rebellious direction away from God. Satan has flooded the world with wickedness and this is the world we are all born into (Psalms 51:5; Isaiah 28:17; 1 John 2:15-17 and Revelation 12:13-17). The idea of being sanctified, different, or set apart from the world of sinners as a holy and royal priest is not something that is very attractive to most (see 1 Peter 2:9; 4:4, and 12). The teraphim were a very popular method of finding out outcomes of future matters even among the kings of the day. False religion is attractive because it represents the majority.

Secondly, false religion is attractive because it offers immediate comfort. While God's words demand a stringent lifestyle of holiness, obedience, self control, and abstinence the religions of the world tell men to live as you please (see Acts 24:25). Most people want comfort now rather than waiting for it in the unforeseen future. Hananiah was a false prophet in the days of Jeremiah that spoke lies in order to comfort the people. He told the people of Judah that the yoke of Nebuchadnezzar would be broke in two years and all the treasures of the temple would be restored along with those who had been taken captive (see Jeremiah 28:1-4). These words were what the people wanted to hear. The people of Judah did not want to hear of more disaster and hardships to come by Jeremiah. They wanted to hear the prophets tell them smooth things that made them feel good rather than guilty (see Isaiah 30:10 and Jeremiah 14:13). Jeremiah warned of those who strengthen the hands of evil doers with rebellious words of error (see Jeremiah 7:8-11 and 23:13-14).

Thirdly, false religion is so attractive because it involves sin. If sin were not attractive then it would have no real or effective draw. Moses is said to have chosen God over the "*passing pleasures of sin*" (Hebrews 11:24-26). False teachers, prophets, and gods promote rebellion to authorized positions of authority (1 Peter 2:13, 18; 3:1; 5:5; 2 Peter 2:10-12 and Jude 1:8-10). To be subject to others is not perceived as fun and free. False religion promotes freedom from the perceived tyranny of God and his laws. The message of the false teacher mirrors that of Satan in the Garden of Eden when he told Eve that she would not die when God said she would if she disobeyed and at of the forbidden fruit (see Genesis 3:1-5).

"*3 Mine anger is kindled against the shepherds, and **I will punish** the he-goats; for Jehovah of hosts has visited his flock, the house of Judah, and will make them as his goodly horse in the battle*" **(10:3).**

The shepherds of God's people ought to have been leading the flock in a direction of righteousness; however, it is apparent that they had turned to the teraphim as did the nations around them. The wicked shepherds, "*he-goats,*" would be "*punished*" for their refusal to abide by the commandments and hope of God. The Lord is depicted as visiting his true people and making them "*as his goodly horse in the battle.*" The

Lord has earlier referred to Zion as his bow, arrow, and sword at Zechariah 9:13-14. Now the Lord depicts Zion as his battle horse.

A war is being waged between the forces of wickedness and righteousness. Those who put their trust in God, through a meek and obedient spirit, will be divinely protected and defended (see Isaiah 31:4-5 and Zechariah 9:8, 15). Those who look to the power, glory, and wealth of this world will be crushed in every generation (see Zechariah 9:1ff and Revelation 18:1-2).

"*4 From him shall come forth the corner-stone, from him the nail, from him the battle bow, from him every ruler together. 5 And they shall be as mighty men, treading down their enemies in the mire of the streets in the battle; and they shall fight, because Jehovah is with them; and the riders on horses shall be confounded*" **(10:4-5).**

God's "*corner-stone*" would come from Zion. We have identified this divine stone at Zechariah 3:9 as the Christ (see also Isaiah 28:16; Matthew 21:42; Acts 4:11; Romans 9:33 and 1 Peter 2:4-7). The Apostle Paul refers to Jesus as the chief corner-stone (see Ephesians 2:20). "*The nail*" will also come from Zion. A nail is used to firmly fix things to a wall. The people of God could count on God's help as sure as a nail firmly fixes an item in the house (see Isaiah 22:23-25). The nail is likely a representation of God's covenant promises and laws that were to be trusted and counted on.

Recall that the distinction between Zion and the nations of men is that Zion is eternal, spiritual, and concerned with upholding righteousness and justice with a spirit of meekness. The nations of men could care less about righteousness and justice (19h). The world of men are enamored with power, lust of the flesh, riches, and fame (1 John 2:15-16). The saints are depicted as battling this attitude and temptation to be like the world in spiritual apathy. This battle is the primary objective of the book of Revelation. Zechariah helps us not only to identify the battle but also those involved (see Revelation 17:14; 19:19-21 and 20:7ff).

Those who represent the corner stone and nail will fight with great success. The true saints of God will be unstoppable by the enemies of the cross. God will be with them and they will tread down their enemies in the streets. The scene is one of great blood shed and loss of life. Figuratively speaking the battle is spiritual. The wicked challenge the righteous in every generation (see Revelation 20:7-10). Sometimes these battles will be fought on grounds least expected. The saints will find themselves battling the wicked within the church itself (see Acts 20:28-31 and Ephesians 6:10-12). The saints of God are equipped for victory (see 2 Corinthians 10:4 and Ephesians 6:14ff). The saints are not to stand by idly but rather fight with all their might (see 1 Timothy 1:8; 6:12; 2 Timothy 4:7). Finally, know that God's saints will always be victorious (see Psalms 48:1-6). Zechariah had earlier said, "*7 Who are you, O great mountain? Before Zerubbabel you shall become a plain; and he shall bring forth the top stone with shoutings of Grace, grace, unto it*" (Zechariah 4:7). No great mountain of false doctrine, kingdoms and nations that stand opposed to truth, governments that permit filth, and wicked who persecute the Christian shall stand in the way of God's eternal kingdom, city, Zion, and church of the living God (see Daniel 2:44; Proverbs 8:22-26 and Zechariah 1:5-6) (12bb). The saints of God will not lose because "*Jehovah is with them*" and he will protect and defend them (see Zechariah 2:5; 9:8, and 15).

"***6** And **I will strengthen the house of Judah**, and I will save the house of Joseph, and I will bring them back; for I have mercy upon them; and they shall be as though I had not cast them off: for I am Jehovah their God, and I will hear them. **7** And they of Ephraim shall be like a mighty man, and their heart shall rejoice as through wine; yea, their children shall see it, and rejoice; their hearts shall be glad in Jehovah*" **(10:6-7).**

Jehovah assures the remnant from the house of Ephraim (Israel; the Northern Kingdom) that they too shall be victorious as their brothers from Judah. Zion, under the Messianic kingdom, would be as one. All the saints shall gain victory over the foes of this world through Christ and forgiveness. Those forgiven of sins will be as happy as one blessed with the fruit of the vine. Herein we see another distinction between Zion and the world of sinners. Money, fame, glory, and power bring gladness to the hearts of the world yet it is forgiveness that makes the heart glad among the true Zion (19h).

Jehovah will bless Judah and Israel (10:8-12)

"**8** *I will hiss for them, and gather them; for I have redeemed them; and they shall increase as they have increased.* **9** *And I will sow them among the peoples; and they shall remember me in far countries; and they shall live with their children, and shall return*" **(10:8-9).**

The Lord will "*hiss*" or call his people and the true Zion shall faithfully respond to redemption (see Joel 2:32). The Apostle Paul refers to this "*hissing*" as God calling people out of the world with the gospel message at 2 Thessalonians 2:13-14. The called and redeemed shall be planted among the peoples of the world and they shall multiply through the nations desiring to have the blessings that God's people have (Zechariah 8:23).

"**10** *I will bring them again also out of the land of Egypt, and gather them out of Assyria; and I will bring them into the land of Gilead and Lebanon; and place shall not be found for them*" **(10:10).**

The Lord shall bring the captives of sin out of their bondage likened unto the days of Egypt and Assyria. The true Zion shall be redeemed and free from sin in Gilead and Lebanon. So many peoples will be redeemed that there shall no space be found for them. All powers opposed to God and his people shall be defeated (i.e., Egypt and Assyria's pride stand figuratively for all who would oppose the Lord). Each generation of men has their Egypt, Assyria, and Babylon. These forces of ungodliness may succeed in bringing many in the world to perdition yet to the true saints of God they shall fall in defeat in every generation (see Revelation 18:4).

"**11** *And he will pass through the* **sea of affliction***, and will smite the waves in the sea, and all the depths of the Nile shall dry up; and the pride* *of Assyria shall be brought down, and the scepter of Egypt shall depart.* **12** *And **I will strengthen them** in Jehovah; and they shall walk up and down in his name, said Jehovah"* **(10:11-12)**.

The Common English Bible reads, "***They*** *will pass through the sea of distress and strike the sea with waves. All the depths of the river will dry up. The pride of Assyria will be brought down; the scepter of Egypt will turn away."* One may asks whether it is God, his people, or both that are passing through the *"sea of affliction."* The proper answer to this question is that it is both God and his people. God; however, is not being afflicted but rather his people are. The faithful, who passed through the Red Sea when coming out of Egypt, were protected from their enemies in that God collapsed the sea upon the Egyptians as they pursued them. Likewise, God's saints traverse a *"sea of affliction"* today (Revelation 7:13-17). Christians, and all men for that matter, are born into a world of sin and sorrows (see Psalms 51:5). The choice to sin and experience God's plagues of great sorrows is man's to make. Secondly, man is tried and tested by God to see if he truly trust the Lord (Acts 14:22 and 1 Peter 1:6-7 - see also Zechariah 13:9). Those who choose to look to God for help will find divine protection from all their enemies and tempting vises (see Zechariah 2:5; 8:7-8; 9:8, 15). All those who traverse this fiery sea putting their trust and hope in God will come through victorious (see Revelation 4:6 and 15:2). God will *"strengthen"* them through Christ's forgiveness and truth (see Haggai 2:4; Zechariah 4:7; 8:13-15; 10:6 and Philippians 4:13) (20o).

Questions over Zechariah Chapter 10

1. Why is God angry with the Shepherds of Israel?

2. What battle does Zechariah speak of at chapter 10:4-7?

3. How would God "whistle," "hiss," or "call" for the redeemed?

4. How will these redeemed people be compared to God's people that came out of Egypt and Assyria?

5. Compare and contrast the *"sea of affliction"* at Zechariah 10:11 with 1 Peter 4:12 and Revelation 15:1-2.

6. How will God *"strengthen"* those who comprise Zion now and forevermore?

ZECHARIAH CHAPTER 11

Synopsis

Zechariah chapter 11 illustrates the great theme of much of the Bible in relationship to man's obedience. God has always demanded man's obedience (see 2 Samuel 15:22-23; Romans 2:8; 6:16 and Hebrews 5:9 and 13:15 to name a few passages).

Application

The true Zion will love God and seek out his commandments in obedience. Those who walk in meekness will have God's protection (Zechariah 9:8 and Isaiah 31:4-5), his walls of fire and salvation with gates of praise (Zechariah 2:5 and Isaiah 26:1-3), and they will have the Lord defend them (Zechariah 9:15). God will be with his saints in all battles of life (Zechariah 10:5). Those who reject God's commands have no such promises. God breaks his covenant of protection and defense with those who break their promise to keep his commandments.

Zechariah 11

Zechariah is called upon to be a Type of the Good Shepherd to Come (11:1-14)

"*1 Open your doors, O Lebanon, that the fire may devour your cedars. 2 Wail, O fir tree, for the cedar is fallen, because the goodly ones are destroyed: wail, O you oaks of Bashan, for the strong forest is come* down. *3 A voice of the wailing of the shepherds! For their glory is destroyed: a voice of the roaring of young lions! For the pride of the Jordan is laid waste"* **(11:1-3).**

Lebanon is mentioned in the previous chapter signifying the place of the redeemed of God (see Zechariah 10:10). The Lord will, in the future, establish his eternal and indestructible kingdom and call men out of the world to enter in by meekness and righteousness. The prophet of God now returns to his own time. The kingdom of God during the prophet's day is not the Zion of the future. God's current people were filled with sin and worldliness. They were hungry for riches and world renown and sought after the council of Teriphim (Zechariah 9:1-3 and 10:2).

God will be a refuge in the time of storm for the future Zion who trust and love him yet the current house of Judah will be devoured for their uncleanness.

"*4 Thus said Jehovah my God: Feed the flock of slaughter; 5 whose possessors slay them, and hold themselves not guilty; and they that sell them say, Blessed be Jehovah, for I am rich; and their own shepherds pity them not*" **(11:4-5).**

Zechariah is commanded to "*feed the flock of slaughter*." This flock is a people that at one time were a "*strong forest*" yet God now brings them low because of their wickedness (Zechariah 11:2). The flock has been voluntarily cared for by unjust shepherds (their "*possessors*") (see Zechariah 10:2-3). The wealth of the shepherds of Judah caused them to think that God was with them and had blessed them as they cheated and gave faulty spiritual direction to the people.

Micah had touched upon the unjust behavior of Judah's shepherds before Babylon had taken them for their sins. These shepherds were guilty of "*perverting all equity*." Both prophet and priest performed works for money alone. They believed that as long as they received money and riches that God was with them (Micah 3:9-11). Amos said that these shepherds of the people "*oppress the poor and crush the needy*" (Amos 4:1). Their wickedness had caused God to withhold the blessings of rain and harvest yet God's people would not return unto him (Amos 4:6-12). Interestingly, the people are in the same situation as they were before the days of their captivity (see Amos 2:6 and 8:4-6). God calls upon Zechariah to feed the flock of his people who have been mistreated much like Christ would feed the ungrateful in the coming years only to be rejected of those he helped.

"**6** *For I will no more pity the inhabitants of the land, said Jehovah; but. Lo, I will deliver the men every one into his neighbor's hand, and into the hand of his king; and they shall smite the land, and out of their hand I* **will not deliver them**. *7 So I fed the flock of slaughter, verily the poor of the flock. And I took unto me two staves; the one I called Beauty, and the other I called Bands; and I fed the flock*" **(11:6-7)**.

Zechariah fulfills God's request to feed the "*flock of slaughter*" (i.e., the poor and cheated among the people of God that the richer shepherds were taking advantage of). Though these sheep were being taken advantage of they were nonetheless guilty of error for permitting the wicked shepherds to guide them in paths of unrighteousness. God determined to smite the entire land due to their wickedness. God demands personal responsibility from everyone. No man will be able to stand before the Lord and say that his sinful choices were someone else's fault (see Revelation 20:13). Jeremiah had to learn this lesson. The prophet of God did not understand why all the people had to suffer when it was the false prophets who had led the people astray. God responds to his prophet saying, "14 *the prophets prophesy lies in my name; I sent them not, neither have I commanded them, neither spoke I unto them: they prophesy unto you a lying vision, and divination, and a thing of naught, and the deceit of their own heart. 15 Therefore thus said Jehovah* **concerning the prophets** *that prophesy in my name, and I sent them not, yet they say, Sword and famine shall not be in this land: By sword and famine shall those prophets be consumed.* 16 **And the people** *to whom they prophesy shall be cast out in the streets of Jerusalem because of the famine and the sword; and they shall have* *none to bury them--them, their wives, nor their sons, nor their daughters: for I will pour their wickedness upon them*" (Jeremiah 14:14-16).

Zechariah, as shepherd, took not one but two staffs (staves) to shepherd the flock. The prophet of God names the two staffs "*Beauty*" and "*Bands.*" The English Standard Version Bible translates the words beauty and bands as favor and union. The Common English Bible translates the two words delight and harmony. The Revised Standard Version Bible translates the words grace and union. Let us continue to study these verses to understand the meaning and significance of these two words.

"**8** *And I cut off the three shepherds in one month; for my soul was weary of them, and their soul also loathed me.* **9** *Then said I, I will not feed you: that which dies, let it die; and that which is to be cut off, let it be cut off; and let them that are left eat every one the flesh of another*" **(11:8-9).**

While feeding the "*flock of slaughter*" as God commanded over the space of four weeks the prophet grew weary with the treatment of three of the shepherds and "*cut them off.*" Zechariah was disgusted with them and they equally loathed him for his words. Weary with the wickedness of all classes of people the prophet turns them over to fill up the measure of their wickedness by eating each other's flesh in a cannibalistic fashion.

The Lord, throughout history, uses other nations to accomplish his ends (i.e. Egypt, Assyria, Babylon, Medes and Persians, Greeks, Rome etc.) and so he now executes judgment against his own people who are wicked. The prophet Ezekiel tells us that Israel and Judah were consumed by the very nations that she committed spiritual adultery with (see Ezekiel chapters 16 and 23). The Apostle John saw a similar vision at Revelation 17. John writes, "*And the ten horns which you saw and the beast, these shall hate the harlot, and shall maker her desolate and naked, and shall eat her flesh, and shall burn her utterly with fire*" (Revelation 17:16). The "*harlot*" of Revelation 17 is the ungodly forces of worldliness in the form of covetousness, lust for wealth and power, and a desire for fame and glory. When lustful men are finished with the harlot they have no respect for her neither are they willing to care for her at all. She is treated shamefully because she does shameful things.

The wicked turn upon the wicked and consume each other when their opinions and fleshly reason do not mesh. The Apostle Paul wrote of the damage of such opinionated living saying, "*But if you bite and devour one another, take heed that you be not consumed one of another*" (Galatians 5:15). Nebuchadnezzar's dream recorded in Daniel chapter 2 illustrates this truth. Daniel interprets the king's dream revealing the fall of each world empire at the hands of another ungodly one. While the kingdoms of this world and sin end in defeat the kingdom of God is everlasting and ever victorious (see Daniel 2:44). The wicked have one mind in that they are rebellious to God's laws (see Revelation 17:13). This one mind; however, has many ways of going about rebellious works. When the wicked stand in the way of each other they have no problem consuming each other in hatred and pride.

"***10** And I took my staff Beauty, and cut it asunder, that I might break my covenant which I had made with all the peoples. **11** And it was broken in that day; and thus the poor of the flock that gave heed unto me knew that it was the word of Jehovah. **12** And I said unto them, if you think good, give me my hire; and if not, forbear. So they weighted for my hire thirty pieces of silver. **13** And Jehovah said unto me, Cast it unto the potter, the goodly price that I was prized at by them. And I took the thirty pieces of silver, and cast them unto the potter, in the house of Jehovah. **14** Then I cut asunder mine other staff, even Bands, that I might break the brotherhood between Judah and Israel*" **(11:10-14).**

Zechariah saw that the wicked shepherds continued their onslaught of wicked and un-just acts against the poor and so he withdrew his covenant to care for them (Zechariah 9:11-13). He broke the staff of Beauty and Bands to signify the end of the covenant agreement for him to feed them. The covenant God made with man was designed to forgive yet those who seek no forgiveness have no part with such a covenant. Zechariah has revealed God's love for man in that he is willing to protect and defend those who love him (see Zechariah 9:8, 15). Those; however, who refuse repentance and obedience have no hope of having God's divine love, protection, and defense. The staffs, Beauty and Bands, represents God's covenant with man.

Zechariah asks to be paid for the work of feeding the people and they agreed. The people weigh out 30 pieces of silver for his work. The people as a whole had rejected Zechariah even though he was the only one who truly cared for them. They agreed to let him go and gave him money in silver to depart. There are strong ties to the Matthew 27:9 passage where Judas received 30 pieces of silver as he sold out the Christ. Matthew refers to this passage as belonging to Jeremiah; however, there is no such passage in the book of Jeremiah. This is obviously a scribal mistake and the passage belongs rather to Zechariah (1d). Jesus was the true and caring shepherd for God's people yet he was rejected. Likewise Zechariah has been rejected. Let all the true saints of God know today that we too will be rejected by the world of rebellious and wicked men (see John 15:18ff and 1 Peter 4:4).

The Wicked Shepherd (11:15-17)

"**15** *And Jehovah said unto me, Take unto you yet again the* **instruments** *of a foolish shepherd.* **16** *For, lo, I will raise up a shepherd in the land, who will not visit those that are cut off, neither will seek those that are scattered, nor heal that which is broken, nor feed that which is sound; but he will eat the flesh of the fat sheep, and will tear their hoofs in pieces*" **(11:15-16).**

The rejection of a caring and loving shepherd gives way to uncaring and unloving shepherds. Shepherds that care nothing but getting gain for self. Such a shepherd could care less if some suffer or do well because all their actions are centered around gaining self benefit and glory (see John 10:7-18).

The identity of the "*foolish shepherd*" is likely those like Herod who ruled over Palestine or the Pharisees who ruled religion during the days of

Christ. These shepherds ruled yet it was leadership without true care for the kingdom of God. To reject God's care is to get for one's self misery. There are foolish shepherds in the church today who do not truly care for the sheep they shepherd (see Acts 20:28-31). Elders in the body of Christ are charged to be the shepherds yet many are novices in truth and uncaring in their actions. The erring may go astray and the shepherds of the church continue to play golf. The erring may cause great disturbances in the church yet the shepherds say nothing (12w).

"**17** *Woe to the worthless shepherd that leaves the flock! The sword shall be his arm, and upon his right eye: his arm shall be clean dried up, and his right eye shall be utterly darkened*" **(11:17).**

The shepherd's responsibility is to watch over the flock. To have a spirit of indifference over the welfare one is entrusted with will by no means go unpunished. The sword shall come to this man and the eye that should be watchful will be darkened or gouged out (like Zedekiah's eyes).

Let this be a solemn warning to all elders of the body of Christ today. Shepherds are entrusted with the flock of God's people. To ignore the fallen, scattered, and weak with a spirit of indifference is to bring condemnation upon one's self. To permit false doctrines and lies within the church is to fail in one's divinely ordained duty (12w).

Questions over Zechariah Chapter 11

1. What error had the shepherds of God people committed?

2. **True or False:** The shepherds would eat each other's flesh.

3. What was God's "*Beauty*" and "*Bands*?"

4. Why did the people give Zechariah 30 pieces of silver?

5. What correlation do you see between Zechariah 11:12-14 and Matthew 27:9?

6. Who ate the flesh of the fat sheep?

7. What can elders of the church today learn from this chapter?

ZECHARIAH CHAPTER 12

Synopsis

The people of God had lost sight of their grand objective set forth as early as the days of their father Abraham (see Genesis 12:1-4). Zechariah's job has been to redirect and remind them of their most important divine mission of establishing a future king and kingdom (Christ and his church). The prophet Isaiah, long before the days of Zechariah, spoke words of encouragement to the Babylonian captives. Isaiah writes, "*8 But you, Israel, my servant, Jacob whom **I have chosen**, the seed of Abraham my friend, 9 you whom I have taken hold of from the ends of the earth, and called from the corners thereof, and said unto you, You are my servant, **I have chosen you** and not cast you away; 10 Fear not, for I am with you; be not dismayed, for I am your God; I will strengthen you; yea, I will help you; yea, I will uphold you with the right hand of my righteousness*" (Isaiah 41:8-10 see also 43:1, 19-21 and 44:1). These words of Isaiah are the mirror image of the words of Zechariah here at chapter 12.

Application

The prophet is encouraging the people to remember how significant and powerful they are as the household of God. No nation of ungodly men or flood of wickedness will have the power to overcome them as long as they put their faith and trust in God. Zechariah paints a picture of an indestructible, everlasting, and powerful kingdom that they are a part of if they would remember God and his commands. To leave off spiritual matters, such as building the temple of God, was to forget their primary mission in this life. To practice idolatry and unjust dealing with others was to forsake the mercy and grace of God. The call of God by Zechariah is that the people remember who they are and what is at stake with their obedience and or disobedience. God continues this loud call to the saints through his gospel lest we forget who we are and what we represent.

Zechariah 12

Zechariah's Second "Burden" (Oracle or Judgment)

"*1 The burden of the word of Jehovah concerning Israel. Thus said Jehovah, who stretches forth the heavens, and lays the foundation of the earth, and forms the spirit of man within him: 2 Behold, I will make Jerusalem a cup of reeling unto all the peoples round about, and upon Judah also shall it be in the siege against Jerusalem*" **(12:1-2).**

The first oracle was directed at the nations who put their trust in the things of this world (Zechariah 9-11). Zechariah is now given the second oracle or burden (divine judgment) which concerns Israel. The surety of the judgment is made by the facts of Jehovah. The Lord lays the foundation of the earth and spirit of man. Based on these two facts his words concerning Israel are truth. The prophet Isaiah similarly spoke of God being the creator and one who formed man at chapter 43:1. Isaiah looked to the creative power of God to prove that the Lord's people would be redeemed not only from Babylonian captivity but through the precious blood of Jesus Christ (3f).

Jehovah God is the creator of the heavens and earth (Genesis 1:1). God set the boundaries of the sea so that they do not go past the sand (Jeremiah 5:22). The Lord spoke and all things were created (Psalms 33:6-9). God sits above the circle of the earth and all the inhabitants are like grasshoppers to him (Isaiah 40:22). The Lord raises nations and brings them down (Daniel 2:21 and Isaiah 41:23). There is no one that can be compared to the Almighty God (Isaiah 40:18). The Lord has also created man from the dust of the earth in his own image (Genesis 1:24-27). The Lord directs the paths of mankind for their good and in this way *"forms the spirit of man within him"* (see also Jeremiah 10:23). God's forming of man is in the likeness of Christ (see Romans 8:29) (19s). Man has been created and formed by God to be his divine image (see 1 John 4:17). The divine expectation of man is to be godlike (Matthew 5:48; 1 Peter 1:15-16 and 2 Peter 1:4).

The context of the chapter before us shall reveal this to be a time when Israel would be under the Messianic King. The Christ will cause many nations to "*reel.*" The nations of the world believe that Israel is weak and feeble under the new king Jesus. As they drink from the cup of worldliness they reel and stagger as a drunkard for they have drank from the cup of God's wrath. The nations were deceived by Israel's front of weakness when in all reality they are indestructible. Jehovah God makes Zion impervious to the onslaught of wickedness that the nations represent (12bb). Zechariah depicts Zion as a nation or kingdom that is impervious to the pit falls of other nations. The Lord *"defends"* (Zechariah 9:15), protect (Zechariah 9:8 and Isaiah 31:4-5), and be walls of fire and salvation with gates that would permit no wicked man to enter (see Zechariah 2:5 and Isaiah 26:1-3). The true Zion is the *"apple of his eye"* and he will not permit them to fall (Zechariah 2:8). The Apostle Paul said, "*13 There has no temptation taken you but such as man can bear: but God is faithful, who will not suffer you to be tempted above that you are able; but will with the temptation make also the way of escape, that you may be able to endure it*" (1 Corinthians 10:13). God will save his true Zion (Zechariah 8:13).

We have, as Bible students, a tendency to take our minds immediately to the siege of Jerusalem that happened under the wicked king Zedekiah. Babylon laid siege to Jerusalem crushing the city and taking its inhabitants captive. Zechariah; however, cannot be speaking of the literal siege of Jerusalem because that had already taken place. Neither is the prophet speaking of the future siege of Jerusalem when Titus destroys the city during the year 70 AD. The siege of Babylon and Romans on Jerusalem represent failures of God's people where as the siege under consideration here represents victory of God's people. The context of our study suggests that the nations of worldly and ungodly men will rise up against the saints in every generation in the form of Gog and Magog (see next verse below and Revelation 20:7-9). The true saints of God, Zion, shall defeat the enemy with the help of God every time (see notes at Zechariah 10:4-5) (60).

"**3** *And it shall come to pass* **in that day,** *that I will make Jerusalem a burdensome stone for all the peoples; all that burden themselves with it shall be sore wounded; and* **all the nations of the earth shall be gathered together against it**" **(12:3).**

We read the first of sixteen "*in that day*" statements for this section. Each of these "*in that day*" sections reveal the time under consideration to be the church age (i.e., the time when the Kingdom of God is established with his Son reigning as King). During these days the church will be persecuted by ungodly men who are "*burdened*" by the saints and truth. Jesus said, "*9 Then shall they deliver you up unto tribulation, and shall kill you: and you shall be hated of all the* **nations** *for my name's sake*" (Matthew 24:9). The Lord will permit the nations of ungodly encompass the church of saints and he will destroy them (see Ezekiel 38 through 39 and Revelation 20:7-9). The world of men or nations comprises the wicked disposition of Tyre (Zechariah 9:1ff). They see that the saints are different and uncompromising in truth (1 Peter 4:4). Many sinful men will lash out at the saints rather than repenting of their sins (John 15:18 - 16:3). Though the wicked kill the bodies of the saints there will be an eternal crown in heaven for those who remain faithful (Revelation 2:10).

The Jerusalem of Zechariah 12:2 will be conformed to the image of Jesus Christ in these latter days (see notes at verse two above). When man is the mirror image of God the world will hate, despise, and desire to be rid of you.

"*4 In that day, said Jehovah, I will smite every horse with terror, and his rider with madness; and I will open mine eyes upon the house of Judah, and will smite every horse of the peoples with blindness. 5 And the chieftains of Judah shall say in their heart, The inhabitants of Jerusalem are my strength in Jehovah of hosts their God*" **(12:4-5).**

The nations against the church of Christ will be militant. Those who oppose the truth will be as horsemen running throughout the church with weapons of warfare. Jehovah; however, shall smite these horses with blindness and they shall be defeated. Defeating these militant peoples of wickedness who are against the church is contingent upon the church's mutual militant stand against its foes. The truth is our weapon and when it is wielded no enemy has any chance of standing (Ephesians 6:17). Each true member of the kingdom of God must fight knowing that God will not be defeated. The Apostle Paul speaks of this spiritual warfare at 2 Corinthians 10:3-6 saying, "*3 For though we walk in the flesh, we do not war according to the flesh 4 (for the weapons of our warfare are not of the flesh, but mighty before God to the casting down of strongholds)... 6 and being in readiness to avenge all disobedience*" (19b).

"*6 In that day will I make the chieftains of Judah like a pan of fire among wood, and like a flaming torch among sheaves; and they shall devour all the peoples round about, on the right hand and on the left; and they of Jerusalem shall yet again dwell in their own place, even in Jerusalem. 7 Jehovah also shall save the tents of Judah first, that the glory of the house of David and the glory of the inhabitants of Jerusalem be not magnified above Judah*" **(12:6-7).**

"*In that day*" (i.e., the day that the church has been established and the wicked assail it with all their might) the chieftains of the people of God shall consume the wicked by the word of God. No place for pride or self glorification will be given to the people of God. All shall stand on equal ground in the fight against the ungodly forces of the world.

"**8** *In that day shall Jehovah **defend** the inhabitants of Jerusalem; and he that is feeble among them at that day shall be as David; and **the house of David shall be as God**, as the angel of Jehovah before them*" **(12:8)**.

When the enemies of truth assail the church even the feeble among the people of God will have the strength of David. David was a mighty warrior for the Lord. By the strength of God he defeated Goliath and many other foes. No enemy of truth is powerful enough to take even the feeble one down. The Apostle Paul spoke of these falsely perceived weak ones at 1 Corinthians 12:22. Even the saints who have what some would perceive as menial positions or works in the church shall be strong against the enemies of righteousness.

Note the militant disposition of those opposed to Jehovah's Kingdom! They are on the attack and so the Christian must exercise the same disposition toward them in this warfare or they shall be consumed (19b). God will not lose one soul as long as that soul exercises the spirit of humility and asks for forgiveness. The forgiveness of sins will be the ever renewing life of the Christian during the church age. The enemies of God may slay us with the sword yet through prayer and repentance the soldier of Christ is able to rise again and again. The enemy cannot defeat us while God is "*defending*" us (see Zechariah 9:15). The Apostle Paul said that if God is for us no man or nation can stand against us (see Romans 8:31ff).

Zechariah introduces the subject of man's perfection and he will expound upon this in the coming verses and chapter 13. Those of the "*house of David shall be as God.*" The Apostle John would later say, "*17 Herein is love made perfect with us, that we may have boldness in the day of judgment; because as he is, even so are we in this world*" (1 John 4:17) (26a).

"**9** *And it shall come to pass in that day, that I will seek to destroy all the nations that come against Jerusalem.* **10** *And **I will pour** upon the house of David, and upon the inhabitants of Jerusalem, **the spirit of grace** and of supplication; and they shall **look unto me whom they have pierced**;*

and they shall mourn for him, as one mourns for his only son, and shall be in bitterness for him, as one that is in bitterness for his first-born" **(12:9-10).**

The day that the church is established will be a time that all nations of ungodly men wage war against it. At that time, God will **pour** out his *"spirit of grace and of supplication"* upon it. God poured out his Holy Spirit upon the apostles and will continue to do so *"upon all flesh"* in the form of divine revelation (see Acts 2:17-22 and Joel 2:28). God would use male, female, young, old, slave, and free to distribute his message. Those immersed in the Holy Spirit would have the power to speak divinely inspired words of truth. These divine truths will be so powerful that no force of ungodliness may detour their purpose of salvation (Romans 1:16).

The author of Hebrews tells us that God communicated his message to man in "**divers manners**" (Hebrews 1:1). God **spoke directly** to some prophets (Genesis 12:1ff; Exodus 12:1ff. etc.). God *"moved"* some men to speak divine truths by the **Holy Spirit** (2 Peter 1:21). The Holy Spirit *"entered into"* (Ezekiel 2:1-2) and *"fell upon"* (Ezekiel 11:5) the apostles and prophets in times past. Jesus said to his apostles, "8 *When the Spirit of truth is come, he shall* **guide** *you into all the truth: for he shall not speak from himself; but what things so ever he shall hear, these shall he speak: and he shall declare unto you the things that are to come"* (John 16:8ff). Nehemiah records, *"Yet many years did you bear with them, and testified against them* **by your Spirit** *through your prophets"* (Nehemiah 9:30 and also see Ezekiel 1:3; 11:4-7). Others received "**visions**" and "**dreams**" from God to speak a divine message to the people (Daniel 7:1; Obadiah 1:1 and Joel 2:28ff). These men, that were moved by God to speak, **confirmed** their words as being of divine origin by the signs and wonders they performed (see Mark 16:20; John 20:30-31 and Hebrews 2:2-4) (10d).

The Apostle John quoted from Zechariah 12:10 at John 19:37. The Roman soldiers pierced the side of Jesus to make sure he was dead on the cross. John then quotes from Zechariah 12:10 and applies it to Jesus (herein we find the interpretation of Zechariah's second oracle to the people of Israel). When some realize that it is the Christ that they have pierced they will mourn with a grievous sadness over their sinfulness. When the people witnessed the crucifixion of Christ, the miraculous darkness that came over the land, the earth quaking, the dead rising from the graves, and the curtain that separated the holy place from the most holy in the temple of God being torn in two they were terrified. These people ran from the cross smiting their breast in agony as they considered what they had done (see Luke 23:48). The Apostles of Jesus Christ would later preach to these people and convict them of the slaying of the Son of God (see Acts 2:23; 3:13-16; 4:10 etc.). They will be moved, by the grace of God, to repent and asks for his forgiveness.

Note that we see the deity of Jesus in these verses. God is the "*me they have pierced*" and John applies this to Jesus at John 19:37 (5c).

"**11** *In that day shall there be a great mourning in Jerusalem, as the mourning of Hadadrimmon in the valley of Megiddon.* **12** *And the land shall mourn, every family apart; the family of the house of David apart, and their wives apart; the family of the house of Nathan apart, and their wives apart;* **13** *the family of the house of Levi apart, and their wives apart; the family of the Shimeites apart, and their wives apart;* **14** *all the families that remain, every family apart, and their wives apart*" **(12:11-14).**

Some believe the "*mourning of Hadadrimmon in the valley of Megiddon*" to be the day when Josiah lost his life to the Egyptians who were passing through. The whole land mourned the death of Josiah. Likewise, all shall mourn when they realize that they had crucified the son of God. All families small and great shall mourn the death of Jesus upon the cross. The thought of murdering God's holy son would be the cause of great grief among the people. These murderous people will be moved to asks, "What must we do?" (Acts 2:37) Likewise this same mourning over

506

man's wickedness and the power of the gospel moves man today to ask interrogating questions regarding their salvation (see 1 Peter 3:21).

Questions over Zechariah Chapter 12

1. How does Zechariah describe God at the beginning of chapter 12?

2. Why does Zechariah speak of God's work in man's creation and form?

3. What "*day*" is under consideration at Zechariah 12?

4. **True or False:** Wicked men will eventually succeed in destroying the church of Jesus Christ.

5. Who was pierced?

6. What will be the people's reaction when they realize who they have pierced?

7. Zechariah discusses the indestructible nature of God's future kingdom and king. What application do you see of these verses for the Lord's church today?

ZECHARIAH CHAPTER 13

Synopsis

Zechariah gives a more detailed picture of the future Zion or church. The city of David, church, will be comprised of forgiven sinners. The saints will be armed to the teeth with God's truths. All that reject the word of God will be shamed and have no place among the people of Zion. Not even flesh and blood family members will stand between the true saints and God. God will maintain a spirit of perfection among his saints in the city of David by fiery trials and punishment. Many will not be able to endure yet a third of mankind, figuratively, will give up all for Christ and his eternal kingdom.

Application

Once again Zechariah is distinguishing the elect of God from all others. There has been and always will be those who serve God in this life come what may. The faithful will grow in strength while the wicked perish (see Romans 11:1-6).

Zechariah 13

Forgiveness and Perfection "*in that day*" will separate the Saints from the Sinners (13:1-6)

"**1** *In that day there shall be **a fountain** opened to the house of David and to the inhabitants of Jerusalem, for sin and for uncleanness.* **2** *And it* *shall come to pass in that day, said Jehovah of hosts, that I will cut off the names of the idols out of the land, and they shall no more be remembered; and also I will cause the prophets and the unclean spirit to pass out of the land"* **(13:1-2).**

Zechariah has used the phrase, *"in that day"* in several context to this point that look to a future date. This will be a day when God will cause the nations of the world that oppose him to drink the cup of his wrath and reel (Zechariah 12:2). Jerusalem, the saints of God, will burden the world with truth in this day (Zechariah 12:3). The day under consideration will see God fighting against the wicked that come up against his Kingdom and saints (Zechariah 12:3-9). This will be a time when he shall pour out the Spirit of grace upon the righteous who desire it (Zechariah 12:10). The people shall mourn on this day because they had pierced Son of God (Zechariah 12:10-14). Zechariah continues to build upon the future time frame and even more clearly now identifying the time *"in that day"* as the time when the Christ would come into the world, be crucified for the sins of mankind, establish his kingdom and reign as King.

Zechariah tells us that in this day God will open a *"fountain"* that remedy the people's sin and unclean acts. God's fountain will be open to *"the house of David and the inhabitants of Jerusalem."* The house of David and inhabitants of Jerusalem have already been identified as Zion or the church that Jesus will establish (see Zechariah 12). Those forgiven of their sins will be *"the house of David and the inhabitants of Jerusalem."* Forgiven sinners are added to the Lord's church when they comply with God's command to be baptized in the name of Jesus Christ (see Acts 2:37-41). Though the fountain is intended for all mankind not all will be cleansed due to disobedience. There were thousands of people who came to Jerusalem on the Day of Pentecost at Acts chapter 2. Out of these thousands upon thousands of people only three thousand obeyed the instructions of Peter and added to the kingdom of God, Zion, or church that belongs to Christ (see Acts 2:38-44).

The "*fountain*" that God opens to his true people has an undeniable connection to the blood of Jesus Christ (see Isaiah 12:3; 41:17-18; Ezekiel 47:9; Zechariah 14:8; Revelation 7:17 and 21:6) and divine revelation (Zechariah 14:8). Christ's blood would be the remedy for man's sins (for an association of sin, being defiled, and uncleanness see Leviticus 16:16, 30; Numbers 5:3, 13, 27 and 6:9-11) (27e). Man comes in contact with the blood of Jesus Christ through baptism (compare Hebrews 9:11-14 and 1 Peter 3:21).

When sins are forgiven all forms of idolatry will be vanished from the true people of God. Unclean spirits and prophets of error will be pushed out of the kingdom of God. While idolatry and false teaching continues today it will never exists within the true church of Jesus Christ. The true Zion will cause the false prophets and teachers in every generation to be ashamed of their false doctrines. The church will have no place for these wicked men. These erring men and women will "*pass out of the land*." The Apostle John said, "**They went out from us**, *but they were not of us; for if they had been of us, they would have continued with us: but they went out, that they might be made manifest that* **they all are not of us**" (1 John 2:19) (24c).

"**3** *And it shall come to pass that, when any shall yet prophesy, then his father and his mother that begat him shall say unto him, You shall not live; for you speak lies in the name of Jehovah; and his father and his mother that begat him shall thrust him through when he prophesies*" **(13:3).**

The New King James Version of the Bible and the New American Standard Bible translate the first few words of this verse as, "*and if anyone still prophesy*." There is one of two things that this verse identifies. First, during the days of Christ, his kingdom, and the forgiveness of man's sins, divine truths would be revealed and all things for man to be complete in God would be furnished (see 2 Timothy 3:16-17). True divine revelation, or words of prophecy, is confirmed by miracles (Mark 16:20). The NT explains to us that God's revelation is now complete and man has all that he needs to know for salvation (Jude 3). The Apostle Paul tells us that when God's revelation is complete there would be no more need of spiritual gifts such as prophecy, tongue speaking, and miracles in general (see 1 Corinthians 13:1ff) (10d). People during the days of Christ were expected to know this. A father and mother that had a son who laid claims to being able to speak words of prophecy or perform miracles was to be exposed as a liar and such a one would not be worthy to live (10d). The Law of Moses demanded such actions and we see the figurative application in the NT (see Deuteronomy 13:1-11 and Matthew 10:34-39).

Another way this verse may be looked at is that God instructs Zion to value truth over flesh and blood relatives. During the days of Christ's church fathers and mothers would value truth above their own son who taught error. Jesus spoke of this at Matthew 10:37. Zechariah reveals the seriousness of walking by God divine authority as opposed to man made idolatrous doctrines.

When we consider the first two verses of Zechariah 13 it is more likely that the prophecy under consideration is faulty, in relationship to absolute truth. When God opens the fountain of truth regarding the effective blood of Christ there will be no additions or subtractions to it (see Revelation 22:18-19). Moses (Deuteronomy 4:2) and Paul (Galatians 1:6-9) gave similar warnings in relation to adding or subtracting from divine revelation. Man is not at liberty to alter or change God's divine instructions. God's instructions are designed to fabricate a justified man of hope. When man altars God's instructions the result is not a justified man of hope but a fabrication of man's own devices. When false teaching is **added** to truth, as though it represented truth, it is to be identified as a doctrine of demons (see 1 Timothy 4:1ff). **Subtracted** ideas and doctrines only elevate a man to the status of God (2 Thessalonians 2:3-4).

"*4 And it shall come to pass in that day, that the prophets shall be ashamed every one of his vision, when he prophesies; neither shall they wear a hairy mantle to deceive:* **5** *but he shall say, I am no prophet, I am a tiller of the ground; for I have been made a bondman from my youth.* **6** *And one shall say unto him, What are these wounds between your arms? Then he shall answer, Those with which I was wounded in the house of my friends"* **(13:4-6).**

"In that day" divine revelation will stand alone as God's sovereign word. All who oppose God's truths or attempt to altar his divine truths will be made to feel ashamed. The righteous shall take the truth and compare it to the words of all who proclaim spiritual teachings. The duty of the faithful child of God is to test the teachings of men in relation to the word of God (Acts 17:10-11 and 1 John 4:1-3) (19m). Zechariah foresees false teachers who attempt to make inroads in God's Zion, holy city, or church. The true Zion will put these men and their doctrines to the test (Ephesians 5:11 and Titus 1:9). There will be no error within the gates of the true Zion.

The false teacher will be left completely exposed to the point that he shall be embarrassed to admit the things he has taught. He shall deny, lie, and make up stories to cover his sinful past. When the erring man is exposed he is made to feel the sting of shame. If we choose, like so many brethren today, to not shame the teacher then he will continue on his merry way and many shall be made merchandise of (2 Peter 2:1-2). The true Zion will expose the erring doctrines of men (24c).

The will of God is that the good shepherd be killed and the sheep scattered yet called back to God through the Gospel Message (13:7-9)

"**7** *Awake, O sword, against my shepherd, and against the man that is my fellow, said Jehovah of hosts: smite the shepherd, and the sheep shall be scattered; and I will turn my hand upon the little ones"* **(13:7).**

God calls for the sword of death to come upon his shepherd who has been identified as the Christ at Zechariah 11:1-14 and 12:10. To do so will bring the spirit of grace and of supplication (Zechariah 12:10) and will open the *"fountain for sin and for uncleanness"* (Zechariah 13:1).

Summarily, the death of the shepherd brings about eternal blessings for God's kingdom. The Apostle Peter, speaking of Christ said, "*him being delivered up by the determinate counsel and foreknowledge of God, you by the hand of lawless men did crucify and slay:*" (Acts 2:23). God's plan to redeem man came before the foundations of the world (Ephesians 1:3-7) (15b).

Jesus quoted from Zechariah 13:7 at Matthew 26:31 in relation to his death causing a scattering of the sheep. Peter boldly tells the Lord that he would never be offended in him or deny his holy name; however, as Jesus predicted Peter denied the Lord three times that night. God's hand would be turned against his people that he may punish and test their spirit to see who truly loves him. Many would not (will not) pass the test and fall away as they give heed to the desires of the world (1 John 2:16-17). Spiritual death would consequently come to two thirds of all mankind (3e).

"**8** *And it shall come to pass, that in all the land, said Jehovah, two parts therein shall be cut off and die; but the third shall be left therein*" **(13:8)**.

The Apostle John is given a vision of "*thirds*" of people dying by the hands of the angels sounding trumpets at Revelation 8:8-10 and 9:13-21. Two thirds of humanity refuse to test the spirits of error and are content with their walk of spiritual death. The object of the great torment is man's repentance yet many (two thirds - figuratively speaking) choose a life of spiritual death over life (see Revelation 9:20-21). There will always be a remnant of God's people who are not affected by the plagues of God due to their faith and trust in him (see Revelation 7:1-4).

"**9** *And **I will bring the third part into the fire**, and will **refine them as silver** is refined, and will **try them as gold** is tried. They shall call on my name, and I will hear them: I will say, it is my people; and they shall say, Jehovah is my God*" **(13:9)**.

The one third that is not killed by the plagues of Zechariah 13:8 will not get away unscathed. This third represents the elect of God who determine to serve him no matter the circumstances of life. The remnant of God will be persecuted, tempted with worldliness, and be inundated with false doctrines yet they are determined to serve the Lord. Additionally, God will cause them to walk through the fiery sea of trials and tribulation (see Zechariah 3:1-2 and 10:11). The Apostle Peter said that the saints of God would be tried and purified by trials as gold and silver (1 Peter 1:6-7). The Apostle Paul said that, *"through many tribulations we must enter into the kingdom of God"* (Acts 14:22). The Apostle John spoke of these trials in life that refine one to perfection at Revelation 7:13-17.

If passing through the fiery trials of life is the only way into heaven then let us all rejoice when going through them (James 1:2ff) (3e). We rejoice over our trials because we know that they will cause us to be stronger than before. When I fail test it makes me want to do better next time. When I experience heart aches over foolish decisions and actions I am more determined to not let that happen again. We are moved to greater relationships with God when we are tried and tested (see Job 23:10 and 1 Peter 1:6-7) (3e).

To call upon the name of God is to invoke the Lord for help in time of our greatest need. We may call upon the Lord during times of trials and afflictions and we may call upon the name of the Lord when we have sinned against him so that we may be forgiven. The point being that the true purified people will put their trust in Jehovah God and none other (see Joel 2:32).

Questions over Zechariah Chapter 13

1. What "*day*" is Zechariah referring to at chapter 13:1?

2. How would a false prophet's mother and father know that their son was not telling the truth?

3. What will cause the false prophet (teacher) to be ashamed?

4. Why does God call for the death of his shepherd?

5. Who will say, "*Jehovah* (the Lord) *is my God*?"

6. How many people will fall to sin and death?

7. Why will God "*refine*" and "*try*" his people through fire?

ZECHARIAH CHAPTER 14

Synopsis

The end of the book of Zechariah is very similar to the end of the book of Ezekiel. Those who approach the final three chapters of Zechariah without establishing the true meaning of "*in that day*" or "*a day of Jehovah comes*" will be forever confused. Through the last three chapters we have affectively established the identity of the future day under consideration as the day when the church, Zion, is established (Acts 2). You and I are living in the days of these final chapters of Zechariah. The saints of God are battling, with the help of God, the forces of Satan as he seeks to wash away people with a flood of wickedness (Revelation 12:13-17).

Application

Zechariah brings the drought back into view in this final chapter (see Zechariah 14:17). The curse of drought and plagues belong to all who reject the words of God whereas fountains of living waters that eternally sustain the soul belong to those who faithfully wait on the Lord's promises. Zechariah helps us to see that there will be little difference, other than the immortal state of the soul, between those in the true church now and forever in heaven. It matters not what man may teach or do God knows who his true saints are. The Apostle Paul said, "*Howbeit the firm foundation of God stands, having this seal, the Lord knows them that are his: and, let every one that names the name of the Lord depart from unrighteousness*" (2 Timothy 2:19).

Zechariah 14

Though the days seem dark the saints of God are called upon to await the life giving Waters of God (14:1-8)

"**1** *Behold, a day of Jehovah comes, when your spoil shall be divided in the midst of you.* **2** *For I will gather all nations against Jerusalem to battle; and the city shall be taken, and the houses rifled, and the women ravished; and half of the city shall go forth into captivity, and the residue of the people shall not be cut off from the city*" **(14:1-2).**

The context from the previous three chapters reveal the "*day of Jehovah*" to be the days of the NT church. During the church days there will be enemies of the cross of Jesus Christ (see Philippians 3:18). These enemies will pervert the truths of revelation through false doctrines and cause many to follow them (2 Peter 2:1ff). The enemies of the cross will also come in the form of worldliness and persecution. The worldly are those whose hope, purpose, and desire rest with the events, nations, and riches of mankind. Jerusalem opposes their lifestyle and consequentially they are persecuted (see Zechariah 12:3).

Notice that it is God that "*gathers all nations against Jerusalem to battle*." God "*gives*" the wicked their place of power among the saints (see Revelation 13:4-8). The Jerusalem under consideration is the city of God, Zion, the kingdom of God, and or his church (see Zechariah 13:1). Gog and Magog will attempt to wash away the saints and their sanctification through worldliness and false doctrines (Revelation 12:15-17 and 20:7-9). Most of the world will follow after the nations of men rather than God (Revelation 13:3).

"**3** *Then shall Jehovah go forth, and fight against those nations, as when he fought in the day of battle.* **4** *And his feet shall stand in that day upon the mount of Olives, which is before Jerusalem on the east; and the* *mount of Olives shall be cleft in the midst thereof toward the east and toward the west, and there shall be a very great valley; and half of the mountain shall remove toward the north, and half of it toward the south"* **(14:3-4).**

Notice the victorious tone of these last few chapters. The house of Israel is being told, by Zechariah, what to expect in the latter days of the kingdom of God. These will be days of strong victory over sin and death for the saints. God will fight for his people (see Zechariah 12:8-9). Jesus is depicted in the book of Revelation as riding a white horse into battle and slashing the enemy with his sword and their life blood is sprinkled upon his white garments (see Revelation 1:5; 3:14 and 19:11-16).

Zechariah tells us that the rider of the white horse of Revelation is Jehovah (deity of Christ). The Lord stands upon the Mount of Olives on the **east** side of Jerusalem. The prophet Ezekiel writes, "1 *Afterward he brought me to the gate, even the gate that looks toward the east.* 2 *And, behold, the glory of the God of Israel came from the way of the east: and his voice was like the sound of many waters; and the earth shined with his glory.* 3 *And it was according to the appearance of the vision which I saw, even according to the vision that I saw when I came to destroy the city; and the visions were like the vision that I saw by the river Chebar; and I fell upon my face*" (Ezekiel 43:1-3). Ezekiel is taken to the gate of the temple that looks out eastward and he saw "*the glory of the God of Israel*" coming to the temple. Earlier in the book of Ezekiel the prophet sees God's holy throne lifted and removed to the east (Ezekiel 9:18-19 and 10:22-23). Ezekiel, once again, sees the throne of God in all its glory as he did by the river Chebar (see Ezekiel 1:3, 28 and 2:23). When the prophet of God looked out to the east and saw the glorious throne of God he falls to the ground face down. The significance of these visions is that God had removed his fellowship and consequential protection from Jerusalem before she was destroyed by Babylon. God, in the days of the church, has restored his fellowship with this people through the blood of Christ. The Lord is depicted by both Ezekiel and Zechariah as coming from the east.

God is seen as standing over the Mount of Olives that has been split into two with a valley below. The Lord defends and protects the people of this valley.

"**5** *And you shall flee by the valley of my mountains; for the valley of the mountains shall reach unto Azel; yea, you shall flee, like as you fled from before the earthquake in the days of Uzziah king of Judah; and Jehovah my God shall come, and all the holy ones with you*" **(14:5).**

The earthquake in the days of Uzziah must have made a deep impression upon the minds of those who witnessed it and told others about it (see Amos 1:1). The prophet uses this earth shaking event as a comparison to the people now running or scattering as sheep after the piercing of the good shepherd (Jesus) (see Zechariah 12:10 and 13:7). The people are depicted as running as far as Azel. Azel is "a place, evidently in the neighborhood of Jerusalem and probably east of the Mount of Olives (Zechariah 14:5). It site has not been identified, but the LXX rendering 'Iasol' suggests Wadi Yasul, a tributary of the Kidron" (New Unger's Bible Dictionary page 129).

"**6** *And it shall come to pass in that day, that there shall not be light; the bright ones shall withdraw themselves:* **7** *but it shall be one day which is known unto Jehovah; not day, and not night; but it shall come to pass, that at evening time there shall be* **light**. **8** *And it shall come to pass in that day, that* **living waters** *shall go out from Jerusalem; half of them toward the eastern sea, and half of them toward the western sea: in summer and in winter shall it be*" **(14:6-8).**

Again, the day under consideration is the time of Christ, his death, establishment of his kingdom, and the forgiveness of sins. Just when all seems lost, dark, and dreary the Lord pronounces help in the form of light at the evening time of Satan's flood of persecution, worldliness, and false doctrine. The Lord shall provide, "*living waters*" that shall cause the distressed disciples to live (see Revelation 21:6). Jeremiah referred to Jehovah as the fountain of "*living waters*" at Jeremiah 2:13 and 17:13. Jesus, speaking to the Samaritan woman at Jacob's well, referred to "*living waters*" that eternally sustain life. These waters represent the truths of God that man may be saved from the life threatening effects of sin (34). The equivalent of "*living waters*" and "*light*" is apparent (see 2 Corinthians 4:4).

Jehovah is King of His Kingdom and shall consume all those who oppose Him (14:9-15)

"**9** *And Jehovah shall be King over all the earth: in that day shall Jehovah be one, and his name one*" **(14:9).**

The time frame continues to be the days of Christ's kingdom, the church, and or Zion. Jesus would wash away men's sins with his own blood. The Lord will reign as "*king over all the earth*." Isaiah identified the Christ as he who would reign as king over the earth (Isaiah 9:6-7). Jesus told Pilate that he was king (see John 18:36-38) (5c).

The days when the church is established and Christ reigns supreme as king will be a time of oneness between the Father, Son, and Holy Spirit (see John 17:21). The oneness of the Godhead is located in truth. All three are in perfect agreement and unison on the direction of life (3p).

"**10** *All the land shall be made like the Arabah, from Geba to Rimmon south of Jerusalem; and she shall be lifted up, and shall dwell in her place, from Benjamin's gate unto the place of the first gate, unto the corner gate, and from the tower of Hananel unto the king's winepreses.* **11** *And men shall dwell therein, and there shall be no more curse; but Jerusalem shall dwell safely*" **(14:10-11).**

The land of Palestine had in years past been ravished, besieged, burned, and knocked to the ground. Spiritually speaking, God's people had been pummeled as well. When Christ reigns in his kingdom the land (spiritual landscape of the souls of men) would be revitalized and take its spot as a permanent fixture in the kingdom of God.

There will be "*no more curses*" in the city of God or Jerusalem. This sounds much like Revelation 22:3; however it cannot be speaking of the saints exalted in heaven due to John's words at Revelation 21:1-2 and 7). Zechariah saw a flying scroll in his sixth vision that represented man's curse for disobedience in the form of plagues (see Zechariah 5:1-4 notes). The true Zion will be protected and defended from the flood of ungodliness in the form of worldliness and false doctrines (see Zechariah 9:8, 15). The true Zion of the New Testament days will mirror the Zion of the eternal heavens (see Revelation 21:1 - 22:5). The truths of God's word will divide the righteous from the wicked even before they go to the grave.

"**12** *And this shall be the* **plague** *wherewith Jehovah will smite all the peoples that have warred against Jerusalem: their flesh shall consume away while they stand upon their feet, and their eyes shall consume away in their sockets, and their tongue shall consume away in their mouth*" **(14:12)**.

All those who love this world and worldliness with its false doctrines and persecution will be "*plagued*" by God. God will smite all the wicked of the world with plagues that they may repent of their wickedness (see Revelation 15:1 and 16:9-11). Though the wicked of the world that teach false doctrines and persecute the saints are alive and walk on two feet they are nonetheless spiritually dead (see Ephesians 2:1-4). Today the world seems to be infatuated with zombies. Spiritual zombies are those who are physically alive yet they are dead spiritually. God's **curse** belongs to these people as long as they walk in sin.

"**13** *And it shall come to pass* **in that day**, *that a great tumult from Jehovah shall be among them; and they shall lay hold every one on the hand of his neighbor, and his hand shall rise up against the hand of his neighbor.* **14** *And Judah also shall fight at Jerusalem; and the wealth of all the nations round about shall be gathered together, gold, and silver, and apparel, in great abundance.* **15** *And so shall be the plague of the horse, of the mule, of the camel, and of the ass, and all the beasts that shall be in those camps as that plague*" **(14:13-15)**.

The Lord had once caused confusion among the Midianites that numbered as the sand of the sea. A great army had assembled itself against Israel and the Lord smote them by way of Gideon. The Midianites turned their swords upon each other and they were all destroyed (Judges 7:12, 22). Likewise, the Lord will turn the worldly minded, false teachers, and persecutors against each other (see Zechariah 11:8-9 and Galatians 5:15). They will have the plague of death that is shared with the horse, mule, camel, ass, and all the beasts in the camp.

God's Blessings to Man have ever been contingent upon his Obedience (14:16-21)

"*16 And it shall come to pass, that every one that is left of all the nations that came against Jerusalem shall go up from year to year to worship the King, Jehovah of hosts, and to keep the feast of tabernacles*" **(14:16).**

Some of the ungodly who waged war against Jehovah and his kingdom will see the error of their ways and turn to Jehovah. The Apostle Paul was one who waged war against the saints only to feel the sting of his shameful conduct, repent, and he was baptized for the forgiveness of his sins (Acts 22:16). Paul had waged war against the saints of God yet in the end he turned to the church as his eternal hope. Gentiles, and all others who once opposed the church of God, shall come with a spirit of thanksgiving (the feast of tabernacles - see more on this at next verse) and worship "*the King, Jehovah of hosts*" (see Revelation 21:24).

"*17 And it shall be, that whoso of all the families of the earth goes not up unto Jerusalem to worship the King, Jehovah of hosts, upon them there shall be **no rain**. 18 And if the family of Egypt go not up, and come not, neither shall it be upon them; there shall be the **plague** wherewith Jehovah will smite the nations that go not up to keep the feast of tabernacles. 19 This shall be the **punishment** of Egypt, and the punishment of all the nations that go not up to keep the **feast of tabernacles**" **(14:17-19).**

Not everyone would open their eyes to the truths of God's kingdom. All who reject Christ and his kingdom would suffer punishment in the form of a plague of no rain. Zechariah has now completed the argument aimed at the discouraged Jews who have left off building God's temple. The delinquent Jews have been commanded to build; however, they have been discouraged by the Samaritans and size of the foundation of the temple. God assures them of the great importance, in the grand scheme to redeem man, building the temple plays (see Zechariah 4:10).

The lesson to learn is that God's blessings of protection, care, and forgiveness are contingent upon man's obedience. Zechariah has consistently identified a true Zion that is protected and defended by God as opposed to those who wage war with God's people. The curse of plague in the form of drought belongs to those who align themselves with the worldly and erring. The blessings of eternal fountains belong to those who align themselves with God's truths.

The Lord takes the opportunity of Israel's failure to build the temple to teach the remnant of the far reaching doctrine of conditional grace. God has withheld the blessings of rain from them because they have not obeyed (Haggai 1:7ff). The eternal principle is that all those who refuse obedience and worship to Jehovah God in truth will have his blessing of salvation withheld! Nothing but punishment awaits such a foolish one (13b).

Why does Zechariah speak of the Feast of Tabernacles in relationship to the future church (Zion or Jerusalem)? Interestingly, it was the Feast of Tabernacles that was first celebrated by the returning Jews from Babylonian captivity (see Ezra 3:2-4). Ezekiel gives several distinct differences between the work, worship, and organization of the temple under the Mosaic dispensation and the church that Christ would establish in the final 9 chapters of the book. Gone will be the keeping of the Pentecost, feast of weeks, day of trumpets, Day of Atonement and so forth in the new Zion church. The only two set feasts that will celebrated will be the first month at the fourteenth day (a Passover feasts of seven days) and then again in the seventh month at the fifteenth day (feast of Tabernacles) (see Ezekiel 45:21-25).

"**20** *In that day shall there be upon the bells of the horses, HOLY UNTO JEHOVAH; and the pots in Jehovah's house shall be like the bowls before the altar.* **21** *Yea, every pot in Jerusalem and in Judah shall be holy unto Jehovah of hosts; and all they that sacrifice shall come and take of them, and boil therein: and in that day there shall be no more a Canaanite in the house of Jehovah of hosts*" **(14:20-21).**

The prophet concludes by saying that in the day that Jesus reigns as King in the kingdom of God all within the gates thereof shall be clean through the blood of Jesus Christ. There shall be no unclean or sinful person within the true church of Jesus Christ (Revelation 21:27). All shall be "*holy unto Jehovah.*" The Bible uses this phrase quite often depicting the sanctified relationship between a person or thing that is clean and holy with God.

Questions over Zechariah Chapter 14

1. What battle is under consideration at Zechariah 14:1-5?

2. What is the "*light*" that brings hope and salvation to the embattled saints?

3. What do we learn about the deity of Christ from Zechariah 14:9?

4. What is the "*curse*" of Zechariah 14:11?

5. What consequences did the world of sinners face if they did not go up to worship God?

Malachi

Robertson's Notes

Bible book 39 of 66

"For I, Jehovah, change not"

Malachi 3:6

Introduction

Malachi exposes the people's sin. A large part of the book is devoted to manifesting the people's state of delusion. Nine examples are delivered that reveal the people's hardened hearts. God had given commandments, and they had taken the liberty to adjust those commands to fit their lives. When people change law to fit their pleasures, they will inevitably invent new ways. Malachi records the extent of the people's apostasy at chapter 3:5, charging them with sorcery, adultery, false swearers, oppressing laborers, widows, and the fatherless. Said selfishness has no time nor need for being hospitable to strangers. The prophet sums up the people's sin with the statement, *"and they fear me not"* (Malachi 3:5).

Due to Israel's lack of fear, God withholds His blessings from them (Malachi 3:10). The rebellious people do not understand why God would do this since they are attempting to serve Him. They thereby conclude that it is *"vain to serve God"* (Malachi 3:13-14). They see no profit in serving God because all their efforts are only partial services. They only partially do what God wants in their sacrifices (Malachi 1:13-14) and tithes (Malachi 3:8ff). When they perform this partial service to God and do not receive His blessings (Malachi 3:9ff), they become discouraged and conclude that God does not love them (Malachi 1:2). Truly their worship and service to God was done in ignorance to His prescribed ways (cf. Acts 17:23).

The source of the people's apostasy can be traced back to the priests of their day. The priests had the responsibility to teach and uphold God's laws (Lev. 10:8-11; Deut. 33:8-10). Malachi identifies the priests as God's messengers responsible for knowing and turning the erring back to God's ways (Malachi 2:6-7). Rather than performing this duty, the current priests were guilty of causing many people to stumble in sin (Malachi 2:8). Malachi delivers words of hope for the erring and misguided people. Though the current messengers are corrupt, God will send another messenger, John the baptist, who shall prepare the way for righteousness and turn the heart of the people from hardened sinners to obedient loving servants (cf. Malachi 3:1; 4:5-6; Matt. 17:10-13).

Prophet and Date of Writing

Nothing is known about the prophet Malachi. The date of the epistle is difficult to assess. One may consider the sinful and deluded mindset of the people and conclude that it was written around the time of Jeremiah (627 to 584 BC). Other considerations would be that Malachi mentions a "governor" at chapter 1:8 and the people's problems with intermarrying foreigners who worshipped other gods at chapter 2:11. Furthermore, Malachi mentions God withholding blessings from His people due to their sin at chapter 3:10ff. Said factors may cause us to conclude that the letter was written somewhere around the time of Nehemiah (i.e., 435 BC or so).

Theme of Malachi

The theme of the book of Malachi seems to be found at chapter 3:6 where the prophet writes, *"For I, Jehovah, change not."* Though the people changed God's ordinances regarding sacrificing (Malachi 1:13-14) and giving of tithes (Malachi 3:8-10) God did not change. God's laws remain a true constant in all eternity (Rom. 3:3-4; Heb. 13:8; James 1:17). Malachi therefore admonishes the people to, *"Remember the law of Moses"* (Malachi 4:4).

Practical Application of Malachi

The Lord's response to the erring people is, *"I have no pleasure in you, said Jehovah of hosts, neither will I accept an offering at your hand"* (Malachi 1:10). The people vainly offered an abbreviation of God's sacrificial system (Malachi 1:7-8, 13-14) and tithes (Malachi 3:8ff). God's blessings would thereby continue to be withheld (Malachi 3:11-12) until the people repented from a heart of sorrow (Malachi 3:7). Eternal heartaches could be avoided by mankind if only they would look to God's perfect law of liberty and respect it. Men of all ages have tried their hands at changing God's laws to fit their pleasure (cf. II Thess. 2:4). The very existence of denominational bodies is present day proof. Some believe they can worship God using various change agents and the Lord will accept their religious efforts. The lesson of Malachi is that God does not change (Malachi 3:6). Those who change God's laws, even in the name of religion, will be subject to His eternal curse (Malachi 4:6). Malachi writes to the erring people saying, *"Bring the whole tithe"* as opposed to their partial service (Malachi 3:10). Two suggestions for acceptable worship may be gained from Malachi. First, cast off all erring teachers (cf. Malachi 2:1-9; II Pet. 2:1ff). Secondly, let us all serve God with our wholehearted service today that He may be well pleased (cf. Malachi 3:10; Matt. 22:37).

MALACHI CHAPTER 1

Synopsis

Malachi gives the **first of nine incidents** where God makes an observation about the people yet they have a total different view of themselves. It reminds us of a study of Jeremiah. The prophet Jeremiah had exposed the peoples sins yet they considered themselves innocent (Jeremiah 2:35) and wise (Jeremiah 8:8). Those deluded in sin will never see the need for repentance and forgiveness so long as they love sin and hate righteousness.

The people sarcastically ask God how it could be that he loves them while they suffer from a crippling drought. God gives them the answer, as he has always done with man, yet it is not the answer that most people are looking for. God's answer convicts and calls for change yet the rebellious and proud see no need for change. Those who continue in rebellion will continue to experience the divine rod of chastening upon their back.

Application

Chapter one teaches us the meaning of honoring and fearing God. The people of Malachi's day were accused of despising the name of God by way of their disobedience to his divine commandments regarding sacrifices. While God commanded the unblemished first-fruits of their flocks the people gave lame and sick animals. The people expected God to accept their offering yet God called it "*evil*" (Malachi 1:8).

Furthermore the Lord said that those who disobey his commands of sacrifice were "*cursed*" (Malachi 1:14). God's blessings are always with those who obey his commandments as did Jacob (see Romans 9:13 as Paul quotes from Malachi 1:3). Those who conclude that God's gracious promises are freely given to men and women today who reject his holy commandments are gravely mistaken. God's eternal wrath will rest upon those who refuse to acknowledge their sins and repent (see Romans 2:1-10). We show the greatest respect, honor, and fear toward God when we are obedient to his will rather than our own.

Malachi 1

God's Love for Israel (1:1-5)

"**1** *The burden of the word of Jehovah to Israel by Malachi.* **2** *I have loved you, said Jehovah. Yet you say, Wherein have you loved us? Was not Esau Jacob's brother? Said Jehovah: yet I loved Jacob;* **3** *but Esau I hated, and made his mountains a desolation, and gave his heritage to the jackals of the wilderness*" **(1:1-3).**

The word "*burden*" is translated "oracle" in the ASV footnotes which means, "A command or revelation from God" (AHD 873). The LXX translates the Hebrew word to Greek as *lemma* meaning "anything received or income" (LS 471) (LXX 1106). Habakkuk and Nahum similarly begin their words of prophecy.

God's people were currently experiencing a debilitating drought that made them think that God did not care for them. God tells the people; however, that he truly does love them. Many of God's people did not understand that the Lord chastens those whom he loves so that they may repent of sinful deeds (see Revelation 3:19 and 16:8-11). Through out Israel's history God had withheld the rain, caused crops to fail, and brought sword and pestilence upon the people when they were in sin (Amos 4:6-12; Haggai 1:7-11 and Zechariah 8:9-13; 10:1; 14:17). These divine acts against the people should have moved them to acknowledge their sins and repent; however, many did not see that God's grace is conditioned obedience. Their conclusion, "*Wherein have you loved us?*" They considered the curses of their existence as a sign that God did not care for them (17d).

To enlighten the people of Malachi's day about the true love of God for his people the Lord reminds them of his eternal choices and sovereignty. God's choice of Jacob (Israel) over Esau (Edom) stands as a timeless example of how God's promises and expectations have always worked (Genesis 25:21ff). The Apostle Paul's used of Malachi 1:3 at Romans 9:13 serve as a commentary to our immediate text. Paul said, "10 *And not only so; but Rebecca also having conceived by one, even by our father Isaac –* 11 *for the children being not yet born, neither having done anything good or bad, that the purpose of God according to election might stand, not of works, but of him that calls,* 12 *it was said unto her, The elder shall serve the younger.* 13 *Even as it is written, Jacob I loved, but Esau I hated*" (Romans 9:10-13). The value of understanding the Old and New Testaments through statements like this is great (see Romans 15:4). When I understand the context of Old Testament scriptures that are being used by New Testament writers I gain a better understanding of the text under consideration. To understand Malachi's use of Jacob and Esau is to understand Paul's use of the same text in the book of Romans.

Malachi's audience is a people that have suffered at the chastening hands of God by way of drought (see Malachi 3:9-12). The people are not connecting their current hardships with God's tender love. The Lord has cursed them with the plague of drought so that they may be moved to repentance. Though acknowledgement of sins and repentance through sorrow and guilt is the objective with chastisement it does not occur in most men's hearts (see Revelation 16:8-11). The people are experiencing the difficulties of a drought and are looking at God sarcastically saying, "Oh sure you love us... If you love us why are we suffering?" God's answer to them is that he has not changed his divine expectations of the people yet the people have changed. Later the prophet will write of God saying, *"For I, Jehovah, change not; therefore you, O sons of Jacob, are not consumed"* (Malachi 3:6).

God has eternally loved good and hated evil and this fact is brought out at Malachi 1:3 and Romans 9:13. The Lord uses the illustration of Jacob and Esau to prove his point. Though Jacob and Esau came from the same mother and people God said that he loved Jacob yet hated Esau. Why did God hate Esau and love Jacob? The Apostle Paul explains that Jacob represented God's elect remnant whereas Esau represented those who live by the flesh (see Romans 9:6-8, 27, 11:1-7, 25-32). God loves the righteous (his elect remnant known as Jacob and Israel - see Romans 11:26-27) and hates the unrighteous (those who reject his will for their own fleshly ways - see Isaiah 34:8ff; Jeremiah 49:7ff; Ezekiel 25:12ff and Obadiah 1:21). Before either of the boys were born this principle was eternally set (see Proverbs 8:22-26). Esau's choice of living by the flesh rather than a life of righteousness brought him much sorrows and pain in life. Solomon depicted a life of sin as walking through a hedge of thorns (see Proverbs 22:5). God hated Esau because he chose a life of sin (Hebrews 12:15-17).

God is telling the people, through Malachi, that they are experiencing hardships in life because of their choice to sin. As long as they walk in sin they will experience the pains of punishment and chastisement like Esau. The object of chastening, whether it be a parent today or God as our heavenly Father, is designed to move man to acknowledge wrong and do right (see Hebrews 12:5-13). The fascinating part about God's chastening hand against the wicked is that it does not let up. If God let up his chastening hand upon the wicked it would mean that he gives up on them but he doesn't (see 2 Peter 3:9). The wicked will consequentially be punished throughout their lives so long as they choose a life of sin. Malachi's duty is to open the people's eyes to these facts so that they would acknowledge their error and seek out God's divine favor and blessings of peace (see notes on Psalms 85 for an excellent discussion on this subject).

"**4** *Whereas Edom said, We are beaten down, but we will return and build the waste places; thus said Jehovah of hosts, they shall build, but I will throw down; and men shall call them The border of wickedness, and the people against whom Jehovah has indignation for ever.* **5** *And your eyes shall see, and you shall say, Jehovah be magnified beyond the border of Israel*" **(1:4-5)**.

Edom would suffer to the point of death in their rebellion because they would not open their eyes and see the divine cause of their suffering. God's indignation would rest upon the backs of Edom all the days of their lives due to their hardened hearts of sin. The objective of God with chastening punishment is to figuratively break the bones of the sinner so that he may fall to his face in shame, acknowledge his sins, and plead for forgiveness (see Psalms 51:1-3, 8, 17) (17d). Edom was "*beaten down*" by God's strong arm of chastisement yet they continued to rebel.

Edom, and all those who set their face against Jehovah God, would be brought down off their high horse of pride by force (see Jeremiah 49:7-22). As a sick man continues to check the clock throughout the night, anxiously awaiting the end of his illness, so Edom would be as they sought for counsel from Jehovah's watchmen (Isaiah 21:11-12). There would be, however, no relief for the pride-stricken people of Edom. World empire after empire would continue to press them (i.e., Assyria, Babylon, Medes and Persians, Grecians and then the Romans), and eventually they were non-existent (Malachi 1:2-4).

"The archeological evidence also indicates the downfall of Edom by the end of the sixth century. Nomadic tribes infiltrated Edom, and it lost the power to control and profit from the trade between Arabia and the Mediterranean coast and Egypt. In the fifth century, an Arabian tribe, the Nabateans, forced their way into Edom and replaced the Edomites, many of whom went westward to southern Judea (later to become Idumea; 1 Maccabees 5:3, 65), while others were absorbed into the newcomers. By 312 B. C. the area around Petra also was inhabited by the Nabateans" (ISBE, volume 2 page 20).

God Explains Why the People are Suffering (1:6-14)

"**6** *A son honors his father, and a servant his master: if then I am a father, where is mine honor? And if I am a master, where is my fear? Said Jehovah of hosts unto you, O priests, that despise my name. And you say, wherein have we despised your name?*" **(1:6).**

God is considered the "father" of Israel (see Hosea 11:1). The Lord watched as sons and servants gave "*honor*" by way of obedience to their earthly fathers and masters yet they would not do the same for God. To "*honor*" (LXX Greek *timao*) means to "to pay honor to, hold in honor, revere, reverence, to be held worthy of honor, to value or prize" (LS 807). The Lord exposes the priest of Israel for not giving or promoting great value to his glorious name and consequentially little to no "*fear*" in the people. God's chastening hand of punishment ought to have caused panic fear in people so that they immediately stopped their sinful ways. The priest; however, were obviously telling people that the current drought was not divinely caused. The priests were saying that the drought and the people's suffering was more of coincidence and a sign that God really doesn't care about them.

God accuses the priest of "*despising*" (Greek *heksouthenesousin*) his most holy name by not promoting honor and fear. The Greek word *heksouthenesousin* means "to make light of, set at naught, despise, contemn, treat with contempt and scorn, to neglect, and or disregard" (Moulton 148). Fascinatingly, it was Esau that "*despised*" his birthright (Genesis 25:34). Esau did not value his grand spiritual birthright. When the priests and people of God refused to honor and fear God, by way of obedience to his commandments, they displayed a spirit of hatred for him.

The **second of nine statements** that illustrate the people's state of mental delusion is given. The wicked foolishly say, "*Wherein have we despised your name?*" The people's minds were so far removed from God they did not know that their actions were illustrating a spirit of hatred and hostility toward God (see Hosea 4:6). Jeremiah had said that the people of God had become "*sottish*" (i.e., deluded as though intoxicated) (Jeremiah 4:22). While being overtaken by Babylon the people, in a spirit of mental delusion, asks, 'why are these things happening to us?' (Jeremiah 13:22 and 16:10) While Israel considered themselves innocent (Jeremiah 2:35) and wise (Jeremiah 8:8) God said they were rebellious (Jeremiah 6:16) and lacked fear (Jeremiah 5:22-24). Man can get so far removed from God's laws that he may honestly believe things are religiously right in his life while that same law reveals him a condemned sinner.

"**7** *You offer polluted bread upon mine altar. And you say, Wherein have we polluted you? In that you say, The table of Jehovah is contemptible.* **8** *And when you offer the blind for sacrifice, it is no evil! And when you offer the lame and sick, it is no evil! Present it now unto your governor; will he be pleased with you? Or will he accept your person? Said Jehovah of hosts*" **(1:7-8).**

The people's sinful delusion is exposed for a **third** time.

A people who have little knowledge of law and even smaller faith in it are hard to reason with. The people want to know how they have shown to God that they do not honor and fear him. The Lord responds by telling them that their bread upon the altar was polluted (i.e., the sacrifices that they made upon the altar of burnt offering) (see Leviticus 22). The priest were offering blind, lame, and sick animals and saying that there was nothing wrong with this because the "*table of God is contemptible.*" The word "contemptible" (Greek LXX *hexoudenoo*) means "to set at naught" (LS 276). The Greek words of this sentence would literally read, "The table of God is worthless."

Oddly, the people figured that their unlawful sacrifices were justified because God was not blessing them with rain and crops. The people's perspective of God's love was that he would tolerate their wicked practices due to the circumstances. God; however, tells them that their actions are proving that they do not value to the "*table of Jehovah.*" Malachi defines religious ideology of every age at these verses. People today think that religion means love and tolerance based on circumstances (14k). If one is accused of sin they are said to be judgmental and un-Christ like. Jesus and God are viewed as tolerant of all man's words and actions. When such a mind is chastised for sin they are appalled because they believe God to be unconditionally loving. Malachi teaches us that we display a spirit of love and value toward God when we obey his commandments.

The Lord asks the contemptuous priests, "Will the governor accept such offerings?" To offer such worthless sacrifices to the governor of the people would be an insult. God; however, did not really matter to them. Would these same religious people, that set aside God's laws for their own religious ideas, offer a serpent to their child for food and say "accept it or be viewed as intolerant?" This is exactly what Jesus said at Matthew 7:7-12. People are very odd. Often times the only error man sees is that of others and when someone charges them personally with sin it is very offensive. Why not get back to the standards of God's words and measure ourselves and our practices by it alone (see Isaiah 28:17)?

"***9** And now, I pray you, entreat the favor of God, that he may be gracious unto us: this has been by your means: will he accept any of your persons? Said Jehovah of hosts. **10** Oh that there were one among you that would shut the doors, that you might not kindle fire on mine altar in vain! I have no pleasure in you, said Jehovah of hosts, neither will I accept an offering at your hand*" **(1:9-10).**

Would God accept an offering to him that was not according to his will? Some believe that any service directed at God is acceptable to him because it is done in the name of religion (see Matthew 7:21-23). Such a believe leads to great shock when another accuses the sinner of wickedness. Worship and lifestyles that do not take into consideration the will of God is contemptuous and unacceptable (see Amos 4:4-5 and 5:21-24). Not only is the worship service unacceptable but the persons performing the ceremony are rejected! God has no pleasure in such people (see Isaiah 1:13) (29m).

Malachi pleads with the people to open their eyes to their folly. The prophet Haggai similarly called upon the people of God to contemplate why they were suffering a drought at Haggai 1:7-11. If only the people would "*entreat the favor of God*" he would be gracious to them and restore their blessings. The Lord, through Malachi, calls upon at least one person to shut the doors of the temple to the altars and to stop the kindling of vain fire upon the altar of burnt offering (see Joel 2:12-14).

"*11 For from the rising of the sun even unto the going down of the same my name shall be great among the Gentiles; and in every place incense shall be offered unto my name, and a pure offering: for my name shall be great among the Gentiles, said Jehovah of hosts. 12 But you* **profane** *it, in that you say, The table of Jehovah is polluted, and the fruit thereof, even its food, is contemptible*" **(1:11-12).**

A shocking contrast is drawn between the disobedient Jews and a future obedient Gentiles. The Lord proclaims a future day when the Gentiles, through a faith in Jesus Christ, would offer up acceptable spiritual sacrifices unto Jehovah God. The Jews, on the other hand, "*profaned*" the name of God and were unacceptable. The word "*profane*" (LXX Greek *bebeloute*) means "what is open and accessible to all; hence, profane, not religious, not connected with religion; unholy or to violate" (Moulton 69). The Jews had treated the kingdom of God as though it were an open door religion that accepts any and all doctrines while the Gentiles gave honor to the exclusive nature of truth (12cc). These words were designed to open Israel's eyes to their sins and move them to jealousy so that they may fear, honor, and obey the laws of God (see Romans 10:19 and 11:11-14).

What caused the Jews to believe they could offer unlawful sacrifices upon the altar and be accepted by God? The Apostle Paul reveals the Jews problem to be that of entitlement. Many of the Jews came to believe that their heritage placed them in close spiritual proximity to God rather than their obedience, fear, and honor toward him (see Romans 9:6-8). The prophet Isaiah, as well as the Apostle Paul, correct this erroneous thinking by writing, "*If the number of the children of Israel be as the sand of the sea, it is the remnant that shall be saved*" (Isaiah 10:22ff and Romans 9:27). The Jews' idea of religion was that God gave them the right alone to a relationship with him. Such elitist thinking lead to a slothful approach to study and an ignorance of God's words (see Hosea 4:6). The further along they traveled on this road of spiritual supremacy due to their heritage the further away from truth they went. The further from truth they were the further from God they became. The further from God they went the closer they came to their own brand of religion. No man, or even God, dared challenge them because they were the Jews.

"**13** *You say also, Behold, what a weariness is it! And you have snuffed at it, said Jehovah of hosts; and you have brought that which was taken by violence, and the lame, and the sick; thus you bring the offering: should I accept this at your hand? Said Jehovah.* **14** *But cursed be the deceiver, who has in his flock a male, and vows, and sacrifices unto the Lord a blemished thing; for I am a great King, said Jehovah of hosts, and my name is terrible among the Gentiles*" **(1:13-14).**

The **fourth statement** of Israel that depicts their deluded mind is revealed.

Israel had grown "*weary*" (LXX Greek *kakopatheias*) meaning "to be vexed, troubled, or dejected" (Moulton 210). God's ordinances regarding sacrificing were exasperating to the Jew. To take an unblemished animal was to take the best. The Jew reasoned that they may as well substitute a less valuable animal for sacrificing. The people thought that it was a waist of a good animal so they brought their lame, sick, and blemished animals that did not mean much to them or that they would not lose any money over. Such actions, on the part of the Jews, was to "*snuff*" (LXX Greek *hexefusesa*) at God's will for sacrifice. The Greek *hexefusesa* means "to avoid, escape, or to flee out" (Moulton 129). God's own people were "avoiding" God's divine commandments by substituting the lame, sick, and blemished for sacrifices. Keeping

God's laws should have never been viewed as "*weariness.*" The Apostle John writes, "3 *For this is the love of God, that we keep his commandments: and his commandments are not grievous*" (1 John 5:3).

Israel was guilty of elevating personal human reason to a level of divine revelation. Solomon wrote, "5 *Trust in Jehovah with all your heart, and **lean** not upon your own understanding:*" (Proverbs 3:5). To "*lean*" (LXX Greek *epairo*) literally means to "lift or raise" (Liddell and Scott 278). Solomon exposes the error of elevating **our own wisdom** to the level of divine law. The Apostle Paul referred to such daring people as sons of perdition (see 2 Thessalonians 2:3-4). The Apostle Peter refers to the daring as false teachers (2 Peter 2:1-12). Obedience to God's authorized words is a very significant topic in the Bible. God does not tolerate man's efforts to change his divine revelation for his own ideas (13b).

Those who avoided God's laws because they were exasperating would be "*cursed.*" The curse of God is his divine punishment designed to move the wicked to acknowledge their unlawful practices and return to his authorized pattern (please read Deuteronomy 28:58-62 and 29:22-30:1). God is a "*great king*" and will not be treated as though his words mean nothing or are subject to man's change. The king speaks and he expects all to give honor and fear to those words. We show the greatest respect, honor, and fear toward God when we are obedient to his will rather than our own (see John 15:1-10). When people change the words of God to fit their own liking God is fiercely angered and his curses of disobedience lies upon that wretched soul (9f).

Questions over Malachi Chapter 1

1. Compare and contrast Malachi 1:1-5 and Romans 9:6-13.

2. **True or False:** A father and master have the right to expect honor from their children or servants.

3. How was Israel guilty of polluting God's altar?

4. What group of people would view God's name as "*great*?"

5. Who does God curse among those who bring sacrifices to his altar?

6. How can we bring glory and honor to the magnificent name of Jehovah God today?

MALACHI CHAPTER 2

Synopsis

The priests of Malachi's day did not fear and look at the name of God with great awe and reverence. Their knowledge of God's word was weak and they caused the people to err by their preferential treatment given to those they selected. The priests permitted some people to bring lame, sick, blemished, and animals attained by violence to the altar of burnt offering. The priests fostered a spirit of disrespect for God's laws among the people so that some were marrying foreign women of idolatry and others were putting away their wives for unlawful causes. Furthermore the priests were guilty of misrepresenting God to others. While God loves the righteous and hates the wicked the priests were telling people that God delights in people who do wicked things. The Lord had come to be weary with the wicked priests of Judah.

Application

We must all know that God is omniscient. There is not one thing that we say or do that escapes his all seeing eyes and ears (see Jeremiah 23:23-25). God has heard and saw all that the wicked priests of Malachi's day has taught and practiced. Those who teach things contrary to God's laws cause many to stumble in sin (see 2 Peter 2:1ff). False teachers and prophet weary the God of heaven. The Lord knows; however, who it is that belongs to him (see 2 Timothy 2:19). There will always be, in every generation, an elect remnant of faithful followers of God that will do all his divine will in fear and reverence (see Romans 11:1-6).

Malachi 2

God's Judgment against the Priesthood (2:1-9)

"**1** *And now, O you priests, this commandment is for you.* **2** *If you will not hear, and if you will not lay it to heart, to give glory unto my name, said Jehovah of hosts, then will I send the curse upon you, and I will curse your blessings; yea, I have cursed them already, because you do not lay it to heart*" **(2:1-2).**

The prophet of God divinely calls out the priest. The priest were guilty of despising the name of Jehovah God in that they did not keep his commandments and were not promoting an environment conducive to obedience among the people (see Malachi 1:6). We bring "*glory*" to the name of God when we obey his commands (see John 15:5-10). God tells the priests that if they will not glorify his name through their obedience then he would send "*the curse upon you*." The people were already suffering from God's cursed plague of drought (see Malachi 3:10). God would send a cursed plague upon the individual priests if they continue in their rebellion. The sacrifices made to God must be according to his divine will. When the priests approved of lame, sick, and violently attained animals upon the altar of burnt offering they were profaning the Lord's tables (see Malachi 1:14).

"**3** *Behold, I will rebuke your seed, and will spread dung upon your faces, even the dung of your feasts; and you shall be taken away with it.* **4** *And you shall know that I have sent this commandment unto you, that my covenant may be with Levi, said Jehovah of hosts*" **(2:3-4).**

The feast that the priests were participating in was their own rather than God's. Amos similarly condemned the worshippers of his day that sought to please their selves rather than God in worship (see Amos 4:4-5). The Lord uses strong language to denounce the ungodly priest by telling them that he would "*spread dung upon your faces.*" No man would permit the priest to serve at the feasts with dung on their face and so these men would be taken out of the camp and counted unclean. God had set the descendants of Levi aside as priests to fulfill the duties of the tabernacle and temple yet they were not fulfilling this agreement. Those wicked Levite priests would be divinely removed so that faithful ones may serve in their place.

"**5** *My covenant was with him of life and peace; and I gave them to him that he might fear; and he feared me, and* **stood in awe of my name**. **6** *The law of truth was in his mouth, and unrighteousness was not found in his lips: he walked with me in peace and uprightness, and* **turned many away from iniquity**" **(2:5-6).**

The Lord fondly remembers the priests of days gone by. The sons of Aaron were blessed by God and entrusted with taking a lead spiritual role among the people. These men would take care of the temple and offer the people's sacrifices unto God. In return, they received the portion of food through heave offerings and tithes. God's gracious gifts of the priesthood, sustenance, and set aside property was so that these priests may "*fear and stand in awe of my name.*" The Lord recalls how that godly men served in the position of priest and performed well with a spirit of fear and awe. These men spoke according to the "*law of truth.*" There was no unrighteousness found in their speech. The priests of old days walked with God and consequentially "*turned many away from iniquity.*" The influence of the priests upon the people was positive in the sense that they encouraged everyone to uphold the standards of righteousness and justice.

The priests of Malachi's day; however, were perverse. Not only did the priests of Malachi's day accept the lame, sick and violently attained animals upon the altar but they promoted a spirit of contempt for the commandments of God among the people (see Malachi 1:13-14 above).

"**7** *For the priest's lips should keep knowledge, and they should seek the law at his mouth; for he is the messenger of Jehovah of hosts.* **8** *But you* *are turned aside out of the way;* **you have caused many to stumble in the law**; *you have corrupted the covenant of Levi, said Jehovah of hosts.* **9** *Therefore have I also made you contemptible and base before all the people, according as you have not kept my ways, but have had respect of persons in the law"* **(2:7-9).**

The priests were responsible for knowing and teaching God's people the law as his messengers (see Leviticus 10:8-11 and Deuteronomy 33:8-10). God's priests had now found his ways wearisome and consequently caused many to stumble in error due to their half hearted approach to service. When the priests accepted sick, lame, and blemished sacrifices that were attained by violence they were compromising God's divine laws. God had made a covenant to take care of them as they served at the tabernacle in faithfulness; however, the priests violated that agreement.

The Lord gives specifics to the error of the priests. Their sin was to pervert justice and equity by practicing "*respect of persons*." Certain people of choice were permitted to offer blemished sacrifices and others were permitted to do other things against God's laws. Those who were not in favor with the priests would be required to keep the law perfectly. The chief cause of a people who have digressed from the Lord's commandments is the teachers. Elders and preachers today who will not uphold the whole council of God cause many to "*stumble in the law*." These men are often supported by the gospel and receive God's blessings (1 Corinthians 9:14). We may rest assured; however, that when such blessings are taken without doing the proper works that God's anger is kindled (18c).

Judah's Treachery against the Wife of their Youth (2:10-17)

"**10** *Have we not all one father? Has not one God created us? Why do we deal treacherously every man against his brother, profaning the covenant of our fathers?* **11** *Judah has dealt treacherously, and an abomination is committed in Israel and in Jerusalem; for Judah has* *profaned the holiness of Jehovah which he loves, and has married the daughter of a foreign god"* **(2:10-11)**

The first sin that exposed Judah's lack of honor and fear toward God was in the area of their sacrificing. The second sin of the people revolves around marriage and divorce. Judah has *"married the daughter of a foreign god."* To take a foreign woman to wife who worshipped other deities was to provide one's brethren with the opportunity to sin. Nehemiah warned of the opportunistic nature of sinning by means of wedding foreign women who worshipped foreign deities at Nehemiah 13:23ff. Apparently Judah had not only wedded these foreign women but had participated in acts of idolatry with their wives. The idolatry of Judah is identified as *"profaning the holiness of Jehovah."* God's people were to be separate from the world of sinful doers. Once again we see the word *"profane"* in relationship to the exclusive expectations of God from ungodliness (see Malachi 1:12). When Judah opened up their worship to other deities they made God's worship common and open to all.

Marrying the daughters of a foreign deity was a matter of *"treachery"* (LXX Greek *hegkatalipes*) against God's holiness. The Greek *hegkatalipes* means "to leave in a place or situation, to leave behind; to forsake or abandon" (Moulton 113). Judah had abandoned the commandments of God regarding marrying foreign women of other deities. This Greek word is found five times in the LXX at Malachi 2:10, 11, 14, 15 and 16. The New Testament has no such laws. We find Christians married to non-Christians with no instructions to get out of those relationships (see 1 Corinthians 7:13 and 1 Peter 3:1). The lesson learned today is that we should earnestly consider who we are marrying and what type of influence they will have on us. Though it is not a sin to marry an unbeliever it is not wise to do (consider 1 Corinthians 11:16).

*"***12** *Jehovah will cut off, to the man that does this, him that wakes and him that answers, out of the tents of Jacob, and him that offers an offering unto Jehovah of hosts"* **(2:12).**

The man that would take a foreign wife who worships another deity is to be cut off from the people of God. The man who offers an offering to God while maintaining a wife that practices idolatry shall be cut off. Many are they today who offer their spiritual sacrifice to God while wedded to wicked practices.

"*13 And this again you do: you cover the altar of Jehovah with tears, with weeping, and with sighing, insomuch that he regards not the offering any more, neither receives it with good will at your hand. 14 Yet you say, Wherefore? Because Jehovah has been witness between you and the wife of your youth, against whom you have dealt treacherously, though she is your companion, and the wife of your covenant*" **(2:13-14).**

Not only had the people made unlawful sacrifices and unlawfully married foreign women of idolatry but they were unlawfully putting away their wives for no just cause. The men who divorced their wives for no just cause were responsible for their tears upon the altar. The divorced wives hearts were broken because their husbands had left them after years of being faithful in marriage. The wicked man that does such a thing will answer for every tear that his wife shed as she faithfully helped her husband and served Jehovah God.

The **fifth statement** regarding Israel's deluded state of mind is recorded. The men guilty of adultery asks, "*Wherefore*" does God not receive our offerings unto him? The foolishness and destitute of character is revealed in such a question. God had witnessed the vows or covenant that was made between the man and wife and he now witnesses the putting asunder of that covenant agreement. These men have dealt "*treacherously*" (abandoned) with their companion that should have been for life. Once again we see the people's works governed not by God's laws but by their own lust and desires.

There is not much of anything recorded about Jewish wedding process. Apparently the two entered into a covenant agreement (Ezekiel 16:8) in which God (here at Malachi 2:14) and man (Ruth 4:10ff) served as witnesses. The covenant meant that the two were joined together for life (see Matthew 19:3ff) (29i) (33d).

"**15** *And did he not make one, although he had the residue of the Spirit? And wherefore one? He sought a godly seed. Therefore take heed to your spirit, and let none deal treacherously against the wife of his youth*" **(2:15).**

The alternate reading in the margin of the ASV Bible reads, "*And not one has done so who had a residue of the Spirit. Or what? Is there one that sees a godly seed?*" The English Standard Version Bible has a clear reading: "*Did he not make them one, with a portion of the Spirit in their union? And what was the one God seeking? Godly offspring. So guard yourselves in your spirit, and let none of you be faithless to the wife of your youth.*" Malachi brings us back to the beginnings of God's intention or laws for marriage. God initially gave law regarding man and woman becoming "*one flesh*" in the marital relationship in that the woman was taken from the man and joined together by God (see Genesis 2:18-25). Both Malachi and Jesus quote from Genesis 2:24 in relationship to unlawful divorce (see Matthew 19:4-5).

Malachi explains the "why" of God joining man and woman as one flesh in the inseparable bond of marriage. Man and woman were to be "*one*" because God was seeking a "*Godly offspring*." The word "*residue*" (Greek LXX *hupoleimma*) is very helpful here. *Hupoleimma* means "something left behind or a remnant" (LS 844 and Moulton 418). There is a direct correlation between man and woman remaining in the marital bond and God seeking a Godly offspring (spiritually minded men and women who would be recognized as his elect remnant). If man and woman were to adhere to God's laws of marriage and remain together they would raise children in an atmosphere of respect for God's laws. Children would see that their parents remained together just as God commanded and they would be more likely to keep God's laws rather than profaning them. To divorce a wife unlawfully would be to deal "*treacherously*" (abandon) with her and to be inconsiderate of one's own soul. Moses, Malachi, and

Jesus were teaching that it has always been God's command for man and woman to marry and remain married so that they may produce Godly offspring (the elect remnant of God). There is obviously great value in remaining together as man and wife. Divorced families will have greater tendencies to produce ungodly offspring. This is a general truth in God's word such as Proverbs 22:6. The general rule is that if a man and woman remain married they will produce Godly children. Likewise, if we raise our children in a Godly home they will not depart from the truth. Both of these statements are generally true yet God gives man a choice in life as to whether he will fear him in obedience or profane his Holy name in ungodliness (see Proverbs 1:29). The point is that in a home where the parents remain married and teach their children to respect and reverence the name of God the child should grow to be of a "Godly seed" (God's elect remnant of faithful followers).

"**16** *For I hate putting away, said Jehovah, the God of Israel, and him that covers his garment with violence, said Jehovah of hosts: therefore take heed to your spirit, that you deal not treacherously*" **(2:16).**

To abandon or forsake the wife is technically identified as "*putting away*" (LXX *hexaposteiles*) meaning to "send away or dismiss" (Moulton 144). Consider the reason God does not permit a man that has been joined to a woman in marriage to put her away. First, it is a profaning of the covenant of our fathers (Malachi 2:10). Secondly, putting away the wife of one's youth is an abomination to God (Malachi 2:11). Thirdly, such an unlawful act will bring a multitude of tears upon the innocent wife as she cries out to God at the altar (Malachi 2:13). Fourth, God does not permit a man to divorce the wife of his youth because she is the man's companion and you made a covenant with her and God to remain one (see Malachi 2:14). Fifth, God does not permit divorce so as to assure the man and wife "*Godly offspring*" (Malachi 2:15). The sixth reason God gives for not permitting divorce is that he "*hates*" it (Malachi 2:16). Lastly, God does not permit divorce because it is a matter of "*treachery*" that violates his divine will (Malachi 2:10-16) (29i).

Malachi divinely associates putting away a wife for causes other than adultery (see Matthew 19:1-10) a matter of "*covering one's garments with violence*" (see Genesis 2:21-25; Matthew 19:1-10; Romans 7:1-4 and 1 Corinthians 7:39). Throughout the Old Testament similar statements are made in relationship to men and women being clothed with various sins rather than righteousness (see Psalms 73:6; Isaiah 59:6 and Zechariah 3:4). The mind that would put away his wife is a mind of sinfulness.

"*17 You have wearied Jehovah with your words. Yet you say, Wherein have we wearied him? In that you say, Every one that does evil is good in the sight of Jehovah, and he delights in them; or where is the God of justice?*" **(2:17)**.

Malachi exposes the **sixth question** that illustrates the people's delusion.

Malachi reveals another sin of the people. God's people are guilty of making profane sacrifices of lame, sick, blemished and violently attained animals. Secondly, they were guilty of marrying foreign women of idolatry. Thirdly, they were guilty of unlawfully divorcing their wives. A fourth sin is now exposed. The people's "*words*" were sinful in that they misrepresented God to others. The wicked people of Judah were telling others that evil people were good in the sight of Jehovah. While God condemned the works of the people they accepted and even said that God accepts them.

Malachi writes, "*Where is the God of justice?*" The God of justice was not known by the sinful people. The word "*justice*" (LXX *krima*) means "judgment, a sentence, administration of justice, execution of justice, or an administrative decree" (Moulton 241). God has eternally been all about law. Law; however, was a far thing from the minds of sinful Judah.

Questions over Malachi Chapter 2

1. Why does God curse the priests?

2. What should the priest have been busy doing?

3. Who did Judah marry?

4. How did the people of God deal treacherously with the wife of their youth?

5. Compare and contrast Matthew 5:31 and 19:4-5 with Malachi 2:15-16.

MALACHI CHAPTER 3

Synopsis

God is doing much for a deluded and hard hearted people that have disappointed him in their sin. The Lord's eternal expectation of all men is perfect obedience to his laws. God has never changed this eternal principle (see Malachi 3:6). If only the people would receive this instruction and return to the Lord in faithful obedience he would restore their rain and crops (Malachi 3:10). To receive God's blessings the people would need to give God the whole tithe rather than partial gifts. Secondly, the people's mind toward God must be corrected. To conclude that it is vain to serve God because he demands perfect obedience is great folly and failure. Malachi's point is that with the help of God man can achieve God's divine directive of obedience.

Application

The issue of establishing Bible authority is defined in this chapter. People often want to know what they can and cannot do in religious service to God or in any part of living life. We are told to establish divine authority for all that we do because it will be the laws of God that judge us in the last day (John 12:44). Those who do not establish authority for their every work will be washed away in judgment (see Isaiah 28:17). What will cause people to establish authority for all that they do today?

There are three things that will move a man to establish Bible authority for all that they do. **First**, people must come to recognize the supreme authority of God in this world we live in. **God is a great King** and demands man's subjection (Malachi 1:14 and 1 Timothy 6:15-16). The Lord establishes this fact by way of creation so that no man has a valid excuse for not believing and obeying his laws (see Romans 1:20 and Revelation 14:7). Divine creation, as opposed to evolution and chance, is so obvious that God uses this to prove his eternal power and divinity. **Second**, man comes to demand Bible authority in his life and the lives of others by seeing the **value** of the Word of God. When we value the Word of God we manifest a value in our eternal souls. God saves man by instructing us through his divine laws. If eternal salvation is attained through truth then these principles should be held in highest esteem (see Proverbs 4:7; 23:23 and Matthew 13:44-45). **Third**, we are moved to establish Bible authority for all that we do when we are divinely chastised for our sins (see Psalms 32:4-5 and Hebrews 12:5-13). Living in sin is like walking through a hedge of thorns in that God chastens sinners with trouble (see Proverbs 22:5). No man in his right mind wants to go through trouble over and over again in life. The incentives to living Godly and happily are obvious (9I). The Apostle Paul had these principles in mind when he wrote, "17 *whatsoever you do in word or in deed do all in the name of the Lord Jesus giving thanks to God the Father through him*" (Colossians 3:17). Those who live by God's laws will be happy now and forevermore (Malachi 3:12).

Malachi 3

The God of Justice Comes with His Words of Instructions for those who would be Saved (3:1-6)

"**1** *Behold, I send my messenger, and he shall prepare the way before me: and the Lord, whom you seek, will suddenly come to his temple; and the messenger of the covenant, whom you desire, behold, he comes, said Jehovah of hosts*" **(3:1).**

The very last verse of Malachi chapter 2 reveals the Lord to be the God of justice (the administrator of law). God would delegate his authoritative laws to his "*messenger*" that would have the job of "*preparing the way*" for him. Jesus quotes from Malachi 3:1 at Matthew 11:10-14 and identifies John the Baptist as this messenger. While Malachi reveals that John the baptizer was to prepare the way for Jehovah to come Jesus refers to John's preparatory work being for him. This conclusively illustrates the deity of Jesus Christ (5c). The God of justice shall appear suddenly in his kingdom, the church, in these days.

Interestingly, Mark begins his account of the life of Christ by quoting from Malachi 3:1 in relationship to the coming of Christ into the world (Mark 1:2). The use of Malachi 3:1 by Matthew, Mark, and Luke 7:27 illustrates the nature of Christ's work when he came into this world. Jesus would represent law, justice, righteousness, and equity. Malachi speaks of the current situation with the people of God being that of a casual approach to God's authorized pattern for worship and Godly living. Christ, not at all unlike the God of the Old Testament, would come into this world with divine authoritative laws and encourage all men to be subject to it for their eternal salvation.

Notice the contrast in the messengers of Malachi 2:1-2 (i.e., the priests who did not practice nor teach just things and turned many away from truth) and the messenger mentioned here who shall prepare the way for the coming of Jesus. The priests of Malachi's day "8 *turned aside out of the way and caused many to stumble in the law*" (Malachi 2:8). John would preach a message of law and righteousness to prepare the way for Jesus to come into the world and establish his kingdom, the church. John's objective would be to turn many to the law rather than away from it. The people of John's day had faulty expectations of John and Jesus as did the priests of Malachi's day. To think that God does not expect his people to hold stringently to his divine laws is to greatly err (see Matthew 5:48 and 1 Peter 1:15-16).

"**2** *But who can abide the day of his coming? And who shall stand when he appears? For he is like a refiner's fire, and like fullers' soap:* **3** *and he will sit as a refiner and purifier of silver, and he will purify the sons of Levi, and refine them as gold and silver; and they shall offer unto*

Jehovah offerings in righteousness. **4** *Then shall the offering of Judah and Jerusalem be pleasant unto Jehovah, as in the days of old, and as in ancient years"* **(3:2-4).**

The Lord Jesus will come and refine men in fire to purify them. The Apostle Peter speaks of this refining process saying that Christians would be put to grief by many trials. Peter writes, "7 *that the proof of your faith, being more precious than gold that perishes though it is proved by fire, may be found unto praise and glory and honor at the revelation of Jesus Christ*" (1 Peter 1:7 see also 1 Corinthians 3:13-15). As the saints are tried, proved, and strengthened in the faith they will, as God's priests (1 Peter 2:9), offer up sacrifices of righteousness that are well pleasing to God (see Hebrews 13:16). The sacrifices of the priests of Malachi's days were polluted and an abomination to the Lord; however, the priests of Christ day would make sacrifices that are "*pleasant unto Jehovah.*"

What made the people's sacrifices viewed as either polluted and or pleasant? Those who fulfilled God's authorized commandments are viewed as pleasant and those who reject God's commands for their own ways are an abomination to him (see Malachi 1:13-14). Authority is established in this manner. Often people want to know if a practice is lawful or unlawful (right, wrong, good and or sinful). Malachi teaches us that God is a great king that rules by law (Malachi 1:14). What ever man does in this life must be authorized by God's laws (see Colossians 3:17). The Apostle Paul reveals Jesus to be "15 *the blessed and only Potentate, the King of kings, and Lord of lords*" (1 Timothy 6:14-16). Man is subject to the authorized laws of this great King because he has created this world that we live in and no man has the right to question his laws (see Romans 9:19-21). David writes, "1 *O LORD, our Lord, how majestic is your name in all the earth! You have set your glory above the heavens*" (Psalms 8:1). The Apostle John writes, "7 *Fear God, and give him glory; for the hour of his judgment is come: and worship him that made the heaven and the earth and sea and fountains of waters*" (Revelation 14:7). Furthermore the sons of Korah sing "1 *Great is the LORD and greatly to be praised in the city of our God! His holy mountain,* 2 *beautiful in elevation, is the joy of all the earth, Mount Zion, in the far north, the city of the great King*" (Psalms 48:1-2) (9l). God's true people will be concerned with keeping the law of their divine king.

"**5** *And **I will come near to you to judgment**; and I will be a swift witness against the sorcerers, and against the adulterers, and against the false swearers, and against those that oppress the hireling in his wages, the widow, and the fatherless, and that turn aside the sojourner from his right, and **fear not me**, said Jehovah of hosts*" **(3:5).**

The world of men are called to court by the Almighty Potentate King and creator of this world. God's laws will be the criterion used to "*judge*" man of good and evil. Jesus would later say, "48 *the word that I spoke the same shall judge you in the last day*" (John 12:48). The "*words*" of Jesus, as the Potentate King, are deemed law. The Apostle Paul writes, "2 *Bear you one another's burdens and so fulfill the **law of Christ**"* (Galatians 6:2). God's laws are consequentially referred to as, "**the Word of God**" (see Matthew 15:6; Acts 11:1; 13:5; 2 Corinthians 2:7 and so on). John the baptizer would receive this law, the word of God, and he would prepare the way for Jesus. Luke writes, "2 *the **Word of God** came unto John the son of Zacharias in the wilderness*" (Luke 3:2). Jesus is so connected with truth that he is called the "Word of God" at John 1:1, 17 and Colossians 1:25-2:2.

The God of justice shall pronounce a condemning judgment against the sorcerers (those who practice the arts of witchcraft and seek answers to life's problems through enchantments rather than turning to God), adulterers (those who divorce their wives and take on others unlawfully), and false swearers (those who break their vows / see Numbers 30 and Zechariah 5:4). God will judge those who cheat the laborers, widows, and fatherless. The Lord will also judge those who do not exercise hospitality to the traveler.

Summarily, Micah tells us that God will judge those who do not "*fear*" him. Solomon defines the fear of God very well at Proverbs 1:1-7. The fear of God is the ability to receive and apply wisdom and instruction in righteousness, justice, and equity in one's life. A spirit of meekness is one's ability to be voluntarily and fearfully subject to the laws of God. God gives man laws and those pleasing to the Lord will be subject to those authorized laws.

"**6** *For I, Jehovah, change not; therefore you, O sons of Jacob, are not consumed*" **(3:6).**

There is one thing certain about God and that is that he does not change. While men may change their perspective about certain things God does not. God has eternally established truth and it has said the same thing throughout all eternity (Proverbs 8:22-26).   The author of Hebrews writes, "8 *Jesus Christ is the same yesterday and today, yea and for ever*" (Hebrews 13:8). James said, "17 *Every good gift and every perfect gift is from above, coming down from the Father of lights, with whom can be **no variation**, neither shadow that is cast by turning*" (James 1:17). The eternal word of God proves his love and divine expectations for his creation. The wicked men of Judah foolishly accuse our unchanging God, that has never changed his laws or expectations of men, of not loving them (see Malachi 1:2).

The "*sons of Jacob*" are not "*consumed*" because God does not change. While God has and does consume the wicked in his fierce anger the "*sons of Jacob*" are not crushed in his wrath. Throughout the Old and New Testament the name "*Jacob*" stands as a figure of those who represent the elect remnant of God that have made their determination to meekly follow God's laws manifest by their obedient actions (see Psalms 14:7; 53:6; Isaiah 59:20; here and Romans 11:26-27). The eternal unchanging God has ever promised to save Jacob. The unlawful; however, will ever be consumed in the fires of God's wrath. The righteous shall shine into eternity with peace in heaven (see Matthew 25:31-46) (9l).

God's Blessings are contingent upon man's Obedience (3:7-12)

"*7 From the days of your fathers you have turned aside from mine ordinances, and have not kept them. Return unto me, and I will return unto you, said Jehovah of hosts. But you say, Wherein shall we return?*" **(3:7).**

Again, God is a great King and the creator yet the people of Malachi's day have treated him as though he were on par with them as far as authority goes. The great God of law and judgment is coming so that the world will give account for their behavior in relationship to the Lord's laws. The omniscient Lord sits above the circle of the earth and watches as his people "*turned aside from mine ordinances*" (see also Isaiah 40:22). Though God's divine wrath is due to the lawless he is nonetheless patient, longsuffering, and merciful (see James 4:8). God, like the father of the prodigal son parable, is watching and waiting for every man to acknowledge their error, repent, and return to him (see Luke 15:11-32). The Lord gives the lawbreakers a chance to "*return unto me*" so that they may be considered part of his elect remnant "*Jacob*." Malachi will reveal a time; however, when God's mercy and patience ends (see Malachi 4:1).

The **seventh** "*but you say*" statement is now recorded. God establishes one fact over and over throughout his revelation to man. Those who sin against his holy word are separated from his divine holiness and blessings (see Isaiah 59:1-2). Blinded by their error and hardened in their sin the people say, "*Wherein shall we return*?" Such an attitude displays a spirit of the fool that Solomon spoke of at Proverbs 1:7. Jeremiah said that the erring people had no shame of their sin (Jeremiah 6:15). While guilty of sin they considered themselves innocent (Jeremiah 2:35) and wise (Jeremiah 8:8). There is a stalemate between God and man. God accuses of sin and man says he has no sin. Let the unchanging God's eternally established law answer the question of right and wrong (see John 12:44).

"**8** *Will a man rob God? Yet you rob me. But you say, Wherein have we robbed you? In tithes and offerings.* **9** *You are cursed with the curse; for you rob me, even this whole nation.* **9** *Bring the* **whole** *tithe into the* *store-house, that there may be food in my house, and **prove me now** herewith, said Jehovah of hosts, if I will not open you the windows of heaven, and pour you out a blessing, that there shall not be room enough to receive it"* **(3:8-10).**

The **eighth deluded statement.** The people of God had robbed him by not giving *"the whole tithe"* as the Lord had commanded (see Leviticus 27:30ff). The inference in the text is that they were only bringing partial tithes. Every thing the people did they did in the name of spiritual service yet they had done things contrary to God's laws. It was not acceptable to the Lord for the people to offer sacrifices of blemishes even though it was done in the name of religion (Malachi 1:13-14). It was not acceptable to God for the people to offer an offering that did not measure up to the tithe even though it was a partial sacrifice on their part (Malachi 3:8). God demands that people follow the whole law else they are in sin (see 1 John 3:4). There are no degrees of sin or lawlessness. If one does not fulfill any part of God's laws, even what some may consider the smallest matters, the action is sinful. James said, "10 *for whosoever shall keep the whole law, and yet stumble in one point, he is become guilty of all*" (James 2:10). Again, it was not God that had changed but the people (9l). Denominational church bodies in our world today do many things that would be considered lawful; however, it is their unlawful practices that God condemns (see the seven churches of Asia). The Apostle Paul said that he declared the *"whole council of God"* because he knew that man was subject to all God's laws not just a select few (see Acts 20:27).

The lesson is one for the ages! God's blessings are contingent upon man's perfect obedience to his words. Yes, man will falter in his attempts to do so; however, the unchanging God of mercy will always be there to call the erring soul back by repentance and prayer (Romans 3:23 and 1 John 1:8-10). This is the message of Haggai and Zechariah to the erring people who, through a spirit of repentance, had returned to building the temple yet did not turn to God with their whole hearts. God does not want partial service! He desires our whole hearted obedience out of a heart that truly desires and loves him. When the people prove God's statements with their whole hearted obedience God would restore the rains to their lands!

"**11** *And I will rebuke the devourer for your sakes, and he shall not destroy the fruits of your ground; neither shall your vine cast its fruit before the time in the field, said Jehovah of hosts.* **12** *And all nations shall call you happy; for you shall be a delightsome land, said Jehovah of hosts*" **(3:11-12).**

The devourer is no doubt the blasting of mildew upon the crops (Amos 4:9) and drought (Haggai 1:11). The fruit of the field would return unto the people as they obeyed the voice of God (see Zechariah 8:12ff and 10:1). Those who refuse obedience shall ever have God's blessings withheld (Zechariah 14:17). Those who obey God are depicted as "*happy*" because God blesses them now and forevermore.

The clear message of the Minor Prophets is that God's blessings are contingent upon man's obedience through a heart of love and fear. When God's people live in such a way to receive his blessings the nations shall take notice and shall desire to have what they have (see Zechariah 8:20-23 and Revelation). The people of God are being watched by the world. When we consistently follow God's laws and live happily in the blessings of God the world is impressed. We may not have much sustenance yet they watch as we are happy and content because we are confident that as we follow God's laws we will be in heaven. Such a life is very impressive to the world of sinners and they shall come to desire the blessed life of Christians (19e).

The People draw Faulty Conclusions due to Faulty Knowledge (3:13-18)

"**13** *Your words have been stout against me, said Jehovah. Yet you say, What have we spoken against you?* **14** *You have said, It is vain to serve God; and what profit is it that we have kept his charge, and that we have walked mournfully before Jehovah of hosts?* **15** *And now we call the* *proud happy; yea, they that work wickedness are built up; yea, they tempt God, and escape"* **(3:13-15).**

The "*words*" of the sinful people are put in contrast to the eternally established "*words*" of God (see Malachi 3:5 notes above). God's words are laws while the people's words have no eternal weight. To place eternal significance on one's own words, as though they were law, is to make one's self a law giver. To make one's self a law giver is to be deity and to claim deity is the height of folly (see 2 Thessalonians 2:1-4).

The **ninth** and final statement that illustrates the people's delusion is given. The Lord makes his charge against the people. The people's words have been "*stout against me.*" Once again, in a state of delusion, the people say, "*What have we spoken against you?*" The people are so calloused in sin and hardened in heart that they do not recognize their folly. The people believe that they have "*kept God's charge*" (i.e., laws). God is the great Potentate King yet they treat his words as though they were from common man. Their day to day conversations with each other have yielded speech that reveals their harsh feelings toward God. They said strong things against God to one another. Their conversation may have been something like, "God's expectations are unreasonable, nobody is perfect" or "No one can keep God's laws perfectly" or then again someone may have said, "No one can know all these laws." The people concluded that if they just threw some sort of effort God's way that he would be pleased. The people lost sight of having to stand before the judgment seat of God and give account for all their deeds and words (John 12:44).

The Lord reveals their stout words against him saying that they say within their hearts that it is "*vain to serve God.*" They saw no profit in serving God because all their efforts were only partial services. They only partially did what God wanted in their sacrifices (Malachi 1:13-14) and tithes (Malachi 3:8ff). When they performed this partial service to God and did not receive his blessings (Malachi 3:9ff) they became discouraged and concluded that God did not love them (Malachi 1:2).

The wicked confused people believed that God should just accept them for what they were. God's people cast aside his divine laws for their own opinions and expected God to fall in line with them. When the unchanging God did not bend his laws to fit their opinions the people concluded that there is no profit in serving him. Their worship and service to God was done in ignorance to his prescribed ways (see Malachi 2:17 and Acts 17:23).

What a sad state of the mind to conclude that it is vain to serve God because I am not living happy and blessed. The right response of the people would have been to "*consider*" why they were not receiving rains and abundant harvest (see Haggai 1:6-11). Pride and arrogance has a way of squashing the mind of humility. The humble minded man would rightly take a personal assessment of his life to see if there were any areas that he violated the God that sends blessings to man. If God is the source of blessings and those blessings are contingent upon one's position to this divine law then it makes sense to see to it that I am following his laws.

"**16** *Then they that feared Jehovah spoke one with another; and Jehovah hearkened, and heard, and a book of remembrance was written before him, for them that feared Jehovah, and that thought upon his name.* **17** *And they shall be mine, said Jehovah of hosts, even mine own possession, in the day that I make; and I will spare them, as a man spares his own son that serves him.* **18** *Then shall you return and discern between the righteous and the wicked, between him that serves God and him that serves him not*" **(3:16-18).**

Though the people, for the most part, were hardened in sin there were a few that did not share this deluded mindset. There were people (and there are in all generations) who "*fear God*" and keep his commandments (see Romans 11:1-6). God saw that there were some who feared his name and he wrote their names in a "*book of remembrances*." These elect priests are the "*possession*" of God (see also 1 Peter 2:9). These men and women will love and know the laws of

God. The elect priests will cast judgments upon the acts of men and determine whether they are wicked or good (see John 7:24). Though the wicked today believe we should not judge others God calls upon his elect saints to do that very thing (20j).

Questions over Malachi Chapter 3

1. Who is the messenger of Malachi 3:1?

2. Compare and contrast the priests of Malachi's day with the priest of the latter days.

3. What significance do you see to the statement, "*For I, Jehovah, change not; therefore you, O sons of Jacob, are not consumed*?" - Remember context of book

4. What would God do for the people if only they would acknowledge their sins and repent?

5. **True or False:** The people had spoken kindly to God and he was pleased.

6. Who would God spare?

MALACHI CHAPTER 4

Synopsis

The final words of the Old Testament identify the righteous and the wicked. The eternal abode of each are discussed. God warns the wicked that there will come a day when all of his patience and mercy will run out. Let the people remember the Law of Moses and live!

Application

Fortunately for all who read these words there remains God's mercy and patience. Those who are living in sin can still be saved if only they would turn to the Lord in obedience. To insure that the world has hope through God's laws he sends Elijah (John the baptizer of the New Testament). John's work would be to speak divine laws to the people so that they would know what to properly expect in Christ. Christ would represent law and his divine expectations of men to keep those laws. Those who see the value of their souls and the value of law will turn to the Lord in obedience. The lesson for the ages is that if we obey God's laws we live and if we are rebellious we shall be eternally ruined.

Malachi 4

The Nature of the Coming Kingdom of God (4 all)

"**1** *For, behold, the day comes, it burns as a furnace; and all the proud, and all that work wickedness, shall be stubble; and the day that comes* *shall burn them up, said Jehovah of hosts, that it shall leave them neither root nor branch"* **(4:1).**

There comes a day in the future where the patience, mercy, and longsuffering of God ends for the wicked. The Lord is not willing that any perish but that all would come to repentance (see 2 Peter 3:9). God; however, is not ever suffering toward the lawless. Those who refuse to open their eyes to the obvious expectations of God will forever be ruined by a flaming furnace in hell (see Revelation 20:10-15). The wicked that miss out on God's mercy will be left with neither neither "*root nor branch*" in that there will be nothing to revive. There is no hope for those who continue in their sins.

"**2** *But unto you that fear my name shall the sun of righteousness arise with healing in its wings; and you shall go forth, as gambol as calves of the stall*" **(4:2).**

The day that comes is the day of Christ kingdom and the separation of the wicked from the righteous. No unclean sinful man or woman shall be considered a part of God's kingdom or in fellowship with the eternal God. God's light of the gospel message shall shine upon the righteous and they shall receive it with glad hearts and be blessed.

3 *And you shall tread down the wicked; for they shall be ashes under the soles of your feet in the day that I make, said Jehovah of hosts*" **(4:3).**

The antecedent to "*you*" is the people who are identified as Jacob, the elect remnant, and those fear the name of God (see Malachi 4:2 above). The elect of God shall "*tread down the wicked.*" The prophet Zechariah gives commentary on this subject at chapter 10:5 when he writes, "5 *And they shall be as mighty men, treading down their enemies in the mire of the streets in the battle; and they shall fight, because Jehovah is with them; and the riders on horses shall be confounded*" (Zechariah 10:5). Zechariah, like Malachi, painted a picture of a distinctly different people with a different approach to life. These different people are sanctified from the world of sinners in that they love and obey the Word of God.

The nations of men in the world; however, could care less about righteousness and justice. The world of men are enamored with power, lust of the flesh, riches, and fame (1 John 2:15-16). Saints are depicted as battling the temptation to be more like the majority of sinners in the world. Worldliness is very attractive. This battle is the primary objective of the book of Revelation. Zechariah and Malachi help us not only to identify the battle but also those involved (see Revelation 17:14; 19:19-21 and 20:7ff).

The true saints of God will be unstoppable by the enemies of the cross. God will be with them and they will tread down their enemies in the streets. The scene is one of great blood shed and loss of life. Figuratively speaking the battle is spiritual. The wicked challenge the righteous in every generation (see Revelation 20:7-10). Sometimes these battles will be fought on grounds least expected. The saints will find themselves battling the wicked within the church itself (see Acts 20:28-31 and Ephesians 6:10-12) or within their own homes (see Matthew 10:36). The saints of God are equipped for victory (see 2 Corinthians 10:4 and Ephesians 6:14ff). The saints are not to stand by idly but rather fight with all their might (see 1 Timothy 1:8; 6:12 and 2 Timothy 4:7). Finally, know that God's saints will always be victorious (see Psalms 48:1-6). Zechariah powerfully writes, "*7 who are you, O great mountain? Before Zerubbabel you shall become a plain; and he shall bring forth the top stone with shoutings of Grace, grace, unto it*" (Zechariah 4:7). No great mountain of false doctrine, kingdoms and nations that stand opposed to truth, governments that permit filth, temptations to practice worldliness, and wicked who persecute the Christian shall stand in the way of God's eternal kingdom, city, Zion, and church of the living God (see Daniel 2:44; Proverbs 8:22-26 and Zechariah 1:5-6) (12bb). The saints of God will not lose because "*Jehovah is with them*" and he will protect and defend them (see Zechariah 2:5; 9:8, and 15).

"**4** *Remember the law of Moses my servant, which I commanded unto him in Horeb for all Israel, even statutes and ordinances*" **(4:4).**

The final OT words reveal instructions, promises, and warnings. God instructs his people to remember the "*law of Moses*." God had always intended for the people to know and keep the law perfectly (Galatians 3:10). The "*law of Moses*" would help men come to be strong in the faith and counted as the elect of God. The Apostle Paul tells us that the Old Testament Scriptures are very valuable to our eternal souls (see Romans 15:4).

"*5 Behold, I will send you Elijah the prophet before the great and terrible day of Jehovah come. 6 And he shall turn the heart of the fathers to the children, and the heart of the children to their fathers: lest I come and smite the earth with a curse*" **(4:5-6).**

God promises his people that Elijah is coming (he who prepares the way for the Christ / see Malachi 3:1). John the Baptist (Matthew 17:10-13), or Elijah, was to prepare the people's minds to be receptive of the Law of Christ and the kingdom of God (see Matthew 11:13-15). Those who fear God would turn to the Lord in obedience and repentance seeing his forgiveness through the blood of Jesus Christ (see Matthew 26:26 and Luke 1:17). Fear and reverence for God would be this man's objective as opposed to the current messengers, the priests of Malachi's day, who led many astray (again, see Malachi 2:1).

The last words of the OT are words of warning. Those who do not obey the words of God have only a curse to look to. God's blessings will be withheld so long as man chooses sin over a life of righteousness (see Haggai 1:6-11).

Questions over Malachi Chapter 4

7. Who would be left with neither root nor branch?

8. Who will tread down the wicked?

9. Why should the people "remember the Law of Moses?"

10. Who will God send before the great and terrible day?

11. Why would God send this messenger?

Bible Topics Index

1. **The Bible**
    a. How we Got the Bible
    b. How to Study the Bible
    c. Unrecorded Epistles
    d. Discrepancies
2. **Creation**
3. **God**
    a. Sovereignty
    b. Providence
    c. Nature
    d. Love
    e. Test or Proves Man
    f. Evidences
    g. View of Sin
    h. Omniscience
    i. Expectations of man
    j. Omnipotent
    k. Concern for Poor, Fatherless, and Widows
    l. Confident in Man
    m. Wrath and Anger

- n. Mercy
- o. Omnipresence
- p. Godhead
- q. Identity
- r. Work
- s. Trustworthy
- t. Jealous
- u. Indwelling of Godhead
- v. God of all Flesh
- w. Glory
- x. Just in Condemning the Wicked
- y. Patient and Longsuffering
- z. Creator
- aa. Not a respecter of Persons
- bb. A Rock of Refuge

4. **God the Father**
    - a. Identity
    - b. Father Figure to Man

5. **Jesus, The Son of God**
    - a. Identity
    - b. Prophecy

- c. Deity
- d. Work
- e. Second Coming
- f. Indwelling
- g. Resurrection
- h. Authority
- i. Our Example
- j. He Never Quit
- k. Preeminence
- l. He Alone Saves
- m. Ascension into Heaven
- n. The Cross
- o. The Fullness of Christ
- p. Humanity
- q. The Perfect Sacrifice

6. **Holy Spirit**
   - a. Indwelling
   - b. Gift
   - c. Work
   - d. Baptism
   - e. Identity

- **f.** Receiving
- **g.** Deity
- **h.** Filled With
- **i.** Blasphemy Against

7. **Angels**
   - **a.** Identity
   - **b.** Fallen
   - **c.** Michael
   - **d.** Gabriel
   - **e.** Cherubim and Seraphim

8. **Devil**
   - **a.** Identity
   - **b.** Work
   - **c.** Tools
   - **d.** Temptation
   - **e.** Demons
   - **f.** Antichrist

9. **Bible Authority**
   - **a.** Direct Statements
   - **b.** Apostolic Examples / Example
   - **c.** Necessary Inference

- d. Expediency
- e. The "Law of Equivalence"
- f. My Attitude Toward
- g. The Example of Christ
- h. Things done, "In the Name"
- i. Expansion of Teaching
- j. Silence
- k. The Pattern
- l. Establishing

10. **Truth**
    - a. Identity - Law / Covenants / Law of Moses / Law of Christ / Gospel of Jesus Christ
    - b. Standard (Righteousness and Justice)
    - c. Distinct
    - d. Inspiration / Complete
    - e. Nature - Power / eternal
    - f. Designed for All
    - g. We Can and Must Know Truth Alike
    - h. Things we Cannot Know
    - i. Reaction to / response
    - j. Making a distinction between the Faith and Liberty

- k. No Man Above the Laws of God
- l. Revelation
- m. Calling of God
- n. Old Testament Laws binding in the New Testament
- o. Not Determined by Popular Preacher
- p. No Man may Change
- q. Type and Antitype
- r. Not Defined by Personal Conscience, Opinion, or Conviction
- s. General Truths
- t. Value of Old Testament
- u. Everlasting Covenant
- v. No Grey Areas
- w. Transforms Lives
- x. Simplicity of
- y. Value of

11. Faith
    - a. Bible Belief
    - b. Trust
    - c. Confidence
    - d. Obedience
    - e. Works

  f. Delusions

  g. Evidences of our Faith

  h. Preconceived Religious Faith

  i. Developing Faith

12. **The Church**

  a. Identity

  b. Name

  c. Organization

  d. Work

  e. Worship

  f. Autonomy

  g. Problems

  h. Prophecy

  i. Establishment

  j. Role of Women

  k. Benevolence

  l. God's Expectation

  m. Nature of

  n. God's Love For

  o. Discipline

  p. Local and Universal

- q. Worship
- r. Associated with Truth
- s. Associated with Life
- t. Letter of Commendation
- u. Music
- v. Determining the Soundness of a Church
- w. Elders / Bishops
- x. Growth
- y. Eternal
- z. Deacons
- aa. building
- bb. Indestructible
- cc. Exclusive

13. **Grace**
    - a. Identity
    - b. Relationship to Works or Obedience

14. **Sin**
    - a. Identity
    - b. Nature
    - c. Sin Separates Man from God
    - d. Why People Choose to Sin

- e. My Attitude Toward Sin
- f. Hard Hearts
- g. Affects of Sin
- h. Shame
- i. Bondage of Sin
- j. Sins of Ignorance
- k. Situational Ethics
- l. Apostasy
- m. Guilt Associated with Sin
- n. Consequences of Sin
- o. Stumbling Blocks
- p. Spiritual Adultery
- q. Sinful Thoughts
- r. Sincerity
- s. Blasphemy
- t. When the Wicked are more Righteous than God's People
- u. Faction
- v. Spiritual Death

15. **How Does One Become a Christian?**
    - a. Christian's Identity (elect or remnant)
    - b. Redemption

- c. Justification
- d. Reconciliation
- e. Steps of Salvation (hear, believe, repent, confess, be baptized, remain faithful)
- f. Transformation of the Mind from fleshly to spiritual
- g. Few find Justification
- h. Calling on the Name of God
- i. God's Promise to Justify the Faithful
- j. Conditioned upon obedience
- k. Baptism Special Study
- l. Free Will

16. **The Christian's Never Quit Attitude**
    - a. Quitting is not an Option
    - b. Pressing Forward in Life
    - c. Developing and Maintaining Conviction and Faith
    - d. Purpose Driven Christian
    - e. Endurance
    - f. Jesus and the Apostles' Never Quit Attitude
    - g. Waiting on God's Promises

17. **The Suffering Saints**
    - a. Why The Christian Suffers Persecution and Hardships

b. Purpose of Suffering

  c. Enduring Suffering

  d. The Lord Chastens those he Loves

  e. Tried and Tested

18. Preachers and Preaching

  a. Identity of the Preacher

  b. Authority for the Local Preacher

  c. Work of the Preacher

  d. Compensation of Preachers

  e. Style and Method of Preaching

  f. Handling the Power of the Gospel

  g. Preaching a Distinct Message

  h. Motivation for Preaching

  i. Consequences of Preaching truth in Love

19. Individual Christian Responsibilities

  a. Grow Spiritually / Study

  b. Militant in Truth

  c. Watchmen

  d. Contend / debate for the Faith

  e. Influence / Glorify the name of God

  f. Government

- g. Christian Armor
- h. Sanctification / Distinct
- i. Know Your Place before Jehovah
- j. Relationship to those in the World
- k. Caring for the Poor
- l. Maintain your Salvation
- m. Put all Doctrines to the Test
- n. Personal Evangelism
- o. Restore the Erring
- p. Give God Glory
- q. Repentance
- r. Fight the good fight of Faith
- s. Conformed to the Image of Christ
- t. Fasting
- u. Longsuffering and patient
- v. Sing songs of Praise

20. **Christian Characteristics**
    - a. Spirit or Character of Man
    - b. Meek
    - c. Humble
    - d. Selfless

- e. Integrity
- f. Love Others
- g. Self Control
- h. Christian Virtues
- i. Righteous Indignation
- j. Making proper Judgments
- k. Walk of Life
- l. Work Ethic
- m. Nature or Natural order of Things
- n. Spiritually Minded
- o. Spiritual Strength
- p. Persecuted

21. **Bible Love**

22. **Unity**
    - a. Identity of Unity
    - b. Unity in Diversity

23. **Fellowship**

24. **The False Teacher**
    - a. Identity
    - b. Their Work
    - c. They are to be Exposed and Shamed

    d. Identify them by Name

    e. Debating

    f. Affects of False Teaching

    g. My Attitude Toward False Teachers

    h. Their Tireless Work Ethic

    i. Why do People Teach False Doctrines?

25. **Worldliness**

    a. Homosexuality

    b. Foul Language

    c. Fornication and Adultery

    d. Lust of the Flesh

    e. Drugs and Alcohol

    f. Prejudice

    g. Gossip

    h. Dangers Associated with Riches

    i. Pride

    j. Immodest Dress

    k. Revenge

    l. Rebellion

    m. Hypocrisy

    n. Respecter of Persons

- o. Envy
- p. Ungrateful
- q. Anger
- r. Flattery
- s. mind of
- t. Putting God to the Test
- u. Bragging

26. **Bible Perfection**
    - a. God's Great Expectation for his Saints

27. **Forgiveness**
    - a. Pray for
    - b. No Sin to Hard for God to Forgive
    - c. Unforgivable Sin
    - d. Forgive Others
    - e. Attaining Forgiveness

28. **Miracles**
    - a. Spiritual Gifts
    - b. Purpose of Miracles
    - c. Are People still Performing Miracles?
    - d. Signs to instill Faith

29. **Various Erroneous Doctrines**

- a. The Spirit of Error
- b. Judaism
- c. Calvinism
- d. Institutionalism
- e. Premillinnialism
- f. Humanism
- g. Denominationalism
- h. One Cup No Bible Class
- i. Marriage, Divorce, and Remarriage
- j. Predestination
- k. 70 A.D.
- l. Once Saved Always Saved
- m. Unacceptable Worship

30. **Bible Characters**
    - a. Noah
    - b. Abraham
    - c. Enoch
    - d. Jacob
    - e. Job
    - f. Moses
    - g. Joseph

- **h.** Samuel
- **i.** Saul
- **j.** David
- **k.** Solomon
- **l.** Jeroboam
- **m.** Ahab
- **n.** Joab
- **o.** Elijah
- **p.** Elisha
- **q.** Joshua
- **r.** Caleb
- **s.** Jehoshaphat
- **t.** Jehu
- **u.** Hezekiah
- **v.** Ahaz
- **w.** Zedekiah
- **x.** Nehemiah
- **y.** Zerubbabel
- **z.** Ezra
- **aa.** Daniel
- **bb.** Nebuchadnezzar

    cc. Jesus

    dd. The Apostle Paul

    ee. Peter

    ff. Judas

    gg. John the Baptizer

    hh. King Herod

    ii. Pharisees

    jj. Sadducees

    kk. Scribes

    ll. Chief Priests and Elders

    mm. Timothy

    nn. Jeremiah

    oo. Jehoiakim

    pp. Ezekiel

    qq. Jews

31. A Battle for the Souls of Men

32. When Jesus, the Church, and God's Word do not meet Man's Expectations

33. Bible Homes

    a. The Husband in the Home

    b. The Wife in the Home

     c. Children's Responsibility in Home

     d. Parents Responsibility to Each other and Children in Home

     e. Marriage

34. **Hope**
35. **Prayer**
36. **Fear of God**
37. **Resurrection**
38. **Spiritual Delusion**
39. **A Worthy Woman**
40. **A Worthy Man**
41. **The Apostles**
42. **Bible Doxologies**
43. **Dating**
44. **Drugs and Alcohol**
45. **Wisdom**
46. **Bible Heart**
47. **Conscience**
48. **Lasting Impressions**
49. **Nations of the World in History**

     a. Assyria

     b. Babylon

    c. Egypt

    d. Roman Empire

    e. Edom

    f. Medo Persian Empire

    g. Grecian Empire

50. **Sarcasm in the Bible**

51. **World View of the Church and Christian**

52. **The Fool**

53. **Edification**

54. **Hades**

55. **Idolatry**

    a. Modern Day Idolatry

    b. Dagon

    c. Baal

    d. Asherah

    e. Diana of the Ephesians

    f. True Identity

56. **Heaven**

    a. Identity

    b. The Glorious Heavenly Body

    c. What will we Do in Heaven?

d. Reward for the Faithful

57. **Hell**

   a. Identity

   b. Eternal place for the Wicked

58. **Day of Judgment**

   a. End of Time

   b. No one Escapes

   c. No Acceptable Excuses for not Obeying the Lord

   d. No Money, Fame, Nation, Person, or amount of Power will Save the Wicked

   e. Outcome based on my Works or Actions

59. **Eternity**

   a. Time frame

   b. What Happens after we Die

60. **Victory**

61. **Miscellaneous Bible Topics**

   a. The Death Penalty

   b. Does God hear the Prayers of Sinners?

   c. Celebrating Christmas, Easter, and other Holidays

BIBLIOGRAPHY

Greek Works

Arndt, William F., and F. Wilbur Gingrich. A Greek-English Lexicon of the New Testament and Other Early Christian Literature. Chicago: University of Chicago Press, 1957.

Brenton, Sir Lancelot C. L. The Septuagint with Apocrypha: Greek and English. Hendrickson Publishers. Peabody, Massachusetts fifteenth printing October 2013.

Liddell, H. G. and Scott. Liddell and Scott's Greek – English Lexicon (Seventh Edition); An Intermediate Greek – English Lexicon. Oxford University Press: Great Clarendon Street, Oxford, New York 1889 – 2000.

Marshall, A. The Interlinear Greek – English New Testament (The Nestle Greek Text with a Literal English Translation). Zondervan Publishing House; Grand Rapids, Michigan 1958.

Moulton, H. K. The Analytical Greek Lexicon Revised (1978 Edition). Zondervan Publishing House: Grand Rapids, Michigan 1978.

Strong, James LL.D., S.T.D. The New Strong's Exhuastive Concordance of the Bible. Thomas Nelson Pulbishers, Nshville, Tennessee 1982.

Thayer, J. H. Thayer's Greek – English Lexicon of the New Testament: Coded with Strong's Concordance Numbers. Hendrickson Publishers: Peabody, Massachusetts 1996.

Dictionaries and Encyclopedias Consulted

Berube, M. S. The American Heritage Dictionary (Second College Edition). Houghton Mifflin Company: Boston 1982.

Bromiley, G. W. The International Standard Bible Encyclopedia (Four Volumes). William B. Eerdmans Publishing Company: Grand Rapids, Michigan 1979.

Unger, M. F. The New Unger's Bible Dictionary. Moody Press; Chicago 1998

Bible Consulted and used as main text of study (unless otherwise stated)

1901 American Standard Version Bible. Old and New Testaments Translated out of the original tongues. Being the version set forth A. D. 1611 compared with the most ancient authorities and revised A. D. 1881 – 1885. Newly Edited by the American Revision Committee A. D. 1901. Star Bible Publications, Inc. Fort Worth, Texas 1929.

Made in the USA
Columbia, SC
21 February 2022